The Battle of Jutland

The Battle of Jutland

Richard Osborne

Frontline Books

THE BATTLE OF JUTLAND
History's Greatest Sea Battle Told Through Newspaper Reports,
Official Documents and the Accounts of Those Who Were There

This edition published in 2016 by Frontline Books,
an imprint of Pen & Sword Books Ltd,
47 Church Street, Barnsley, S. Yorkshire, S70 2AS

ISBN: 978-1-84832-453-4

For more information on our books, please visit
www.frontline-books.com,
email info@frontline-books.com
or write to us at the above address.

Printed and bound by CPI Group (UK) Ltd, Croydon, CR0 4YY

Typeset in 10.5/12.5 Palatino

Contents

Foreword

For most British people brought up believing in the invincibility of the Royal Navy, Jutland, which was the largest naval action and the only full-scale clash of battleships in the First World War, was probably the most disappointing battle fought during the Great War. The battle took place at a time when the British Grand Fleet had been awaiting an opportunity to face the German High Seas Fleet for almost two years since the outbreak of the war. Furthermore, the Royal Navy and the British public expected that the High Seas Fleet would suffer very severe losses as a result of any fleet encounter. Unfortunately, by 1916, to the British public the Royal Navy seemed to be scarcely involved in the war, especially when compared with to the casualties suffered by the Army. Consequently, the failure to destroy the German fleet at Jutland had an adverse effect on public opinion, and confidence in the Royal Navy suffered accordingly.

The heaviest British losses occurred during the first phase of Jutland when a force of six battlecruisers and four modern fast battleships commanded by Vice Admiral Sir David Beatty, lost two battlecruisers and two destroyers while engaging a German squadron of five battlecruisers which lost just two destroyers. Once the main action was joined, the ratio of capital ships was seven to five in favour of the Royal Navy. The latter lost one battlecruiser, three old armoured cruisers and six destroyers while the Germans lost one battlecruiser, one pre-dreadnought battleship, four cruisers and three destroyers. Furthermore, the High Seas Fleet suffered far more damage than it inflicted, in terms hits on surviving ships, and once Scheer encountered the full might of the Grand Fleet he had only one aim, namely to avoid further combat and get back to base under the cover of darkness.

While the Germans could claim a tactical victory in the initial battlecruiser duel, it is also clear that they were defeated once the Jellicoe's battleships joined the fray. Furthermore, despite sinking more British ships and causing more fatalities, the Germans suffered a strategic defeat from which they never recovered. In one respect Jutland assisted the Royal Navy by shattering the over-confidence in materiel while at the same time revealing deficiencies in leadership and training. A second 'Trafalgar' on 31 May 1916, would have, in all probability, restored British naval supremacy for decades but, the failure to annihilate the High Seas Fleet meant that the Royal Navy began to lose its prestige both at home and abroad and has been in decline ever since.

The aim of this book is to record and evaluate what people thought during and after the Battle of Jutland using official records, newspaper reports and personal accounts. However, it was never my intention to repeat the detailed personal accounts of the battle found in the earlier works by Fawcett and Hooper[1] and Steel and Hart[2] or discuss matters such as the development of the dreadnought battleship and the arms race that it triggered, or describe how the deterioration in the relationship between the United Kingdom and Germany forced the former into an understanding with its long-standing enemy France. Instead, for the first part of this book I have opted to provide an account of the battle derived mainly from the despatches[3] and informed by John Campbell's[4] excellent analysis of the actual fighting.

This brings us to the vexed question of the quality and reliability of the official sources available at the National Archives and elsewhere. Like most others writing about Jutland I have chosen to use despatches as my primary source because it was the first to be published and appears to offer a basic and objective evidence of the course of the battle. This source contains original despatches, track charts, a list of signals and other raw data from which it is difficult to provide an understandable account. In February 1919, the then First Sea Lord Admiral Sir Rosslyn Wemyss, allocated that task to a committee led by the Director of Navigation, Captain John Harper, but publication of the so-called 'Harper Record' was abandoned when Beatty became First Sea Lord. Instead, the latter arranged for the despatches to be published in 1920 but once it became known that Beatty had ordered Captain Harper to make alterations, opponents of the new First Sea Lord became alarmed that he might to be writing his own biased account under the guise of it being the considered verdict of the Admiralty. Subsequently, Harper discussed Beatty's corruption of the first proposed account of the 'Harper Record' in his *The Truth About Jutland*, which was published in 1927 and accurately informed the readers of how the public had been seriously misled.[5] Despite evidence of Beatty's interference, the despatches are generally assumed to be accurate and impartial even though all despatches from ships of the Battlecruiser Fleet were sent to Beatty prior to being forwarded to London. No doubt much original material was destroyed decades ago and it is now no longer clear to what extent the original despatches are an accurate reflection of what took place. There can be little doubt that Beatty interfered with every one of the official publications but to what extent remains unclear. Beatty's actions post-Jutland appeared to be aimed at achieving a favourable public image of the Battle Cruiser Fleet's role and his leadership of this force. In effect he seems to been trying to show that his operational ideas had been more successful than they actually were, thereby making them appear preferable to Jellicoe's cautious approach.

Another weakness of the despatches concerns the variable quality of the reports from Flag and Commanding Officers. Those used to reading 'Reports of Proceedings' from the Second World War, will be disappointed by the lack of accuracy and detail. At the time of Jutland commanding officers were only required to submit a report and there was no obligation or expectation to use as much evidence as possible or make it as accurate as possible by confirming times, reporting fire-control data and information from other ships.

Because of the absence of a Naval Staff, Jellicoe was able to set up self-seeking and self-serving Grand Fleet Committees to learn from the experience of Jutland. The work done by these committees was instrumental in improving the battle-worthiness of the Royal Navy such that by 1918 the latter would have crushed the High Seas Fleet had it encountered the Grand Fleet. However, for all their good work, these committees chose to ignore the dangerous magazine practices that had been allowed to develop in the years leading up to Jutland, preferring to blame a lack of armour for the loss of the battlecruisers. Researchers hoping to find documentary evidence of the lax attitude to cordite and its explosive consequences will be disappointed because, sadly, most of it seems to have been weeded out many years ago. All that remains are a few fragments from larger reports.

Newspaper reports after Jutland make for interesting reading because of the initial panicky response when it appeared that the Grand Fleet might have been defeated. Thereafter, as the 'truth' was gradually revealed and German 'lies' exposed, the tone of the British newspapers changed. This change in attitude was particularly obvious in the United States press where the Germans suffered a massive public relations disaster once it was realised that they had been economical with the truth. It also interesting to see how some reports in the German press claimed victory but then went on to ask for a resumption of unrestricted submarine warfare. The latter was a clear sign that the High Seas Fleet had not won the Battle of Jutland and that its leaders realised that it would be able to defeat the Grand Fleet and so break the blockade that was throttling the German war effort.

In the penultimate chapter I have discussed the likely cause of the loss of the battlecruisers using those contemporaneous sources that still remain while at the same time showing that a conscious decision must have been made by the senior officers of the Grand Fleet to ignore the cordite factor and blame inadequate armour protection instead. This scapegoating of the battlecruisers was apparently done to protect the morale of the officers and men of the Grand Fleet – while at the same time protecting those responsible for the lax attitude to cordite from richly deserved censure.

Finally, the above comments show the difficulties encountered in compiling a coherent account of Jutland and its aftermath. There is a desperate need for new material some of which may lurking in the papers of former naval personnel whose descendants have little or no idea as to its significance. Fortunately, thanks to the work of marine archaeologist and historian Dr Innes McCartney, the Jutland 'battlefield' has been mapped using modern multi-beam sonar. His work,[6] which is in press, will be the first to identify the location of most of the ships sunk at Jutland and, in so doing, will enable the accuracy of despatches and other publications to be evaluated.

Richard Osborne,
Cavelossim, Goa, 2016

Acknowledgements

My thanks go to Dr Innes McCartney, Dave Sowdon, Andrew Smith and Harry Spong for the help and advice that they have given me during the compilation of this work. I thank John Grehan and Martin Mace of Frontline Books for me giving me the opportunity to explore a controversial subject. I am also indebted to John Grehan for his editorial role. Any errors that remain are mine and mine alone.

Parts of this book could not have been written without the author receiving the benefit of the knowledge and experience of the late David K. Brown (1928–2008) of the Royal Corps of Naval Constructors during a quarter of a century of friendship. David was particularly interested in how well warships performed in action and we exchanged numerous letters and e-mails on the subject. In particular he strongly believed that British battlecruisers were the equal of their German contemporaries and that their losses suffered at Jutland were the consequence of appallingly lax magazine practices.

I thank the World Ship Society for allowing me to use photographs from their extensive photo library.

Finally, I thank my wife Chris for her patience and support throughout the many months of research and writing.

Glossary of Technical Terms and Abbreviations

AB	Able Seaman.
Abaft	A relative term used to describe the location of one object in relation to another in which the object described is farther aft than the other.
Abeam	The bearing of an object 90 degrees from ahead (in a line with the middle of the ship).
APC (Shell)	Armour Piercing Capped, an armour-piercing shell. Such shells must withstand the shock of punching through armour plating. Shells designed for this purpose have a greatly strengthened case with a specially-hardened and shaped nose, and a much smaller bursting charge. The problem with British APCs at Jutland was that their casings were too brittle and their burster too sensitive. APC is now little used in naval warfare, as modern warships have little or no armour protection.
Athwartships	Across the ship, at right angles to the centreline.
Barbettes	Structures upon which gun turrets rotate. Shells and propellants are passed up to the guns from the shellrooms and magazines.
Beam	The registered breadth of a vessel measured at the outside of the hull amidships, or at its greatest breadth.
Bearing	The direction of an object with reference to you, your ship or another object.
Bulkhead	A vertical structural partition in a vessel's interior dividing it into various compartments for strength and safety purposes.
Bulkhead gland	Gland which allows bulkhead penetration by cables etc. without compromising the bulkheads watertight integrity

Bulwark	Barrier of stiffened plating at the outboard edge of the main or upper deck to prevent or inhibit the entry of the sea.
Burster (Burster Charge)	Explosive charge within a shell. The well-known failure of British APC to penetrate German armour at Jutland was partly caused by the sensitive nature of their Lyddite bursters which caused many of these shells to detonate immediately upon contact with the target. After Jutland a new weaker, but less sensitive burster called 'Shellite', a 50:50 mixture of Lyddite and dinitrophenol (DNP) was developed but was found to cause insufficient fragmentation. Tests with 60% Lyddite and 40% DNP bursters were satisfactory and it was this combination that was used in the 'Greenboy' projectiles issued in early 1918. After the war a 70% Lyddite:30% DNP mix was found to give improved fragmentation while at the same time maintaining an adequate margin against premature detonations. This mixture was used on all subsequent British 15-inch APCs.
	The burster charge varied according to the type of shell. At Jutland, the 15-inch Mk 1a fired a 1,920 lb shell with the APC variant containing a burster charge of just 60.5 lb of Lyddite, the CPC shell containing 129.3 lb of black powder (later TNT) and the HE shell containing 216.5-224 lb of Lyddite.
Cable (length)	100 fathoms or 600 feet.
Capstan	Steel warping drum rotating on a vertical axis for the handling of mooring lines and, optionally, anchor cable.
C-in-C	Commander-in-Chief.
CO	Commanding Officer.
Communications Number	A member of the gun crew who received information about the range and bearing of a target.
Compass Points	There are 32 compass points named in a clockwise direction. Ordering a 16 point turn is the equivalent to ordering a reversal of course while a ship turning 32 points has steamed in a circle.
Compartment	A subdivision of space or room in a ship.
CPC (Common) shell	Common Pointed Capped. A semi-armour piercing shell. On bursting, common shells tended to break into relatively large fragments which continued along the shell's trajectory rather than laterally. Their black powder burster also had some incendiary effect. After Jutland, German reports suggested that many British shells had broken into large pieces and contained black

	powder thereby indicating that the shell was of the CPC type rather than an APC.
Crossing the 'T'	Crossing the 'T' is a classic tactic in naval warfare used from the late-nineteenth to mid-twentieth centuries, in which a line of warships crosses in front of a line of enemy ships, allowing the crossing line to bring all their guns to bear while receiving fire from only the forward guns of the enemy. The advent of steam-powered battleships, with rotating turrets, which were able to move faster and turn more quickly than sailing ships, made the tactic theoretically possible. However, as was demonstrated several times at Jutland, when too many ships engaged the same target, spotting each ships' fall of shot became next to impossible with a resultant decrease in hitting. Thus the German cruiser *Wiesbaden* was fired on by many Grand Fleet battleships simultaneously but suffered relatively little damage until engaged solely by the battleship *Marlborough* which soon reduced the cruiser to a floating wreck. After Jutland the Grand Fleet developed fire-concentrating techniques to overcome this problem.
CS	Cruiser Squadron.
Deck	A platform or horizontal floor which extends from side to side of a vessel.
Displacement	The weight of the water displaced by a ship. This weight is the same as the weight of the ship when afloat. Standard displacement is the displacement of a warship complete, fully manned and equipped ready for sea including all ammunition, equipment, provisions, miscellaneous stores and fresh water for the crew but without fuel or reserved boiler water on board. Full load is standard displacement plus fuel and reserve boiler water on board.
Director	In the First World War era the Royal Navy's Vickers Tripod-Mounted Director, often situated in a 'light aloft tower' housing four crew, a director layer, a director trainer, a sightsetter, and a talker. The latter was equipped with a telephone headset and often a flexible speaking tube from the spotting top above. He acted as a communications interface.
	The sightsetter had a follow-the-pointer sight to adjust to the range and deflection being continually indicated upon it from the transmitting station.
	The director trainer would use his handwheels to rotate

the entire director assembly and the top of the external housing until he saw the target aligned in his telescope. The director layer would use his handwheel to elevate his crosshairs, whose elevation had been altered as the sightsetter dialled in the desired gun range. When the target was aligned and a small 'gun ready' display board showed a sufficient number of guns were ready to fire, the director layer would pull a trigger with his free hand to signal the firing impulse.

DF	Destroyer Flotilla.
DNI	Director of Naval Intelligence.
DNO	Director of Naval Ordnance.
Draft (draught)	The depth of a vessel below the waterline measured vertically to the lowest part of the hull, propellers or other reference point.
Engine Room	Space where the main engines of a ship are located.
Fathom	A seagoing unit of measure equivalent to six feet.
Fearnought screens	Flashtight screens that prevented flash from burning cordite entering magazines.
Fearnought sleeves	Flashtight sleeves that prevented flash from burning cordite entering magazines.
FO	Flag Officer.
Gunner	Warrant Officer given training as a gunnery instructor with particular emphasis on Direction.
Gunner (T)	Warrant Officer trained as a gunnery instructor but with the emphasis on torpedoes .
Gunnery Control Tables	Mechanical computers used for fire control of, for example, the 15-inch guns in HMS *Warspite*.
Halliards or Halyards	Ropes used for hoisting gaffs, sails and signal flags.
HE (Shell)	High Explosive
HMS	His Majesty's Ship.
IHP	Induced Horsepower.
LS	Leading Seaman.
Lt	Lieutenant.
Lt Cdr	Lieutenant Commander.
Lt Cdr (G)	Gunnery Lieutenant Commander.
List	To lean to one side.
Lyddite	Picric acid (2,4,6-trinitrophenol, TNP), like other highly nitrated compounds is an explosive, and was first manufactured at Lydd in Kent. Lyddite bursters were able to withstand the shock of being fired from a gun but were vulnerable to the concussive effects of the shell's impact with its target leading to premature explosions in many British APCs used at Jutland.

	German ships hit by Lyddite-containing shells had yellow stains on their sides and superstructures.
Mile	Where 'mile' is used in this book as a distance at sea, the nautical mile or sea mile should be assumed – one minute of latitude, equivalent to 6,080 feet (usually rounded off to 2,000 yards in naval practice and 1.8532 kilometres. The English land mile is 1,760 yards (5,280 feet).
nm	nautical mile.
Outboard	In a direction towards the side of the ship.
OS	Ordinary Seaman.
Pendants	A length of wire or rope secured at one end to a mast or spar and having a block or other fitting at the lower end.
Pennants	A long, thin triangular flag flown from the masthead of a warship.
PO	Petty Officer.
Port side	The left hand side of the ship looking forward.
Prize Law	During wartime belligerent states often attempted to interfere with maritime commerce to prevent ships from carrying goods that benefited the war effort of their opponent. After being captured ships were sent to a friendly port where a Prize Court would determine the legality of the seizure and the fate of the ship and its cargo. If the ship could not be sent to a friendly port the ship could be sunk. A neutral vessel on the high seas or in a belligerent's territorial waters may be stopped and searched if suspected of carrying contraband and may be condemned as prize if any contraband is found.
Prize Rules	Although enemy warships could be sunk on sight, international law expected that merchant ships could be stopped for inspection and, if necessary, a prize crew put aboard to sail the ship to a friendly port for adjudication by the local Prize Court. It was understood that merchant ships should only be sunk once the crew had been given a chance to take to their boats. During 1915 the German U-boats demonstrated that sinking the merchant ships of the Entente and neutral nations on sight and without having to surface could have a very damaging effect on British maritime trade. Prize Rules required the U-boat to surface, stop the merchant ship and put a search party aboard. This exposed the surfaced U-boat to attack by disguised armed merchant ships (the so-called 'Q' ships), destroyers and aircraft.
Quarter	A side of a ship between the main midship frames and the stern.

RMLI	Royal Marine Light Infantry.
RN	Royal Navy.
Sight Setter	The person who keeps a settable gun sight set to the proper range and deflection to establish the proper angles on the sighting telescopes to place shells on target.
SHP	Shaft Horse Power.
SS	Steam Ship.
Starboard side	The right hand side of the ship looking forward.
S/Lt	Sub Lieutenant.
Superimposed Guns	The concept of superfiring is to locate two turrets in a line, one behind the other, but with the second turret located above (i.e. super) the one in front so that the second turret could fire over the first. This configuration meant that both forward or aft turrets could fire at any target within their sector, even when the target was in the same vertical plane as the turrets.
Trim	To modify the angle of a vessel to the water by shifting cargo or ballast; to adjust for sailing; to assume, or cause a vessel to assume, a certain position, or trim, in the water.
TS	Transmitting Station – A compartment between decks which housed the fire-control predictors. They were fed target information (range, bearing, elevation) from optical instruments (sights and rangefinders) trained on the target; they calculated the future position of the target; and they transmitted to the gun mountings the predicted ranges, bearings and elevations for the guns to hit the target. At Jutland in larger ships the TS was concerned with surface fire control for the main guns only.
Turrets	Structures designed for the mounting and handling of guns of a warship constructed so as to revolve (usually on barbettes) about a vertical axis usually by means of electrical or hydraulic machinery.
WO	Warrant Officer.

A Tale of Two Communiqués

During the afternoon a series of heavy engagements developed
between Skagerrak and Horn Reefs which were successful for us.[1]

The Battle of Jutland started at 14.20 hours GMT on 31 May 1916, when the light cruiser *Galatea* reported enemy ships in sight and ended just over twelve hours later the following day with the ships of the German battle fleet passing or having passed Horn Reefs en route to their home ports.

The fact that the battle took place much nearer to their home bases enabled the German Admiralty to release an official communiqué a full day before their British counterparts. Consequently, their Official Report, dated 1 June 1916, and published the following day, was received in neutral countries and commented upon in their Press at least twenty-four hours before any news was forthcoming from British sources. The communiqué read:

During an enterprise directed northward our High Seas Fleet encountered on May 31 the main part of the English fighting Fleet, which was considerably superior to our own forces. During the afternoon a series of heavy engagements developed between Skagerrak and Horn Reefs, which were successful for us and which also continued during the whole of the night. In these engagements, as far as is known up to the present, were destroyed by us the large battleship *Warspite*, the battlecruisers *Queen Mary* and *Indefatigable*, two armoured cruisers of the *Achilles* type, one small cruiser, the new flagships of the destroyer squadrons, the *Turbulent*, *Nestor* and *Acasta* and one submarine. By observations, which are free from any objections, it was stated that a large number of English battleships suffered damage from our ship's artillery and from attacks of our torpedo-boat flotillas during the day and night engagements.

Among others, the large battleship *Marlborough* was hit by a torpedo, as has been confirmed by prisoners. Several of our ships rescued portions of the crews of the sunk English ships among whom were the only two survivors of the *Indefatigable*. On our side the small cruiser *Wiesbaden* was sunk by hostile artillery fire during the day engagements and the *Pommern* during the night by a torpedo. The fate of the *Frauenlob*, which is missing, and of some torpedo-boats which have not yet returned, is unknown. The High Seas Fleet returned to our ports during the day.[2]

The German communiqué had significant omissions and exaggerations because they deliberately did not admit to the loss of the battle cruiser *Lützow*, the grounding of her compatriot *Seydlitz* and the sinking of the light cruisers *Rostock* and *Elbing*. Furthermore, despite German claims to the contrary, the British did not lose either a large battleship or a light cruiser and, with the exception of four ships of the 5th Battle Squadron and *Colossus*, none Jellicoe's battleships was damaged by German shellfire. However, with the German communiqué already in circulation on the Continent and elsewhere there was no point in stopping its publication in the British Press.

The first British communiqué about the Battle of Jutland was written by Arthur Balfour, the First Lord of the Admiralty, and issued to the Press on the evening of 2 June 1916. It read:

On the afternoon of Wednesday May 31, a naval engagement took place off the coast of Jutland. The British ships on which the brunt of the fighting fell were the Battle Cruiser Fleet, and some cruisers and light cruisers supported by four fast battleships. Among those the losses were heavy. The German battlefleet, aided by low visibility, avoided prolonged action with our main forces, and soon after these appeared on the scene, the enemy returned to port, though not before receiving severe damage from our battleships.

The Battle Cruisers *Queen Mary*, *Indefatigable*, *Invincible*, and the cruisers *Defence* and *Black Prince* were sunk. The *Warrior* was disabled, and after being towed for some time, had to be abandoned by her crew. It is also known that the destroyers *Tipperary*, *Turbulent*, *Fortune*, *Sparrowhawk* and *Ardent* were lost, and six others are not yet accounted for. No British battleships or light cruisers were sunk. The enemy's losses were serious. At least one battlecruiser was destroyed, and one severely damaged; one battleship was reported sunk by our destroyers during a night attack, two light cruisers were disabled and probably sunk. The exact number of enemy destroyers disposed of during the action cannot be ascertained with any certainty, but it must have been large.[3]

Unfortunately, this candid, accurate and restrained communiqué caused dismay in the United Kingdom because it gave no indication of the level of success actually attained, provided no vision of the effect of the battle on the outcome of the war, and was therefore interpreted by many as a defeat. To a nation nurtured in the belief of its naval invincibility, a defeat was unthinkable and its possibility triggered a great deal of comment, some of which was most uncomplimentary to the Royal Navy and those responsible for its leadership and management.

Faced with a concerned and critical populace, just six hours later, the British Admiralty issued an updated communiqué in which the list of British destroyer casualties was corrected and then went on to claim that three German capital ships had been sunk instead of the two claimed earlier. Surprisingly, this turned out to be substantially true because in addition to the battlecruiser *Lützow* and the pre-dreadnought battleship *Pommern*, the heavily damaged *Seydlitz* had sunk in shallow water on her return journey. Had the latter been fifty miles further from her home base she would have indeed been lost.

Clearly, a major naval battle between the world's two largest navies using much untested technology and untried tactics, had occurred somewhere in the North Sea. However, the competing claims of the combatants meant that it was difficult to understand the outcome and its consequences or how well that novel technology and its associated tactics had withstood the test of war.

The Opening Moves

Had I been defeated, it is impossible to say what the consequences might have been.[1]

The above quotation might well have come from Admiral Sir John Jellicoe speculating about the consequences of the defeat of the Grand Fleet, which had it happened, could have led to the defeat of Great Britain within a relatively short period. In fact, the words were spoken by Vice-Admiral Sir Robert Calder at his Court Martial in December 1805. During an indecisive action off Cape Finisterre on 22-24 July 1805, Calder's fleet of fifteen ships-of-the-line had inflicted losses on Villeneuve's superior force of twenty ships but had then allowed them to brush past him into harbour. Sadly, his apparent lack of determination resulted in Calder being court martialled in December of that year. The charges of cowardice and disaffection against him were absurd but he was found guilty of an error of judgement, sentenced to be severely reprimanded and was never to be employed again. In reality and despite his misgivings, Calder's fleet was but one of several British fleets and its defeat would not have given the French any long term naval superiority.

In comparison, Jellicoe's fleet was the only modern British battlefleet and very serious losses would have greatly undermined any subsequent effort to maintain the seaways vital to the nation's survival. Furthermore, it was the presence of the battleships of the Grand Fleet that enabled the armed merchant cruisers of the 10th Cruiser Squadron to impose an economically damaging starvation blockade on Germany.

Strict comparison between Calder and Jellicoe is difficult because the weapons and tactics employed by the former had been established at least 250 years earlier. The Battle of Tsushima in 1905, although small in comparison with Jutland, was the only large battle between steamships and during the subsequent ten years there had been a revolution in battleship size, speed, armour and firepower. Consequently, it is possible to argue that Jellicoe had no established tactical doctrine upon which to fall back once battle commenced. However, as in the sailing era, skilful use of geography and speed could force battle on a reluctant enemy and, on the evening of 31 May 1916, Jellicoe was able to put the Grand Fleet between the High Seas Fleet and its bases. Had those commanding his light forces passed on vital information during the night of 31 May / 1 June it is quite possible that Jellicoe would have been able to renew the action at dawn with devastating consequences for the German battlefleet.

Unfortunately, Jellicoe seems to have been a natural pessimist and was unable to accept that the German battlefleet also suffered from ships that broke down, needed refits and gunnery practice – just like the ships of his own Grand Fleet. Consequently, because the Germans could always choose the most opportune moment to sortie into the North Sea, he was concerned that a combination of break downs, refits and work ups would so reduce the strength of his battlefleet that it risked defeat. Furthermore, he seems not to have understood that with a 2:1 superiority, random losses would actually increase his advantage. For example, if thirty ships face fifteen and each force loses five vessels the superiority will rise from 2:1 to 2.5:1.

It can be argued that Jellicoe had no need to destroy the High Seas Fleet because he retained control of the seas equally well if the Germans remained in harbour, but the actual exercise of command of the sea required the Grand Fleet to put to sea and thereby risk losses to mines and submarines. Clearly, such considerations weighed heavily on Jellicoe's mind not least because before the Battle of Tsushima Admiral Togo lost two of his six battleships to mines.[2] Jellicoe was equally concerned that isolated British battle squadrons might be cut off and annihilated during an encounter with the entire High Seas Fleet.

However, despite these concerns, in reality, Jellicoe had every reason to take risks in battle so as to avoid the greater risk of his numerical superiority being reduced by attrition prior to a fleet action. While Jellicoe was only too aware that he held Britain's Shield he may not have been so conscious that he also held the sword. Successful use of the latter would therefore free up huge resources including a large number of destroyers attached to the Grand Fleet. The latter could then be used to counter the submarine threat.

The German Aim
The German's initial foray into unrestricted submarine warfare in 1915 had been abandoned because of the fear of bringing the Americans into

the war on the 'Entente' side. In particular, the sinking of the *Lusitania* on 7 May 1915 followed by that of *Arabic* on 19 August caused the Germans to give up the U-boat campaign west of England. Admiral von Pohl, the C-in-C of the High Seas Fleet asked to be released from his office because 'he held to be impossible to give up the U-boat campaign, which was the only effective weapon against England that the Navy possessed'[3] The U-boat campaign dragged on until the end of the year although with only moderate success because of the need to obey Prize Rules.

When Admiral Scheer took over command of the High Seas Fleet in January 1916 he was assured by the Chief of the Naval Staff on 1 February that the unrestricted U-boat campaign would be inaugurated on 1 March but diplomatic concerns intervened. Scheer records that the decisive session at General Headquarters took place on 4 March when the Chief of the Naval Staff informed him:

> For military reasons, the unrestricted U-boat campaign against England, which alone promises full success, must begin on April 1. Till then the Imperial Chancellor must set in motion all political and diplomatic machinery to make America understand our position, with the aim of securing our freedom of action.[4]

On 24 March 1916, SS *Sussex*, with 300 passengers on board, was torpedoed in the English Channel while en route from Folkestone to Dieppe. There were several American citizens amongst her passengers and their presence caused the US Government to deliver a very strongly worded note to their German counterpart threatening to break off diplomatic relations if unrestricted submarine warfare was not abandoned. Subsequently, on 20 April the German Naval Staff were ordered to conduct submarine warfare in accordance with Prize Law thereby rendering the U-boat campaign ineffective.

Now that submarines could not be employed to destroy British maritime trade, the only alternative was to employ the High Seas Fleet against the numerically much stronger Grand Fleet in an attempt to break the British blockade. Scheer must have known all along that a full-scale encounter between the British and German fleets could have only one outcome, namely disproportionally larger losses on the High Seas Fleet. It is possible to argue that Scheer was forced to risk his battle squadrons to show Germany's political masters that their surface fleet could not overcome British command of the sea. This would demonstrate the need to resume unrestricted submarine warfare regardless of the risk in a desperate attempt to impose a German peace on the 'Entente' powers before American forces were able to intervene effectively.

The German objective prior to Jutland was simple and envisaged drawing the Grand Fleet or at least a significant part of it over a force of submarines while at the same time engaging an isolated detachment of it with the whole High Seas Fleet. The trap was to be baited by a bombardment of Sunderland by Hipper's battlecruisers because previous raids on the east coast had brought out Beatty's battlecruisers supported by one or more battle squadrons. If all went well, British numerical superiority would be reduced significantly and thereby loosening British command of the sea. Scheer's order issued on 18 May assumed that bombardment of the English east coast would be certain to 'call out a display of English fighting forces as promised by Mr Balfour'[5]:

> The bombardment of Sunderland by our [battle]cruisers is intended to compel the enemy to send out forces against us. For the attack on the advancing enemy the High Seas Fleet forces to be south of the Dogger Bank, and the U-boats to be stationed for attack off the East Coast of England. The enemy's ports of sortie will be closed by mines. The Naval Corps will support the undertaking with their U-boats. If time and circumstances permit, trade-war will be carried on during proceedings.[6]

However, to achieve actual command of the sea, the High Seas Fleet would have to repeat this operation successfully on several occasions.

Scheer intended to bombard Sunderland with Hipper's five battlecruisers. This more northerly attack would greatly increase the chance of action against a pursuing British force while at the same time increasing the risk of meeting the whole Grand Fleet based in Scottish waters. To protect against such an encounter, Scheer stationed seventeen submarines to mine the approaches to British bases while at the same time reporting the movements of the Grand Fleet. The attack on Sunderland was planned for 17 May but was delayed until 29 May because repairs to the battlecruiser *Seydlitz* were incomplete. Furthermore, the submarine force would have to be withdrawn on 1st June and, in view of the danger of the voyage to and from Sunderland without airship scouting, an alternative plan for bad weather was drawn up. Thus, the High Seas Fleet was to show itself off Norway in the expectation that this would be sufficient to draw a significant British force out of its bases and over his submarines even if there was little possibility of the defeat of an isolated detachment.

The Grand Fleet

The only force which could catch Hipper's battlecruisers was Beatty's Rosyth-based Battle Cruiser Fleet which had been weakened by the departure of Rear-Admiral the Hon. Horace L.A. Hood's 3rd Battle Cruiser Squadron (*Invincible, Indomitable* and *Inflexible*) to Scapa Flow for long overdue gunnery training. However, Beatty had been reinforced by the Rear Admiral Evan-Thomas's 5th Battle Squadron composed of the fast, 15-inch gun-armed ships of the Queen Elizabeth-class. The latter were at that time the fastest and most powerful battleships in the world and represented a significant reinforcement of the Battle Cruiser Fleet. Unfortunately, he did not have enough time to fully integrate this powerful squadron with the rest of his forces, and Beatty was well aware of the risks of being lured onto the guns of the High Seas Fleet and was determined to avoid such a confrontation.

In the event that a battlecruiser action resulted in the Grand Fleet encountering the High Seas Fleet, Jellicoe had made it clear in a letter, sent on 30 October 1914, to the Admiralty that because the German fleet was superior in submarines, torpedoes and mines, he would (a) fight the action in the northern North Sea, (b) avoid close pursuit, (c) fight a long range gunnery duel outside of torpedo range and (d) only fight at short range once the Germans had been weakened significantly. If the latter were not willing to engage in such an action, Jellicoe was not willing to force it upon them.[7] Because Jellicoe's margin of superiority was small in late 1914, the Admiralty had no hesitation in approving his ideas[8]. However, by 1916, the Grand Fleet's measure of superiority had increased significantly, and Jellicoe's justifiable caution of eighteen months earlier was no longer applicable.

In early 1916 the Admiralty wanted to concentrate the Grand Fleet in the Firth of Forth where it would be better placed to counter German raids on the east coast. The Lowestoft raid of 25 April triggered concerns that the Germans might venture even further south while at the same time forcing Arthur Balfour, the First Lord, 'to announce publicly that should German ships again venture to show themselves off the British coast, measures had been taken to ensure their being severely punished'.[9]

Jellicoe's meticulously-detailed and highly proscriptive Grand Fleet Battle Orders envisaged a long range gunnery duel between fleets sailing on parallel course. His subordinates were neither trained to nor expected to show initiative in the rigidly hierarchical structure that the Royal Navy had become. Furthermore, despite having a considerable superiority in light cruisers and destroyers, the Royal Navy showed little or no interest in fighting night actions fearing that they would become something of a lottery from which the weaker Germans would be the main beneficiary. The lack of training in night fighting would have serious consequences.

The Grand Fleet Sails

At 15.40 hours on 30 May the ships of the High Seas Fleet anchored in Schillig Roads were sent a signal from Scheer ordering them to put to sea the following day and sail towards the Sakagerrak. Scheer was unaware that the British were monitoring his radio signals and that their direction finding stations and decoding experts in Room 40[10] would soon tell Jellicoe the position and most of the content of his signal. The intercepted signal, which was available to the Admiralty at 17.00 that day, showed that a major deployment was intended by the High Seas Fleet. At 17.40 Jellicoe was informed by the Admiralty that the Germans were likely to put to sea the following day. A later German signal on 30 May clarified their intentions and Jellicoe was ordered to concentrate the Grand Fleet ten miles east of Aberdeen. The Official Despatches record that:

> At.9.30 p.m., 'Iron Duke,' First and Fourth Battle Squadrons, Third Battle-Cruiser Squadron, Second Cruiser Squadron, Fourth Light-Cruiser Squadron, Commodore (F), Fourth and Twelfth Flotillas, and four destroyers of Eleventh Flotilla, 'Canterbury' and 'Chester' left Scapa.
>
> At 10 p.m., the Second Battle Squadron, First Cruiser Squadron and remainder of the Eleventh Flotilla left Cromarty.
>
> At 10 p.m. 'Lion,' First and Second Battle-Cruiser Squadrons, First, Second and Third Light-Cruiser Squadrons, 'Fearless' and nine boats of First Flotilla, 'Champion' and ten of Thirteenth Flotilla, eight destroyers of Harwich force and 'Engadine', left Rosyth.
>
> At 10.40 p.m., the Fifth Battle Squadron (four ships) left Rosyth.[11]

Consequently, the Grand Fleet and Beatty's Battle Cruiser Fleet were at sea by 22.30 hours – two and half hours before Hipper sailed from the Jade Estuary!

During the night of 30 May, the British fleet was in three main groups with the 1st (*Lion, Princess Royal, Queen Mary* and *Tiger*) and 2nd Battle Cruiser Squadrons (*New Zealand* and *Indefatigable*) and the 5th Battle Squadron (*Barham, Valiant, Warspite* and *Malaya*) leaving the Firth of Forth, the 2nd Battle Squadron (1st Division: *King George V, Ajax, Centurion, Erin,* 2nd Division: *Orion, Monarch, Conqueror* and *Thunderer*) sailing from Cromarty and the 4th Battle Squadron (3rd Division: *Iron*

Duke, Royal Oak, Superb, Canada, 4th Division: *Benbow, Bellerophon, Temeraire, Vanguard,* 5th Division: *Marlborough, Revenge, Hercules, Agincourt,* 6th Division: *Colossus, Collingwood, Neptune* and *St. Vincent*) plus the 3rd Battlecruiser Squadron (*Invincible, Indomitable* and *Inflexible*) departing from Scapa Flow.

The seaplane carrier *Campania,* which was lying in an isolated anchorage in Scapa Flow, did not receive the order to sail and did not notice the departure of the Grand Fleet, and was left behind. This was the first of many signalling failures that were to plague the British over the next two days as well as being an example of the lack of initiative that pervaded the Royal Navy at that time. Common sense suggests that having been warned that the Grand Fleet was about to sail *Campania* should have taken all steps necessary to maintain communication.

Scheer had planned that two U-boats in the Pentland Firth would intercept the Grand Fleet as it put to sea while eight more were stationed to cover the egress of the Battle Cruiser Fleet from Rosyth. In practice, only two U-boats sighted the British ships and only one of these attempted to attack. The first part of Scheer's plan had failed completely leaving him unaware that the whole Grand Fleet was at sea and en route to intercept his force off Norway.

The 2nd Battle Squadron joined Jellicoe during the morning of 31 May and the Grand Fleet steamed steadily onwards for their rendezvous with Beatty's battlecruisers. At 14.00 the Grand Fleet was in position 54°45' N 4°15' E and while Beatty was to be at 56°40' N 5° E sixty-nine miles south-south-east of Jellicoe at the same time. Although this wide separation has been criticised, it was an inevitable consequence of the problem of attempting to intercept German battlecruiser raids. Thus concentration too far north ran the risk of missing the Germans altogether while a deployment further south could mean that the British would arrive too late. Success was dependent upon an efficient link between the two British forces which in 1916 meant a visual link. Unfortunately, Jellicoe and Beatty both failed to deploy their fast cruisers so as to establish a positive location of each other's ships as soon as possible.

A second British failure of communication occurred on the morning of the 31 May when Captain Thomas Jackson of the Operations Division asked Room 40 for the present location of the German call sign 'DK' only to receive the unhelpful but correct reply 'in Wilhelmshaven'. 'DK' was the harbour call sign of the C-in-C High Seas Fleet and was shifted to a shore station whenever Scheer left harbour aboard his flagship *Friedrich der Grosse.* Unfortunately, such was the level of mutual contempt between Jackson and the civilians manning Room 40 that the latter did not bother to ask the reason for the request. The effect of Jackson's stupid question and its equally stupid answer was to deprive Jellicoe of any sense of urgency. Thus at 12.30 Jackson sent the following signal to Jellicoe:

> Directional wireless places flagship in Jade at 11.0 GMT. Apparently they have been unable to carry out airship reconnaissance which has delayed them.[12]

Unsurprisingly, this signal led Jellicoe to believe that the High Seas Fleet was still in port and that he was engaged on yet another uneventful sweep.[13] Jellicoe cannot therefore be blamed for his disbelief in the efficacy of radio direction finding when just a few hours later he had Scheer's flagship *Friedrich der Grosse* in front of him.

The Scapa and Cromarty forces proceeded for the 14.00 rendezvous ordered by Jellicoe in 57° 45′ N, 4° 15′ E, but they actually met at 11.15 at 58° 13′ N 2° 42′ E. Meanwhile, the Rosyth force continued towards their rendezvous in latitude 56° 40′ N longitude 5° E.

At 14.00 hours. on 31 May,[14] Jellicoe's 'Dreadnought' battlefleet was in position 37° 57′ N 3° 45′ E, in Fleet Organisation No. 5, with divisions in line ahead disposed abeam to starboard (in other words from left to right) in the order 1st, 2nd, 3rd, 4th, 5th and 6th divisions screened by the 4th, 11th and 12th Destroyer Flotillas with the 4th Light Cruiser Squadron (*Calliope, Constance, Caroline, Royalist* and *Comus*) three miles ahead of the battlefleet. Sixteen miles ahead of the battlefleet and spread eight miles apart on a line of direction N 40° E, and S 40° W, in the order from east to west were the 2nd Cruiser Squadron (*Cochrane, Shannon, Minotaur* and *Hampshire*) and 1st Cruiser Squadron (*Warrior, Defence, Duke of Edinburgh* and *Black Prince*).

The 3rd Battle Cruiser Squadron was about twenty miles ahead of the Grand Fleet, with the light cruisers *Canterbury* five miles ahead and *Chester* five miles on his starboard beam as scouts while the destroyers *Shark, Acasta, Ophelia* and *Christopher* formed an anti-submarine screen ahead. The whole force was steering south at fifty degrees east, zig-zagging, with a speed of advance of fourteen knots.

At 14.00 hours Beatty's force was in position 55° 46′ N 4° 40′ E, course north by east at a speed of nineteen and a half knots with *Lion* and the 1st Battle Cruiser Squadron in single line ahead, screened by *Champion* and ten destroyers of the 13th Flotilla (*Nestor, Nomad, Narborough, Obdurate, Petard, Pelican, Nerissa, Onslow, Moresby, Nicator, Turbulent* and *Termagant*). The 2nd Battle Cruiser Squadron was in single line ahead, three miles east-north-east of *Lion*, screened by six destroyers of the Harwich force (*Lydiard, Liberty, Landrail, Laurel, Moorsom* and *Morris*) with the 5th Battle Squadron, in single line ahead, five miles north-north-west of *Lion*, screened by *Fearless* and nine destroyers of 1st Flotilla (*Acheron, Aerial, Attack, Hydra, Beaver, Goshawk, Defender, Lizard* and *Lapwing*).

Ships of the 1st (*Galatea, Phaeton, Inconstant* and *Cordelia*), 2nd (*Southampton, Birmingham, Nottingham* and *Dublin*) and 3rd (*Falmouth, Yarmouth, Birkenhead* and *Gloucester*) Light-Cruiser Squadrons formed a screen astern, eight miles south-south-east from *Lion*, with the cruisers spread on a line of direction east-north-east and west-south-west five miles apart, in the order from, west to east,

Southampton	*Nottingham*	*Falmouth*	*Birkenhead*	*Inconstant*	*Galatea*
Birmingham	*Dublin*	*Gloucester*		*Cordelia*	*Phaeton*

The seaplane carrier *Engadine* was stationed between *Gloucester* and *Cordelia* while *Yarmouth* of the 3rd Light Cruiser Squadron acted as linking ship between *Lion* and the Light-Cruiser screen.[15]

At 13.58 Beatty was ten miles short of his rendezvous position but, in accordance with orders to join Jellicoe if nothing was in sight by 14.00, made a signal to alter course to north by east at 14.15. At that moment Hipper's First Scouting Squadron was fifty miles east although the screening cruisers were just sixteen miles apart and contact would have been made at about 15.00.

Contact Made

At about 13.00 hours the DFDS passenger and cargo steamship *N.J. Fjord* which was on a voyage from Leith-Fredrikshavn with coal, was overflown by a German Zeppelin when not far north of the Jutland Bank some seventy miles off the Skagerrak.[16] At about 14.00, while at her full speed of fifteen knots, *N.J. Fjord* was sighted by the German light cruiser *Elbing* from the extreme westerly flank of the scouting forces eight miles ahead of Vice Admiral Hipper's battlecruisers. *Elbing* ordered the Danish steamer to stop for inspection and sent the torpedo boat *B110* covered by *B109* to discover whether the ship was British and whether or not she was carrying contraband in her hold. With her engines stopped *N.J. Fjord*'s safety valves blew off and the escaping steam mixed with her funnel smoke to produce a cloud which, in time, would become visible for miles in the clear sky.

B110 went alongside *N.J. Fjord* and sent a search party aboard while *B109* lay off covering the DFDS ship with her gun and torpedo tubes. A short time later a signal from *B109* led to the recall of *B110*'s boarding party after which both destroyers left the scene at increasing speed while at the same time ordering *N.J. Fjord* to await further orders.[17]

Fifteen minutes earlier the light cruiser *Galatea*, in company with her sister *Phaeton*, had been steaming towards her place at the extreme easterly wing of the screen which Vice Admiral Beatty, in his flagship *Lion*, had extended to cover the northward movement of the Battle-Cruiser Fleet. At 14.18 hours in position 56° 52′ N 5° 21′ E, *Galatea* and *Phaeton* had just reached their station on the port wing of Beatty's light cruiser screen when *Galatea* sighted the cloud of smoke and steam, about twelve miles distant, emanating from the hove-to *N.J. Fjord*.[18] Both cruisers increased to full speed and proceeded to investigate the smoke arising from a vessel which was apparently stopped – the usual indication of a German submarine was at work.

Galatea and *Phaeton* had intended to resume their fleet formation as soon as they had completed their investigation but while speeding towards *N.J. Fjord's* smoke, they sighted not only the merchant ship, but the German torpedo boats *B110* and *B109*, pulling away from her vicinity. Furthermore, cruisers of the German 2nd Scouting Group were sighted and at 14.20 hours and *Galatea* signalled 'Urgent. Two cruisers, probably hostile, in sight bearing ESE course unknown' and hoisted 'Enemy in sight' flags. *Galatea* and *Phaeton* closed to the attack and at 14.28 both cruisers opened fire on the two destroyers who proceeded to the Northward at speed.[19]

One of the officers aboard the Danish steamer reported the 'daring spirit of the British' on sighting the two British torpedo boats [actually the cruisers *Galatea* and *Phaeton*] which approached at full speed just as thirty German warships hove into sight. The officer noted that 'without hesitation the two British destroyers attacked', thus opening the great battle.[20]

As the German cruiser *Elbing* hurried to support the torpedo boats *B109* and *B110* which had been forced to flee from the 6-inch guns of *Galatea* and *Phaeton*, she notified Hipper and the High Sea Fleet of the presence of hostile vessels, and, in doing so, broke the wireless silence which the Germans had observed since leaving harbour. *Elbing's* report was detected by British listening and direction-finding stations and her position relative to the Grand Fleet plotted.[21]

The Official Despatches record that at 14.32 'a three-funnelled cruiser [*Elbing*] opened fire at 15,000 yards, salvoes falling both sides of *Galatea* and *Phaeton*, but only one 5.9-in. shell hit *Galatea*: this did not burst'.[22] The German shell hit *Galatea* just below the bridge, failed to explode and went on to penetrate two decks before coming to rest in the disengaged side of the cruiser.[23] The Germans had scored the first hit of the battle but the shell was a dud.

Galatea and *Phaeton* then altered course until they were steering north-west in an attempt to draw the enemy away from German waters and into the arms of the British Battle Cruiser Fleet, a manoeuvre calculated to enable *Galatea*'s supporting ships to cut off the German retreat. At 14.40 *Galatea* reported a large quantity of smoke bearing east-north-east in the distance and by 15.00 was able to signal that the smoke appeared to be coming from seven cruisers and destroyers steering north.[24] It would appear that a considerable German force was at sea and that there was a possibility of luring it to destruction at the hands of Beatty's battlecruisers.

Meanwhile, on seeing the German torpedo boats being chased off, the crew of *N.J. Fjord* restarted the engines and took their twenty-year old ship out of harm's way as fast as her ageing machinery would allow. Had *N.J. Fjord* not been intercepted by the Germans it is highly probable that the two fleets would still have encountered one other albeit sometime later. However, the tactical situation with regard to the light, sea state and visibility, would have been quite different. As it was, this premature contact between the Beatty's and Hipper's light forces was most beneficial for the Germans because, but for the fortuitous presence of the Danish steamer, contact would have been delayed until the British battle fleet would have been able to participate almost at once rather than several hours after the battlecruiser action had begun. As it was, the trap had been sprung too early with Jellicoe still sixty-five miles away to the north while, Scheer who was fifty miles away, was steaming north with the German battleships blissfully unaware that he was steaming towards the whole Grand Fleet.

The Run to the South

There seems to be something wrong with our bloody ships today.

Almost immediately after receipt of *Galatea*'s signal of 14.20 hours Beatty ordered the destroyer screen to reform on a course of south-south-east, the heading for Horn Reef, so as to place his force between the Germans and their base. At 14.32, the general signal to take this course was made by flags.

Unfortunately, Rear Admiral Evan-Thomas in *Barham*, commanding the 5th Battle Squadron, did not act on this signal until 14.40 and maintained his course of north by east at nineteen knots thereby increasing the distance between *Lion* and his flagship by about five miles. The reasons for Evan-Thomas' failure to turn to south-south-east seems to be:

> *Lion*'s signals were difficult to read because of her arrangement of masts and yards.
>
> *Barham* was almost astern of *Lion* and visibility on this bearing was reduced by funnel smoke.
>
> *Tiger*, the nominated repeating ship, failed to pass on the signal by searchlight to *Barham*.
>
> The signal staff of *Lion*, which was nearer to *Tiger*, failed to obey Grand Fleet Battle Orders or use their common sense and therefore did not repeat the change of course to *Barham* by searchlight.
>
> No one seems to have told Beatty that the 5th Battle Squadron had not acknowledged the signal. Beatty was used to his battlecruisers following the leader almost without orders.
>
> Evan-Thomas was used to the more formal battle fleet procedure and would not act without receiving precise orders. Evan-Thomas believed that his squadron was being kept on a Northerly course to prevent the enemy from escaping.

Fortunately, by 14.40 Evan-Thomas had realised that something was not quite right and, at last, turned the 5th Battle Squadron to join the battlecruisers but he was now about ten miles astern. The delay in getting these powerful ships into action would be a cause of regret later that afternoon.

At about 14.33 Commodore Alexander-Sinclair, commanding the 1st Light Cruiser Squadron (LCS) in *Galatea*, reported seeing a large cloud of smoke bearing east-north-east and then turned to the north-west with the intention of drawing the German ships with her.[1] This was the first of many instances on 31 May when British scouting forces allowed themselves to be diverted from their primary function of seeking out and reporting the composition, speed and course of enemy forces.

Initially the Germans followed her but by 14.45 they moved onto a more northerly course.

Beatty had gradually altered course, at first to the East such that by 15.00 he believed that he had cut off the Germans from the Horn Reef Channel. In response to further reports from *Galatea* Beatty turned more and more to the North while Evan-Thomas took a short cut and closed the gap between his squadron and the battlecruisers to about six miles.

Galatea's report made at 14.35 suggested that the enemy force was considerable and not merely and isolated squadron of light cruisers and consequently, at 14.45 Beatty ordered the seaplane carrier *Engadine* to send up a seaplane with orders to scout to the north-north-east.[2] This order was carried out very quickly, and by 15.08, a Short 184 seaplane[3] piloted by Flight Lieutenant F.J. Rutland, RN with Assistant Paymaster G. S. Trewin, RN, as Observer, was airborne and their first reports of the enemy were received in *Engadine* at about 15.30. Unfortunately, low cloud limited the machine to 900 feet and consequently, it was unable to add much to what could be seen from the surface. Furthermore, in order to identify four enemy light cruisers, the seaplane had to fly to within 3,000 yards of them whereupon the ships opened fire on the machine with every gun that would bear. A German account of the incident was published some time later and described their response to the intrusion of the flimsy Short 184 seaplane into the airspace adjacent to their ships:

> A small dark speck appears far off in the grey sky. It approaches visibly and becomes larger and larger and clearer. A powerful battle-plane brought over the sea by the aeroplane parent ship *Campania* [actually *Engadine*], the Cunard liner, rushes up. The armoured body gleams and flashes. Now the anti-aircraft guns are trained on to it. The shrapnel explode around it like a wreath of black and white

points. His way is barred by a sheaf which keeps growing denser. Now one of them appears to have hit. Its body seems to stumble and lay still for a second. It has had enough of it. It rises sharply, turns in a small curve and disappears again in the direction from which it came.[4]

However, the exploding shrapnel in no way interfered with the clarity of their reports from the seaplane and subsequently both Flight Lieutenant Rutland and Assistant Paymaster Trewin were congratulated on their achievement by Vice Admiral Beatty who went on to observe that their achievement 'indicates that seaplanes under such circumstances are of distinct value'.[5] At 16.00 engine trouble forced the machine to return to *Engadine* but because of the latter's slow speed no more seaplanes were sent aloft and the carrier retired to the north accompanied by two destroyers. Sadly, although *Engadine* received their radio reports, the seaplane carrier was unable to pass them on to *Lion*.

Meanwhile, the 1st and 3rd LCSs had closed on *Galatea* thereby leaving the area to the eastward unsearched and consequently, Hipper's 1st Scouting Group, with five battlecruisers at its core, was actually first sighted by *Lion* at 15.30. In the meantime, the 2nd LCS (*Southampton*, *Birmingham*, *Nottingham* and *Dublin*) had come in at high speed and was able to take station ahead of Beatty's Battle Cruisers steering east-south-east, the course on which they first engaged the enemy.

Commander G.J. Mackenzie-Grieve aboard the light cruiser *Birmingham* recorded that:

We went to 'Action' Stations and fell out and went to tea when everything was ready. Up to this time I had no idea that anything was going to happen, and rather looked on the enemy as a small squadron that would fly through the Skagerrak. However, they did not, and five enemy battle cruisers were made out heading roughly S. Easterly. 'Action' was sounded and the Commodore [Goodenough] signalled that the 2nd L.C.S. was to prepare to attack the van of the enemy. The *Lion* turned to the Southward followed by the remainder of the Battle Cruisers, and as they were doing so the enemy opened fire. The enemy consisted of five Battle Cruisers [*Lützow, Derfflinger, Seydlitz, Moltke* and *Von der Tann*] , and they appeared to be accompanied by a considerable number of destroyers, and some light cruisers which kept clear on their far side, and I saw nothing more of the latter.

Our forces consisted of six Battle Cruisers, the *Lion, Tiger, Queen Mary, Princess Royal, Indefatigable* and *New Zealand*: the First, Second and Third L.C.S. and a considerable number of destroyers. The First,

Second and Third L.C.S. proceeded to the Northward, and we, the Second L.C.S., deployed ahead of the Battle Cruisers with the destroyer force on their starboard bow.

The sun was fairly low and over our line, the light in consequence being very favourable indeed for the enemy and extraordinarily bad for us.[6]

Beatty's appreciation of his situation was more upbeat and he reported that:

The visibility at this time was good, the sun behind us and the wing S.E. Being between the enemy and his base, our situation was both tactically and strategically good.[7]

Despite his potentially good strategic position, Beatty's tactical situation was far less favourable because once again, British ships, silhouetted against the sun and in need of gunnery practice, were be pitted against Germans ships that were well-drilled in gunnery and hard to see in the fading light.[8]

Because of the better visibility to the westward, Hipper's force had sighted his British opponents twelve minutes earlier and signalled Scheer 'Enemy battle fleet in sight'. At this time the 1st Scouting Group was steering north-west and Beatty north-east some fourteen miles away. Beatty immediately altered course to the east and a few minutes later altered to east-south-east before forming the Battle Cruiser Fleet into a line of battle.

Hipper realised that on this course the British battlecruisers would cross his wake and thereby cut him off from Scheer's supporting battle squadrons. This he could not allow and at 15.33 Hipper had turned about and was heading south-east in an attempt to draw the British battlecruisers under Scheer's guns. By this time the battlecruisers were converging at a rate of about 150 – 200 yards per minute but Beatty held fire until the Germans were in range of the 12-inch guns of his oldest ship (*Indefatigable*, 18,500 yards) and consequently, Hipper was the first to open fire at 15.47 at an estimated range of 15,000 yards. This turned out to be a considerable over-estimate and was blamed by von Hase[9] on the excitement of the operators of the stereo-rangefinders and several corrections were required before a straddle was obtained. Hipper must have been concerned lest the British opened fire beyond the maximum range of his battlecruisers. Fortunately for the latter, the British squandered the advantage conferred by their possession of longer-ranged guns firing significantly heavier shells. *Lion* replied to the Germans at 15.48.[10]

Captain A.E.M. Chatfield, commanding Beatty' flagship *Lion*, explained why the British 13.5-inch gun armed battlecruisers were so tardy in opening fire despite having the considerable advantage of longer-ranged weapons:

> We were now steaming at 19 knots on a south-south-easterly course. The enemy battle-cruisers were rapidly closing us steering south-westerly. The range-receiver on the bridge showed 20,000 yards. I was on the compass platform with my navigator, Commander The Hon. Arthur Strutt, and my small staff. Beatty remained for a time on his own bridge, below me, with Commodore Bentinck, Commander Bailey and Spickernell, his secretary. I wanted him to come on the compass platform and sent a message to Seymour [Beatty's Flag Lieutenant], telling him to advise Beatty that the range was closing rapidly and that we ought almost at once to be opening fire. This was a duty that I had actually handed over to the Chief of Staff [Bentinck]. But I could get no reply, the Vice Admiral was engaged in sending an important message to the Commander-in-Chief. 18,000 yards. I told Longhurst to be ready to open fire immediately. The turrets were already loaded and trained on the leading enemy ship, the *Lützow*. At 3.45 the range was 16,000 yards. I could wait no longer and told Longhurst to open fire. At the same moment the enemy did so.[11]

Beatty's Battlecruisers Defeated During the Run South

Unfortunately, as at Dogger Bank, the Battle Cruiser Fleet had misinterpreted a distribution of fire signal which should have resulted in *Lion*, *Princess Royal*, *Queen Mary*, *Tiger* and *New Zealand* engaging *Lützow*, *Derfflinger*, *Seydlitz*, *Moltke* and *Von der Tann* respectively leaving *Indefatigable* free to take on *Moltke* or *Von der Tann*. Unfortunately, *Queen Mary* and *Tiger* missed Beatty's signal and in the general confusion, *Lion* and *Princess Royal* engaged *Lützow*, and *Queen Mary* missed out *Derfflinger* and engaged *Seydlitz* while *Moltke* was targeted ineffectually by *Tiger* and *New Zealand* and *Indefatigable* took on *Von der Tann*.

This left *Derfflinger* undisturbed but it was some time before her shooting became effective. In comparison, the four leading German battlecruisers engaged their opposite numbers with *Lützow* opposing *Lion*, *Derfflinger* firing on *Princess Royal*, *Seydlitz* engaging *Queen Mary* and *Moltke* shooting at *Tiger* while *Von der Tann* missed out *New Zealand* and engaged *Indefatigable*. Despite the rapid closing of the range, the original estimates by both sides were so far out that it was several minutes before either side scored a hit. The first German ships to score hits were *Lützow* and *Moltke* which were both of the ships being engaged by two British battlecruisers.[12]

Moltke was the first to score hitting *Tiger* at 15.50 on the forecastle and at 15.51 on the shelter deck and hitting both 'Q' and 'X' turrets and temporarily put both out of action by 15.55. All told, *Tiger* had been hit nine times by *Moltke* by 16.00 hours. As John Campbell pointed out:

> *Moltke* made two hits in the first three minutes and continued hitting in one of the most accurate spells of firing in the whole battle.[13]

Meanwhile, *Lion* was hit by *Lützow* at 15.51 and 15.52. Commander G.J. Mackenzie-Grieve aboard *Birmingham* observed that:

> Both our own fire and that of the enemy seemed good, indeed that of the enemy will ever seem good! But whereas we had behind us to the westward a clear sky and a horizon which silhouetted our ships clearly, the enemy ships were difficult to discern. Behind them to the eastward there was a dull grey sky and a misty horizon; spotting for us was therefore difficult and for him much easier. During the run south, therefore, the Battle-Cruiser Force had a severe disadvantage, especially under the conditions of range and speed.
>
> The enemy's shooting was good and our line was soon straddled. Personally I thought that our B.C.s were shooting very short. For some time nothing of very much importance happened except that the leading enemy Battle Cruiser started sending up a number of white Very's lights, as many as half a dozen at a time.[14]

By 15.54 the range had shortened to 13,000 yards and the action was very fierce with *Derfflinger*, for example, firing 12-inch salvoes every forty seconds and 5.9-inch salvoes every seven seconds. It is possible that at this time both Admirals were concerned about the possible effects of secondary armaments and turned away thereby opening the range. Despite their concerns, there is little evidence that these weapons caused any significant damage to battlecruisers at any stage of the battle.

At 16.00 *Lützow* hit *Lion*'s 'Q' turret putting it out of action – its guns had fired a total of just twelve rounds by then. The turret was hit at the junction of the front plate and the roof, and cordite charges within the turret caught fire. Although mortally wounded, the turret officer, Major Harvey RM, gave orders for the magazine to be flooded and consequently, when flames from the turret fire ignited charges in the hoist, the ship did not blow up.

Princess Royal was hit at 15.58 when two shells from *Derfflinger* struck her, one of which put her Argo fire control system out of action temporarily. Another hit at 16.00 hours struck near 'B' barbette. By 16.00 the German battlecruisers had hit their British counterparts fifteen times and received only four in return. These included two on *Lützow* by *Lion* and two on *Seydlitz* by *Queen Mary*. Immediately thereafter, *Lützow* scored three hits on *Lion* between 16.01 and 16.03.[15]

The Loss of *Indefatigable*

At about 16.02 or 16.03 *Indefatigable* was hit by two successive salvoes from *Von der Tann* at a range of about 15,500 – 16,000 yards. These caused a fatal magazine explosion and the ship staggered out of line sinking by the stern. Only two men out of her crew of 1,017 were picked up three and three-quarter hours later by the German torpedo boat *S16*.[16] The exact cause of her loss remains unclear but it is likely that cordite charges in 'X' turret were ignited by a shell strike and the flash passed down to the magazine below. One of the two survivors was Signalman C. Falmer who witnessed the event from his position in the spotting top on the mainmast and then experienced a 180-foot fall into the sea as the mainmast collapsed:

> There was a terrific explosion aboard the ship – the magazines went. I saw the guns go up in the air just like matchsticks – 12" guns they were – bodies and everything. She was beginning to settle down. Within half a minute the ship turned right over and she was gone. I was 180 feet up and I was thrown well clear of the ship, otherwise I would have been sucked under. I was practically unconscious, turning over really. At last I came up on top of the water. When I came up there was another fellow named Jimmy Green and we got a piece of wood. He was on one end and I was on the other end. A couple of minutes afterwards some shells came over and Jim was minus his head – so I was left on my lonesome.[17]

Commander G.J. Mackenzie-Grieve aboard *Birmingham* witnessed the destruction of *Indefatigable* and the highly accurate German gunnery:

> Shortly after this an enormous column of smoke [*Indefatigable*] rose from down our line, many hundreds of feet into the air. I could see no ship except *Lion*, and the *Tiger* a little out of the line nearer the enemy. The enemy's shooting at the *Lion* became extremely accurate, and she sheered a little to starboard, the effect of the fall of shot being very noticeable.[18]

The shooting of the British battlecruisers was not very effective between 16.00 and 16.20 but fortunately for Vice Admiral Beatty the 5th Battle Squadron was about to enter the fight. Thus, *Barham* had opened fire on the German light cruiser *Frankfurt* at 15.58 at a range of 17,000 yards. Her sisters *Valiant* and *Warspite* joined in shortly afterwards firing on the cruiser *Pillau* and her escorting destroyers which had to use smokescreens to affect their escape.[19]

At 16.05 Evan-Thomas sighted the German 1st Scouting Group and *Barham* opened fire on *Von der Tann* at range of 19,000 yards. The 5th Battle Squadron's shooting was excellent and the ships soon registered hits with their 1,920lb 15-inch shells on *Moltke* and *Von der Tann*. The latter was hit on the stern below the waterline and when the shell exploded it hurled sections of armour plate through several compartments causing serious flooding and damaging the steering engine. Emergency repairs kept *Von der Tann* in the line but she had 600 tons of water in her after compartments and a distinct list.

Meanwhile the pressure on Beatty's battlecruisers was such that at 16.09 Beatty ordered the 13th Destroyer Flotilla to attack the German battlecruisers. Hipper countered at 16.14 by ordering his torpedo boats to attack Beatty's Battle Cruiser Fleet.

At 16.11 the British battlecruisers experienced a submarine scare when there was the sighting of a supposed periscope by the destroyer *Landrail*, one of the destroyers screening Beatty's capital ships. Beatty reported that:

> It would appear that at this time we passed through a screen of enemy submarines. In evidence of this a torpedo was sighted passing astern of 'Lion' from starboard to port. The destroyer 'Landrail' of 9th Flotilla, who was on our Port beam trying to take station ahead, sighted the periscope of a submarine on her Port quarter, and at the same time the track of a torpedo which passed under her and crossed the line of the Battle Cruisers between 'Tiger' and 'New Zealand'. Though causing considerable inconvenience from smoke, the presence of 'Lydiard' and 'Landrail' undoubtedly preserved the Battle Cruisers from closer submarine attack. 'Nottingham' also reported a submarine on the Starboard beam.[20]

Despite the panic experienced by the British, examination of German records post-war revealed that no U-boats took part in the battle.

Soon afterwards the ships of the 5th Battle Squadron were ordered to concentrate in pairs on the two rear German ships such that *Barham* and *Valiant* engaged *Moltke* and *Warspite* and *Malaya* fired at *Von der Tann*. By

16.15 all four battleships were firing and *Moltke* soon began to suffer, being hit by a 15-inch shell which destroyed a 5.9-inch gun at 16.16. Ten minutes later she was hit on her armoured belt by another 15-inch shell. Meanwhile at 16.23 *Tiger* scored a hit on the stern of *Von der Tann* which obscured the latter from the attentions of *Warspite* and *Malaya*.[21]

The shooting of the 5th Battle Squadron was much more impressive than that of the battlecruisers with salvoes of closely-spaced shells being fired at very short intervals. Otto Groos remarked that 'the 15-inch salvoes possessed too little spread'.[22] The German battle cruisers zigzagged at very short, irregular intervals in an attempt to disrupt British fire control.

Encouraged by their support Beatty once again closed the range and fierce fighting broke out with *Queen Mary* coming under fire from both *Derfflinger* and *Seydlitz*. *Queen Mary* was firing rapid, tightly grouped eight gun broadsides at *Derfflinger* which was straddled twice suffering one hit each time.

The Destruction of *Queen Mary*

With the light in their favour the German gunners continued to hammer the British ships, with *Lion* suffering several more hits which caused flooding and fires while *Princess Royal* had her after turret put out of action. Meanwhile, *Queen Mary* had scored four hits on *Seydlitz* two of which were particularly punishing. The first of these penetrated the side armour and exploded causing many fires while the second exploded in the aftermost turret igniting four charges which killed the turret crew. Fortunately flash-tight doors prevented the fire from penetrating the magazine.

In return she was hit by at least four 11-inch shells from *Seydlitz* in the first thirty minutes, including one on the after 4-inch battery and possibly another near 'X' turret. The ammunition fire observed by *Seydlitz* suggests that there was considerable damage in the 4-inch battery. Petty Officer Ernest Francis remembered that:

> There was a heavy blow, I should imagine in the after 4-inch Battery and a lot of dust and pieces flying around the top of 'X' turret.[23]

At 16.21, about five minutes before she blew up *Queen Mary* received a 12-inch hit from *Derfflinger* on 'Q' turret which put the right gun out of action although the left gun continued firing. Midshipman Jocelyn Storey observed that:

> Everything went beautifully until 4.21, when 'Q' turret was hit by a heavy shell and the right gun put out of action. We continued firing

with the left gun for two or three minutes and then a most awful explosion took place and the ship broke in half by the foremast. Our left gun broke off outside the turret and the rear end fell into the working chamber; the right gun also slid down. The turret was filled with flying metal and several men were killed. A lot of cordite caught fire and blazed up and several people were gassed.[24]

This hit was followed by another two from *Derfflinger* at 16.26, one of which struck 'A' or 'B' turret and the subsequent explosion shook the ship. Hydraulic pressure also failed in 'Q' turret.[25] Seconds later, 'A' and 'B' magazines exploded, blowing the ship in two. The forward part sank immediately; the after part, with the stern clear of the water and the screws still turning, remained afloat briefly until another explosion blew it up. The destroyer *Laurel* picked up seventeen survivors, *Petard* picked up one and the German torpedo boat *G8* two more but 1,266 of *Queen Mary*'s crew were lost.

Petty Officer Ernest Francis described his experiences of *Queen Mary*'s final moments thus:

I put my head through the hole in the roof of the turret and nearly fell through again. The after 4-inch Battery was smashed out of all recognition, and then I noticed that the ship had got an awful list to port. I dropped back again into the turret and told Lieutenant Ewert the state of affairs. He said, 'Francis, we can do no more than give them a chance, clear the turret.'

'Clear the turret,' I said, and out they went. PO Stares was the last I saw coming up from the Working Chamber, and I asked him whether he had passed the order to the Magazine and Shell Room, and he told me it was no use as the water was right up to the trunk leading to the shell room, so the bottom of the ship must have been torn out of her. Then I said, 'Why didn't you come up?' He simply said, 'There was no order to leave the turret.'

I went through the Cabinet and out on top and Lieutenant Ewert was following me; suddenly he stopped and went back into the turret. I believe he went back because he thought someone was inside.

I was halfway down the ladder at the back of the turret when Lieutenant Ewert went back. The ship had an awful list to port by this time, so much so that men getting off the ladder went sliding down to port. I got to the bottom rung of the ladder and could not, by my own efforts, reach the stanchions lying on the deck from the ship's side, starboard side. I knew if I let go I should go sliding down to port like some of the others must have done, and probably get smashed up sliding down. Two of my turret's crew, seeing my difficulty, came to my assistance. They were AB Long, Turret Trainer, and AB Lane, left gun No 4. Lane held Long at full length from the ship's side and I dropped from the ladder, caught Long's legs and so gained the starboard side. These two men had no thought for their own safety; they knew I wanted assistance and that was good enough for them. They were both worth a VC twice over.

When I got to the ship's side, there seemed to be quite a fair crowd, and they didn't appear to be very anxious to take to the water. I called out to them, 'Come on you chaps, who's coming for a swim?' Someone answered, 'She will float for a long time yet,' but something, I don't pretend to know what it was, seemed to be urging me to get away, so I clambered over the slimy bilge keel and fell off into the water, followed I should think by about five more men. I struck away from the ship as hard as I could and must have covered nearly fifty yards when there was a big smash, and stopping and looking round, the air seemed to be full of fragments and flying pieces.

A large piece seemed to be right above my head, and acting on impulse, I dipped under to avoid being struck, and stayed under as long as I could, and then came to the top again, and coming behind me I heard a rush of water, which looked very like surf breaking on a beach and I realized it was the suction or backwash from the ship which had just gone. I hardly had time to fill my lungs with air when it was on me. I felt it was no use struggling against it, so I let myself go for a moment or two, then I struck out, but I felt it was a losing game and remarked to myself, 'What's the use of you struggling, you're done, and I actually ceased my efforts to reach the top, when a small voice seemed to say, 'Dig out'.

I started afresh, and something bumped against me. I grasped it and afterwards found it was a large hammock, but I felt I was getting very weak and roused myself sufficiently to look around for something more substantial to support me. Floating right in front of me was what I believe to be the centre bulk of our Pattern 4 target. I managed to push myself on the hammock close to the timber and grasped a piece of rope hanging over the side. My next difficulty was to get on top and with a small amount of exertion I kept on. I managed to reeve my arms through a strop and I must have become unconscious.

When I came to my senses again I was halfway off the spar but I managed to get back again. I was very sick and seemed to be full of oil fuel. My eyes were blocked up completely with it and I could not see. I suppose the oil had got a bit crusted and dry. I managed by turning back the sleeve of my jersey, which was thick with oil, to expose a part of the sleeve of my flannel, and thus managed to get the thick oil off my face and eyes, which were aching awfully. Then I looked and I believed I was the only one left of that fine Ship's Company. What had really happened was the *Laurel* had come and picked up the remainder and not seeing me got away out of the zone of fire, so how long I was in the water I do not know. I was miserably cold, but not without hope of being picked up, as it seemed to me that I had only to keep quiet and a ship would come for me.

After what seemed ages to me, some destroyers came racing along, and I got up on the spar, steadied myself for the moment, and waved my arms. *Petard*, one of our big destroyers, saw me and came over, but when I got on the spar to wave to them, the swell rolled the spar over and I rolled off. I was nearly exhausted again getting back. The destroyer came up and a line was thrown to me, which, needless to say, I grabbed hold of for all I was worth, and was quickly hauled up on to the deck of the destroyer.[26]

Upon seeing the magazine explosion which broke *Queen Mary* in half Beatty remarked to Chatfield that 'There seems to be something wrong with our bloody ships today' and then ordered a turn two points towards the enemy.[27]

After the loss of *Queen Mary*, *Seydlitz* shifted her fire to *Tiger* while *Derfflinger* targeted *Princess Royal* and the latter was hit at 16.27 and 16.32 hours and probably once more. *Tiger* was hit by *Moltke* at 16.22 and 16.24 suffering three hits during this period. *Von der Tann* hit *New Zealand* on 'X' barbette at 16.26 but the British battlecruisers were also inflicting damage in return with *Princess Royal* hitting *Lützow* at 16.15, *Tiger* hitting *Von der Tann* at 16.20 and 16.23 and the 5th Battle Squadron hitting *Moltke* at 16.23 and 16.26.[28]

The Cordite Fire in *Lion's* 'Q' Turret

At 16.28 hours a serious cordite fire blazed up in *Lion's* 'Q' turret which had been hit and put out of action at twenty-eight minutes earlier. Fortunately, the magazine had been flooded before the fire broke thereby saving Beatty's flagship from the fate of her sister *Queen Mary*. Commander G.J. Mackenzie-Grieve aboard *Birmingham* reported that:

> I saw an enormous plate which I judge to be the top of a turret blown into the air. It appeared to rise very slowly turning round and round and looking very like an aeroplane. I should say it rose some four or five hundred feet and looking through glasses I could distinctly the

holes in it for the bolts. My attention was drawn from this by a sheet of flame by her second funnel which shot up about 60 feet and soon died down but she did not immediately disappear. It seemed to have no effect on the ship except that her midships turret seemed out of action. One gun was about horizontal and the other one at a considerable angle.[29]

Captain Chatfield aboard *Lion* remembered that:

It was not long after the disaster to the *Indefatigable*, that I heard a resounding clank behind me. Turning round from the compass which I was watching carefully to ensure that the Chief Quartermaster below in the conning tower was steering that steady course which is so important for gunnery, I saw a large flame spring up from Q turret (some hundred feet abaft the bridge). Those on the bridge who had been looking after told me the armoured roof of Q turret had gone up in the air and fallen on the upper deck.

Realising that the magazine might be in danger, I told the C.T. to order Q magazine to be flooded immediately. My order, however, had been forestalled by Major Harvey R.M.L.I., the turret commander.[30]

In his autobiography, Chief Gunner Alexander Grant of *Lion* wrote that:

There were four [turrets] named A, B, Q and X. Each one had four separate magazines. As soon as fire had opened I made for A and B magazines. They were in the fore part of the ship and in close proximity to each other. I found everything quite satisfactory, no delay, only one door opened, and not more than one full charge in the handing room. The supply was meeting demand. I left orders that if there was a lull in the firing, the party must not forget to close the door of the magazine in use.[31]

He then made for 'Q' magazine which was in the centre of the ship and on entering the handing room found the magazine door closed and the crew standing about in silence.

When I asked what was the matter, the Sergeant in charge said that something had gone wrong in the turret and that the Major in charge of the turret had ordered the magazine to be flooded. I inquired how long the valves for flooding had been opened and when I learned that they had been opened for some time I was convinced that the magazine was now completely flooded. It was also reported that the supply cages were full. It would therefore appear that there was outside the magazine at least two full charges in the supply cages and there may have been two more in the loading cages in the working chamber which was immediately under the guns.

While Grant was elucidating what had happened men from the working chamber came down the trunk into the handing room and explained that 'Q' turret had been pierced by a shell which exploded inside killing the gun's crews and putting the turret out of action. They told how the mortally wounded Major Harvey had ordered the magazines to be flooding thereby safeguarding the ship, a deed for which he was posthumously awarded the Victoria Cross.

Grant then made his way to 'X' magazine finding everything in order and then decided to return to 'Q' because he felt uneasy about the flooded magazine.

> I had reached the hatchway leading to the flat above the magazine and by the providence of God had only one foot on the step of the Jacob's Ladder, when suddenly there was a terrific roar, followed by flame and dense smoke. Had I been a few seconds earlier and thus further down the Ladder, I would have met the same fate as all those fine men below who were burned to death.

All the cordite charges outside of *Lion's* 'Q' magazine had caught fire and deflagrated but their combined explosive force was not powerful enough to sink the battlecruiser thereby vindicating Grant's safety measures which had left just eight charges exposed to ignition. It is quite possible that if Grant's cordite safety procedures had been in use throughout the Beatty's force, none of his battlecruisers would have been sunk by magazine explosions.

The German 1st Scouting Squadron, having damaged *Lion* and sank *Indefatigable* and *Queen Mary*, now had complete tactical control of the battlefield. Their superior Zeiss rangefinders enabled them to repeatedly hit all the British battlecruisers silhouetted in the late afternoon sun with fast and accurate fire, while leading them onto destruction towards the oncoming High Seas fleet with its battleships. The British squadron meanwhile, struggled to identify the German fleet's range, hidden in the murk of the clouds and funnel smoke. Fortunately, for Beatty, the powerful 5th Battle Squadron was coming to his rescue and Jellicoe's Grand Fleet battleships were not far behind.

The Destroyer Action

As the hard-pressed British battlecruiser drew out of range to repair damage and extinguish fires and to ease his situation Beatty ordered his destroyers, led by the light cruiser *Champion*, to attack Hipper's ships. The Official Despatches record that:

> Eight destroyers of the 13th Flotilla, 'Nestor,' 'Nomad,' 'Nicator,' 'Narborough,' 'Pelican,' 'Petard,' 'Obdurate,' 'Nerissa,' with 'Moorsom' and 'Morris' of 10th Flotilla, 'Turbulent' and 'Termagant' of the 9th Flotilla, having been ordered to attack the enemy with torpedoes when opportunity offered, moved out at 4.15 p.m. simultaneously with a similar movement on the part of the enemy.
>
> The attack was carried out in a most gallant manner and with great determination. Before arriving at a favourable position to fire torpedoes they intercepted an enemy force consisting of a Light Cruiser and 15 Destroyers. A fierce engagement ensued at close quarters, with the result that the enemy were forced to retire on their Battle Cruisers, having lost two destroyers sunk, and having their torpedo attack frustrated. Our destroyers sustained no loss in this engagement, but their attack on the enemy Battle Cruisers was rendered less effective owing to some of the destroyers having dropped astern during the fight. Their position was therefore unfavourable for torpedo attack.[32]

At about the same time, the German light cruiser *Regensburg* led the 9th Torpedo-Boat Flotilla and part of the 2nd Torpedo-Boat Flotilla toward Evan-Thomas' 5th Battle Squadron in an attempt to relieve the pressure on Hipper's battlecruisers.

However, the German torpedo boats were thwarted by the advance of their British counterparts and a fierce destroyer action which had begun at about 16.30 hours in between the lines of capital ships and lasted for approximately fifteen minutes. Commander Mackenzie-Grieve observed the onset of the destroyer action:

> The Flotillas went on full speed with the *Champion* passing partly through and mostly astern of us (II L.C.S.) steering a course of about four points in from ours towards the enemy. At the same time his destroyers approached mostly from ahead of his line but some from through the line, and a destroyer engagement of a sort appeared to take place.[33]

The primary function expected of British destroyers was to repel an enemy torpedo attack and consequently they were larger than their

German counterparts and carried a heavier gun armament at the expense of torpedoes. A furious battle developed between the destroyers and torpedo-boats with ranges down to as little as 600 yards. The German vessels were unable to break through the British destroyer screen and fired eighteen torpedoes ineffectively at about 9,000 yards scoring no hits.

Nomad was brought to a standstill by a hit in her engine room while *Petard* was hit twice but suffered little damage. Of the German torpedo boats, *V27* was brought to a stop by two hits in her forward engine room, *S36* was damaged by splinters and *V29* was hit aft by a torpedo believed to have been launched by *Petard*. *V29*'s stern soon disappeared but her bows remained afloat for about thirty minutes. *V26* took off *V27*'s crew and then sank her wreck by gunfire before rescuing some of *V29*'s complement. *S35* took aboard the remainder of *V29*'s survivors. The light cruiser *Regensburg* provided gunfire support to the German boats of the 9th Flotilla but 13th Flotilla's light cruiser *Champion* took little if any part in the action while two of the twelve British destroyers, *Narborough* and *Pelican*, did not open fire.

The 19-year-old Sub Lieutenant and Navigator aboard the destroyer *Pelican* described his experiences at Jutland in a letter to seventeen-year-old Midshipman Carbutt who was in hospital having lost a leg during the battle:

> We were attached to the Battle Cruisers and were with them throughout the action, so we were probably in the thick of it, as no doubt you saw in the papers that the battle cruisers stood the brunt of the action, and we were in action for about 3 hours before the battleships arrived upon the scene.
>
> To start with it was all at such long range that the Destroyers were rather out of it, except there were plenty of 15" falling around us, and we just watched; it really seemed rather like a battle practice on a large scale, and we could see the flashes of the German guns on the horizon.
>
> Then they ordered us to attack, so we bustled off at full bore. Being navigator, also having control of all the guns, I was on the Bridge all the time and remained there for 12 hours without leaving it at all.
>
> When we got fairly close I sighted a good looking Hun Destroyer which I thought I'd like to strafe. You know, its awful fun to know that you can blaze off at a real ship and do as much damage as you like. Well, I'd just got their range on the guns and we'd just fired one round when some of our own Destroyers coming from the opposite direction got between us and the enemy and completely blanketed us, so we had to stop firing as the risk of hitting one of our own ships

was just too great – which was rather rot. Shortly afterwards, they recalled us, so we bustled back again. How any Destroyers got out of it is perfectly wonderful.

Literally there were hundreds of progs [projectiles] all round us from a 15" to a 4", and you know what a big splash a 15" [actually German 12-inch or 11-inch shells] bursting in the water does make; we got soaked through by the spray.

Just as we were getting back a whole salvo of big shells fell just in front of us and short of our big ships. The Skipper and I did rapid calculations as to how long it would take them to re-load, fire again, time of flight, etc. as we had to go right through the spot. We came to the conclusion that as they were short they would probably go up a bit and [they] didn't, but luckily they altered deflection and the next lot fell just astern of us. Anyhow we managed to come out of that lot, without the ship or a soul on board being touched.

It's extraordinary the amount of knocking about the big ship can stand. One saw them hit, and they seemed to be one mass of flames and smoke and you think they're gone, but when the smoke clears away they are apparently none the worse for wear and are still firing away.

But to see a ship blow up is a terrible, but wonderful sight; an enormous volume of flame and smoke about 200 ft. high and great heaps of metal etc. blown sky high and then, when the smoke clears away, not a sign of the ship.[34]

The German torpedo boats fired ten torpedoes during 16.33 to 16.35 but the British northward turn at 16.40 took Beatty's battlecruisers out of harm's way. *Nestor* and *Nicator* each fired two torpedoes at the German battlecruisers at a range of 5,000-6,000 yards but failed to hit their targets.[35] Beatty was impressed with the determination of his destroyers and in his despatch wrote:

These destroyer attacks were indicative of the spirit pervading His Majesty's Navy, and were worthy of its highest traditions. I propose to bring to your notice a recommendation of Commander Bingham for the Victoria Cross, and other officers for some recognition of their conspicuous gallantry.[36]

At 16.43 the destroyer action was ended by *Lion* which signalled 'Destroyers Recalled' as the battlecruisers hauled round to the north following an utmost priority signal from Commodore Goodenough leading the 2nd LCS in *Southampton*.

The High Seas Fleet Sighted

At 15.54 Hipper reported being in action with six battlecruisers giving their position, course and speed and at 16.02 Scheer altered course to 302 degrees in an attempt to trap the British force between two German forces. Subsequently, the German battleship *König* reported the British battlecruisers turning to the north. Two minutes later Scheer ordered a twenty-three degree turn which put the High Seas Fleet's battleships into six columns steering 325 degrees. By 16.48 hours the British battlecruisers and the ships of the 5th Battle Squadron could be seen from Scheer's flagship *Friedrich der Grosse* although the latter was well out of range.[37]

During the destroyer action Commodore Goodenough's 2nd LCS, led by *Southampton* with *Birmingham*, *Nottingham* and *Dublin* in company, had been in a position approximately two to three miles ahead of *Lion* and at 16.30 Goodenough reported sighting a light cruiser, then at 16.33 'Battleships SE'. At 16.38 he reported by radio to both Beatty and Jellicoe 'Have sighted enemy battlefleet bearing approximately SE course of enemy N.' Goodenough closed to within about 13,000 yards of the German battleships before the latter identified the cruisers as British and opening heavy fire at a lethal range. Miraculously the four cruisers emerged almost unscathed from their dangerous situation thanks to a combination of weaving wildly and zigzagging. The only casualty was *Southampton* which suffered an oblique hit at 16.50 on the port side aft by an 11-inch shell from the battleship *Nassau* when at a range of 20,100 yards.[38]

Commander Mackenzie-Grieve aboard *Birmingham* recalled the 2nd Light Cruiser Squadron's initial encounter with Scheer's battleships:

> We then sighted the German Battle Fleet coming up from the Southward and steering as I thought about 230° from our course. They appeared to be going quite slowly, and presented a fine sight, in perfect station and making no smoke. It struck me as curious that they were led by the 'Roon' [not present at the battle & more likely to be a four-funnelled light cruiser] and that no other cruisers and destroyers were in sight. The 'Lion' hoisted a signal (I think general) 16 points to starboard. The II L.C.S., however, went on to reconnoitre the enemy's battle squadrons and got in to, I should say, about 12,000 yards though it was probably a little more. I looked astern down when the Battle Cruisers were turning, and could see very little damage in the 'Lion' except that the midships turret was obviously still out of action; the guns appeared black. There was a large mark on her side just before the turret which looked like a large square hole, and a fire was

still burning at the base of her No. 2 funnel. I did not notice the other B.C.s except 'Tiger' which appeared unscathed.

By this time we passed pretty close to the Battle Fleet [i.e. High seas Fleet], and I began to wonder what was going to happen to us when 'Southampton' turned to starboard and I think just when the [German] battleships opened fire. We turned in succession, and in consequence I think we in the 'Birmingham' got closer to them than anyone.

We were very heavily shelled, and the enemy's shooting was very good. We did not reply though the other ships did with I think no possible effect.

Heavy shells falling all round the four ships and to me it seemed unlikely that we should get away at all. One salvo fell all round us abreast the after funnel, three to starboard and two to port, and so close that the ship shook as if we had rammed something. I do not think the three starboard ones fell 20 feet away at the outside. I had the time of flight taken as near as possible and it was about 40 seconds towards the end of the shelling. Splinters were plainly audible and often visible, and the noise of the bursting of the shells was very impressive. Once what appeared to be a half shell passed us ricocheting, seemingly quite slowly but making a noise like an express train and falling in the water some hundreds of yard ahead, and at another a whole shell was plainly visible spinning round on its side beam on to the line of flight.

Soon, though it seemed a considerable time, we got out of range and the 'Southampton' made a signal to close. Salvoes came close several times as we attempted to steer towards her, and once or twice we had to steer off to port, but eventually the squadron formed in line ahead considerably strung out and the Fifth B.S., a welcome sight, appeared on the port bow. Our battle cruisers were out of sight as far as I could see and enemy battle cruisers had evidently turned to the northward too. I could only see flashes from guns from both sides and even Fifth B.S. became very indistinct in the haze. The "Southampton" made a sharp swing to starboard, apparently to sight the enemy battle fleet and on being shelled once more came back to again to a northerly course.[39]

Scheer's battleships, which had been steaming west to entrap Beatty's battlecruisers, had turned to the north-west when Hipper reported the presence of the 5th Battle Squadron. Beatty altered course to close Goodenough and almost at once sighted Scheer and consequently turned his battlecruisers first to north-west and then to north to close

Jellicoe as quickly as possible. He also signalled Jellicoe to report the sighting of the German battlefleet but the signal was garbled/mutilated and only added to Jellicoe's confusion when he came to deploy the Grand Fleet's battle squadrons.

Although it is natural to lead from the front, Beatty's order to turn sixteen points [i.e. reverse course] in succession was of arguable merit because it not only placed his weakest ships in the most exposed position but, with its fixed turning point, could have a target for a German concentration of fire. As it was, Hipper was still in confusion from the British destroyer's torpedo attack and Scheer was not yet in effective range. Unfortunately, Evan-Thomas, who was eight miles astern, had neither seen the signal to turn nor *Southampton's* sighting report, and therefore continued heading south. At 16.48 he passed Beatty heading north and was signalled to turn 16 points to starboard in succession. Worse still, this signal was not made executive [i.e. the flag hauled down] until 16.45 when *Barham* was some distance past *Lion* and consequently, the 5th Battle Squadron was once again separated from the battlecruisers.[40] This time the situation was serious because the turning point was well within range of the leading German battleships and therefore turning in succession made the four ships of the 5th Battle Squadron easy targets. Once again, Beatty and his Flag staff had blundered by making the wrong signal.

Barham and *Malaya* were both hit heavily during this turning manoeuvre and it is possible that latter, the last ship in the line, would have been even more heavily damaged if the commanding officer, Captain Boyle, had not turned her out of line and thereby partially avoiding the German concentration of fire. In meantime Commodore Goodenough was still closing on Scheer's battleships to confirm their course and disposition. Unfortunately, there is no evidence that any signal from *Southampton* giving the composition of the German fleet reached either Beatty or Jellicoe at this time. One can argue that it would have been well worth the loss of a light cruiser or two to get this information.

Beatty's turn to the northwest was followed by Hipper who made a 180 degree turn to take up his station ahead of the High Seas Fleet. Hipper's change of course enabled some of the recalled British destroyers to obey the recall while at the same time engaging the enemy. Thus, *Nicator* and *Petard*, which had delayed to assist the crippled *Nomad* and *Nestor*, fired four torpedoes before retiring. One of these from *Petard* hit *Seydlitz* below her forward armoured belt tearing a huge hole in her stout hull but she was able to remain in the line.

At 16.43 Beatty recalled his destroyers and at 16.50 they were ordered to close and take station ahead but not all boats saw the signal while others could not respond. *Nicator* and *Nestor* again closed on the German battlecruisers firing torpedoes at a range of about 4,000 yards achieving no success in either case. *Nicator* escaped unscathed but *Nestor* was hit twice in her boilers but refused a tow from *Petard*. The latter also made a second attack firing her last torpedo at about 6,500 yards and is usually credited with hitting *Seydlitz* on the starboard side at 16.57, although *Turbulent* also fired three torpedoes at about the same time. The battlecruiser's torpedo bulkhead withstood the explosion and she was able to remain in the line. Meanwhile, the German torpedo boats *G41*, *V44*, *G87* and *G86* made another attack on the British line at 16.50 firing seven torpedoes at a range of 9,000 – 10,000 yards without success.[41]

The Sinking of *Nomad* and *Nestor*

Meanwhile, the immobilized *Nomad* and barely mobile *Nestor* awaited their fate at the hands of the 5.9-inch secondary guns of the oncoming battleships of the High Seas Fleet. Both destroyers lay ahead and to port of the oncoming German battleships. The stationary *Nomad* was the first to be destroyed by a hail of fire from *Friedrich der Grosse*, *Prinzregent Luitpold*, *Kaiser* and *Kaiserin* but still managed to fire her last torpedo before rolling over and sinking at 17.30 leaving her survivors clinging to wreckage. *Nomad's* fore magazine was hit and blew up shortly before she sank.

Meanwhile, Bingham, who had twice refused to endanger other destroyers which had offered to tow *Nestor* clear of the scene and having destroyed confidential books and secret papers, swung his crippled vessel round to face the enemy. He steadfastly steered his crippled ship towards the German waiting until the last possible moment to fire his last torpedo so as to get the closest possible range before being sunk. It is believed that *Nestor* came under the fire of eight battleships including *Prinzregent Luitpold*, *Thüringen*, *Helgoland Ostfriesland*, *Oldenburg*, *Rheinland*, *Posen*, and *Nassau*. Despite being overwhelmed by numerous shells, *Nestor's* last torpedo was sent on its way but, like that of *Nomad*, failed to find a target. *Nestor* sank slowly by the stern at 17.35 after being under fire for twelve minutes. The Germans rescued seventy-two survivors from *Nomad* and eighty from *Nestor*, including both their Captains, a surprisingly high number considering the weight of high explosive and steel that had sunk them. The first destroyer action of the battle was over and, of the thirty-eight torpedoes fired, only two hit which suggested that the menace of torpedo attacks had been overestimated. However, it should be noted that this largely untried weapon exerted considerable tactical effect by causing both battle lines to turn away at a critical moment thereby ending a gunnery duel.

Lieutenant Commander Paul Whitfield the commanding officer of the destroyer *Nomad* was captured by the Germans after the loss of his ship and hospitalized in the Marine Lazarett at Wilhelmshaven. On 8 June, while still in hospital he wrote to Captain Farie, commanding the 13th Flotilla describing the loss of *Nomad*:

Our misfortune lay in getting a shell from one of their Light Cruisers clean through the Main Steam pipe, king instantly the Engineer Officer and I think a leading stoker. At the same time from two boilers came the report that they could not get water.

We then shut off burners from the Upper Deck, engaging the enemy meanwhile. The ship finally stopped though steam to pour from the Engine Room. With the ship stopped bad luck had it that the only gun that would bear was the after one, and that couldn't be fought owing to the steam from the E.R obliterating everything. Several of our destroyers passed close, but I did not signal to them for assistance as I saw they were all wanted and busy.

I then noticed that we had started to list to port considerably, and so I thought that rather than let the torpedoes go down with the ship and the list became too bad, I would give them a run for their money, and fired all four at the enemy's battleships who were on the Starboard beam. I think they were of the Kaiser class, and if any were hit about 3.00 G.M.T. I put a claim in.

Having no one within our gun range, we set to work putting small fires out etc. and I also prepared for being towed, in case a friendly destroyer came along. Just about this the 1st High Seas Fleet spotted us, and started a 'Battle Practice' at us with 6" or bigger guns. Salvo after salvo shook us, and wounded a few. The ship was sinking fast, I gave the order to abandon her and pull clear, and about 3 minutes after, she went down vertically by the stern.

Three German Torpedo Boats picked us up.

It was grand practice for them, but murder for us, and so exasperating as we could not hit back.

The officers and crew behaved splendidly, and while waiting for 'the end', or my order to abandon ship, they might have been having their usual forenoon stand easy, to look at them. I cannot find out names or numbers of our casualties because all my officers and men except for the wounded have gone to some prison camp.

With my usual luck, I met three different salvoes and am wounded as follows:

Upper and lower lips torn pieces (since sewn together). Three teeth removed.

Shrapnel hole through throat – each hole about size of 4/- piece.[42]
Splinter hole in the right forearm and right ear cut.
Shot or splinter hole in the right chest.
Left hand burned – now fit for duty.
This is just a rough description of the last of 'Nomad', and I nearly
cried as she went down.[43]

Major Sturgis described the sinking of the destroyer *Nestor*:

We went into action somewhere about 4.30 in the afternoon and very soon were in the thick of it. I can just remember that before we ourselves came to grips, I looked out and saw two lines of ships, ranging themselves opposite one another, never opening fire, but moving grimly into positions that neither could retire from unless with the enemy's consent and that was unlikely after so much waiting. Then I knew this was no Dogger Bank skirmish, and got my medical ready. Being in action itself was rather commonplace.

Everything went as if we were at practice until we were hit in the engine room. One shell only. Nobody killed. But we were hit in a vital part, and we merely came to a standstill, looking very foolish, I daresay, as the whole High Seas Fleet steamed past. The battle turned the opposite way and we were left.

Up till now we had only three wounded; one man seriously in the leg and two flesh wounds. The ship herself had a searchlight smashed and some wardroom stores had gone afire, but soon was put out. Half an hour later their battleships opened fire on us with their secondary armament and once they had got our range, the poor old 'Nestor' was a shrieking hell of crumpled iron and flaming explosives. The Captain realised that discretion was the better part of valour, so we took to the boats, of which only one, mine was seaworthy. The men behaved absolutely heroically, unselfish to the last degree, obedient, calm and methodical when removing my eight wounded, and acting up to the traditions of our Navy, quite unconscious that they were doing more than duty.

In my last round of the ship to see that no wounded were left a shell burst amidships and struck the engineer just as he was emerging from the engine-room hatch, leaving his beloved kettles for the last time. I pulled him out, found his skull smashed in, and went away. He had been killed outright.

By this time the German fire was a bit hot, and before I knew where I was someone pushed a life belt over my head and shoved me into the boat. I was no sooner in and we were about to shove off when someone shouted 'What about Freeman'? This man had been left on the bridge with his leg half shot away, so I rushed up on top only to find poor Freeman dead. In about 30 seconds more I was in the boat again. There was a frightful shriek and the whole bridge crashed over the side. If Freeman had been alive and it had been necessary for me to carry him, I would have assuredly have gone that time, for he was a heavy man and the going was none too easy. We were now out of the frying pan into the fire, as we had no oars and couldn't shove off from the 'Nestor', while the wash from the shells dropping into the sea close to us nearly swamped us, not to mention that it half drowned us with the spray. At last we got away, how, I can never remember, but by paddling with our hands I should think. Then I seemed to be conscious of the fact that the Captain and Rowe were in the boat and the gunner was in the water hanging on to the gunwhale. After that things seemed to become more or less clear again, and I saw the 'Nestor' about 30 or 50 yards away badly down astern; then she sank, gradually and with dignity until her bow remained out of the sea, for all-the world like a sentry box. She remained like this for about 5 minutes, then disappeared gently and without fuss. As she went under the men sang 'Tipperary' and gave three cheers for the Nestor.

By this time our horizon extended a bit, to include three German torpedo boats, who came along and picked us up and in a few minutes we were standing on her deck. A very foolish crowd. Indeed I never spent so embarrassing a five minutes as these five. Then we were sent down below and given coffee and food.[44]

Beatty Turns North to Avoid Certain Destruction

The sighting of Scheer's battleships at 16.30 ended the first phase of the battle with Beatty having succeeded in doing his primary job of locating the main German fleet while at the same time having been beaten decisively by Hipper's numerically much smaller 1st Scouting Squadron. Thus, Beatty had lost of two battlecruisers and almost all of their crews while severe damage had been inflicted on *Lion* and *Tiger*. In comparison, the Germans, with the light in their favour, had scored forty-two hits on British battlecruisers and received only eleven in return. The poor gunnery of the British battlecruisers is emphasised by the performance of *Moltke* which scored more hits in this phase of the battle than all six British ships combined! While much of this discrepancy in hitting ability can be ascribed to the light conditions at the time, both Jellicoe and Beatty had been well aware of the Battle Cruiser Fleet's lack of gunnery practice which was why the 3rd Battle

Cruiser Squadron had been at Scapa and the 5th Battle Squadron had been accompanying the battlecruisers.

During this engagement by the opposing battlecruiser forces, Hipper had been heading south towards Scheer's battleships, and at 16.30 the light cruiser *Southampton* sighted the German battle fleet. This was a nasty surprise for Beatty, who, like Jellicoe, had been led to believe the German ships were still in port.

To escape the certain destruction of his ships Beatty turned north, thus ending the first phase of the battle, known as 'The Run to the South'. The unpalatable truth was that Hipper, who was outnumbered two to one in heavy ships, had scored a notable success. The 'first round' had most definitely gone to the Germans.

The Run to the North

The leading German light cruiser fired two salvoes before Chester fired.

This phase of the battle is defined by the period that started with the 5th Battle Squadron's turn to the north at 16.54 and ended at 18.15 with Jellicoe's signal deploying the Grand Fleet to meet Scheer's battleships.

During the 'Run to the North', Beatty's four remaining badly bruised battlecruisers were able to escape destruction at the hands of Hipper's five capital ships while, the four powerful ships of the 5th Battle Squadron not only avoided disaster but in so doing were able to cause considerable damage to the pursuing German battlecruisers and the leading German battleships.

The Withdrawal of Beatty's Battlecruisers

Hipper turned to close Beatty at 16.52 just before the 5th Battle Squadron made its turn and thereafter intermittent exchanges of fire occurred between the battlecruisers until 17.10 when the action ceased because the poor visibility meant that the range became too great for effective gunnery. Beatty was steaming north at twenty-five knots so as get ahead of Hipper and prevent him from sighting the Grand Fleet too soon.

At 16.57 when the range was approximately 17,500 yards Beatty altered course so as to parallel Hipper's battlecruisers but his flagship was soon hit by her opposite number. At 17.02 Hipper reduced speed for four minutes and as a result of this and the manoeuvres undertaken by the British and German battlecruisers, the distance between *Lion* and *Lützow* had increased to 21,000 yards by 17.10 Hipper's failure to pursue Beatty's four battlecruisers as soon as his 1st Scouting Group turned to the north allowed his already badly battered opponent to avoid further action at ranges which could have caused yet more losses.

However, as Beatty's ships gradually drew away they were further hammered by the Germans who took full advantage of the favourable light and between 16.59 and 17.02 *Lützow* scored three more 12-inch hits on *Lion*, one of which caused a cordite fire in her after 4-in gun battery while another destroyed the sick bay. By this stage, *Lion* was in a poor condition with fires raging in several places, fire hoses and fire mains shredded by shell splinters and water that should be available to put out her fires cascading onto her decks. Her 'Q' turret and its associated magazine trunking, main deck and 4-in gun batteries, were littered with the dead and wounded while wreckage hindered the work of damage-, fire-control and stretcher parties. Smoke and cordite fumes permeated throughout the ship which was lit by only oil battle-lanterns and the flames from the many fires because the electric lighting had been knocked out. *Princess Royal* and *Tiger* had also suffered considerable damage but neither former nor *New Zealand* was hit at this time but *Tiger* was hit by an 11-inch shell from *Seydlitz* at about 16.58. More seriously, the right gun of *Tiger*'s 'A' turret suffered a defect which put it out of action for the rest of the battle. Fortunately, their hulls and machinery remained sound and they were able to use their speed to gradually draw away from Hipper's squadron. Hipper again reduced speed for a further four minutes at 17.17 hours, probably to avoid getting too close to the 5th Battle Squadron without support from the High Seas Fleet 3rd Battle Squadron.[1]

The Fifth Battle Squadron to the Rescue

Hipper's 1st Scouting Group was faster than the 5th Battle Squadron and could have closed the range but he was wary of the power of their 15-inch guns and consequently, during the 'Run to the North' range between the German battlecruisers and the four 'Queen Elizabeths' was at least 17,000 yards. However, the longer ranged 15-inch guns of the 5th Battle Squadron continued to fire intermittently as they gained occasional glimpses of Hipper's battlecruisers with *Lützow* and *Seydlitz* being particularly hard hit.

The withdrawal of Beatty's battlecruisers left the 5th Battle Squadron to take on Hipper and Scheer by themselves. *Barham*, engaged by *Derfflinger*, was the first to be hit when at 16.58 a heavy shell wrecked her medical store and auxiliary wireless office as well as causing a cordite fire and heavy casualties in the starboard 6-inch gun battery. Another hit at 17.01 on the superstructure abaft the mainmast caused very severe damage to the light structure and put the main wireless out of action. A third hit at 17.08 on the side plating aft below the main deck caused severe damage to light structures and main deck while a fourth

41

hit at 17.10 damaged the main deck about four feet forward of the centreline of 'B' barbette.[2]

Valiant seemed to lead a charmed life and suffered no damage unlike her sisters *Warspite* and *Malaya*. At about 17.27 the former was hit about four feet abaft 'Y' barbette by an 11-inch shell from *Seydlitz* which caused considerable local damage without affecting her fighting efficiency. Another shell passed through the upper part of the fore-funnel at about the same time.

Malaya, the rear ship of the line, received concentrated fire from a number of battleships suffering seven hits, the first of which at 17.20 struck the starboard side at the waterline abaft 'A' barbette without causing serious damage. A shell struck the roof of 'X' turret at 17.27 bursting on impact without causing serious damage. Although the first hit at 17.30 caused minor damage to the ship's starboard forward superstructure, the second shell caused a serious cordite fire in *Malaya*'s starboard 6-inch gun battery which was put out of action for a time with 102 casualties. Two shells struck close together abreast the forward boiler room just below the main armour belt at 17.35 with one passing out through the double bottom without exploding while the other exploded just after entry. Wing compartments were flooded for a length of over fifty feet causing a list of about four degrees which gradually corrected by pumping oil from starboard to port bunkers. A seventh shell is known to have struck and damaged armour between 'A' and 'B' barbettes.[3]

In return, and despite initially having the disadvantage of the light, *Barham* and *Valiant* engaged Hipper's battlecruisers hitting *Lützow* four times, *Derfflinger* three times and heavily damaging *Seydlitz* with six hits. Neither *Moltke* nor *Von der Tann* was hit although the latter's remaining last turret (port wing) failed because of a mechanical breakdown at 17.15. *Warspite* and *Malaya* fired at and hit the leading German battleships *König* and *Grosser Kurfürst* once and *Markgraf* three times.[4] During this successful fight they scored eighteen hits on the German ships during 16.45 to 18.15 and with their advantage of speed over the German battleships they gradually opened the range and by 17.30 could not be reached by German heavy guns.

Beatty Returns to the Fray

During the period when Beatty's battlecruisers had withdrawn from the action, their track lay about a mile to the eastward of the 5th Battle Squadron and apart from being engaged intermittently by *Lützow* until 17.27 they were otherwise left alone. The crews of the heavily damaged *Lion*, *Princess Royal* and *Tiger* took advantage of this lull in the fighting put out fires and generally restore their ships' battle-worthiness.

At 17.35 Beatty altered to north-north-east in preparation for deploying ahead of Jellicoe's battleships and to force Hipper further away from the Grand Fleet. Beatty's despatches record that:

> At 5.35 p.m. our course was N.N.E., and the estimated position of the Grand Fleet was N. 16 W, so we gradually hauled to the North Eastward, keeping the range of the enemy at 14,000 yards. He was gradually hauling to the Eastward, receiving severe punishment at the head of his line, and probably acting on information received from his Light-Cruisers which had sighted and were engaged, with the Third Battle-Cruiser Squadron. Possibly Zeppelins were present also. At 5.50 p.m ., British Cruisers were sighted on the port bow, and at 5.56 p.m., the leading battleships of the Grand Fleet bearing North 5 miles. I thereupon altered course to East and proceeded at utmost speed. This brought the range of the enemy down to 12,000 yards. I made a visual report to the Commander-in-Chief that the enemy Battle-Cruisers bore South East. At this time only three of the enemy BattleCruisers were visible, closely followed by battleships of the 'Konig' class.[5]

For the first time, the visibility favoured the British with the low sun in German eyes and, with the range closing, Hipper's ships were clearly visible and as the range came down to 12,000 yards *Lützow* was hit by *Princess Royal* at 17.45 while *Derfflinger* was heavily hit forward and only survived because of the closure of all watertight doors and openings as well as the evacuation of her forepart. The already badly damaged *Seydlitz* was hit repeatedly and set on fire as the 1st Scouting Group, which had outrun Scheer's supporting battleships, was now suffering at the hands of Beatty's eight ships which were all but invisible and consequently turned away to the north-north-west and then north and ordered his torpedo-boat flotillas to attack.

More trouble was at hand for Hipper because at about 15.00 Rear Admiral Hood with the 3rd Battlecruiser Squadron (*Invincible*, *Indomitable* and *Inflexible*) had left Jellicoe and steamed to join Beatty's embattled force. This squadron was originally stationed twenty miles ahead of the battlefleet, with the light cruiser *Chester* acting as linking ship between the squadron and the cruiser line.[6] Subsequently, Hood stationed the light cruisers *Canterbury* five miles ahead and *Chester* five miles on his starboard beam as scouts, while the destroyers *Shark*, *Acasta*, *Ophelia* and *Christopher* formed an anti-submarine screen ahead. At 16.05 Jellicoe ordered the 3rd Battlecruiser Squadron to support Beatty and Rear Admiral Hood increased speed to twenty-four knots.

Hood had anticipated Jellicoe's order and his course and intuition later proved to have been very fortunate because it enabled his 3rd Battlecruiser Squadron and its attached destroyers to intervene in the battle with an effect quite disproportionate to their limited strength.[7]

Chester Ambushed by German Light Cruisers

However, because of an error in Beatty's signalled position, Hood's force was steering to the east of the course necessary for a direct approach to the Battle Cruiser Fleet and was on a collision course to meet Admiral Bödicker's 2nd Scouting Group stationed on Hipper's disengaged bow. At 17.30 *Chester*, which was five miles north seventy degrees west of the 3rd Battlecruiser Squadron, reported to *Invincible* by searchlight that she had heard firing and seen flashes of gunfire to the south westward, where the 5th Battle Squadron was fighting Hipper's battlecruisers on their run to the north. *Chester* immediately turned to investigate.

Soon afterwards, at 17.36, the dim shape of a three-funnelled cruiser accompanied by some destroyers appeared out of the mist on *Chester's* starboard bow.[8] With the range coming down to 6,000 yards three more cruisers appeared astern of the one first sighted and all four opened fire on *Chester* which at once took violent evasive action and turned onto a north-easterly course to put her adversaries astern. Her assailants were Bödocker's light cruiser squadron consisting of his flagship *Frankfurt* accompanied by *Wiesbaden*, *Pillau* and *Elbing* and *Chester* was soon smothered in shell splashes, splinters and hits. In his report written on 13 June, *Chester's* Commanding Officer, Captain R.N. Lawson, wrote:

> The leading German light cruiser fired two salvoes before CHESTER fired. The fact that the ship being of high speed and under helm was the cause of delay, as the control officer gave prompt orders to open fire before receiving orders from me, as soon as he had assured himself that the leading cruiser and destroyer were enemy ships.
>
> Steady firing was carried out by the after gun, which was the only gun which could be kept continuously bearing. Lieutenant Arthur George Curtis R.N., stationed at the after control, left his control after a few minutes having found it impossible to get the after guns P.3, S.3, P.4 and S.4 on the enemy owing to rapid changes of bearing, and owing also to casualties and the stunning effect of salvoes which had burst in the batteries. After visiting these guns, which he found somewhat depleted, and many men stupid from shock, he settled down to spot for the after gun, but found it a most difficult matter owing to the mass of enemy shorts. The after gun fired about 18

rounds, but I fear with little or no effect. But Lieutenant Curtis evidently kept a cool and practical appreciation throughout, and if the enemy was hit it is due to the calm judgement of this officer under very heavy fire.

The other after guns were unable to accomplish much, as the enemy's bearing altered from one quarter to the other. Marines guns' crew at P.3 and S.3 did what was possible, under the direction of Acting Captain Edward Bamford R.M.L.I. This officer remained in his station in the after control for a few minutes after Lieutenant Curtis had left. He was slightly burnt about the face with a cordite fire which occurred close below the after control and was in the after control when it was wrecked by a shell which burst inside; then went to S.3 gun and assisted to work it, many of the crew being killed and wounded; directed P.3 gun when its turn came to fire, and assisted in extinguishing a fire abaft the after funnel.

Communication with the guns by voice pipe from the fore top and transmitting station was lost by the cutting of the voice pipes within 8 minutes of opening fire, and possibly some minutes earlier than this. The control officer, Lieutenant Charles E.B. Simeon R.N., did not leave his stations, he had seen that the Commander was wounded and was in momentary expectation of seeing the bridge (with Captain and navigating officer) shot away. His intention was to con the ship from aloft, by voice pipe to lower conning tower (via the transmitting station), where the quartermaster was stationed. He did not bring up the extra guns crews from the supply parties, as he considered the circumstances such that this would mean additional carnage, with no compensating advantage.[9]

Captain Lawson went on to deplore the 'lack of experienced ratings in the ship's company drafted to this ship' before adding,

> no case of actual flinching or deserting a post had come to my notice although 47 out of 100 men at the guns crews were killed or wounded. But confusion undoubtedly occurred among guns crews – utterly inexperienced in all that appertains to sea life – when they found themselves on an open deck, with mutilated men all round, officer of the battery either killed or wounded, and apparently no enemy to shoot at.

This must have been a terrifying baptism of fire for the young and inexperienced crew of this newly commissioned cruiser but her gun crews fought on until, in several cases the last man had been killed. Boy

First Class Jack Cornwell was a sight-setter and communication number at one of *Chester's* 5.5-inch guns and despite receiving a mortal wound remained at his post adjusting gun sights and passing orders until, with the last of the gun's crew killed or injured, his weapon fell silent. During a lull in the fighting he was found standing erect at his post awaiting orders despite the severity of his wound. His courage and determination was rewarded by the award of a posthumous Victoria Cross.

The 3rd Battle Cruiser Squadron Enters the Fray

On hearing gunfire abaft of his starboard beam Hood altered course to the north-west and soon sighted *Chester* ahead and under fire. The Official Despatches record that:

> At 5.40 p.m., the Third Battle-Cruiser Squadron, which until then had been steering about S. by E., sighted enemy cruisers to the westward and turned to about W.N.W. It is apparent that the Rear-Admiral Commanding, Third Battle-Cruiser Squadron, was misled by the difference in reckoning between the battlefleet and battle-cruiser fleet and had gone too far to the eastward, actually crossing ahead of the two engaged battle-cruiser squadrons until meeting the enemy advanced cruisers. At 5.52 p.m., the Third Battle-Cruiser Squadron and 'Canterbury' engaged three enemy light-cruisers which were then administering heavy punishment to 'Chester'.[10]

With the range no more than 8,000 the battlecruisers opened fire on *Chester's* tormenters reducing *Wiesbaden* to little more than a wreck with her engines out of action. *Pillau* was hit by a 12-inch shell which put four of her boilers out of action, caused a fire in her stokeholds and reduced her speed to twenty-four knots. However, despite this damage she managed to escape with the rest of her squadron.

At 17.56 Hipper who had turned east to escape Beatty's fire found himself almost immediately under heavy fire from the north-east as Hood entered the battle. Thinking that Hood was the Grand Fleet, Hipper turned south-west to rejoin Scheer and by 18.10 the 1st Scouting Group had taken station ahead of the High Seas Fleet and all were steaming NE. Before Hipper's disengagement was complete, the 2nd Scouting Group had been hammered by Hood's battlecruisers which crippled the cruiser *Wiesbaden* and damaged two others.

Hipper's torpedo-boat attack planned against Beatty was launched against Hood in the belief that his ships were Jellicoe's battleships. *Regensburg* led the thirty-one vessels of the 2nd, 6th and 9th Flotillas against Hood's three battlecruisers launching a mere twelve torpedoes. Some of the latter were sighted and a turn away by Hood prevented any hits. The complete failure of this heavy attack was due largely to the bravery of Commander Loftus Jones whose four destroyers, *Shark*, *Acasta*, *Ophelia* and *Christopher*, mounted a counter-attack against the attacking German flotillas losing *Shark* and the gallant Loftus-Jones in the process. *Acasta* was also severely damaged during the engagement

William Griffin the former Torpedo Coxswain of *Shark* provided a graphic account of the demise of his ship:

> We were in company with the Battle Cruisers 'Invincible' &c., also four destroyers (including the 'Shark'); during the day of 31st of May we were told by the Captain that we would probably meet the enemy. During the afternoon, about 3 o'clock, I should say, the report of the enemy was sighted, which was in great number, and action stations was rung on the alarm bell. We then proceeded at a speed of 25 knots.
>
> The signal was made open fire, in which we altered course to Port, the course being N.E., the Starboard guns being used. Again we altered course to Port, the course being N., it was then that our steering was hit, I report steering gear gone, Sir, the captain gave orders to me to man the after wheel, it was then that I got wounded in the head and over the right eye, we then went to Starboard making use of our guns on the Port side, this was when the Forecastle gun's crew were completely blown away, gun and all; about this time the 'Acasta' arrived, and the captain of the 'Acasta' asked if he could assist us, and the captain replied don't get sunk over us, we then with our steering gear and engines out of action, she was helpless and with only one gun firing which was the midship gun, and the captain came off the bridge and spotted for the midship gun, during that time he gave me orders for the boats and rafts to be lowered and got out, but the boats were useless, he also gave orders for the collision mat to be got out, which was done all this time the enemy's Light Cruisers and destroyers were constantly shelling us; several of the enemy destroyers came very close to us in line formation, the range being about 600 yards, we were still firing our only gun, by this time the gun's crew consisted of three men, the Midshipman, T. Smith, R.N.R., J. Howell, A.B., Gunlayer II., and C. Hope, A.B. The captain was then wounded slightly in the leg, but he managed to control the gun, myself remaining there for orders from the captain.
>
> I must say that during the first part of the action the foremost and after torpedo were fired, and the spare torpedo was just hoisted up in line with the tube when a shell hit the air chamber and exploded. We

were about half an hour in action when our engines stopped, she was battered about by shell, and began to settle down at the bows. At this time the gunlayer, J. Howell, A.B., was wounded in the left leg, it was about a minute afterward, the captain had his leg shot away, the shell not exploding. C. Hope, A.B., left the gun and assisted the captain. It was about five minutes afterwards that the ship sank. Captain gave orders to save yourselves, the two rafts were filled up (the third raft could not be got out owing to shell fire), and as time went on the men began to gradually die away with exposure, the water being very cold. While we were in the water we saw a number of our ships and destroyers pass us at full speed chasing the enemy. At 10 o'clock (old time) we were picked up by the Danish steamer, S.S. 'Vidar', bound for Hull, there was seven of us, one, Ch. Sto. [Chief Stoker] Newcombe, who died on board. Nearly everyone on board wore lifebelts or lifesaving collars, which proved a great success, and the rafts were also of great service to us, carrying about twelve.[11]

The water was very cold and the survivors gradually succumbed until about 22.00 when they were picked up by the Danish S.S. *Vidar*, only seven were alive. The seventh, a Chief Stoker (Pensioner) died after getting on board S.S. *Vidar* and his body was taken to Hull. The survivors were treated very well by the Captain and crew of *Vidar*. The Captain of the *Vidar* told survivors that a little while before he picked them up he saw

what looked like the bow of a big German Man-of-War standing out of the water: the draught marks were in metres. After being picked up they passed a large (presumably German) Man-of War heavily on fire.[12]

One of the survivors, Able Seaman Charles Smith reported that:

They were in company with the following vessels: *Acasta*, *Ophelia*, *Contest* or *Christopher* or *Cockatrice*, and at 6 p.m. they engaged a four-funnel German cruiser. *Shark* fired one torpedo at her, which Charles Smith, who was stationed at the after tube, states that he saw hit the cruiser and explode, and he further states that the ship stopped and seemed to be on fire.[13]

The survivors reported that at 18.00 *Shark* and her three compatriots engaged a four-funnel German cruiser and that *Shark* fired a torpedo at her. At this time *Invincible*, *Indomitable* and *Inflexible* were from two to four cables on the starboard beam and they also fired at the German cruiser.

About 18.15 *Shark* eased down and stopped owing to the pipes to the oil suctions having been damaged. The fore steering gear was also put out of action at this time and shortly afterwards was shot away altogether. Two light grey painted enemy destroyers now attacked *Shark* which had been left behind by the other vessels. One of them was driven off by gunfire from *Shark*'s midship gun which was the only one left in action.

The second German destroyer was also hit, but succeeded in firing two torpedoes at *Shark* from a range of about 1,500 to 1,800 yards and one of them hit her abreast the after funnel. *Shark* took a heavy list and sank almost immediately at about 19.00. Stoker Petty Officer Filleul reported that before the ship was torpedoed the Captain gave orders for all men not engaged at the guns to lie down on the deck. He stated that:

> 'Shark' at this time was between the opposing Battle Fleets and that shrapnel was being fired at them. This is confirmed by the fact that the two wounded men are suffering from shrapnel wounds — not severe. The boats were all riddled and useless, but two Carley Floats floated off and 14 or 15 men got into each. While they were in the water about ten or more enemy battle cruisers or battleships passed about 5 miles off, followed by a large number of our battle ships within a mile who were engaging the enemy heavily. A lot of enemy shells were falling 'over' our ships.
>
> The Captain – Commander Loftus Jones had his left leg shot away before the vessel sank, and although he had a life-belt cannot have survived long.[14]

Arrival of the Battle Fleet

The main fleets were almost in sight and Beatty had led an unsuspecting Scheer onto Jellicoe's guns while at the same time preventing Hipper and the 1st and 2nd Scouting Groups from sighting the Grand Fleet. It is difficult to understand Scheer's surprise at meeting Jellicoe because if a defeated Beatty really was running from the Germans why was he heading north and later even east of north? Presumably with an inferior British force in sight Scheer and Hipper had forgotten about the possibility of encountering the full might of the Grand Fleet. Beatty had only fallen short in one respect because he failed to maintain close contact with the High Seas Fleet and report its disposition and movements to Jellicoe. Either *Malaya*, the rear ship of the line, or better still Goodenough's cruisers should have been given this role and thereby kept Jellicoe fully informed.

It is possible to excuse Beatty for doing nothing, in the heat of battle, to get in visual contact with Jellicoe but Sinclair and Napier commanding the 1st and 3rd light cruiser squadrons were in the right direction and were not engaged. Jellicoe was probably more at fault because he could have sent Le Measurier's 4th Light Cruiser Squadron to find and fix Beatty's force. As was to be shown at 18.15 that day, the armoured cruisers of the 1st and 2nd cruiser squadrons were too slow and too vulnerable to perform this duty.

The Official Despatches describe the arrival of the Grand Fleet's battleships and their supporting vessels in the following terms:

At 5.45 p.m., 'Comus', of the Fourth Light-Cruiser Squadron, then three miles ahead of the battlefleet, reported that heavy gunfiring was heard from a direction south. The flashes of guns were shortly afterwards observed S.S.W., and at 5.56 p.m., some vessels, subsequently seen to be the British battle-cruisers, were seen bearing S.S.W. from 'Marlborough', steering E., heavily engaged with an unseen enemy.

At 6.0 p.m., 'Iron Duke's' position was latitude 57° 11' N., longitude 5° 39' E., course S.E. by S., speed twenty knots; battlefleet in divisions in line ahead disposed abeam to starboard (Organisation No. 5), columns eleven cables apart. It was apparent on meeting that the reckoning of the battlecruiser fleet was about twelve miles to the eastward of 'Iron Duke's' reckoning. In consequence of this the enemy were sighted on the starboard bow instead of ahead, and some twenty minutes earlier than was anticipated.

At 6 p.m., the Vice-Admiral Commanding, Battle-Cruiser Fleet, reported enemy battle-cruisers bearing S.E., and at 6. 14 p.m., in reply to a signal, he reported the enemy battlefleet in sight, bearing S.S.W. Owing to the uncertainty as to the position of the enemy battlefleet, it had not been possible to redispose the guides of columns on any different bearing. Consequently, the deployment was carried out under some disadvantage, and, indeed, it was not easy to determine the correct direction of deployment until the battlefleets were almost in contact.

At this stage it was not clear whether the enemy battlefleet was ahead of our battlefleet or on the starboard beam, as heavy firing was proceeding from ahead to the starboard beam and the cruisers ahead were seen to be hotly engaged. In order to take ground to starboard a signal was made at 6.2 p.m., to alter course by 9 pendant to South, but it was then realised that the enemy battlefleet must be in close proximity, either ahead or on to allow the battle-cruisers, which were before the starboard beam, to pass ahead.[15]

Shortly after 18.00 that day, individual torpedo attacks were made the British destroyers *Onslow* and *Acasta*:

At about 6.5 p.m., 'Onslow', being on the engaged bow of 'Lion' sighted an enemy Light-Cruiser at a distance of 6,000 yards from us, apparently endeavouring to attack with torpedoes. 'Onslow' at once closed and engaged her, firing 58 rounds at a range of from 4,000 to 2,000 yards, scoring a number of hits. 'Onslow' then closed to within 8,000 yards of the enemy Battle-Cruisers, and orders were given for all torpedoes to he fired. At this moment she was struck amidships by a heavy shell, with the result that only one torpedo was fired. Thinking that all his torpedoes had gone, the Commanding Officer proceeded to retire at slow speed. Being informed that he still had three torpedoes, he closed the Light-Cruiser previously engaged and torpedoed her. The enemy's Battle-fleet was then sighted at a distance of 8,000 yards, and the remaining torpedoes were fired at them; having started correctly, they must have crossed the enemy's track. Damage in her feed tank then caused 'Onslow' to stop.[16]

During this gallant sortie *Onslow*, commanded by Lieutenant Commander J.C. Tovey, a future C-in-C Home Fleet during the Second World War, was struck by three 5.9-inch shells from the battlecruiser *Lützow*, two of which hit her boiler room and one exploded further aft. In return she launched a torpedo at 3,500 yards which hit the already crippled cruiser *Wiesbaden* aft. She also two fired torpedoes at the battleship *Kronprinz* a range of 8,000 yards but both missed although one of them passed ahead of *Kaiser* at 18.25. While withdrawing from this second attack, *Onslow* was hit by two 4.1-inch shells from the cruiser *Rostock* but survived being eventually towed home by the destroyer *Defender*.

Soon after *Onslow* launched her solo attack, the destroyer *Acasta* also attacked the German battlecruisers from a position on their starboard bow firing one torpedo a *Lützow* at a range of 4,500 yards. The torpedo missed and *Acasta* came under fire from *Lützow* and *Derfflinger* being hit by two 5.9-inch shells in her engine room which also damaged her steering. Fortunately, *Acasta* was spared further damaged because she was hidden from the German gunners by smoke and was eventually able to return to port with the assistance of the destroyer *Nonsuch*.[17]

Jellicoe's Deployment

Jellicoe was steaming southeast with his fleet of twenty-four battleships in six columns of four ships. His flagship, *Iron Duke*, was leading the third column from the left but Jellicoe knew neither the strength nor the position of the High Seas Fleet and was equally uncertain about Beatty's position thanks to errors in their respective flagships. From 16.30 to 17.00 Jellicoe had received five enemy reports, three of which were from the 2nd Light Cruiser squadron, and then nothing until 17.40 when three more reports came in from Goodenough. *Invincible* and *Chester* both failed to report their actions and Beatty's only report at 16.45 was received as '26-30 battleships probably hostile, bearing SSE steaming SE'.

Consequently, Jellicoe believed that he had to face all completed German ships consisting of eighteen (sixteen) dreadnoughts, ten (five) pre-dreadnoughts and six (five) battlecruisers (actual figures in brackets). However, the pre-dreadnoughts had little fighting value and were known to the Germans as the 'five minute ships' because that was how long they were expected to survive in battle. Worse still the pre-dreadnoughts slowed down Scheer's fleet speed. Actually, Jellicoe had a considerable superiority in dreadnoughts of twenty-eight to sixteen and an overwhelming superiority in gun size with 15-inch, 14-inch, 13.5-inch and 12-inch guns compared to the German 12-inch and 11-inch weapons. Furthermore, the size of the explosive burster-charge contained within a shell increased rapidly with the size of the shell.

At 17.50 *Marlborough*, leading the starboard wing column, reported heavy gun flashes on her starboard bow and at 18.00 reported battlecruisers in sight. Jellicoe had been expecting *Lion* to be twelve miles dead ahead and now found that she was five-and-a-half-miles on the starboard bow. Consequently, instead of meeting Scheer dead-ahead at 18.30 Jellicoe realised that contact would be about twenty minutes earlier and somewhere on the starboard bow.

It seems to have been at about this time that Jellicoe decided to deploy on the port column because at 18.01 he ordered destroyer disposition No. 1 which put the bulk of his flotillas on the port side. Almost simultaneously *Iron Duke* sighted *Lion* and asked what should have been the unnecessary question 'Where is the enemy battlefleet?' Beatty didn't know because *Lion* hadn't seen them since about 17.00 and could only reply 'Enemy battlecruisers bearing SE' without even giving a range. This was received by Jellicoe at about 18.06 who had wisely decided to ignore an incorrect message from Goodenough just before 18.00 which suggested that Hipper was south-west of Scheer. At 18.10 Jellicoe repeated his question to Beatty, who on sighting the main fleet, had turned east and soon sighted the leading German ships and signalled 'Have sighted Enemy Battlefleet bearing SSW'. This signal, which was received at 18.14, contained no estimate of the range but Jellicoe, who had had *Iron Duke's* rangefinders estimate the visibility in various directions interpreted Beatty's sighting as five miles [actually 7] on the starboard bow.

On receipt of *Lion's* message, Jellicoe almost immediately made the signal to deploy on the port wing column, course south-east by east and told his Flag Captain to put *Iron Duke's* helm over. The signal was hauled down [i.e. executed] at 18.15. It would appear that Jellicoe had chosen the port column before 18.00 and the receipt of *Lion's* signal at 18.14 merely confirmed his thinking Jellicoe wanted to engage the High Seas Fleet to the south of the Grand Fleet as his rangefinder tests had shown that visibility was in his favour in that direction. Deployment to starboard would have achieved that as well as to port but he would not have been between Scheer and his bases. Deployment to starboard would place the turning point of the Grand Fleet very close to an enemy, whose exact course and position was unknown, and risked exposure to the possibility of massed torpedo attacks. Many distinguished authorities have argued in favour of other deployments but, to this writer, the decision to deploy to port was both inevitable and entirely logical, given the novelty of the ships and weapons involved, the limited visibility and the incomplete information available to Jellicoe.

Windy Corner

Your firing is very good, keep at it as quickly as you can,
every shot is telling.

A s the Grand Fleet battleships undertook their stately deployment, fierce fighting broke out between the fleets. As the various British forces coalesced to meet the oncoming High Seas Fleet, there was a brief period when the ships of the 5th Battle Squadron, a light cruiser squadron, various destroyers as well as the oncoming ships of Arbuthnot's 1st Cruiser Squadron and Beatty's battlecruisers were gathered in a small area into which the Germans were concentrating all available fire. Those on the receiving end of this deluge of shells described the area as 'windy corner'. Yet because of the deteriorating visibility, and despite the number of shells fired, very few ships were hit. More surprisingly is that there were no collisions despite the rapid evasive manoeuvres being performed.

It is also worth remembering that in those days before the advent of radar and modern communications, newly arriving Grand Fleet squadron commanders could see very little of either the enemy or their own ships and knew next to nothing of the German positions, course, strength or dispositions. This ignorance, coupled to impetuosity, led to disaster when Rear Admiral Robert Arbuthnot turned two of his ships, *Defence* and *Warrior*, on to a course parallel to Beatty's and glimpsed Bödicker's 2nd Scouting Group fleeing from Hood's 3rd Battlecruiser Squadron. The German light cruiser *Wiesbaden*, which had been disabled by Hood's battlecruisers, was sighted by the brave but incompetent Rear Admiral Arbuthnot in *Defence*, who led his elderly armoured cruisers to attack her. Without a moment's thought he closed the range so fast that he forced *Lion* to swing away so as to avoid his ships and then, after firing on *Wiesbaden*, found himself less than 8,000 yards from the High Seas Fleet. The latter punished Arburthnot's stupidity by causing *Defence* to blow up, with the loss of all on board, and reducing *Warrior* to little more than a wreck.

The sorry story is told succinctly in the Despatches:

> At 5.52 p.m., Rear-Admiral Sir Robert Arbuthnot, in 'Defence', signalled that the battlefleets would shortly be engaged. Rear-Admiral Herbert L. Heath, in 'Minotaur', with the Second Cruiser Squadron, made a sweep to the eastward to ensure that no enemy minelayers were at work in that direction, and proceeded to take up deployment station two points on the engaged van of the battlefleet, being joined there by 'Duke of Edinburgh' at 5.17 p.m. At 5.50 p.m., the cruisers on the right flank of the cruiser line had come in contact with the enemy cruisers.
>
> A large three-funnelled enemy light-cruiser [*Wiesbaden*] was engaged and disabled by 'Defence' and 'Warrior'. She drifted down between the lines, being fired on by the battlefleet, and was subsequently seen to sink by several independent observers. 'Defence' and 'Warrior' of the First Cruiser Squadron, which vessels had turned to starboard during the engagement with the light-cruisers, passed between our own and the enemy battle-cruisers and battlefleet, and the two ships found themselves within comparatively short range of the enemy's heavy ships.
>
> At 6.16 p.m., 'Defence' was observed to be heavily hit and blew up; 'Warrior' was badly hit and disabled, but reached the rear of the battlefleet and was taken in tow by 'Engadine' It is probable that Rear-Admiral Sir Robert Arbuthnot did not realise the proximity of the German battlefleet, and coming across it at short range in the mist was unable to extricate his squadron before his flagship was sunk and the 'Warrior' disabled.[1]

The number of hits scored on *Wiesbaden* by Arbuthnot's ships is not known but has been estimated to be six 9.2-inch or 7.5-inch[2] before they ran into German capital ships including *König* and *Seydlitz* at a range of just over 6,000 yards. *Defence* was hit by several heavy shells and exploded sending flames and debris hundreds of feet into the air. *Warrior* was lucky to survive but her upperdecks were reduced to tangled wreckage, fires were started between decks and her starboard engine room badly damaged. As to the rest of Arbuthnot's squadron, *Duke of Edinburgh* opened fire on *Wiesbaden* at 18.08 but was prevented from following *Defence* by Beatty's oncoming battlecruisers while *Black Prince* was observed to turn to port at 17.42 presumably to avoid Beatty's ships. Unfortunately, *Black Prince* was lost with all hands

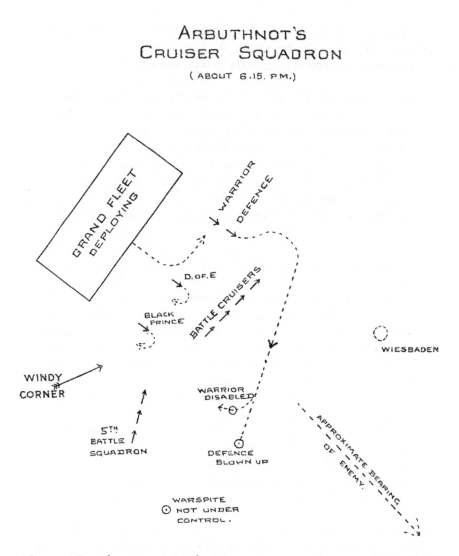

ARBUTHNOT'S CRUISER SQUADRON

(ABOUT 6.15. PM.)

GRAND FLEET DEPLOYING

WARRIOR

DEFENCE

D. OF. E

BATTLE CRUISERS

BLACK PRINCE

WIESBADEN

WINDY CORNER

WARRIOR DISABLED

5TH BATTLE SQUADRON

DEFENCE BLOWN UP

APPROXIMATE BEARING OF ENEMY.

WARSPITE
NOT UNDER CONTROL.

Above: Map showing Arbuthnot's cruiser squadron at about 18.15 hours on 31 May 1916.

during the night but *Warrior* probably sighted her astern of the Grand Fleet at 19.00 and at 20.45 she reported an imaginary submarine to Jellicoe.[3]

Captain Molteno of *Warrior* described the fatal action in his report written on 7 June 1916:

At 6.5 Port guns had opened fire on the same enemy [*Wiesbaden*]. I saw her hit both by 'Warrior's' and 'Defence's' 2nd salvo, and she appeared to be crippled, and very soon nearly stopped.

'Defence' continued to close her to about 5,500 yards before turning away to Starboard at 6.17, and 'Warrior' closed to about 3 cables of 'Defence' going about 135 revolutions (just 22 knots).

At 6.19 'Warrior' turned to Starboard, and 'Defence' was observed to be hit by two salvoes in quick succession. A huge furnace appeared to be under her fore turret for quite an appreciable time (10 secs, perhaps) and then she blew up and disappeared. From the time of about 6.7 onwards 'Defence' and 'Warrior' were being straddled by heavy salvoes (11-in. to 14-in.).[4]

At 6.17 I ordered the Lieut. -Commander (N) to work the ship from the conning tower, and entered it myself and continued to work the ship from that position till the action was over, Lieut.-Commander (T) and Signal Bosn. remaining just outside, as there was no room for them inside. A shell a few moments afterwards wrecked the bridge and wounded Lieut.-Commander (T) outside the C.T, 'Defence' having gone at about 6.20 p.m. and light cruiser Russian type[5] sinking just afterwards, I decided to withdraw and obstruct the fire of the B.C. fleet and 5th B.S. as little as possible, but I noticed that the ship was losing her speed as I turned away, and sent a message to keep the engines going at all costs.

At 6.32 I received a report that Starboard engine room was disabled, and at 6.33 that both engine rooms were disabled, and shortly afterwards that there were two or three fires on the Main Deck, one especially bad round the Ship's and Armament offices, which blocked access to the Engine Rooms. During the whole time the 'Warrior' was withdrawing she drew the fire of at least four of the enemy's heavy ships, first they appeared to be Battle Cruisers, but latterly were certainly Battle Ships. I passed some distance astern of the 5th B.S. except 'Warspite,' who was considerably astern of the remainder of 5th B.S. and to Starboard (enemy's side) of the line. I should have passed astern of her also had she not turned to Starboard and passed under my stern, thereby screening me from the enemy's fire. This was a particularly gallant act as the 'Warspite' had just been having a very severe pounding herself, and she probably saved 'Warrior' being sunk then and there.

'Warrior' then passed the rear of our own Battle Fleet and observed one of our armoured cruisers almost astern of the Battle Fleet, about 4 miles away.[6]

Vice-Admiral A. Burney in *Marlborough* reported that:

> One of our armoured cruisers, probably 'Warrior', was observed passing down the engaged side, making for her position in rear of the line. When near the end of the line she turned up parallel to it and engaged the enemy at short range. Heavy enemy salvoes were observed to fall all round her; she then turned about 14 points to port, a salvo struck her and a large flame was seen to burst from her quarter deck and she then passed astern.[7]

Warrior was saved from instant annihilation by the battleship *Warspite*. Evan-Thomas had sighted *Marlborough* at 18.06 and once he appreciated that the fleet was deploying to port he had to give up the idea of taking station in the van and consequently had to take his alternative position at the rear of the line. In order to reach this position, he had to undertake a large turn to port and, during this manoeuvre, *Warspite*'s steering gear jammed and she made two complete circles about 10,000 yards from the High Seas Fleet. *Warspite* was hit by thirteen heavy shells which caused severe damage and when at 19.00 her steering gear jammed again she was ordered home. However, her circles had taken her between the leading German ships and the damaged *Warrior* and had saved the latter for the rest of the day.

By 18.30, the 5th Battle Squadron (less *Warspite*), was formed astern of *Agincourt* in the battle line. At 18.33 Jellicoe increased speed to seventeen knots which was maintained until the Fleet left the scene for its bases on 1 June.[8]

The Loss of *Invincible*

At about 18.10, the 3rd Battle-Cruiser Squadron sighted the battle-cruiser fleet, and at 18.21, took station ahead of the Vice-Admiral Commanding, Battle-Cruiser Fleet, in *Lion*, with the *Chester* then taking station astern of the Second Cruiser Squadron and remaining with that squadron for the night.

At 18.23 Hood sighted the 1st Scouting Group at 9,000 yards and *Invincible* opened fire on both *Lützow* and *Derfflinger* causing fatal damage to the former when two 12-inch shells struck below the waterline in or near the broadside torpedo flat. Two more shells struck *Lützow* below the waterline further forward and, as a result of these four hits, practically the whole of the ship below the armour deck forward of 'A' turret became flooded. However, *Lützow* struck back at 18.32 when *Invincible* blew up following a hit on 'Q' turret. The turret roof was blown

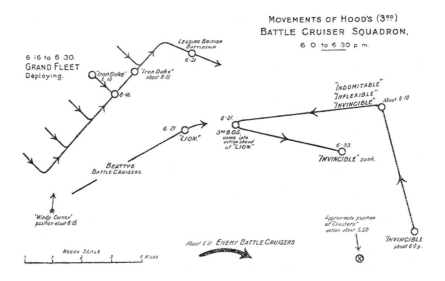

Above: Map showing the movements of Hood's 3rd Battle Cruiser Squadron.

off and flash from the resulting cordite fire reached the magazines which exploded and the dreadful sight of a fine battlecruiser sinking in two halves was seen once again. Captain F.W. Kennedy the Commanding Officer of *Indomitable* who assumed command of the 3rd Battlecruiser Squadron after *Invincible*'s loss described the flagship's final minutes in a report written for Vice Admiral Beatty on 12 June 1916:

> The First Battle Cruiser Squadron was then sighted on our port bow, heavily engaged with some enemy whom I could not see owing to the mist. At 6.13 p.m. 'Invincible' turned to starboard, apparently stopped, and large quantities of steam were observed to be escaping from her escape pipes. At the same moment 'Inflexible' turned to port and tracks of torpedoes were observed by 'Indomitable' coming from the enemy's light cruisers with whom we had been engaged. The range at which I engaged them was about 12,000 yards. I turned away from the torpedoes and increased to full speed. One torpedo actually ran alongside this ship at a distance of about 20 yards, which we managed to outrun. As we turned, two torpedoes passed close to the stern of the ship, but they had run their distance, for I managed to turn ahead of them and resume my place in the Squadron as did

'Inflexible' astern of 'Invincible', which ship was then again going ahead, having turned to about 153°. In all about 5 torpedoes' tracks were seen coming from the enemy's light cruisers.

At 6.14 p.m. 'Invincible' while steam was escaping, hoisted the 'Disregard' but hauled it down at once and followed it by hoisting 1 flag and the squadron got into proper order again. About 6.20 p.m. at a range of 8,600 yards the leading ship of the enemy's battle cruisers was seen firing at the 3rd Battle Cruiser Squadron. They were promptly engaged, and I realised that 'Invincible' could have sustained little or no damage from a torpedo, as I had thought she had when she stopped at 6.13 p.m., for I had to go 20 knots to regain station in the line; 6.32 p.m. shells were falling about 'Indomitable' from the enemy's battle cruisers, which were distant about 8,000 yards. At 6.33 p.m. 'Invincible' was straddled by a salvo and was hit in the after part; 6.34 p.m. a salvo or one shot appeared to hit her about 'Q' turret, and she immediately blew up. Wreckage, &c. was thrown about 400 feet in the air. She appears to have broken in half immediately, for, when the smoke cleared and we had got to the position, the bows were standing upright about 70 feet out of the water and 50 yards away the stern was standing out of the water to a similar height, while in a circle round was wreckage and some few survivors. The visibility, which I have before said was sometimes up to 14,000 yards, was now generally much less than that.[9]

Captain Kennedy was also able to comment on the effectiveness of *Invincible*'s gunnery shortly before her loss:

We were steering 153°. The enemy's battle cruisers were disappearing out of sight, but were still firing on 'Indomitable' and 'Inflexible' The Director Gunner, reported that about this time one of the 'Derfflinger' class fell out of enemy's line and he saw her sink. The Lieutenant-Commander (G) in the Control top at same period remarked that she was very low in the water.[10]

On 2 June 1916, Commander H.E. Dannreuther, the senior surviving officer of *Invincible* wrote an account of his ship's last minutes:

I DEEPLY regret to report that H.M.S. 'Invincible' commanded by Captain A. L. Cay, R.N., and flying the flag of Rear-Admiral the Hon. Horace L. Hood, Rear-Admiral Commanding the Third Battle Cruiser Squadron, was blown up and completely destroyed when in action with the enemy at 6.34 p.m. on Wednesday the 31st May. The total

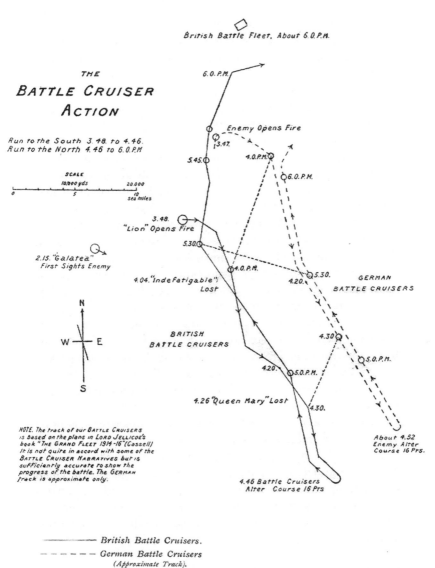

British Battle Fleet, About 6.0.P.M.

THE

BATTLE CRUISER ACTION

Run to the South 3.48. to 4.46.
Run to the North 4.46 to 6.0.P.M

SCALE
10,000 yds   20,000
0   5   10
sea miles

2.15. "Galatea"
First Sights Enemy

Enemy Opens Fire

6.0.P.M.

3.47.

5.45.

4.0.P.M.

6.0.P.M.

3.48.
"Lion" Opens Fire

5.30.

4.0.P.M.

5.30.

4.04. "Indefatigable"
Lost

4.20.

GERMAN
BATTLE CRUISERS

N

W — E

S

BRITISH
BATTLE CRUISERS

4.30.

5.0.P.M.

4.20.

5.0.P.M.

4.30.

4.26. "Queen Mary" Lost

NOTE. The track of our BATTLE CRUISERS
is based on the plans in LORD JELLICOE'S
book "THE GRAND FLEET 1914-16" (Cassell)
It is not quite in accord with some of the
BATTLE CRUISER NARRATIVES but is
sufficiently accurate to show the
progress of the battle. The GERMAN
track is approximate only.

About 4.52
Enemy Alter
Course 16 Prs.

4.46 Battle Cruisers
Alter Course 16 Prs

————————— British Battle Cruisers.
— — — — — German Battle Cruisers
(Approximate Track).

Above: Map showing the battlecruiser actions.

number of officers and men on board at the time was 1,031. Of these only six survived.

The circumstances of the destruction of the ship are briefly as follows:—

The 'Invincible' was leading the 3rd B.C.S. and at about 5.45 p.m. first came into action with an enemy light cruiser on the port bow. Several torpedoes were seen coming towards the ship, but were avoided by turning away from them. 'Invincible's' fire was effective on the light cruiser engaged, and a heavy explosion was observed. A dense cloud of smoke and steam from this explosion appeared to be in the same position some minutes later.

'Invincible' then turned and came into action at about 6,15 p.m. with the leading enemy battle cruiser, which was thought to be the 'Derfflinger'. Fire was opened at the enemy at about 8,000 yards, and several hits were observed. A few moments before the 'Invincible' blew up Admiral Hood hailed the Control Officer in the Control Top from the fore bridge: 'Your firing is very good, keep at it as quickly as you can, every shot is telling'. This was the last order heard from the Admiral or Captain who were both on the bridge at the end.

The Ship had been hit several times by heavy shell, but no appreciable damage had been done when at 6.34 p.m. a heavy shell struck 'Q' turret and, bursting inside, blew the roof off.

This was observed from the control top. Almost immediately following there was a tremendous explosion amidships indicating that 'Q' magazine had blown up. The ship broke in half and sank in 10 or 15 seconds. The survivors on coming to the surface saw the bow and stern of the ship only, both of which were vertical and about 50 feet clear of the water.

There was very little wreckage, the six survivors were supported by a target raft and floating timber till picked up by H.M.S. 'Badger' shortly after 7 p.m. Only one man besides those rescued was seen to come to the surface after the explosion, and he sank before he could reach the target raft. The 'Badger' was brought alongside the raft in a most expeditious and seamanlike manner, and the survivors were treated with the utmost kindness and consideration by the officers and men.[11]

Despite the destruction of two obsolete armoured cruisers and the world's first battlecruiser, this phase of the battle had been far more satisfactory for the British because the German fleet had been brought within Jellicoe's reach without Hipper realising his precarious position. Furthermore, the 15-inch gunned armed ships of the 5th Battle Squadron had not only escaped from Hipper's battlecruisers but had also inflicted very heavy damage upon them.

Thereafter, the arrival of Hood's weak squadron consisting of the oldest battlecruisers in either fleet had exerted a powerful influence out of all proportion to their actual battle strength. Finally, despite her loss, the already obsolescent prototype battlecruiser *Invincible* had inflicted lethal damage to the powerful and brand new *Lützow* which was more akin to a fast battleship than a lightly armoured battlecruiser.

The loss of the latter was of far greater significance to the German Navy than was the combined loss of *Invincible, Defence* and *Warrior* to the Royal Navy.

Main Fleet Action

Battle cruisers at the enemy. Give it everything!

Jellicoe's initial report of the action resulting from the meeting of the two battlefleets shows that while his deployment was complete by about 18.40 many Grand Fleet battleships were in action by 18.30 at ranges of about 12,000 yards:

> The First Battle Squadron, at the rear of the battle line and the furthest to the westward during deployment, came into action almost immediately the deployment signal had been hauled down. At 6.15 p.m., a salvo pitched short of and over the forecastle of 'Hercules', deluging the bridge and conning tower with water.
>
> The enemy at this time were made out by our rear ships to be in a single line, steering to the eastward, their battle-cruisers leading, followed by four 'Konigs' four or five 'Kaisers' and four 'Helgolands', the remainder of the line being invisible owing to the large overlap we had established, and to the converging course. 'Marlborough' and her division opened fire at 6.17 p.m. on one of the 'Kaiser' class. 'Hercules' opened fire at 6.20 p.m. on the second 'Kaiser'. 'Colossus' and her division opened fire at 6.30.
>
> The practice from the First Battle Squadron was very satisfactory under the conditions and severe punishment was administered to the enemy. 'Marlborough' continued her fire with great success even after the ship had assumed a considerable list after being torpedoed; 'Agincourt's' powerful armament was used with good effect, and other ships were also observed to be scoring frequent hits.[1]

Many of the battleships initially fired at the stationary *Wiesbaden* including *Colossus, Collingwood, Conqueror, Temeraire* and *Hercules*, the latter firing her first salvo at the disabled cruiser. *Marlborough*, the flagship of Sir Cecil Burney commanding the 1st Battle Squadron, began firing at the cruiser at 18.25 followed a minute later by *Superb* which claimed hits from her third and fourth salvoes. Her sister *Bellerophon*, which fired intermittently for fifteen minutes, also shot at the crippled ship but didn't claim any hits.

The new Royal Sovereign-class battleship *Revenge* fired intermittently during 18.22-18.39, engaging *Wiesbaden* for some of the time. Her sister *Royal Oak* opened fire on the cruiser at 18.29 firing four salvoes and claiming a hit aft with her third, at 18.30. At about the same time, *Monarch* joined in firing three salvoes while *Vanguard* commenced shooting at 18.32 firing forty-two shells in thirteen minutes at *Wiesbaden* claiming several hits from her fourth and successive salvoes. *Agincourt*, which carried fourteen 12-inch guns, opened fire on the cruiser at 10,000 yards while the 14-inch gun-armed battleship *Canada* despatched two salvoes at about 18.40 towards the German cruiser which was still afloat at 18.45 and had just fired a torpedo at her tormentors.[2]

In fact too many ships were firing at *Wiesbaden* which was also attacked by some of the lighter British units as she came into range with both *Falmouth* and *Yarmouth* opening fire at 18.15 before engaging two of *Regensburg*'s destroyers. About ten minutes later the cruisers engaged *Lützow* and *Derfflinger* with 6-inch guns and torpedoes scoring a few hits with 6-inch shells on the battlecruisers. Of the other units of the 3rd Light Cruiser Squadron, *Birkenhead* fired eight or nine salvoes at *Wiesbaden* before turning her attention to the two battlecruisers.

With so many ships firing at the *Wiesbaden* spotting was almost impossible and few hits were scored thereby confirming pre-war trials during which two ships fired at the same target. The British claimed twelve hits on the light cruiser at this time but the reality was probably less. Clearly, with the control arrangements available in 1916, concentrated fire was impossible at anything beyond point blank range and this fact makes nonsense of arguments about 'Crossing the T'. Additional evidence for this comes from the few hits scored by the High Seas Fleet on the 5th battle squadron turning at 16.50 and the fact that *Warspite* survived her pirouette in front of the High Seas Fleet. As will be seen in later chapter, this lesson was learned and by the end of the war the Grand Fleet was capable of concentrating fire even when the target was not visible to all the ships firing at it.

Jellicoe's flagship *Iron Duke* opened on *Wiesbaden* at 18.23 firing four salvoes one of which straddled her at 18.25. Gunner F.W. Potter R.N. who was stationed in *Iron Duke*'s 13.5-inch gun director tower aloft on the tripod foremast, described the early stages of the main fleet encounter:

> At 4 p.m., Action being sounded, I repaired to the 13.5-in. Director Tower, and Tested all Circuits. I then received information from T.S. that our Destroyers were engaging the Enemy's Battle Cruisers, and that we should probably be in action in about one hour's time. Also that 4 ships of the 5th Battle Squadron were engaging the enemy, and the German High Sea Fleet were standing North.
>
> At about 5.25, I observed flashes from Guns, bearing about Green 60, and about 6 p.m. the Battle Cruisers could be seen heavily engaged with the enemy. 6.25 we opened fire at a three funnelled Cruiser,[3] which looked like the 'Augsburg' Class, Range 11,500. The first was short, the second over, and the third straddled.
>
> After this the shooting appeared to be good, but unfortunately the enemy got obscured by smoke. About this time three Battleships of the 'Koenig' Class appeared bearing Green 70. I then received the order to train Green 70, Battleship of the 'Koenig'[4] Class, and fire was opened on her. About six hits were obtained in the vicinity of 'A' and 'B' Turrets, one salvo causing a big fire on the fore part of the ship. The last salvo fired was a straddle short, as I distinctly saw one shot hit the ship's side and explode. The enemy now turned away [not seen by Jellicoe or anyone near him on top of the chart house – turn seen at about 18.40] and were obscured by the mist, and the order 'check fire' was given.[5]

The First Encounter

In fact, Jellicoe had achieved a very useful concentration with his twenty-four ships occupying five and two-third miles[6] against Scheer's nine-mile line of twenty-two ships. Scheer must have been astonished to find Jellicoe deploying the Grand Fleet across his path and horizon to horizon appeared to be a wall of fire from innumerable heavy guns. His leading ships immediately suffered heavy punishment, particularly from the 3rd Battle Cruiser Squadron. *Lützow*, her bow under water, fell out of line at 18.37 while *Derfflinger*, the new leader (Captain Hartog), was in little better condition. When Hipper tried to transfer to *Seydlitz* he found her awash to the middle deck forward while *Von der Tann* had no turrets left in action but gallantly remained in the line to draw fire from her colleagues. Only *Moltke* remained effective and Hipper couldn't board her until 21.50.

During 18.15 to 19.00, British ships received thirty-six hits, none of which were on Grand Fleet battleships while thirty-three were on

Invincible, Defence, Warrior and *Warspite*. In comparison, the Germans received twelve hits from battlecruisers and ten from battleships.

With the arrival of the Grand Fleet's battleships, Beatty's battlecruisers returned to the fray and *Lion* began again at 18.17, firing a total of ten salvoes at *Lützow* in four-and-a-half minutes at 10,800 yards. She reopened fire at 18.28 targeting the head of Scheer's 3rd Battle Squadron firing seven salvoes in four minutes before the German ships vanished into the mist. *Princess Royal* reopened just after *Lion* but only fired a few salvoes at intervals at uncertain targets while *Tiger* reported directing a few salvoes at her opposite number from 18.19 to 18.29 as well as firing her 6-inch guns at *Wiesbaden* from 18.19 to 18.24. *New Zealand*, the sole surviving ship of the 2nd Battlecruiser Squadron is thought to have engaged what appeared to be a battleship for a short while at 18.19 before shooting at *Derfflinger* and checking fire at about 18.28. Because of the mist and smoke at this time, gunnery conditions for the four battlecruisers were poor and they scored just two hits on *Lützow* at 18.19.

One of the ships in the 3rd Battlecruiser Squadron's screen was the brand new destroyer *Ophelia*, which was making her first voyage since being delivered from her builder's yard to Scapa Flow. She fired a torpedo at 18.29 at 7,500/8,000 yards at a target on her starboard quarter which was probably a unit of the German 3rd Squadron. *Ophelia* escaped unscathed, but *Marvel* of the 12th Flotilla and *Defender* of the 1st Flotilla were each struck by 12-inch shells which failed to explode. *Marvel*, which was hit right forward at 18.15 suffered little damage but the hit in *Defender's* forward boiler room at about 18.30 caused marked reduction in her speed.[7]

No British capital ship was hit over 10,000 yards after 17.40, but *Hercules* was straddled at 18.16, *Vanguard* reported shells falling near during first ten minutes of engagement, and *Royal Oak* was straddled at 18.33. In comparison, British guns were still hitting at ranges up to 17,000 yards even though the visibility was still poor from a Grand Fleet perspective because occasional clearings in the mist would allow a few salvoes as targets presented themselves.[8]

For example, *Marlborough* opened fire on Kaiser-class ships at 18.17, firing seven salvoes in four minutes and claiming hits from her fifth and seventh salvoes but it is not believed that any did actually strike home. *Revenge*, meanwhile, opened fire at 18.22 hours and checked, after firing intermittently for seventeen minutes. Similarly, *Hercules* opened fire at 18.25 on a Kaiser-class ship at 12,000 yards firing seven or eight salvoes. *Iron Duke* opened fire at 18.30 on *König*, which was 12,000 yards away and lit up by the sun, firing nine salvoes of CPC (Common Shell – i.e. Semi-Armour Piercing) totalling forty-three rounds in four minutes fifty seconds before *König* appeared to turn away. Shells from her second, third and fourth salvoes were thought to have hit with six hits being claimed and seven made which severely damaged *König* forward and ignited a number of 5.9-inch cordite charges. *Orion* fired the first of four salvoes of APC (Armour Piercing) at *Markgraf* at 18.32 the last of which scored a hit at 13,300 yards. Her sister *Monarch* sighted three Königs and two Kaisers at 18.33, firing two salvoes of APC at the *König* scoring one hit. *Benbow* opened at 18.30 and fired intermittently for ten minutes but was hampered by haze firing only six two-gun salvoes from her forward turrets. *Bellerophon* may have fired briefly at the German battleships at about this time while *Colossus* opened at 18.30 and fired three salvoes at the German line which was difficult to see. At 18.39 *Marlborough* fired one salvo at a supposed Kaiser-class ship and a minute later *Neptune* fired two salvoes at 11,000 yards on a battleship which was barely visible in the mist.[9]

Jellicoe's report in the Official Despatches give a vivid impression of the damage that he believed his battleships were causing to their opposite numbers and in particular the ships of the modern König-class:

> At 6.30 'Iron Duke' shifted her fire to the leading battleship (one of the 'Konig' class) bearing S.W., range 11,000 yards, and hit her several times in the third and fourth salvoes at 6.33 p.m. The remainder of the third division also opened fire on the leading enemy battleships of 'Konig' class. 'Benbow' and the fourth division opened fire at 6.30 p.m., and 'Orion' and certain ships of the Second Battle Squadron also opened fire at this time on the rear enemy battle-cruisers and leading battleships. At 6.40 p.m. the second 'Konig' was seen to be heavily hit and to be ablaze fore and aft, then to turn 16 points to starboard, the original third ship passing her. The ship then settled by the stern and was observed to blow up by independent witnesses in 'Thunderer', 'Benbow', 'Barham', 'Marne', 'Morning Star', and 'Magic' at 6.50 p.m.[10]

As it happened, Jellicoe and his independent witnesses were wrong as the ship in question neither blew up nor sank and several British officers must have been surprised to see all four ships of the König-class present when the High Seas Fleet surrendered in November 1918.

During the period from 18.40 to 19.00 there was little actual fighting compared with the previous twenty-five minutes because of the poor visibility and because at 18.33 Scheer ordered a *Gefechtwendung* or battle turn-about that took the High Seas Fleet out of the range of the British capital ships. Consequently, firing ceased at about 18.40 because smoke and haze considerably hindered both sides. Jellicoe's despatches record that:

> At this time the visibility was about 12,000 yards, and for ranges about 9,000 yards. The light was, however, extremely baffling, partly due to misty clouds appearing and dissolving, and partly due to layers of smoke from funnels and ships firing. The direction of the wind was W.S.W., force 2.[11]

The loss of contact did become obvious to Jellicoe fairly quickly but countering Scheer's manoeuvre presented difficulties. Thus, turning the fleet towards the enemy's last position would place the German torpedo-boats in an ideal attacking position on the British bow.

Jellicoe correctly considered the risks posed by destroyer attacks in limited visibility to be too great to make it worth following the retreating German battleships which could also fire torpedoes at his dreadnoughts. He could not know that all available German flotilla vessels had taken part in the attack on Hood's 3rd battlecruiser squadron and were in disorder following *Shark's* gallant counter attack. Another factor influencing Jellicoe's caution was that German capital ships were all believed to carry mines, and might reasonably be expected to lay them as they retired[12] but, surely no one really believed that any competent Admiral would take a fleet to sea with heavy loads of high explosive on the upper deck?

Submarine Scares Prior to the Second Encounter

Jellicoe solved his dilemma by deciding to place the Grand Fleet across the German line of retreat to the Heligoland Bight and at 18.44 altered course by divisions to 122 degrees. At 18.55 Jellicoe altered course again to 167 degrees and the 3rd and 4th divisions passed on either side of the wreck of *Invincible* about two minutes later. Subsequently, this wreck, which was located on 3 July 1919 in 57° 03'N, 6°07'45"E, provided the datum point for charts of the battle.[13]

Jellicoe's despatch written soon after the battle describes events at this time as the High Seas Fleet once more hove into view under the guns of the Grand Fleet battleships thanks to Scheer's signal of 18.55 which ordered an about turn to starboard at 18.55. Consequently, by 19.00 the already damaged *König* was once again leading the High Seas Fleet battle line eastwards:

> At 6.55 p.m. the course of the Fleet was altered by divisions to south, conforming to the movements of the battle-cruiser squadrons and with

a view to closing the enemy. Firing was general in the battlefleet, but the use of distribution of gunfire signals was out of the question, only three or four ships being in sight at a time from the van and centre, although more were visible from the rear. Ships fired at what they could see, while they could see it. Hitting had by this time become general.

At 6.54, the Vice-Admiral Commanding, First Battle Squadron, in 'Marlborough' reported that his flagship had been struck by a torpedo or mine. Later evidence pointed to it being a torpedo, possibly discharged from a submarine. This is supported by the report of 'Revenge'.

Officers in the transmitting station, 'A' and 'Y' shell rooms, the director tower and spotting tower all felt a shock as if the ship had struck something. A few minutes after the 'Marlborough' was torpedoed. A large patch of oil, with an upheaval in the middle and portions of wreckage, came to the surface. 'Revenge, on seeing 'Marlborough' struck, had hauled out of the line to port about a cable and probably struck and sank a submarine. [none present – torpedo came from crippled *Wiesbaden*]

At this time the destroyer 'Acasta' was passed in a disabled condition. She signalled that she was holed fore and aft and unable to move her engines. In spite of her condition her ship's company were observed to be cheering as the battlefleet passed. At 6.55 p.m. 'Iron Duke' passed the wreckage of 'Invincible'. The ship was split in two, the bow and stern standing out of the water, the centre part resting apparently on the bottom. The position of the wreck was latitude 57° 6' N., longitude 5°02' E. 'Badger' was picking up survivors. In order to guard against the risk of secret documents being recovered by the enemy should the position of the wreck be located by remaining above water, a submarine was sent from Blyth to search for and if necessary, sink the wreck. She was unable to find it, and there is no doubt that the vessel sank.[14]

At 18.54 Beatty reported sighting an imaginary submarine and about this time the armoured cruiser *Hampshire* fired at a 'periscope'. The incident was recorded in a letter written on 4 June by Midshipman Clement Stanley Bertram Mallet RNR to his parents.

Dear Mater & Pater,
Just a few lines to let you know that I am still in the land of the living after last Wednesday's stunt. We went in to action in great form and luckily came out ditto not touched. We were fired at several times but as I have said they all missed. We sank a light cruiser and accounted for

two submarines,[15] one we rammed and the other by gunfire. Really it was a very fine sight and everybody was full of life even the boys some only fifteen years old. I will never forget it in all my life – there was 'some' noise specially when the Battle Fleet opened fire. Our losses are very heavy but I am sure by what I have seen the Huns have lost more than have been reported the truth will probably come out later.[16]

Sadly, Mallet lost his life a few days later when *Hampshire*, with Lord Kitchener aboard, was mined and sunk off the Orkneys while en route to Russia. The fears about the presence of submarines seemed to have been confirmed at 18.57 when *Marlborough* signalled that she had been struck by a mine or a torpedo, confirming that it was a torpedo about a minute later.

Although the torpedoes were sighted and avoided by various British capital ships between 18.40 and 19.01, they were attributed initially to submarine(s), whereas they were more likely to have been fired by the stationary *Wiesbaden* and the crippled *V48*. *Marlborough* was struck at 18.54 by a torpedo from *Wiesbaden* abreast the starboard diesel generator room causing a list of seven to eight degrees to starboard. Water entered the forward boiler room causing fires to be drawn, but she was still able to make seventeen knots and remained in the battle line for the time being. Unlike Jellicoe who believed that *Marlborough* had been torpedoed by a submarine (see above), Vice-Admiral Burney recognised very early on that the likely culprit was the disabled cruiser *Wiesbaden* and his damaged flagship hit back hard:

> Shortly after being struck, 'Marlborough' opened fire on an enemy cruiser passing down the line which was suspected of having fired the torpedo. The 3rd and 4th salvoes both hit and appeared to open up her side, as a deep red flame could be seen inside her hull. A torpedo was fired at her at 7.10 p.m. During this time the 'Acasta' was passed disabled on the port side, and 'Marlborough' avoided 3 more torpedoes by the use of the helm.[17]

The later torpedoes, and that seen by *St Vincent* at 19.00, came from *V48*.

At 19.00 Beatty signalled by searchlight that the High Seas Fleet was to the westward although they had been out of sight from *Lion* for about twenty-five minutes and had not been seen by the 3rd Light Cruiser Squadron for about the same period of time. However, the 3rd Light Cruiser Squadron failed to undertake any scouting and it was left to the indefatigable Commodore Goodenough and his 2nd Light Cruiser Squadron to seek out the Germans. In the meantime, there occurred a strange incident as Beatty moved further away from Scheer when, at 19.00, *Lion* led the battlecruisers through a 360 degree turn.[18] Compass error and a lack of attention on *Lion's* bridge were blamed for this strange manoeuvre which, despite evidence to the contrary, Beatty always denied had taken place.

Unsurprisingly, Goodenough's 2nd Light Cruiser Squadron was the only one of the four light cruiser squadrons to move out to the last known German position and, during another daring and typically competent reconnaissance, *Southampton* came under fire from the High Seas Fleet before withdrawing at 19.04. Prior to retreating from the German battleships, *Southampton* sent a signal at 19.00 reporting that that the German battlefleet was steering 100 degrees bearing 190 degrees, number unknown, and gave her position as 57° 02'N 6° 07'E which was correct to within four miles. Regardless of its accuracy, the 2nd Light Cruiser Squadron was visible to the 1st Battle Squadron and possibly even Jellicoe in *Iron Duke*. More importantly, *Southampton's* signal gave due warning of the likelihood of a resumption of the battle within a matter of minutes.[19]

In fact, Jellicoe had ordered another turn at 18.44 to the south and, although neither knew it, he had led the Grand Fleet into a crescent across Scheer's route to Wilhelmshaven.

The Second Encounter

It was about this time that Scheer ordered his fleet to turn again and head east thereby taking him into the centre of the British line a mere 10,000 yards away. Various explanations have been offered for this strange manoeuvre the least likely being that a gun and torpedo attack followed by another turn away would drive the Grand Fleet to the east thereby giving the High Seas Fleet more room to escape after dark. A far more likely explanation is that Scheer was thoroughly confused during the earlier encounter and had no idea of the course and position of the British fleet. It is possible that the unexpected arrival of the 3rd Battle Cruiser Squadron added to his confusion. While it is possible to excuse Scheer's manoeuvre on the grounds of confusion during the poor visual conditions then obtaining, it goes far to destroy any remaining claim of his ability as a tactician.

At 19.10 the rear divisions of the Grand Fleet which were the furthest north and west sighted enemy battleships to the south west at a range of about 10,000 yards and began to fire on them. Within five minutes the leading ships of the High Seas Fleet and, in particular the already badly mauled battlecruisers of 1st Scouting Group and Behncke's 3rd Battle Squadron were once again under heavy fire from Jellicoe's dreadnoughts at a range of 10,000 -14,000 yards. Once again British shooting was better and for a short period the Grand Fleets' battleships were able to fire with considerable effect with very little damage being done in return. Jellicoe's despatches record his impressions of this successful phase of the battle:

> At 7.10 p.m. 'Marlborough' and several other ships were firing at the second of the three of the remaining 'Konig' class ('Marlborough' fired fourteen salvoes). At 7.18 a ship turned out of the line very low in the water aft and sinking. An Officer in the torpedo control tower in 'Colossus' saw this ship sink at 7.30 p.m., his evidence being confirmed by 'Benbow', 'Superb', 'Colossus, and 'Malaya'. At 7.12 p.m. enemy battle-cruisers also emerged from the mist at 10,000 yards range on the starboard beam of the 'Colossus 'division, which opened fire on them. A ship of the 'Derffiinger' class was observed to be hit several times by 'Colossus' and 'Neptune', and listed over and passed out of sight obscured by heavy smoke and mist. 'Colossus' was hit, but only suffered trifling damage. At the same time a ship of the 'Seydlitz' class was also fired at and hit by 'Collingwood'. 'Revenge' also fired at and hit a battlecruiser supposed to be 'Von Der Tann', which then turned away.[20]

Vice Admiral Burney in *Marlborough* was another he believed that a German battleship had been sunk at this time:

> 'Marlborough' then engaged a ship of the Konig class, firing 14 salvoes. Distinct hits were seen in four salvoes. This ship finally turned out of the line, very low in the water aft, and was apparently sinking. A destroyer was observed to place herself on her engaged side, and make a dense smoke in order to screen her.
>
> Shortly after this a heavy smoke screen was observed at what appeared to be the head of the enemy battlefleet, and it was soon apparent that the destroyers were attacking under its cover.[21]

Once again those who reported the loss of a German battleship were in error although their evidence must have convinced Jellicoe to claim the sinking of two battleships in his despatches. The battleship *Colossus* was heavily involved in the second fleet encounter and her commanding officer, Captain A.D.P.R Pound R.N. a future wartime First Sea Lord, provided a detailed account of his ship's experiences:

7. p.m.—Opened fire on enemy 3-funnelled cruiser (ex 'Greek') steaming opposite course on Starboard Beam, 9,700. Other ships of Battle Fleet also firing. Fired 3 salvoes.

7. 2 p.m.—Passed wreck of 'Invincible' port hand. Broken in two pieces. 'Oak' standing by. Two survivors in sight near propellers.

7. 3 p.m.—'Benbow' firing 6-in. on enemy Destroyer Starboard Bow. 3 points to Starboard together.

7. 5 p.m.—Battle Cruiser Fleet opened fire Starboard Bow. Ships not actually in sight. Opened fire 12-in. and 4-in. on enemy Destroyer coming down on Starboard Bow, 4,000 yards. Hit Destroyer, which disappeared apparently sunk. 'A' turret also fired on several Destroyers further off.

7.10 p.m.—Altered course 3 points to Port together.

7.12 p.m.—Suddenly observed 'Derfflinger' class ship emerge from mist 10,000 yards Starboard Beam accompanied by two (possibly more) Battle Cruisers. Attention of ships generally concentrated on enemy Destroyer. Immediately shifted to leading Battle Cruiser and opened fire at 9,000 yards range, closing at

7.16 p.m. to 8,400. —'Colossus' hit in superstructure just abaft funnel (foremost) by 12-in. shell which exploded and caused fire in port gun decks and signal deck. Cordite chief cause of fire, extinguished in a few minutes. Another 12-in. shell hit sounding platform on Port Signal Deck, but apparently passed overboard without bursting.

7.17p.m.—Heavy shell burst 30 yards short abreast 'A' turret. Splinters penetrated foremost funnel and unarmoured parts of ship in about 20 places and wrecked S. 1 Searchlight, burst fire main in Captain's Cabin Flat and caused unimportant damage. Rangetaker fore Upper Bridge severely wounded, one Marine look-out same position slightly wounded. Leading Signalman in Fore Top severely wounded.

7.18 p.m.—Hit in Fore part of ship by splinters from heavy shell, which burst short.

7.15 p.m. —Fired 5 salvoes at 'Derfflinger' (or 'Liitzow') on beam, steering same course, 8,000-9,000 yards

7.20 p.m. In range. Observed at least 4 direct hits (4th and 5th salvoes) (2 hits on water line). Enemy vessel obscured by heavy smoke and mist, but just previously observed to have listed.

7.25 p.m.—Firing ceased.

7.35 p.m.—'Colossus' turned to port to avoid torpedo coming from Starboard.[22]

Battlecruisers at the Enemy. Give it Everything!

As the High Seas Fleet encountered the full might of the Grand Fleet for the second time that day Scheer must have known that he faced disaster. Furthermore, he must have realised that any attempt at successful evasion must therefore be predicated by darkness because to run from the Grand Fleet would, at very least, expose the six eighteen-knot pre-dreadnoughts of the 2nd Squadron, with their inadequate armour and reciprocating machinery, to annihilation at the hands of Jellicoe's dreadnoughts and super-dreadnoughts. Furthermore, eight[23] of the dreadnoughts in the 1st Squadron were also powered by steam reciprocating machinery with its inherent inability to give full speed for more than a few hours.

In comparison, Jellicoe's fleet of turbine-engine battleships could maintain their maximum speed of twenty-one knots without difficulty for prolonged periods. Scheer was therefore very fortunate that Jellicoe chose to fight the battle at sixteen – eighteen knots thereby throwing away his speed advantage over the older German ships.

In effect, only one opening remained to Scheer, namely a simultaneous turn away under cover of a smoke screen and attack by his light forces. Jellicoe was aware of this German manoeuvre because of the code book taken from the *Magdeburg* but because of the poor visibility he did not notice the 'turn away'. However, it is quite clear that this was seen by other Grand Fleet ships and also by officers aboard *Iron Duke* but not one thought to check that his Admiral had seen the German manoeuvre through the haze. Possibly the worst example was *Falmouth* of the 3rd Light Cruiser Squadron whose duties should have been to report the enemy movements, but she failed to signal that she had seen the leading German ships turn away. Undoubtedly, some of the blame can be placed on Jellicoe, whose initiative-stifling Grand Fleet Battle Orders said that when the ships of the battle fleet were in sight of one another reports were not required, although another order said that ships sighting enemy movements which might not be visible to the C-in-C should report.

In his extreme danger it appeared to Scheer that a torpedo-boat attack alone would not deter Jellicoe from hot pursuit. Consequently, at 19.13 he sent the dramatic signal '*Schlacht Kreutzer ran an den Feind. Voll einsetzen*' (Battle cruisers at the enemy. Give it everything!) to his already badly damaged battlecruisers ordering them to attack Jellicoe's centre regardless of the consequences and in so doing draw the British fire from the German battleships. Captain Hartog leading the four remaining battlecruisers in the badly damaged *Derfflinger* complied, closing to within 7,700 yards of the British battleships which they could only see as a line of flashes. During the so-called 'death ride' the already badly battered German battlecruisers attracted the greater part of the British fire which but for their presence would have been aimed at the battleships as they turned away. At 19.17 Scheer signalled the battlecruisers to operate against the enemy's van and Hartog was able to turn away and open the range thereby saving his ships.

At 19.15 he ordered his torpedo-boat flotillas to attack the British line and finally at 19.18 he ordered a second battle about-turn so as to withdraw his battleships from British gunfire. Meanwhile, until these manoeuvres were complete, his ships would have to endure a deluge of heavy shells, without being able to offer any effective reply.

Of the British battleships, seven fired at German battleships, eighteen at the 1st Scouting Group and three at *Lützow*. The battlecruisers bore the brunt of the British cannonade with *Von der Tann* being hit by a 15-inch shell at 19.19, *Seydlitz* was hit five times between 19.14 and 19.27 and *Derfflinger* was hit by fourteen shells, eleven of which struck during 19.14 and 19.20 while *Moltke* escaped unscathed.[24] The 1st Scouting Group was also engaged ineffectually by the British battlecruisers with *Lion* firing four salvoes from 19.14 at a range of 16,000 – 18,000 yards and *Princess Royal* firing for three minutes at the same unidentified target. Neither ship scored a hit. *Tiger* was in action against a German battlecruiser from 19.16 – 19.20 at a range of between 19,750 – 20,200 yards, also without success.

Of the German battleships, *Grosser Kurfürst* was hit seven times, *König*, *Markgraf* and *Helgoland* once each and *Kaiser* twice. The hits on *Markgraf* and *Kaiser* were probably scored by *Agincourt*. The already doomed *Lützow* came under fire from and *Monarch*, *Orion* and *Centurion* from 19.14, suffering five hits before her seven escorting torpedo-boats were able to lay down an effective smoke screen.

Gunner Potter who was in the director control tower atop *Iron Duke*'s tripod foremast recalled:

> A large Cruiser of the 'Moltke' Class came into view, accompanied by about seven Destroyers. I was put on to the Cruiser, which made a splendid Target, but she was very soon screened by the Destroyer's smoke, so I reported the Enemy obscured. It seemed that as soon as she saw the Fleet she turned about and disappeared.[25]

During this period of intense shelling Hipper, who was still trying to board his replacement flagship, had to remain in the torpedo-boat *G39* because once firing restarted he was unable to board *Moltke* which had become the most effective unit of the 1st Scouting Group.

With poor visibility, the British battleships could not be engaged effectively and the Germans made only two hits at 19.16 when two shells from *Seydlitz* struck *Colossus* at 8,000 yards. Altogether, four salvoes fell close to *Colossus* causing additional splinter damage forward. *Agincourt* was straddled at 19.17 and several other battleships reported shells falling nearby. Meanwhile, the light favoured the British who took full advantage of it to hammer the leading ships of the German line scoring about twenty-seven hits of which nineteen were on the already seriously damaged battlecruisers.

Of the British battleships and battlecruisers, *Erin* did not fire her main armament while *Conqueror*, *Vanguard*, *Inflexible* and *New Zealand* did not engage any capital ships. *Wiesbaden* remained a target for some ships including *Marlborough* whose four salvoes fired at 9,800 – 9,500 yards from 19.03 seemed to have effectively wrecked the German cruiser with hits being obtained from the third and fourth salvoes. Ships that fired at *Wiesbaden* during this period included *Agincourt*, *Revenge*, *Colossus*, *Neptune*, *Collingwood* and *St Vincent* but, once again, too many ships were shooting at the same target.

Meanwhile, while carrying out Scheer's simultaneous turn away, the ships of the German 3rd Squadron were too close together and were also under a considerable weight of fire from four or five British battleships. The resulting congestion meant that for a short while several German battleships were very close to one another, line abreast and proceeding at a slow speed. *König* laid a smoke screen at 19.25 and *Kaiser* joined suite at 19.28 but, the volume of British fire had largely died away by then.

The German Torpedo-boats Attack
At 19.15 Scheer ordered his torpedo-boat flotillas to attack and the ten boats of the 6th and 9th flotillas, stationed near the head of the German line and having already expended twenty-one of their sixty torpedoes, moved in. Jellicoe's despatches describe the situation that developed as see from his flagship:

At about 7.10 p.m. a flotilla of enemy destroyers supported by a cruiser was seen approaching 'Iron Duke', bearing from 'Iron Duke' S. 50° W. (60° green). The Fleet was turned away two points by the 'Preparative' and subsequently another two points, fire being opened on the flotilla with 4-in, 6-in., and turret guns at a range of about 10,000 to 8,000 yards. When at about 8,000 yards range, the destroyers fired their torpedoes, turning towards the rear of their line and disappearing in a smoke screen. No torpedoes hit. One destroyer [S35] was observed to sink.

At about 7.25 p.m. another enemy's destroyer attack was observed approaching the rear of the battle line from a bearing about 120° green, 9,000 yards from 'Iron Duke', and was heavily engaged by the four rear divisions of the battlefleet and Fifth Battle squadron. The Eleventh Flotilla and Fourth Light-Cruiser Squadron had advanced to counter the former enemy destroyer attack and were in a favourable position to counter the second attack during which at 7.22 p.m. they sank an enemy destroyer.

They were recalled at 7.40 p.m. In addition, the third destroyer from the left was observed to sink, and the left-hand one to be struck and turned bottom up approximately at 7.35 p.m. At 7.45 p.m. a division of the Twelfth Flotilla, consisting of 'Obedient', 'Mindful', 'Marvel', and 'Onslaught', proceeded to attack, and sink an enemy 'V'-class destroyer [the already disabled V48] flying a Commodore's pendant near the rear of the Fifth Battle Squadron.[26]

The 6th Flotilla fired just eleven of its sixteen remaining torpedoes between 19.22 and 19.24 at a range of 7,500 to 9,000 yards with G41, which was hit by a 6-inch shell, firing two, while V44, G87 and G86 each fired three. They achieved no hits but G87 was hit by a 6-inch shell which passed through the ship and G86 was damaged when a heavy shell burst very near to her starboard side. The 9th Flotilla which had twenty-three torpedoes remaining fired ten torpedoes at about 19.26 with V28, S36 and S51 each firing one, V26 and S35 launching two each and S52 firing three. Once again, they achieved no hits but V28 was hit by a 6-inch shell, S51 and S52 being damaged by splinters while S35, which was hit by two 13.5-inch shells from Iron Duke, broke in two and sank.[27]

The demise of S35 was witnessed by Gunner Potter from his station in Iron Duke's 13.5-inch director tower at the top of her tripod foremast:

> I then received the order to Train Green 110 a Destroyer, followed by the order 'Green 120, a Destroyer' After Ranging for a few moments, the order 'Open Fire' was given. The only Salvo was a straddle short.
> When the splash cleared, the Destroyer had disappeared altogether. The order 'Check Fire' was given at about 7.30. Several bearings were given to me during this time, but no further firing took place.[28]

Gunner Herbert D. Jehan, who was stationed aloft controlling Iron Duke's 6-inch guns, saw a destroyer being hammered by the flagship's secondary armament:

A Destroyer attack was observed coming towards the Fleet, starboard bow. The order was given by the Captain from Conning Tower 'Destroyer 63 Green, Open fire when ready.'

The Guns were given the Bearing of the Leading Destroyer at an estimated range of 10,000 yards, and 600 closing, fire was opened by salvoes, first salvo was over and out for line. This was corrected the next salvo being short, and the third salvo straddled, the fourth hit the Destroyer which appeared to stagger and Independent firing was ordered. No less than four hits were observed and the Destroyer sank. The 6-in. were ordered to Check Fire and shift to another Destroyer bearing 84 Green, Range 9,000. This Destroyer appeared to be hit once by the 6-in., but not disabled, and turned away. Range increased rapidly to extreme Gun Range, and the 6-in. were ordered to Check Fire.

The second attack came from aft, the order given by the Captain from Conning Tower was 'Destroyers 135 Green, Open Fire when ready.' This was passed to Battery, and 10,000 put on the Sights. 'Salvoes Commence' being ordered. The guns appeared to be a long time before opening fire. One Gun fired, and I could not see the Fall of Shot. A Check Bearing was given 115 Green, and it appeared to me as if the after guns were on the second Destroyer, and the foremost guns on the leading Destroyer. I did not check fire, as I thought it would be waste of time. It was most difficult to spot through the firing of the ships.[29]

The 3rd and 7th German flotillas tried to attack the British rear but at 19.22 Jellicoe ordered them to be counter-attacked by the 4th Light Cruiser Squadron as well as by *Castor* and part of the 11th destroyer flotilla and they managed to fire only one torpedo. All told, 150 rounds of 12-inch to 15-inch were expended against the 6th and 9th Flotillas as well as a larger number of 6-in shells in an action which demonstrated the uselessness of the 4-inch secondary gun batteries during a daylight action.

British battleships which sighted and/or took avoiding action against torpedoes between 19.30 and 19.45 included *Colossus*, *Collingwood*, *Marlborough*, *Revenge*, *Hercules*, *Agincourt*, *Barham* and *St Vincent*.[30]

Vice-Admiral Burney observed the German turn away during the attack by their torpedo-boats:

I immediately hoisted the signal 'NM', informing our flotillas astern that the enemy flotillas were making an attack. At the same time the preparative was hoisted, and I turned my division away.

As far as I could judge the whole squadron opened fire on the attacking destroyers with the whole of the secondary and some of the main armament, and the attack was checked, and they turned away, but not before they were able to fire some of their torpedoes, which, however, were avoided. Two of the enemy's destroyers were observed to be hit by 'Marlborough's' 6-inch gun fire alone, and there must have been others as the fire was so intense.

As the destroyer attack developed the enemy battlefleet in sight were observed to turn at least 8 points until their sterns were towards our line. They ceased fire, declined further action, and disappeared into the mist.[31]

The German 2nd and 7th flotillas were unable to attack because of their position and consequently out of fifty torpedo-boats potentially carrying 224 torpedoes only twenty-two weapons were fired and none hit. From Jellicoe's perspective, the situation must have looked grave when a large number of German torpedo-boats appeared out of a thick smoke screen. He believed that the Germans could have eighty-eight torpedo boats each carrying six torpedoes and, unsurprisingly, the threat posed by 528 torpedoes or the actual 224 must have appeared terrifying.

Pre-war exercises and crude mathematics suggested that the only counter was to turn away from such a threat with some torpedoes being outrun while the relative speed of the remainder would be reduced thereby making avoidance much easier. At that time, the 'turn away' was used by all admirals in both fleets and there had been no criticism when Jellicoe had written it into the Grand Fleet Battle Orders. Post-war exercises, and more subtle calculations, showed that a turn towards would be at least as effective and would not expose vulnerable sterns of ships to torpedoes. With the knowledge available then, a turn away was the safest short term action but, in the presence of a disorganised enemy with little daylight remaining, a case can be made for a turn forward.

At 19.22 Jellicoe turned away two points and a further two points at 19.25 on a course south-easterly course. Some British ships sighted approaching torpedoes and individual avoiding action involved a further turn away. Some ships had narrow escapes. The effect of each turn was to open the range by 1,200-3,800 yards depending on which squadron and when. Combined with Scheer's smoke enshrouded turn away this meant that contact was lost. All the British light cruisers lost touch with the enemy except for those of Goodenough and for once he failed to make a sighting report.

At 19.35 Jellicoe turned five points towards the enemy and followed this with a signal to form line. At 19.40 a turn of three points toward was ordered followed at 20.00 with a change to course west and speed increased (!) to seventeen knots. At this time the Grand Fleet was still between the High Seas Fleet and its home bases. Much discussion has ranged around Beatty's 'follow me' which appeared to be intended to lead the battle fleet into close action with the enemy. At the time it was sent Beatty had no enemy in sight and although Jellicoe responded very quickly telling Vice-Admiral Jeram in *King George V* to follow Beatty, the battlecruisers were no longer in sight. The debates that have raged around this incident seem to be at best trivial not least because, while everyone acted quickly and sensibly, events moved far too fast for the primitive signal systems then available.

The Last Daylight Actions
Jellicoe's despatches record the final actions as darkness fell:

> At 8 p.m. firing had practically ceased except towards the rear of the line, where some of the ships of the First and Fifth Battle Squadrons were still engaged. Whilst the battlefleet had been turned away from enemy torpedo attacks, the Vice-Admiral Commanding, Battle-Cruiser Fleet, had continued engaging the head of the enemy line, gradually hauling round to S.W. by S. and then S.W. to keep in touch.
>
> At 7.32 p.m. 'Lion's' course was S.W., speed eighteen knots, the leading enemy battleship bearing N.W. by W. The battle-cruiser fleet were inflicting considerable punishment on the enemy, so much so that the enemy torpedo-boat destroyers were called upon to cover the capital ships by emitting volumes of grey smoke. Under cover of this smoke, the enemy were lost sight of at 7.45 p.m.[32]

Just after 20.00 Scheer was heading south, passing ahead of the British fleet steaming west. Beatty, to the south west was heading south-west with a light cruiser squadron (Napier) ahead. At 22.09 Napier reported that the cruiser fight between the 4th Scouting Group and the 3rd Light Cruiser Squadron which was scouting ahead of the battleline, occurred between 20.20 – 20.32.

This was also heard by Beatty who turned towards the sound of gunfire sighting the 1st Scouting Group and opening fire on *Derfflinger* at 20.23, obtaining a hit at 20.28 which temporarily jammed her 'A' turret. *New Zealand* fired on *Seydlitz* scoring three hits before checking fire at 20.31. *Derfflinger* and *Seydlitz* were rescued by appearance of the six old pre-dreadnoughts of the 2nd squadron. The latter closed to within 6-8,000 yards of Beatty's ships before disappearing into the haze at 20.35, thereby ending the last capital ship battle of the war.

During this final encounter, *Hannover* was struck by fragments of a 13.5-inch armour piercing shell from *Princess Royal*, *Schleswig-Holstein* was hit by a shell from *New Zealand*, *Schlesien* was hit by splinters from a short salvo from *New Zealand*, and *Pommern* was hit by *Inflexible* which ceased fire soon afterwards at 20.33 because the light was too poor for the fall of shot to be seen. The Official Despatches record that:

> The enemy was last seen by 'Falmouth' steaming to the westward. At 8.40 p.m. all battle-cruisers felt a heavy shock, as if struck by a mine, torpedo, or sunken wreckage.[33]

Sunset occurred at 20.19, but there was still enough light for the 4th Light Cruiser Squadron to make brief contact with the German line at 20.45. The British continued to miss chances although when the 4th Light Cruiser Squadron sighted enemy battleships at 20.45 it was initially thought they were pre-dreadnoughts but they were actually the *Westfalen*, *Nassau* and *Rheinland*.

The cruisers *Caroline* and *Royalist* fired two and one torpedoes respectively (though against Vice Admiral Jerram's orders) at 21.05 and 21.10 at the centre ship of the three in sight but unfortunately scored no hits. The actions of *Caroline* (Captain Cooke) and *Royalist* (Captain The Hon. H. Meade) represent one of the few occasions when British ships attacked the enemy at Jutland regardless of orders to the contrary. Jerram had sighted these same enemy ships at 10,000 yards but refused to open fire because he thought that they were Beatty's battlecruisers. Commodore Hawsley with the 11th flotilla would not attack in daylight without gunfire support and missed the chance to do considerable damage with his powerful flotilla. By 21.00, as night fell, the leading British and German battleships were five miles apart on converging courses.

Night Action and Inaction

Here and there flames would shoot up on board the burning
British destroyers.

The action on the night of 31 May / 1 June 1916 was full of stories of incredible courage but, from a British perspective, what happened was of little importance compared to those actions which did not take place.

With command of the sea already assured by the numerically superior Grand Fleet, the Royal Navy had no need to indulge in risky night-fighting, and it was therefore something the fleet was not experienced in. The actions that night would also reveal that, for all their courage, the British destroyers at Jutland were poorly trained when it came to carrying out torpedo attacks and their performance that night was also limited by the relatively primitive communications then available and by the stultifying effects of Jellicoe's voluminous Grand Fleet Battle Orders which discouraged initiative. Thus, those commanding British warships were loath to attack on their own initiative in the absence of a direct order while at the same time being reluctant to report enemy sightings back to their Commander-in-Chief who they had been brought up to believe was all-seeing and all-knowing.[1]

As darkness fell, the British and German commanders faced totally different problems with Scheer's High Seas Fleet having to reach the swept channels through the minefields in the Heligoland Bight in time to avoid being brought to battle by the whole Grand Fleet the next day. In comparison, Jellicoe had to prevent his battleships becoming embroiled in close-range night fighting while at the same time ensuring that he was in position to intercept the High Seas Fleet before it could enter the mined area the following morning. Scheer's approach to the problem he faced was particularly single-mined, the units comprising his fleet being ordered return using the shortest route via the Horn Reef.

Furthermore, his heavy ships were to keep on heading for their bases regardless of the opposition encountered while his torpedo-boats were ordered to attack any British forces they met. Scheer was confident that the night-fighting capabilities of his dreadnoughts would be more than adequate to brush aside attacks from British destroyers – and so it proved.

Jellicoe could not know which way Scheer would attempt to reach home but rightly assumed that the long route to the north of Denmark would be impossible for any seriously damaged ships. Jellicoe believed that there were four (actually three) routes through or round the minefields to Wilhelmshaven and, from the west-south-west course of the Germans when they were last seen, he believed that they were taking the Ems route. British submarines had frequently been seen off the Horn Reef and it was assumed that the threat posed by these boats would mean that Scheer was unlikely to take this route even though it was the shortest. By steaming slowly south Jellicoe believed that the Grand Fleet would cover all routes except that via Horn Reef. The destroyer *Abdiel* had been sent to lay mines in this route as a precaution.

Jellicoe's Night Disposition

Jellicoe started the night with the Grand Fleet situated between the High Seas Fleet and its bases and with this in mind he continued on a course of 167 degrees at seventeen knots throughout the night confident of meeting his opponent early the next morning. Jellicoe formed his fleet into three columns with *Marlborough's* division straggling and the 5th battle squadron, less *Warspite*, also somewhat behind.

Furthermore, he stationed his destroyers, other than those with Beatty, five miles astern of the battlefleet so as to screen the latter from attack by German torpedo-boats while at the same time decreasing the likelihood of a blue-on-blue incident in which British destroyers mistakenly attacked their own heavy ships. They were also tasked with preventing Scheer from getting round the Grand Fleet but, sadly no one seems to have told the destroyers what they were supposed to do or informed them as to the position of the enemy. The disposition also meant that the British battleships could treat all destroyers as hostile. Jellicoe's despatches written soon after the battle reveal his intentions for the night and the following morning:

> Darkness was now rapidly setting in, the mist was increasing and it became necessary to decide on the future course of action.
> The British Fleet was between the enemy and his base. Each side possessed a considerable number of destroyers, it being most

probable that the enemy was largely superior in this respect, in numbers, as it was logical to assume that every available torpedo-boat destroyer and torpedo-boat had been ordered out as soon as contact between the fleets became probable. I rejected at once the idea of a night action between the heavy ships, as leading to possible disaster owing, first, to the presence of torpedo craft in such large numbers, and, secondly, to the impossibility of distinguishing between our own and enemy vessels. Further, the result of a night action under modern conditions must always be very largely a matter of pure chance.

I was loth to forego the advantage of position, which would have resulted from an easterly or westerly course, and I therefore decided to steer to the southward, where I should be in a position to renew the engagement at daylight, and should also be favourably placed to intercept the enemy should he make for his base by steering for Heligoland or towards the Ems and thence along the north German coast. Further, such a course enabled me to drop my destroyer flotillas astern, thus at one and the same time providing the battlefleet with a screen against attack by torpedo craft at night, and also giving our flotillas an opportunity for attacking the enemy's heavy ships should they also be proceeding to the southward with the object of regaining their bases.

Accordingly, at 9 p.m., the fleet was turned by divisions to south (speed seventeen knots) the second organisation being assumed, and the fleet formed in divisions line ahead disposed abeam to port, columns one mile apart, the object of the close formation being that the divisions should remain clearly in sight of each other during the night, in order to prevent ships mistaking each other for enemy vessels.[2]

Jellicoe's dispositions for the Grand Fleet that night were as follows:

At 9.24 p.m., the Vice-Admiral Commanding, Battle-Cruiser Fleet, in latitude 56° 29' N., longitude 5° 27' E., turned to south. At 9.27 p.m., the destroyer flotillas were ordered to take station five miles astern of the battlefleet.

At 9.32 p.m., 'Abdiel' was directed to lay mines in wide zig-zags from a position fifteen miles 215° from the Vyl light vessel in a mean direction 180°, ten mines to the mile. This operation was successfully accomplished without observation, and 'Abdiel' then proceeded to Rosyth to replenish with mines. At 10 p.m., 'Iron Duke's' position was: latitude, 56° 22' N., longitude, 5° 47' E., course, south, speed, 17 knots, the order of the fleet from west to east being as follows : Battle-

Cruiser Fleet; Cruiser Squadrons; Battlefleet (in divisions, disposed abeam to port, columns one mile apart, in Organisation No. 2) First Light-Cruiser Squadron four miles one point before the starboard beam of the Battle-Cruiser Fleet; Second Light-Cruiser Squadron astern of the Fifth Battle Squadron and Second Battle Squadron ; Third Light-Cruiser Squadron on starboard bow of the Battle-Cruiser Fleet: Fourth Light-Cruiser Squadron ahead of the Battlefleet; Destroyer Flotillas—five miles astern of the Battlefleet in the order, west to east—Eleventh, Fourth, Twelfth, Ninth, Tenth, Thirteenth.[3]

The minelaying destroyer *Abdiel* duly laid her eighty mines in a position about fifteen miles bearing 215° from the Vyl Lightship in a position which was approximately nine miles west-south-west of a similar minefield that she had laid on 4 May 1916. However, unlike her earlier field, the mines laid between 01.24 and 02.04 on 1 June caused no damage to the retreating Germans.

As a result of Jellicoe's dispositions, the 4th Light Cruiser Squadron continued to lead the Grand Fleet while the 2nd Light Cruiser Squadron took up a position on the fleet's starboard quarter. Regarding the British destroyer flotillas, the 11th Flotilla (*Castor, Kempenfelt* and fourteen M-class destroyers) were the most westerly with the 4th (*Tipperary, Broke* and ten K-class destroyers), 13th (*Champion* and seven M-class destroyers plus *Termagant* and *Turbulent* of the 10th Flotilla)), 9th (four L-class destroyers plus *Morris* of the 10th Flotilla) and 12th (*Faulknor, Marksman* and thirteen M-class destroyers) in order to the eastward. All the destroyers and flotilla leaders present had their full complement of torpedoes except for those in the 13th Flotilla where *Petard* had none, *Turbulent* and *Nicator* one each, *Nerissa* two and *Moresby* three. Unfortunately, the 11th Flotilla was out of position because of its action with German light cruisers and the brunt of the fighting fell on the significantly weaker 4th Flotilla.

Jellicoe, who received no information as to the position of the German battlefleet from any of his ships, was also let down by the Admiralty which for most of the night had known that Scheer was making for Horn Reef but either failed to pass him the information or, alternatively sent him an edited form which lacked meaning. The first signal, sent at 21.58, was seen by Jellicoe an hour later and gave an obviously incorrect position for the High Seas Fleet thereby adding to his distrust of radio intelligence. Between 21.00 and 22.40 three signals were intercepted by the Admiralty. The first asked for Zeppelin reconnaissance at Horn Reef at dawn and, if passed to Jellicoe would have enabled him to be at Horn Reef at the same time. Instead, at 22.41, the Admiralty sent:

MAP OF THE NIGHT FIGHTING

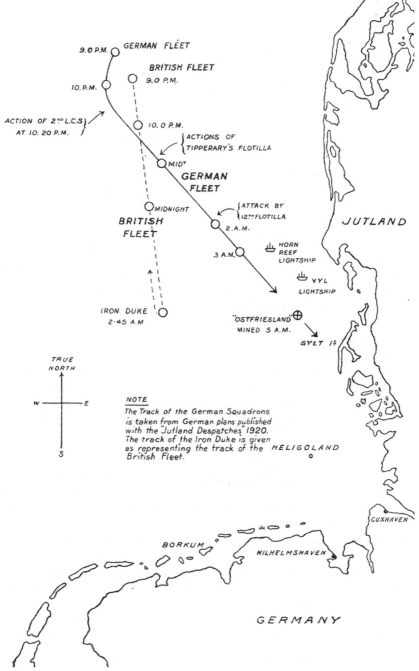

GERMAN FLEET

9.0 P.M.

BRITISH FLEET
9.0 P.M.

10. P.M.

ACTION OF 2ND L.C.S
AT 10.20 P.M.

10.0 P.M.

ACTIONS OF
TIPPERARY'S FLOTILLA

MIDT

GERMAN
FLEET

MIDNIGHT

BRITISH
FLEET

ATTACK BY
12TH FLOTILLA
2.A.M.

3 A.M.

HORN
REEF
LIGHTSHIP

VYL
LIGHTSHIP

JUTLAND

IRON DUKE
2·45 A.M.

"OSTFRIESLAND"
MINED 5 A.M.

SYLT IS

TRUE
NORTH

W ——— E

S

NOTE
The Track of the German Squadrons
is taken from German plans published
with the "Jutland Despatches" 1920.
The track of the Iron Duke is given
as representing the track of the
British Fleet.

HELIGOLAND
o

CUXHAVEN

BORKUM

WILHELMSHAVEN

GERMANY

> German Battle Fleet ordered home at 21.14, Battle cruisers in the
> rear. Course SSE three-quarters E. Speed 16 knots.

In retrospect, if plotted from the 21.00 position this meant Horn Reef
but this was not obvious to Jellicoe at the time. Between 23.15 and 01.25
the Operations Division received eight more deciphered signals but
only one, that giving *Lützow*'s course, position and speed was passed
on. Even one calling for a destroyer rendezvous at Horn Reefs was not
passed on.

The end result was that Jellicoe was unable to form a clear picture of
the likely position of the High Seas Fleet early on 1 June.[4]

German Dispositions

The night formation of the German battlefleet was completed by 22.30
with twenty-four capital ships is a single line ahead led by *Westfalen*
and followed by *Nassau, Rheinland, Posen, Oldenburg, Helgoland,
Thüringen, Ostfriesland, Friedrich der Grosse, Prinzregent Luitpold, Kaiserin,
Kaiser, Markgraf, Kronprinz, Grosser Kurfürst, König, Deutschland,
Pommern, Schlesien, Schleswig-Holstein, Hessen, Hannover, Von der Tann*
and *Derfflinger*. The brunt of the night-fighting en route for the Horn
Reef light ship would be borne by the dreadnought *Westfalen* and her
sisters *Nassau, Rheinland* and *Posen*. The cruisers of the 2nd and 4th
Scouting Groups were to the east of the battleships with *Regensburg*
astern of *Derfflinger*.

The exact courses taken by *Moltke* and *Seydlitz* are unknown but they
were steaming the west and east respectively of the course steered by
Scheer's battleline. The crippled *Lützow* was able to steer southwards at
seven knots for a couple of hours after which it became clear that she
could not be saved.[5]

Like his British counterpart, Scheer received only limited information
as to the whereabouts of the British battlefleet but thanks to British
stupidity he did receive the first two letters of that night's reply ('UA')
to any challenge. Apparently the source of this was *Princess Royal*'s reply
to a flash-lamp signal from *Lion* requesting the challenge and reply then
in force because her own data had been lost. Once again, it would
appear that British naval success was hampered by the flawed
signalling organisation in Beatty's flagship although, there is some
evidence that the Germans knew the British recognition signals used
that day much earlier.[6]

The night was punctuated by a series of short and violent clashes as
the retreating High Seas Fleet demonstrated its superiority in
recognition and night fighting as it passed through an area occupied by

numerous British destroyers without encountering any serious opposition. Despite being offered numerous opportunities for torpedo attacks, the performance of the British Flotillas was lamentable and, quite correctly, has been described as 'disastrously ineffective'.[7]

The first action occurred at about 21.50 when the 4th Flotilla, which was en route to take up its station five miles astern of the Grand Fleet, encountered the German 7th Flotilla which fired four torpedoes before disengaging to the south. The destroyer *Garland* sighted the Germans and made one of the few destroyer reports that night.[8]

Castor in Action

Castor (flagship of Commodore (F)) and the 11th Flotilla, had turned south to follow the Grand Fleet when, at about 22.13, the German light cruisers *Hamburg*, *Elbing* and *Rostock* encountered *Castor* and opened fire. The latter was hit by about ten shells but her side armour protected her from serious damage and, in return, she hit *Hamburg* with three 6-inch shells causing only minor damage.

For some unknown reason only *Castor* and the destroyers *Magic* and *Marne* of the 11th Flotilla fired torpedoes. Three of the British destroyers reported hearing a violent explosion in their engine rooms but the cause is unknown. Sadly, the remaining ships of the 11th Flotilla deigned to participate in the action probably fearing they might be engaging British ships. Thereafter the actions of the 11th Flotilla during the subsequent two hours are unclear although they proceeded south without following the enemy.[9]

The 2nd Light Cruiser Squadron Encounters the 4th Scouting Group

At about 10.30 the 2nd Light Cruiser Squadron, which was coming up astern of the Grand Fleet, sighted ships on a parallel course and, soon afterwards, the British ships were involved in a violent action with the four light cruisers of the 4th Scouting Group plus *Hamburg*, *Elbing* and *Rostock* at ranges reported to be between 800 and 2,500 yards. Fire was opened at 22.35 and the action lasted a mere three-and-a-half minutes, during which *Southampton* was engaged by *Stettin*, *München* and *Rostock* while *Stuttgart* fired at *Dublin*, and *Elbing* fired at both *Southampton* and *Dublin*.

Although *Southampton* had the worst of this fire-fight she released a torpedo from a submerged torpedo tube which hit the obsolete light cruiser *Frauenlob* in the port auxiliary engine. The damage proved fatal and *Frauenlob* quickly heeled to port but continued firing until she capsized and sank with the loss of all but nine of her complement. In return, *Southampton* was damaged by two 5.9-inch and eighteen 4.1-inch shells while *Dublin* was hit by five 5.9-inch and eight 4.1-inch shells. Of the German cruisers, *Stettin*, *München*, *Hamburg* and *Elbing* were hit by two, three, one and one 6-inch shells respectively suffering only minor damage.[10]

The 4th Flotilla Encounters the High Seas Fleet

During the ninety minutes from 23.30 onwards, the German battlefleet passed to eastward astern of the Grand Fleet and only the 4th Destroyer Flotilla opposed their passage although the old armoured cruiser *Black Prince* blundered into the German battlefleet with tragic consequences. Unfortunately, none of the British ships that sighted the German battleships at during this time felt the need to inform their Commander-in-Chief of the momentous events unfolding to the rear of his battleships.

The post-action report of the 4th Flotilla provides a vivid, if sometimes inaccurate and incomplete account of the night's events:

'Tipperary', 'Broke' and the Fourth Flotilla came in contact with enemy cruisers at 11.30 p.m., the enemy being on a south easterly course; a heavy fire was opened on the flotilla resulting in 'Tipperary' being set on fire forward; she sank at 2.0 a.m. 'Broke' was badly hit, and her steering gear and engine room telegraphs disabled, and before she could be got under control she rammed 'Sparrowhawk'. Both vessels were under a very heavy fire, and 'Sparrowhawk's' injuries were such that her crew were taken off and she was sunk on the following morning. 'Broke' reached the Tyne. One four funnelled enemy cruiser [*Rostock*?] was torpedoed by 'Spitfire' (next astern of 'Tipperary') and took a heavy list, and appeared to be in a sinking condition. 'Spitfire' also rammed a light cruiser [actually the battleship NASSAU] and carried off 29 feet of her skin plating. She had two cranes and three funnels, a red band being painted on each of the latter.

The remainder of the flotilla altered course to the eastward and then southeastward, and at midnight came in contact with an enemy battle squadron consisting of ships of the Deutschland class. One enemy ship was torpedoed, either by 'Ardent', 'Ambuscade' or 'Garland', and was observed to list over considerably. It is probable that she was sunk. 'Fortune' was sunk during this attack.

The flotilla was eventually driven off by gunfire and obliged to retire to the northward. Shortly after turning off 'Ardent' sighted four more large German ships crossing her bows and steering N.N.E. 'Ardent' attacked and fired a torpedo, but could not observe the result as a devastating fire was opened on her, and she sank with colours flying after a gallant fight, her commanding officer being picked up by 'Marksman' on the following morning after being five hours in the water.[11]

The German ships that bore the brunt of the fighting against the 4th Flotilla were the leading four battleships *Westfalen*, *Nassau*, *Rheinland* and *Posen* plus the cruisers *Rostock*, *Stuttgart*, *Elbing* and *Hamburg* and the destroyer *S32* which were to port of the capital ships.

The 4th Flotilla sighted the leading German battleships at 23.30 and soon afterwards *Tipperary* challenged *Westfalen* which immediately switched on her searchlights and opened fire with her secondary guns at a range of about 2,000 yards. *Westalen*'s first salvo destroyed *Tipperary*'s fore guns and bridge while subsequent hits cut steam lines and started major fires leaving the battered ship to drift astern. *Nassau*, *Rostock*, *Elbing*, *Hamburg* and *S32* fired at *Tipperary* and the destroyers astern of her while *Rheinland* engaged *Black Prince* with her 5.9-inch guns at 23.35 at 2,400 to 2,800 yards.[12] The battleships turned away and in the confusion the cruiser *Elbing* tried to pass through the German battle-line only to be rammed on her starboard side by the battleship *Posen*. Both of the cruiser's engine rooms were flooded, her steering engines and dynamos put out of action and *Elbing* drifted down to starboard of the German line.

Spitfire, which was astern of *Tipperary*, fired two torpedoes at a target about 1,000 yards away and also fired on the searchlights of those ships shooing at *Tipperary*. *Garland* and other destroyers also used their 4-inch guns against German searchlights. In the meantime, *Spitfire* circled round to the head of the German line only to find that the German battleships[13] had resumed their original course and that *Nassau* was a mere 450 yards distant and heading straight for her. *Spitfire* managed to turn to meet the battleship port bow to port bow. *Nassau* heeled five to ten degrees to starboard with the impact of the collision and consequently two 11-inch shells fired from her fore turret at maximum depression passed through the destroyer's bridge screens and the bottom of her second funnel. *Spitfire* was heavily damaged forward but her third bulkhead held and she was able to limp to the Tyne carrying twenty feet of *Nassau*'s upper side plating on her forecastle.[14]

A graphic account of *Nassau*'s experiences that night was published in a German newspaper soon after Jutland:

If any of us had believed that we should now have a quiet night journey, they were badly mistaken. Flashes suddenly darted out from the head of our line. British destroyers were trying to attack us under cover of darkness. 'Switch on searchlight! Fire!'

A few flashes and a roar as of thunder, and one of the enemy destroyers was in flames. She had been discovered too soon. But what is that, gliding along the horizon like a shadow? Black on black? Our foremost gun fires into the darkness.

Silently and once more in darkness, our ships steam on. But again and again, at longer intervals, nimble destroyers bobbed up to right and left of us. Burning ships, like flaming torches, drifted ahead and astern of us, and on either side. It was a grand sight and would have been a beautiful one, had not the occasion been so bitter earnest.

Here and there flames would shoot up on board the burning British destroyers, there would be one or two sharp explosions, which for the moment would transform the whole horizon into a sea of flame, and then again the heavy pall of darkness would descend over the spot. The greedy waves had closed, bubbling and hissing, over their fresh prey, and had hidden it in the insatiable wide grave of the ocean.

In the morning we found the hawse pipe of the destroyer [*Spitfire*] in the hole torn in our side plating by the force of the collision.[15]

Sparrowhawk, *Garland*, *Contest* and *Broke*, which were following *Spitfire* in that order, each fired a torpedo but of those following *Broke*, namely *Achates*, *Ambuscade*, *Ardent*, *Fortune*, *Porpoise* and *Unity*, only *Ambuscade* fired one while *Unity* lost touch with her compatriots.

However, the destroyer's 4-inch guns did some damage when S32 was hit by two shells one of which cut the main steam pipe in her after boiler room with the other hitting below her bridge. The torpedo-boat managed to get under way again about an hour later, albeit with seawater in her boilers and eventually reached the Danish coast near Lynvig. The battleships *Westfalen* and *Nassau* both suffered damage to their searchlights.[16]

Broke then led the remaining ships of the 4th Flotilla to the south only to find that the Germans had resumed their previous course with the light cruiser *Rostock* 1,100 yards on *Westfalen*'s port beam. *Broke* challenged *Rostock* which replied by switching on her searchlights and smothering the destroyer in a hail of shells. The cruiser then turned to starboard to give *Westfalen* and *Rheinland* a clear field of fire but was hit by a torpedo on the port side between her first and second boiler rooms which filled with water, temporarily stopping her main turbines, steering engine and dynamos. The crippled *Rostock* drifted astern passing through the line of the 2nd Battle Squadron causing considerable disorganisation amongst the pre-dreadnoughts.

Westfalen sighted *Broke* at 23.50 and immediately opened fire. However, the destroyer had already been badly hit forward by *Rostock* and her helm jammed and steering telegraphs put out of action. Consequently, she rammed *Sparrowhawk* just forward of the bridge cutting almost halfway through her. Worse was to follow because while the two destroyers were still locked together *Contest* rammed the unfortunate *Sparrowhawk* aft cutting five feet off her stern as well as jamming her rudder. *Broke*, which had been hit at least seven times, had three boilers out of action and had suffered heavy casualties, managed to reach the Tyne on 3 June despite of another encounter with the Germans. In comparison, *Sparrowhawk* had been reduced to little more than a wreck and was scuttled eventually.

Achates now led *Ambuscade*, *Ardent*, *Fortune*, *Porpoise* and *Garland* about three miles to the east and then turned southward and at about 00.10 *Westfalen* sighted *Fortune* approaching abaft of her port beam. The well-drilled battleship challenged the approaching ship, lit up *Fortune* with her searchlights and opened fire turning away at maximum speed. *Westfalen* fired for just twenty-eight seconds quickly reduced her opponent to a blazing wreck which became a target for other German ships. *Rheinland*, *Posen*, *Oldenburg* and *Helgoland* also fired on the approaching British destroyers including *Ardent* and *Porpoise*. The latter, which was partially screened by the doomed *Fortune*, was hit by at least two shells which damaged her steering gear as well as causing the air chamber of her spare torpedo to explode holing her main steam pipe. Despite having two boilers out of action *Porpoise* was able to return home.[17]

After this encounter the 4th Flotilla was reduced to just four destroyers, one of which, *Achates*, still had three torpedoes, turned to the east believing she was being pursued by cruisers. *Ardent* with two torpedoes remaining turned to the south while *Garland*, with just one torpedo sped off to the north-east.

The Sinking of the Armoured Cruiser *Black Prince*
During the afternoon the armoured cruiser *Black Prince* had signalled Rear Admiral Arbuthnot in *Defence* that she was experiencing electrical problems. At about 17.42 she was seen to turn about twelve points to port, fell far astern and was not seen again.[18] After dark, she was still astern of the Grand Fleet and quite by chance was in the path of the oncoming High Seas Fleet and tragedy now ensued at about 00.10 because *Black Prince* strayed too close to the German battleships being sighted on *Thüringen*'s port bow. The latter switched on her searchlights and opened fire on the hapless armoured cruiser firing a total of ten 12-

inch, twenty-seven 5.9-inch and twenty-four 3.5-inch shells at 750 to 1,100 yards. The first salvo destroyed *Black Prince's* after turret while the following salvoes raked the cruiser from stem to stern. After the battleship's penultimate salvo *Black Prince* was rocked by a massive explosion and sank with the loss of all 857 of her complement. The battleships *Nassau, Ostfriesland* and *Friedrich der Grosse* also fired on *Black Prince* whose sinking wreck forced *Nassau* to turn to starboard and, in so doing, nearly collided with *Kaiserin*.[19]

The End of the 4th Flotilla
At 00.25 *Ardent* again encountered the head of the German line firing a torpedo at *Westfalen* which opened fire with her 5.9-inch guns on the destroyer at 900 yards wrecking her forward as well as causing a boiler and steam-pipe explosion. The doomed *Ardent* was also heavily hit by *Posen, Rheinland* and *Oldenburg*.

By now the 4th Flotilla had been well and truly dispersed and defeated mainly by *Westfalen's* skilful use of her searchlights in combination with her secondary armament. Furthermore, the Germans considered that the British destroyers had not been trained in torpedo attack with far too many of them attacking separately and firing their torpedoes while still closing. Unfortunately, the black-painted British destroyers stood out against the night sky while their inadequate black-out measures made them even more visible to the German gunners who were well-trained in night-fighting techniques.[20]

At about the same time, the German destroyers *S53, S54* and *G88* came upon the burning wreck of the *Tipperary* with *S53* rescuing nine of her survivors from a raft before sighting the badly damaged *Broke*. *S53* and *G88* fired on the crippled ship hitting her twice amidships and each torpedo-boat fired a torpedo at ranges estimated to be 650 and 350 yards respectively. Both torpedoes missed but the Germans broke off the action believing *Broke* to be in a sinking condition. *Tipperary* did not sink until sometime after the departure of the German torpedo-boats and most of her survivors were picked up by the crippled *Sparrowhawk*.[21]

13th Flotilla in Action
The Thirteenth Flotilla took station astern of the battlefleet and during the night all except *Obdurate* and *Moresby* lost touch with the cruiser *Champion*. The Official Despatches record that:

> At 0.30 a.m. the destroyers which had become detached and were then under the orders of 'Narborough' came under heavy fire from an enemy ship, which was at first mistaken for one of our light-cruisers

or a ship of 'Warrior' class. The 'Turbulent' was rammed and sunk by gunfire.[22]

The situation was a rather more complex because at about 00.35 the German battleship *Westfalen* sighted the destroyers *Petard* and *Turbulent* at 1,100 yards on her port bow and made straight for the two ships. *Petard*, which had no torpedoes left, was hit by four shells fired by the battleship's starboard battery causing a serious oil fire but no vital damage. The destroyer sped away at twenty-eight knots although the German gunners believed that they had sunk her in eighty seconds.

Turbulent was not so lucky being savaged by *Westfalen*'s port battery. Both *Narborough* and *Pelican* sighted the leading German battleships mistaking them for British cruisers even though there was an action taking place about 1,000 yards distant and neither destroyer, which still had all four torpedoes available, intervened. Meanwhile the burning *Turbulent* was sighted at 2,400 to 2,600 yards to port by *Thüringen* which fired eighteen 5.9-inch and six 3.5-inch shells at the unfortunate destroyer which was sighted on fire at about 01.00 by the torpedo-boats *V71* and *V73*. After rescuing thirteen survivors *V71* fired two torpedoes at the burning hulk which sank soon afterwards.[23]

Pelican's navigator remembered that:

We saw one rather extraordinary sight. Of course you know the N.S. [North Sea] is very shallow. We came across a Hun Cruiser absolutely on end. His stern on the bottom and his bow sticking up about 3′ above the water, and a little further on a Destroyer in precisely the same position.

But the night was far and away the worst time of all, and an awful strain. It was pitch dark, and of course, absolutely no lights and the firing seems to be much worse at night as you could see the flashes absolutely lighting up the sky, and it seemed to make much more noise, and you would see ships on fire and blowing up; of course we shewed absolutely no lights.

One expected to be surprised any minute – and eventually we were. We suddenly found ourselves within 1,000 yards of two or three big Hun Cruisers. They switched on their searchlights and started firing like nothing on earth. They put their searchlights on us, but for some extraordinary reason they did not fire on us, as of course we were going full speed we'd lost them in a moment, but I must say that I, and I think everybody else, thought that was the end, but one does not feel afraid or panicky. I think I felt rather cooler then than at any other time. I asked lots of people afterwards what they felt like and they all said the same thing. It all happens in a few seconds, one hasn't got time to think, but never in all my life have I been so thankful to see daylight again – and I don't think I ever want to see another night like that – it's such an awful strain; one does not notice it at the time but it's the reaction afterwards. I never noticed I was tired till I got back to harbour, and then we all turned in and absolutely slept like dogs. We were 72 hours with little or no sleep. The skipper was perfectly wonderful, he never left the bridge for 24 hours and was either on the Bridge or in the Chart House the whole time we were out, and I've never seen anybody so cool and unruffled. He stood there sucking his pipe as if nothing out of the ordinary were happening.

One quite forgot all about time. I was relieved at 4 a.m. and on looking at my watch found I had been up there nearly 12 hours, and then discovered I was rather hungry. The Skipper and I had some cheese and biscuits, ham sandwiches and water on the Bridge and then I went down and brewed some cocoa and ship biscuits.[24]

The Sinking of *Lützow*, *Wiesbaden*, *Elbing* and *Rostock*

Lützow's crew was taken off by the torpedo-boats *G40*, *G38*, *V45* and *G37* from 00.55, and at 01.45 *G38* was ordered to finish off the water-logged battlecruiser which heeled over to starboard and sank in two minutes, about forty-five miles astern of *Westfalen*. The shattered wreck of the light cruiser *Wiesbaden* also sank at about this time or an hour later and there was only one survivor who was rescued by a Norwegian steamer late on 2 June.[25]

The majority crew of the light cruiser *Elbing*, which had been unable to restart her turbines following her collision with *Posen*, was taken off by the torpedo-boat *S53*. The small party left aboard the stricken ship rigged a sail in an attempt to get her nearer to the coast but when sighted at 02.00 by British destroyers to the south the order was given to scuttle *Elbing*. Her sinking was witnessed by *Sparrowhawk* which was lying disabled nearby.[26]

Rostock was taken in tow by *S54* and for a short time managed to make ten knots on a southerly course but eventually she had to be scuttled at about 04.30 in response to the approach of *Dublin* of the 2nd Light Cruiser Squadron. *Dublin* had been sighted at 03.55 and the torpedo-boats *S54*, *V71* and *V73* were ordered to take off *Rostock*'s crew. At 04.05 *S54* sailed eastwards and about ten minutes later sighted *Dublin*, which did not close, while *S54* continually made 'UA', the first two letters of the British challenge. *Dublin* replied and steamed away at high speed thereby allowing *S54* to make for Horn Reefs. *V71* and *V73* had remained near *Rostock* and fired three torpedoes (two from *V71*) to hasten the cruiser's sinking after which both sped off towards Horn Reefs.[27]

The 12th Flotilla Joins the Fray

The 12th Flotilla formed astern of the First Battle Squadron, which was on the port flank and somewhat astern of station because *Marlborough*'s speed had been reduced by damage. Jellicoe's despatches record that:

> At 11.30 p.m. the flotilla was obliged to alter course to clear Another flotilla—probably the Fourth Flotilla—which was crossing on a southeasterly course, and this alteration caused the Twelfth Flotilla to be about five miles to the eastward and ten miles to the northward of the First Battle Squadron by midnight. At 1.45 a.m. an enemy battle squadron was sighted on the starboard bow, steering S.E., consisting of six ships, the first four of which were thought to be of the Kaiser class (it is interesting to note that this points to there being only six ships of the enemy's Third Battle Squadron left, thus confirming the evidence already given that two were sunk during the day action).[28]
>
> The Captain (D), Twelfth Flotilla, altered to a parallel course and increased to 25 knots, leading round in order to attack on a northwesterly course. The attack was carried out most successfully, torpedoes being fired at 2 a.m., at a range of about 3,000 yards, at the second and third ships of the fine, the latter vessel being particularly conspicuous by a torpedo boat being stationed close under the quarter. Torpedoes took effect on the third ship, which blew up, the magazine having apparently exploded. Enemy cruisers astern of the battle line attacked the flotilla and obliged the Captain (D) to alter course to north. The cruisers were shaken off and the flotilla altered round to south to resume its course after the battlefleet.[29]

The 12th Flotilla's attack on the German 2nd and 3rd battle squadrons was the last major action of the battle with the destroyers being momentarily sighted at about 01.47 by *König* which opened fire. However, the destroyers disappeared into the mist after a few minutes when *Grosser Kurfürst* reported sighting six four-funnelled destroyers at 02.04 attacking at high speed in a single line ahead and opened fire hitting *Nessus* at about 2,200 yards.[30]

Meanwhile, *Faulknor* had fired her first torpedo at 02.02 followed by a second two minutes later, *Obedient* fired one at 02.04 and another five minutes later and *Marvel* fired two just after 02.04 and her remaining pair at about 02.08. *Onslaught* directed all of her torpedoes at the 2nd

Battle Squadron, which was composed of the elderly and vulnerable pre-dreadnoughts, firing two at 02.08/09 and two more three minutes later.

Her efforts were rewarded when the first of her four actually hit *Pommern* at 02.10 causing a series of explosions that occurred in rapid succession. *Pommern* broke in two with the loss of her entire complement of 844. In return, *Schleswig-Holstein* opened fire on *Onslaught* hitting the latter on the bridge with a 6.7-inch high-explosive shell which started a fire and mortally wounded her commanding officer. Subsequently, *Maenad* and *Narwhal* fired three and two torpedoes respectively but without success. The 12th Flotilla's attack was altogether more skilful than that of the 4th Flotilla but, even so, only one hit was made from the seventeen missiles fired.[31] Subsequent research showed that firing a full spread of four torpedoes would have had much greater chance of hitting a target than firing them singly or in pairs.

Jellicoe records that following signal was sent to the Commander-in-Chief by the Captain (D) of the 12th Flotilla:

> 'Enemy battlefleet steering S.E., approximate bearing S.W. My position ten miles astern of First Battle Squadron. 0152.'
>
> This signal was unfortunately not received in the battlefleet owing to telefunken interference. Whilst the main torpedo attack by the Twelfth Flotilla was being made, 'Maenad', having anticipated that the attack on the enemy would be made with tubes bearing to starboard, was not ready when the turn was made and port tubes brought to bear. He, therefore, held on the southeasterly course and turned later to fire one torpedo from the port side when the tube was trained. He then trained both tubes to starboard, turned and went ahead, closing in again to between 4,000 and 5,000 yards from the enemy and firing two more torpedoes. The second torpedo struck the fourth ship in the line. There was a heavy explosion, the flames topping the mast heads, and the ship was not seen again, though those ahead and astern were distinctly visible. The time of this attack was twenty-five minutes later than the main attack. It seems therefore certain that two battleships were hit and there is considerable probability that both were sunk by the Twelfth Flotilla. It is to be noted that six ships were observed by the Captain (D) at the commencement of the attack—only five were seen by 'Maenad' when 'Maenad's' attack was made, and only four were visible after 'Maenad's' attack. The report from 'Maenad' was sent to me from Rosyth, before her commanding officer had seen the Captain (D), Twelfth Flotilla, or knew that he had reported having blown up one of the battleships.'

Jellicoe summarised the actions of his destroyers thus:

> Firing was heard astern, searchlights were seen in use, and a fair number of star shells were fired by the enemy, which gave out a brilliant illumination, and it was evident that our destroyer flotillas and light-cruiser squadrons were in action.
>
> From reports received subsequently it is fairly certain that the German battlefleet and battle-cruisers crossed astern of the British battlefleet and made for the Horn Reef channel. In crossing the rear of the British battle line, the enemy fleet came in contact with the British flotillas, which seized the opportunity to deliver a series of brilliant and gallant attacks.[32]

By 03.00 *Westfalen* leading the German line was approximately thirteen miles 240 degrees from the Horn Reef lightship.[33]

The High Seas Fleet had successfully passed through an area filled with British destroyers and survived the confusion caused by repeated short-range encounters while at the same losing one pre-dreadnought battleship, three light cruisers and one torpedo-boat. In return they had sunk one armoured cruiser and five destroyers.

The passage of the High Seas Fleet through the destroyer screen astern of the Grand Fleet was aided by the destroyer's inability to distinguish between friend and foe coupled a lack of divisional training and gun/torpedo practice. Worse still, British destroyers were painted black which it was realized during the night actions at Jutland is the most visible colour at night. After Jutland, the Commanding officer of the destroyer *Moresby* recommended that: 'Destroyers be painted light grey; black is very visible at night'. Subsequently, soon after Jutland orders were given that destroyers were to be painted grey.[34]

Grand Fleet 02.00 – 03.00, 1 June 1916
Jellicoe was hopeful of renewing the battle early on 1 June and therefore set about forming a line of battle:

> At 2.0 a.m. a report was received from the Vice-Admiral Commanding, First Battle Squadron, that 'Marlborough' had been obliged to ease to twelve knots on account of stress on bulkheads at the higher speeds. The remainder of the divisions continued at seventeen knots. The Commander-in-Chief ordered 'Marlborough' to proceed to the Tyne or Rosyth by 'M' channel. The Vice-Admiral Commanding, First Battle Squadron, called the 'Fearless' alongside 'Marlborough', shifted to 'Revenge' in the 'Fearless', and detached

'Fearless' to escort the 'Marlborough'. The weather was very misty at daylight, visibility being only three to four miles, and I deemed it advisable to disregard the danger from submarines due to a long line of ships and to form line of battle at once in case of meeting the enemy battlefleet before I had been able to get in touch with my cruisers and destroyers. The battlefleet accordingly altered course to north at 2.47 a.m. and formed line of battle. The Fourth Light Cruiser Squadron was in company, but the sixth division of the battlefleet comprising the 'Revenge', 'Hercules' and 'Agincourt' had lost touch owing to 'Marlborough's' reduction in speed and was broad on the eastern flank of the fleet during the day.[35]

As dawn broke, Jellicoe quickly learned that his opponent had fled the scene and had almost reached the safety of his bases. It is reported that the visibility at Horn Reef at dawn on 1 June was so poor (less than four miles) that a successful battle would have been impossible but, if only the Admiralty and all the ships that had sighted the enemy during the night had told Jellicoe, a second 'Glorious First of June' might still have been possible.

After 03.00 on 1 June there were two more brief contacts between the fleets, one involving the sinking of *Rostock* (see above) and the other the four torpedo-boats carrying *Lützow*'s crew namely, *G40*, *G38*, *V45* and *G37*.

They were sighted by the light cruiser *Champion* and the destroyers *Obdurate*, *Moresby*, *Marksman* and *Maenad* at about 03.25 and a brief action developed on nearly opposite courses at a range of 2,400 – 7,400 yards. *G40* was hit by a 6-inch shell from *Champion* which damaged her after turbine but was able to maintain twenty-six knots for some ten minutes before coming to a stop and being taken in tow by *G37*. The Official Despatches record that:

> At 3.25 a.m. four enemy destroyers were sighted, steering to the southeastward, and at 3.30 a.m. were engaged at a range of approximately 3,000 yards. The enemy passed and disappeared in the mist, after firing torpedoes at 'Champion'. At 4.30 a.m. 'Obdurate' picked up two survivors from the 'Ardent'. At 5.0 a.m. two rafts were sighted and 'Moresby rescued seven men and 'Maenad' eleven men, survivors from the 'Fortune'. 'Marksman' was detached to the assistance of the 'Sparrowhawk' at 6.0 a.m. and the flotilla proceeded to Rosyth.[36]

At 03.00 the Zeppelin *L11* detected units of the Grand Fleet taking station astern of them. Subsequently, several British units engaged *L11* shaking her with near misses before she lost sight of all British ships at 04.20. Jellicoe reported that:

> At 3.44 a.m. course was altered to west, heavy firing being heard in that direction. At 4.0 a.m. a Zeppelin was bearing S.E. She approached the fleet, but was driven off by gunfire.
>
> At 4.10 a.m. the battlefleet formed divisions in line ahead disposed abeam to starboard. The Vice-Admiral Commanding, Battle Cruiser Fleet, in accordance with orders, closed the Commander-in-Chief at 5.40 a.m. and was directed to sweep to the northward and eastward, whilst the Commander-in-Chief swept with the battlefleet first to the southward and eastward and then northward. At 3.0 a.m. the 'Sparrowhawk' was lying disabled in approximately lat. 55° 54' N., Long. 5° 59' E., when a German light-cruiser with three high straight funnels equally spaced, two masts and a straight stem (probably 'Kolberg')[37] was sighted two miles East steaming slowly to the northward; after being in sight about five minutes she gradually heeled over and sank slowly bows first.[38]

Battleship *Ostfriesland* Mined

Neither British nor German submarines played any significant role in the battle. However, a minefield laid by the destroyer *Abdiel* on 4 May 1916 was more successful. In his report Jellicoe wrote:

> The estimated course of the enemy fleet was S.E./E., and the estimated time of the last battle squadron passing the Horn Reef light-vessel abeam, eighteen miles distant, was 3.45 a.m. Submarine 'E55', on the bottom to the west of the Horn Reef light-vessel, heard eleven explosions between 2.15 and 5.30 a.m. on the 1st June. The estimated time of the last of the enemy's heavy ships passing over 'Abdiel's' minefield is 5 a.m.[39]

The exact nature of the explosions heard by *E55* is unknown but they were not caused by German ships striking one of *Abdiel's* mines. It is much more likely, they were premature explosions from the minefield laid by the destroyer earlier that morning. However, at 05.20 the battleship *Ostfriesland* detonated a mine, from the field laid by *Abdiel* on 4 May 1916, on her starboard side. The explosion caused little damage but reduced her maximum speed to fifteen knots.

Unfortunately, at 11.20 when about five miles from Heligoland, *Ostfriesland* turned sharply to avoid an imaginary submarine thereby increasing the rent in her already damaged torpedo bulkhead. More water entered the battleship which listed four-and-three-quarters degrees to starboard and had to reduce to slow speed.[40]

The Crippled *Seydlitz* Limps Home

Seydlitz took station astern of the 2nd Squadron at 06.05 on 1 June but could not maintain the fleet speed of fifteen knots having to reduce first to ten knots and then seven knots. By this time the battlecruiser was so low in the forward that large amounts of water entered compartments above the armoured deck between the forward citadel and the forward boiler room bulkheads via the battery deck which had been seriously damaged on the starboard side by the first shell which had struck the ship.

Just after 09.00 *Seydlitz* grounded off Hörnum at the southern end of the Sylt but thanks to counter-flooding the ship came off before high water. Thereafter the battlecruiser made slow but steady progress stern first until at 03.25 on 3 June she anchored in the Vareler Deep and divers were then able to examine the underwater damage and undertake some patching. The ship's own drainage system was now able to pump out some of the flooded compartments, damaged bulkheads were shored up and as much weight as possible was removed. This included both 11-in guns, the roof and some of the armour plate from 'A' turret. Thereafter, damage repair and pumping made steady progress and at 14.30 on 6 June *Seydlitz* entered, stern first, the South Lock of the Third Entrance after which rapid progress was made with patching. Eventually at 05.40 on 13 June *Seydlitz* was towed from the lock and at 08.15 was in the large Wilhelmshaven floating dock.

During her struggle to get home, *Seydlitz* touched bottom several times but because she was re-floated and returned to service she is not usually listed as sunk. However, she was lucky that the bottom was so close because nothing could disguise the fact that she could not have crossed the North Sea.

The Grand Fleet Returns to its Bases

The Grand Fleet's passage to its bases must have been something of an anti-climax, leaving those manning the ships feeling that they had been robbed of success by a combination of bad luck and the weather. Jellicoe's despatches outline the Fleet's return:

> The Commodore (T) with the Harwich force had been ordered at 3.20 a.m. by the Admiralty to proceed to join the Commander-in-Chief to replace vessels requiring fuel. The Commander-in-Chief gave directions for four torpedo boat destroyers to be detached to screen 'Marlborough', whose 4.30 a.m. position was Lat. 55° 30' N., Long. 6°

3' E., course S.W., speed fourteen knots. At 9.0 a.m. the Commander-in-Chief ordered the Vice-Admiral Commanding, Battle Cruiser Fleet, who was to eastward of the battlefleet, on a northerly course, to sweep as far as Lat. 57° 30' N., Long. 5° 45' E. At 9.36 a.m. the Admiralty directed the Third Battle Squadron and Third Cruiser Squadron to return to harbour and revert to usual notice. At 10.31 a.m. the Fifth Battle Squadron joined up with the remainder of the battlefleet.

At 1.15 p.m. the battlefleet, having swept out the area south of the scene of the action, proceeded N.W. for Scapa, the battlecruiser fleet and 'Valiant' proceeding to Rosyth. At 4.0 p.m. the Commander-in-Chief informed the Commodore (T) that the Admiralty had been told that there was nothing left for the Harwich force to do. He was ordered to strengthen 'Marlborough's' screen by two destroyers and return to Harwich.

At 10.0 p.m. the Commander-in-Chief directed the Vice-Admiral Commanding, Orkneys and Shetlands, to send out at daylight any destroyers available to meet and screen the fleet, approaching on a bearing 82° from Pentland Skerries.

The battlefleet, Fourth Light Cruiser Squadron, Fourth, Eleventh and Twelfth Flotillas arrived at Scapa between 10.30 a.m. and noon on 2nd June. On arrival 'Titania' was directed to send a submarine as soon as the weather permitted to sink by torpedo, gunfire, or explosive charge, the portion of wreck of 'Invincible' in approximately Lat. 57° 06' N., Long, 6° 02' E., if still showing above water. 'G. 10' sailed at 3.0 a.m. 3rd June, and returned to Blyth at 9.20 p.m., 6th, reporting that after searching for forty-eight hours nothing could be found.

At 9.45. p.m. [2 June] the Commander-in-Chief reported to the Admiralty that the battlefleet was again ready for action and at four hours' notice.[41]

Although the Germans were about to claim a stunning victory, was Admiral Scheer in a position to make a similar claim on behalf of the High Seas Fleet?

Ready For Action?

At 9.45 Admiral Jellicoe reported to the Admiralty that the Grand Fleet was at its base, refuelled with steam at four hours' notice and ready for sea.

As darkness fell on 31 June 1916, Jellicoe knew that the Grand Fleet was between the German Fleet and its bases and he must have been reasonably confident of being able to renew the battle at first light the next morning.

Instead, British ships searching for Scheer's battlefleet found only empty sea, the Germans having broken through the rear of the Grand Fleet and escaped towards the Heligoland Bight. Consequently, Jellicoe had no choice but to order his fleet's return to its bases.

Return of the Damaged British Ships

During the return passage Jellicoe must have been gradually made aware of the losses sustained by his fleet including damaged ships that might have difficulty making port. Jellicoe's despatches provide an excellent narrative of return of his disabled ships and in particular that of the battleship *Marlborough* which had been damaged by a torpedo:

> At 2 a.m. on 1st June, 'Marlborough' reported that her speed was reduced to 12 knots and at 2.30 a.m. she was directed by Commander-in-Chief to proceed to Tyne or Rosyth by 'M' channel. At 3.0 a.m. Vice-Admiral Commanding, First Battle Squadron was directed to send his division to join Commander-in-Chief, keeping one ship as escort if necessary. He reported that he had transferred to 'Revenge' and that 'Marlborough' was proceeding with 'Fearless' in company.
>
> At 7.0 a.m. Commander-in-Chief ordered Commodore (T) to detach four destroyers to screen 'Marlborough' her 4.30 a.m. position being in latitude 55° 30′ N., longitude 6° 3′ E. Course S.W., speed 14 knots.

At 6.50 p.m. 1st June 'Marlborough' reported—All compartments between 78 and 111 stations starboard from outer bottom to middle or main deck probably flooded. All double bottom compartments between these stations on starboard side vertical keel damaged and probably double bottom compartments vertical to 2nd longitudinal on port side also damaged. Boilers, auxiliary machinery in 'A' boiler room not damaged, except air blower and Diesel engine oil pump. 'A' boiler room partially flooded but water is being kept under. At 9.30 p.m. Admiralty directed 'Marlborough' to proceed to Rosyth for temporary repairs. At midnight 1st-2nd June 'Marlborough' reported her position to be in latitude 54° 40′ N., longitude 0° 53′ E., and that she was making for Flamborough Head. Owing to bad weather the water was gaining.

The Commander-in-Chief requested the Senior Naval Officer Humber to send powerful tugs to her and also directed 'Canterbury, who was proceeding to Harwich, to proceed to her assistance. 'Canterbury' sighted 'Marlborough' E of the Humber at 7.30 a.m. 2nd June, when she was informed that her assistance was not required. At 4.0 a.m. 'Marlborough' reported her position to be in latitude 54° 10′ N., longitude 0° 2′ E., course South, speed 11 knots; water was being kept under-control. 'Marlborough' arrived in the Humber at 8.0 a.m. 2nd, screened by 'Fearless' and 8 destroyers from Harwich, having been unsuccessfully attacked by enemy submarines whilst en route.[1]

The battleship *Warspite*, which had received considerable punishment while performing a pirouette in front of the massed guns of the High Seas Fleet's capital ships, had been ordered back to Rosyth soon after her rudder control had been restored. As the Official Despatches show, her return journey was eventful:

At 9.0 p.m. 31st May, 'Warspite' reported that the damage reduced her speed to 16 knots. The Commander-in-Chief ordered her to proceed to Rosyth. At 6.10 a.m. 1st June, 'Warspite' reported to the Commander-in-Chief that she had many holes from shellfire, that the ship was tight and on an even keel. Several compartments were full, but the bulkheads were shored. The ship was being steered from the engine room.

At 9.0 a.m. 1st June the Commander-in-Chief asked the Commander-in-Chief, Rosyth, to send local destroyers to screen 'Warspite'. She arrived at Rosyth at 3.0 p.m. on 1st June having been unsuccessfully attacked by enemy submarines en route.[2]

Unfortunately, by the evening of 1 June sensational rumours of a British defeat were spreading all over the country. These rumours had originated from Rosyth dockyard where preparations had been underway since 1 June to receive Beatty's damaged ships and, as the badly damaged *Warspite* limped into the dockyard, railwaymen on the bridge above hurled coal down at the battered ship, believing that she had run away.

Worse was to follow because when Beatty's damaged flagship *Lion* slowly entered her berth, Rosyth dockyard workers jeered and booed her tired and battle-stained crew in the belief that the Royal Navy, the pride of the nation, had been defeated. Exactly what the sailors thought about being judged *in absentia* by those who they fighting so hard to protect is probably unprintable but, in a letter to Eugénie Godfrey-Faussett written on 19 June, Beatty wrote, 'My poor sailors were terribly upset at first at the injustice.'[3]

Eventually the story of how heroic servicemen returning from battle had been mistreated began to come to attention of the public at large thereby generating letters of the type sent to the editor of the *Portsmouth Evening News* on 22 July:

THE HEROES OF THE JUTLAND FIGHT.
Dear Sir, —I have with the utmost astonishment read the statement that some of our wounded heroes of Jutland Battle were abused and jeered at when returning from the scene of battle to one our British ports. Even if had been a defeat instead of glorious victory, where are our vaunted traditions sportsmen? Is the losing team in a well - contested football cricket match hissed when the result is declared? Likewise is the loser in hard fought boxing contest hissed as he leaves the ring with the scars of battle still him? Shame on those who are responsible for this disgraceful proceeding. I consider that the name of the town or towns in which this took place should made public, that all decent feeling public may shun and avoid them.
Yours truly, D. SAVINS (Naval Pensioner). Sultan Road, Portsmouth.

The flotilla leader *Broke*, which had been crippled during the night action, was the subject of a search to try and find her on 1 June:

At 11.24 a.m. 1st June the Commodore (F) reported that 'Broke's' midnight position was in latitude 57° 49' N., longitude 3° 50' E., course N.W. speed 7 knots; that she was damaged forward and would like escort if available. At 1.30 a.m. 2nd June, 'Active' was dropped astern of fleet and proceeded to search for 'Broke'. She was informed that two destroyers would be sent as soon as 'Broke' had been located.

At 5.0 a.m. the Commander-in-Chief directed the Commodore Commanding, Fourth Light-Cruiser Squadron, to detail one Light cruiser to assist 'Active' in search for 'Broke'. 'Constance' proceeded at 5.30 a.m. 2nd June. At 6.30 a.m. 2nd June the Rear-Admiral Commanding, Second Cruiser Squadron was ordered to abandon the search for 'Warrior' and sweep to find 'Broke'. At 9.15 p.m. 2nd June orders were given for the search to be continued next day to the South and S.W. of the area already searched.

At 1.0 a.m. 3rd June 'Constance' and 'Active' were ordered to return to Scapa. At 3.0 a.m. 3rd June 'Broke' reported her position to be in latitude 56° 21' N., longitude 0° 12' E., course West, speed knots, and the Vice-Admiral Commanding, Battle Cruiser Fleet, was ordered to send four destroyers to meet and screen her. They sailed at 8.0 a.m. 3rd June.

The Second Cruiser Squadron was ordered to return to the base. This squadron arrived at 6.30 p.m. the same day. The 'Broke' arrived in Tyne at 6.0 p.m. 3rd June.[4]

The armoured cruiser *Warrior* had only survived the fate of her flagship *Defence* because the German gunners were distracted by *Warspite* after the latter's steering gear had jammed forcing her to undertake an involuntary circling manoeuvre.

The crippled cruiser sailed past the Grand Fleet battle squadrons and out of harm's way but it was soon clear that she would need assistance if she was to return home:

At 8.0 p.m. 31st May 'Engadine' took 'Warrior' in tow in about latitude 57° 10" N., longitude 5° 45' E., steering W.N.W. 'Warrior' was abandoned at 7.45 a.m. 1st June in approximately latitude 57° 34' N., longitude 2° 56' E., 'Engadine' proceeding alongside to take the crew off. The latter arrived at Rosyth at 1.35 a.m. 2nd June with 35 officers, 681 men, 25 cot cases and two walking cases from 'Warrior'.

At 8.45 a.m. 1st June the Commander-in-Chief, not having received information that 'Warrior' was abandoned, informed the Commander-in-Chief, Rosyth, that she was in tow of 'Engadine', completely disabled, in latitude 57° 18' N., longitude 3° 54' E., course W.N.W., speed 7 knots, and requested that tugs should be sent.

At 9.55 a.m. 1st June, the Rear-Admiral, Invergordon, informed the Commander-in-Chief that yacht 'Albion., in charge of two tugs, had been ordered to leave Peterhead and proceed to the assistance of

'Warrior'. 'Engadine's' 11.0 p.m. position on 31st May was in latitude 57° 10′ N., longitude 2° 17′ E. At 1.45 p.m. 2nd June, the Rear-Admiral, 'Cyclops', reported that yacht 'Albion III' with three tugs had been unable to find 'Warrior'. At 4.30 p.m. the Commander-in-Chief informed the Rear-Admiral Commanding, Second Cruiser Squadron, of the state of affairs about 'Warrior' and directed him to search for her and if impossible to salve, to sink her. If the tugs sent out from Peterhead were not required for 'Warrior' they were to be sent to tow 'Acasta', who was in tow of 'Nonsuch', a little to the Eastward of 'Warrior's' position.

At 2.30 p.m. the Commander-in-Chief directed Unit 42 from Peterhead to be diverted to search for 'Warrior'. At 3.0 p.m., the Rear-Admiral Commanding, Second Cruiser Squadron, reported no sign of 'Warrior' in area 17 miles south of and 40 miles north, west and east of her last position given. Good visibility. Wind, N.W., 6 to 7. Somewhat heavy sea. Second Cruiser Squadron's position at 3.0 a.m., 57° N., 2° 45′ E.

At 8.0 p.m., 2nd June, Third Light-Cruiser Squadron and three destroyers sailed from Rosyth to join in the search for 'Warrior'. At 11.30 p.m. Commander-in-Chief informed the Vice-Admiral Commanding, Battle Cruiser Fleet, that the Second Cruiser Squadron had searched area North of 57° 10′ N. and west of longitude 4° 10′ E., and was now searching N.W. of this area for 'Broke'. He suggested that light-cruisers from Rosyth should search area south of this latitude and east of longitude 3° 50′ E. At 9.30 a.m., 4th June, Rear-Admiral Commanding, Third Light-Cruiser Squadron, reported his position in 56° 15′ N., longitude 3° 0′ E., and proposed abandoning search at 8.0 p.m. and return to harbour. This was approved and squadron arrived at Rosyth 6.0 a.m., 5th June. Captain of Warrior' reported by telegraph that cypher and signal books in use were thrown overboard when ship was abandoned.

When abandoned, the stern of the ship was two or three feet above water. Stem about normal draught, every sea washing over upper deck. At least two feet of water on main deck. Decks and bulkheads terribly shattered by shell fire and no longer watertight; ship settling down and stability gone. No chance of ship remaining afloat in increasingly heavy weather prevailing.[5]

Captain Molteno described the final hours of his crippled cruiser thus:

After passing the rear of our battle fleet I shaped a course for Kinnaird Head, and almost at once sighted the 'Engadine'. I directed her to stand by me, as I was badly disabled. Both engine rooms were filled with water to within 10 ft. of the Main Deck, but the engines continued to revolve, giving the ship a speed of quite 10 to 12 knots.

Having ascertained that there was no possibility of the engines working for more than another hour, at 8 p.m. I directed H.M.S. 'Engadine' to take 'Warrior' in tow, which she did, and proceeded towing at a speed of 8.2 knots for the first hour, and I had good hopes of saving the ship. At 7 a.m. next day, speed was about 6 knots, as 'Warrior' by then had sunk so low aft. Officers and men worked most heroically in shoring bulkheads, stopping shell holes and leaks, and manning the hand pumps, but owing to the rising sea and the list to Port which was increasing, it was impossible to keep the water from rising on Main Deck. At about 7.45 a.m. I decided that unless the ship were abandoned immediately most of the ship's company and all the wounded would perish; I therefore decided to abandon her. However, as I did not know but that a vessel might be close by to tow her, and that the weather might possibly get quite smooth, I closed all the W.T. openings before quitting her. As it turned out the ship was quitted only at the very last moment, after which it would have been impossible for the 'Engadine' to get alongside and take off the ship's company, I consider that two to three hours was the maximum time she could have remained afloat, under the weather conditions that prevailed. Every sea was washing over the upper deck, and her stern was within 3 ft. of the water, and a list of about 6° to Port (Windward).[6]

Warrior's survivors would soon be put to good use because shortly after the battle, the C-in-C Ships and Vessels at Devonport received the following letter from the Admiralty about their future service:

With reference to Admiralty Telegram No. 493 of 10th June last, I am commanded by My Lords Commissioners of the Admiralty to acquaint you that the ship's company of H.M.S. WARRIOR should be kept together and utilised to commission H.M.S. GLORIOUS so far as they are suitable: any ratings not required for H.M.S. GLORIOUS may now be appropriated as necessary.[7]

Jellicoe's despatches provide a succinct record of the fate of the remaining damaged ships:

'CHESTER'
Ordered by Rear-Admiral Commanding, Second Cruiser Squadron, at daylight, 1st to proceed to Humber. She arrived at the Humber at 5.0

p.m., 1st, and reported her damage. Three guns out of action, much damage to upper works and holed four places above water line. Engines, boilers and all machinery almost intact. No serious damage below waterline.

'SPARROWHAWK'

At 7.30 a.m., 'Marksman' reported to the Commander-in- Chief that he was endeavouring to tow 'Sparrowhawk' stern first. At 8.5 a.m. 'Marksman' reported that hawser had parted, and on receipt of approval from Vice-Admiral Commanding, First Battle Squadron, 'Sparrowhawk ' was sunk in 56° 8' N. 6° 10' E.

'NONSUCH' and 'ACASTA'

'Acasta' was with 'Shark', 'Ophelia' and 'Christopher' screening Third Battle-Cruiser Squadron. At 9.45 a.m., 'Nonsuch' reported to Commodore (F) that he was escorting 'Acasta' to Aberdeen at 10 knots, the latter being badly damaged. 'Nonsuch' reported later that she had taken 'Acasta' in tow about noon in position 57° 16' N., longitude 4° 8' E., course W, ½ N., speed about 6 knots. 'Nonsuch' reported her 7.0 p.m. position on 1st, in 57° 8' N., 2° 33' E., speed about 7 knots, all well.

At 8.40 p.m., 1st, Rear-Admiral, Peterhead, was requested to send a trawler unit to screen 'Nonsuch' and 'Acasta' to Aberdeen, and at 6.30 a.m. 2nd, he was requested to direct 'Albion' and tugs which were searching for 'Warrior', to proceed to assist 'Acasta' in tow of 'Nonsuch'. 'Nonsuch's' position at 5.0. p.m., 20 miles East of Aberdeen, speed 8 knots, all well. 'Nonsuch' arrived Aberdeen at 8.0 p.m., and 'Acasta' at 9.15 p.m.

'ONSLOW' and 'DEFENDER'

'Defender' took 'Onslow' in tow between 7.15 and 8.0 p.m., 31st May, 'Defender's' maximum speed being 10 knots. They arrived at Aberdeen at 1.0 p.m. on 2nd June.

Flotillas.

At 7.33 a.m., 1st June, Commodore (F) reported that all destroyers of Eleventh and Twelfth Flotillas and 'Sparrowhawk' were in company. The wreckage of 'Ardent' was passed at 8.20 a.m., 1st, in latitude 55° 58' N., 6° 8' E. At 9.45 a.m. Commodore (F) reported having passed some bodies and lifebuoy marked 'Turbulent' at 8.0 a.m., 1st.

At 8.58 a.m., lat. 56° 3' N., long. 6° 4' E., 'Orion' reported she had passed considerable wreckage and floating bodies, apparently foreigners. 'Dublin', which was with the Battlefleet until 10.0 a.m., reported that at 6.0 a.m., in Lat. 55° 51' N., long. 5° 53' E., she picked up a stoker from 'Tipperary'.[8]

The man rescued was Stoker First Class George Thomas Augustus Parkyn. He later described his experiences:

> I was at work in No. 3 Stokehold, and at about 11.0 p.m. (31st May 1916) I learnt that we were in action with German Torpedo Craft. We had been in action about ¼ of an hour when the Bridge caught fire from shells.
>
> The vessel kept afloat for some time after this, going down about break of day, 1 hours or 2 hours after being hit. When abandoning the ship the Motor Boat was tried, the only boat left, but sank as soon as it touched water. Some men had previously got away on a small raft, and about 17 men got on to the larger raft. I saw neither of these after. 'Tipperary' plunged suddenly, going down by the Bows. I saw no other survivors while in the water.[9]

Repairing Beatty's Battlecruiser Fleet

Warspite, which had arrived at Rosyth on the afternoon of Thursday 1 June, immediately replaced her sister *Queen Elizabeth* in the dockyard so that her damage could be evaluated as soon as possible. Despite having over 150 holes in her and with her riddled funnels looking like colanders, *Warspite*'s effective armour protection had withstood the test of war and her casualties of just four killed and thirty wounded out of a complement of about 950 officers and men were very light. Many of the much smaller and unprotected destroyers suffered far worse casualties from just a few hits.

On 4 June there was a conference was held at Rosyth to discuss repairing the damaged ships. The meeting involved the Commanding Officer of *Lion*, Admiralty Department representatives, Vickers-Armstrong, the Commodore Superintendent of Rosyth and several Dockyard Officers.

Notes taken at the meeting show that it was agreed that:

> LION Repair at Rosyth (except damaged armour plate), at short notice ... 3 weeks
> Then to Tyne to repair damaged armour plate and remove turret ... 2 weeks
> Then back to Rosyth – returning to Tyne for turret to be replaced when ready.

TIGER Repair at Rosyth (damaged turret roof plate being removed and replaced by old one) 3 weeks.

PRINCESS ROYAL Patch at Rosyth to enable her to go to other port for repair. Undesirable take her to Rosyth with present resources. 5 days after receipt of order.

WARSPITE Repair at Rosyth. Time under consideration probably 3 – 4 weeks

SOUTHAMPTON repair at Rosyth 14 days.[10]

Spitfire and a Piece of *Nassau*

The K-class destroyer *Spitfire*, which had survived an 11-inch shell hit and an oblique collision with the German battleship *Nassau*, was repaired on the Tyne where it was found that she was carrying a piece of side plating from her much larger assailant.

While in the hands of the dockyard the German plating was removed leaving the Captain Superintendent wondering how it should be disposed of. Consequently, on 5 August he wrote to the Secretary of the Admiralty:

> Instructions are requested as to the disposal of a piece of plating torn from a German cruiser[11] which collided with H.M.S. SPITFIRE. The plate is about 20 feet in length and apparently consists of the stringer plating for a width of about 2 feet and side plating for a depth 3 feet joined by a deck boundary angle,
>
> It was found jammed in the side plating of SPITFIRE between the forecastle and upper deck at about 18 station on the Port Side.[12]

The reply, dated 28 September, revealed that this small relic of the Jutland battle would be touring the United States:

> With reference to your letter dated 5th August 1916, No. 905, requesting instructions as to the disposal of a piece of plating from a German cruiser which collided with HMS *Spitfire* and which was found jammed in the side plating of the latter vessel, I am to acquaint you that it has been decided to send this piece of plate for exhibition in the British War Exhibit of War Relics, Souvenirs and Munition specimens, to be shown at Allied Bazaars and other Exhibitions which are being arranged in various cities of the United States for the benefit of charities of the Allies.

I am to state that the piece of plate, with a short account indicating
its historic interest affixed thereto should be forwarded to:

> Captain Guy Grant, C.M.G., RN, c/o H.B.M.'s Consulate
> General, State
> Street, New York.

My Lords have decided that on its return from America, the plate is
to be deposited at Portsmouth, to be held available in the event of
any public exhibition of Naval Trophies.[13]

Grand Fleet Ready for Action on 2 June 1916

Despite inflicting more serious losses on the Royal Navy than he could
ever have contemplated, Scheer had been outmanoeuvred, surprised
and outgunned. Not only that, from a German viewpoint, the net effect
the battle had been to increase the Grand Fleet's already large margin of
superiority as a fighting force, instrument blockade and shield against
invasion.

No matter how much the Germans might claim to have achieved a
major victory over the Royal Navy, control of the North Sea remained
in British hands and was likely to remain so for the rest of the war.
Nothing demonstrated this more clearly than the state of the British and
German fleets on the days immediately after the action. The official
historian summed up the British position thus:

> Admiral Jellicoe's Battle Fleet (1st, 2nd, 4th and 5th Battle Squadrons)
> with the 4th Light Cruiser Squadron, the 11th and 12th Destroyer
> Flotillas and part of the 4th Flotilla arrived at Scapa between 10.30 and
> noon on 2 June 1916. At 9.45 Admiral Jellicoe reported to the Admiralty
> that the Grand Fleet was at its base, refuelled with steam at four hours'
> notice and ready for sea. In reply to an inquiry, Admiral Beatty
> reported at 11.20 p.m. on June 3 that three of his ships, the *New Zealand*,
> *Indomitable* and *Inflexible* were ready for action, and three others, the
> *Lion*, *Tiger* and *Princess Royal* were available for action if necessary.[14]

Thus, despite losing the battlecruisers *Queen Mary*, *Indefatigable* and
Invincible which had been sunk and the battleships *Warspite* and
Marlborough which were under repair, Jellicoe still had a significant
superiority over the High Seas Fleet that had sallied forth on 31 May.
Furthermore, the British could expect the battleship *Queen Elizabeth* and
the battle cruiser *Australia* to return to service within a short time while
the new battlecruisers *Renown* and *Repulse* were almost ready to join the

fleet as were the 15-inch gun armed battleships *Royal Sovereign*, *Resolution* and *Ramillies*.

But, what of the effectiveness of the German battleships and battlecruisers post-Jutland?

Repairing German Capital Ships After Jutland

The less seriously damaged dreadnoughts, of which only *Helgoland* required dry-docking, were all repaired at Wilhelmshaven, although, in some cases the work was not started immediately. There are no dates available for the completion of repairs to *Kaiser* and *Oldenburg* while the dates for *Helgoland*, *Nassau*, *Rheinland* and *Westfalen* were 16 June, 10 July, 10 June and 17 June respectively.

The Germans relied largely on floating docks for the repair of their capital ships and as neither Wilhelmshaven nor Kiel possessed a dry-dock that could accommodate *Derfflinger* or *Seydlitz*, while Kiel did not have one big enough for the battlecruiser *Moltke* or a König-class battleship. *Seydlitz* was therefore docked in the large floating dock in Wilhelmshaven and her repairs were completed on 16 September. *Ostfriesland* and *Von der Tann* whose repairs were completed on 26 July and 2 August respectively were accommodated in dry-docks at Wilhelmshaven. *Moltke* spent a short time in dry-dock at Wilhelmshaven before being transferred to Blohm and Voss at Hamburg where she entered a floating dock. Her repairs were completed on 30 July. *Markgraf* and *Grosser Kurfürst* were also accommodated in floating docks in Hamburg and their repairs by Blohm & Voss and Vulkan respectively were completed on 20 and 16 July.

The badly damaged *König* and *Derfflinger* were sent to Kiel where there was only a single floating dock capable of taking ships of their size. *König* was docked from 4 to 18 June and her repairs, which were undertaken by Howaldt, completed on 21 July. *Derfflinger* had been docked for preliminary repairs in the Wilhelmshaven floating dock prior to *Seydlitz* and was in the Kiel floating dock from 22 June to 15 July, but her repairs in Kiel dockyard were not completed until 15 October.[15]

All-in-all, the High Seas Fleet was not in a fit state to engage the Grand Fleet until late July 1916 and the battlecruisers *Seydlitz*, and *Derfflinger* would not be available for several months. Although the German battlefleet would be increased by the battlecruiser *Hindenburg* and the 15-inch gun armed battleships *Baden* and *Bayern*, these new ships were more than countered by British reinforcements.

Discovering the State of the German Fleet Post-Jutland

Unsurprisingly, after Jutland the British went to considerable lengths to ascertain the condition of the German fleet and its combat readiness using secret agents and naval attachés.

For example, an unidentified agent known only as 'R.16' sent the following report from Rotterdam on 27 June:

> In accordance with instructions received from you on June 2nd I went to Bremen travelling from there to Danzig, Kiel, Rostock, Geestemünde, Emden and Sande near Wilhelmshaven, in order to ascertain the exact German losses in the North Sea action of May 31st. The following is the result of my investigation.
>
> The PILLAU arrived at the Weser Werft at 6 a.m. on June 4th and I learned from people of this ship that the LÜTZOW, ROSTOCK and SEYDLITZ had been lost, although this loss was not acknowledged by the German Admiralty. The SEYDLITZ had been in the tow of the PILLAU but, in the outer Weser, the cables had to be cut as the ship was sinking rapidly. I learned afterwards from the men of the SEYDLITZ that the ship had been salved since with the help of the big floating crane of Wilhemshaven, and is now in dock (floating dock) at this latter port.
>
> When the DANZIG, which was still in dock, had come out, the PILLAU took her place. She was hit once under the waterline near the stem and her funnels and superstructure were damaged. She left the dock on June 15th, and on June 25th she was still lying near the Yard to repair the damage on her deck. She also has damage to the furnaces of one of her boilers through the feed pumps getting out of order. She will probably be seaworthy again by the end of the month. The DANZIG will not be ready before August.
>
> The MÜNCHEN which is under repair at the Bremer Vulkan at Vegesack, has only some damage on deck, except for a shot in the stokehold, which damaged a feed pump, and this is probably at present moment ready for service.
>
> On June 5th I went to Sande near Wilhelmshaven, as the latter is closed to traffic. Here I met men of the LÜTZOW and learned that part of her torpedo nets had got entangled in the propellers, which was the cause of her reducing speed, and eventually her loss.
>
> On June 6th I proceeded to Emden. In both docks of the Nordseewerke were destroyers of the latest type, whilst three more destroyers were lying near the docks. All had been hit under the water-line, but they were still seaworthy.
>
> On June 7th I was in Geestemünde. In the dock of the Tecklenborg Werft was a merchant vessel, whilst in both docks of the Selbeck Werft were auxiliary cruisers.

I proceeded the same day to Hamburg. No ships had arrived here yet, with the exception of the STETTIN lying at the Reiheratieg Werft with light damage on deck and in the engine-room. She will be ready end of next month.

On June 8th I arrived at Kiel. Here the FRANKFURT was in dock at the Kaiserliche Werft. She had been hit once under the water-line near the stem, and was ready again for service on June 24th. The BAYERN was also lying at Kiel. This ship did not take part in the action, but she was guarding the Sund during this time.

From June 9th till June 12th I was at Danzig. In the docks of the Kaiserliche Werft were one destroyer of the newest type with three funnels, and one small cruiser with two funnels, one of which had been partially shot away. Near the Schichau Werft were lying seven destroyers, but I was unable to ascertain their damage.

When I arrived in Kiel again on June 14th the following ships were there:

BAYERN	
DEUTSCHLAND	all [3] undamaged
BRAUNSCHWEIG	
SCHLESIEN	all [3] with light damage, are under
SCHLESWIG-HOLSTEIN	repair in the outfitting Harbour of
HANNOVER	the K.W. [Kaiserliche Werft]
KÖNIG	Lying at the Howaldt Werft with some severe damage in the engine room and on deck and will have very long repairs
STRALSUND	Light damage

On June 15th I was again at Hamburg, where in the meantime the following ships had arrived:
At Blohm & Voss:

MOLTKE was in dock (when I went again to Hamburg on June 21st the damage under the water-line had been repaired and the damaged part already had a coat of paint).

MARKGRAF This ship must have been severely damaged and has been hidden away between the floating dock and the giant steal of H.A. L. [Hamburg America Line].

At the Vulkan yard:
GROSSER KURFÜRST is in dock and has received some very severe damage under the water-line from a torpedo. Engines also damaged.

On June 16th I returned to Sande near Wilhelmshaven and learned
that the following ships are under repairs at Wilhelmshaven:
> KAISER, KAISERIN, NASSAU, OSTFRIESLAND,
> THŰRINGEN : in dry dock.
> SEYDLITZ – in floating dock
> All [six] with damage under the water-line. On June 25th three
> of them, the KAISERIN, OSTFRIESLAND and SEYDLITZ were
> still in dock.

Besides the above ships, there were also in Wilhelmshaven, the
VON DER TANN, DERFFLINGER, OLDENBURG, HELGOLAND,
THEINLAND [actually RHEINLAND], WESTFALEN,
REGENSBURG, KÖNIG ALBERT (This latter ship was not in the
action). Of these ships the VON DER TANN has all her turrets out of
action and some severe damage on deck. The DERFFLINGER has also
received severe damage (Vide Kiel later on).

When I arrived back in Bremen on June 18th, the PILLAU had left
the dock, and the MŰNCHEN was still lying at Vegesack.

On June 19th I was at Geestemünde and Einswarden but did not
see any damaged ships.

At Hamburg, where I was on June 20th there were still the same
ships I saw on my previous visit.

I then proceeded again to Kiel where had arrived the:
> ESSEN light damage being repaired at Kaiserliche Werft.
> DERFFLINGER has been hit once under the water-line, forward
> and three times above the water-line; her fore-funnel has also
> been hit, the guns have been taken out of all of her turrets and
> the latter are covered with tarpaulins.

On account of the damage sustained the following will not be
ready for service within the next three months:
> KAISERIN, MARKGRAF, KÖNIG, GROSSER KURFŰRST,
> SEYDLITZ, DERFFLINGER, VON DER TANN, OSTFRIESLAND
> and possibly THURINGEN.[16]

Other sources of information about the damage to the High Seas Fleet
included the Russian Admiralty which sent the following report to
London on 17 June:

Russian Admiralty received following reports dated June 7th:
> SEYDLITZ at HAMBURG has 4 holes below and severely

damaged above waterline. Turrets severely damaged.

At WILHELSHAVEN, 2 battle cruisers in harbour; KAISER and KRONPRINZ [?] in dock, details of damage not given.[17]

A second report dated 4 July was received in early that month:

Following reports dated July 4th, received by the RUSSIAN Admiralty:

Movements of GERMAN ships:

GROSSER KURFÜRST and MARKGRAF: HAMBURG TO WILHELMSHAVEN

DERFFLINGER and KÖNIG ALBERT: WILHELMSHAVEN to LAVARONE

Repairs:

WESTFALEN, NASSAU and OSTFRIESLAND completed.

REGENSBURG, GRAUDENZ, PILLAU and VON DER TANN nearly completed.

OLDENBURG will take four months.[18]

Neutral Denmark was an ideal place for agents to monitor the activities of the German Navy because its western coast bordered the Heligoland Bight while its eastern coast and associated islands covered Kiel and the western part of Germany's Baltic coastline.

Naval movements in the Skagerrak and Kattegat could also be observed from northern Denmark. Consequently, throughout the war a regular supply of information about the German Navy was received in London via Copenhagen. For example, on 19 June the British Naval Attaché in Copenhagen sent the following report:

It is said that in the Naval harbour (Kiel) 3 damaged vessels are lying of the Kaiser class, and that the KÖNIG ALBERT and PRINZREGENT LUITPOLD are lost, or possibly have been so damage that they cannot get through the canal [Kiel Canal]. Another and persistent rumour says that the Kiel Canal is blocked in consequence of a ship having sunk on the 15th. On the other hand another rumour says that only three of the Kaiser class took part in the battle, and that the only one damaged battleship namely the FRIEDRICH DER GROSSE has arrived at Kiel.[19]

The same day the Admiralty's Naval Intelligence Department received information from German Agent 'D.15' who had visited Wilhelmshaven and was able to report that:

118

59 German ships took part in Naval battle most of which are damaged. Worst damage is KÖNIG, MARKGRAF, DERFFLINGER, SEYDLITZ. Damage to these mostly by gunfire.

English cruisers commenced action 26 kilometres: German returned fire at 18 kilometres and found range at 15 kilometres.

German loss 63 officers and 2,414 men killed, 490 wounded.

Corroborates LYNX' report about KÖNIG and DERFFLINGER. Latter and SEYDLITZ are 2 worst damaged ships. Nearly all DEFFLINGER's guns out of action, she will take 8 weeks to repair. Two shells in engine room.

SEYDLITZ nearly sunk entering Wilhelmshaven, but they managed to get her into Vulcan Yard. She has 18 hits. 11 torpedo boats sunk.

Following also damaged: FRIEDRICH DER GROSSE, VON DER TANN, STUTTGART, MŰNCHEN, POSEN, BRANDENBURG, GRAUDENZ. Last three in B &V Yard, Hamburg. POSEN worst damage. Extensive damage superstructure, 5 weeks repair.

FRIEDRICH DER GROSSE was the flag ship; she had only two hits and has to rejoin the fleet.

SEYDLITZ extensive damage to superstructure, propeller shaft and machinery six weeks to repair will go to Germania.

VON DER TANN in Weser Yard, Bremen. She has 2 bad hits and 4 less hits all above the waterline. 5 weeks to repair.

FRIEDRICH DER GROSS and MÜNCHEN go to Vulcan Yard, Wilhelmshaven but no room yet. I should think at least 3 weeks to repair. FRIEDRICH DER GROSSE armour plates much damaged.

MARKGRAF in Vulcan Yard Wilhelmshaven, both funnels shot away, 3 bad hits below the water line, machinery damaged, 8 weeks to repair.

POMMERN collided with ELBING damaging latter.

LŰTZOW was taken in tow and sunk close to Heligoland.

POMMERN sunk by torpedoes.

WIESBADEN by torpedo and gun fire.

HINDENBURG not in battle. She is in Vulcan Yard Wilhelmshaven and will not be ready until end of September.

BRAUNSCHWEIG badly damaged several weeks ago and is repairing Libau. She will be 3 weeks yet.

Many damaged torpedo boats Wilhelmshaven no numbers. It is said S/Ms will have no numbers in future.

New battleship BAYERN lies outside eastern entrance to Kiel Canal.[20]

On 20 June, Agent D.3 commented on damage to German torpedo-boats reporting that:

Of the ten destroyers which returned to Stettin via Belt five were more or less damaged and under repair as follows:

Forward gun and deck wrecked
Funnels bridge and after deck
Engine room bridge and hull
Whole foredeck and bridge
Bridge and hull bottom[21]

On 24 June British Naval Attaché in Copenhagen was told by the Danish Secret Service that the battlecruiser *Hindenburg* had been very seriously damaged at Jutland with all her 12-inch guns destroyed.

The ship in question, which had to be her sister *Derfflinger*, was also reported to have had the port side of her hull very badly damaged as well.[22] The same day Agent N.1 in Copenhagen reported:

NASSAU at Wilhelmshaven badly damaged by torpedo, no room for repair.
KRONPRINZ, Vulcan Yard Hamburg.
KÖNIG is going in Germania Yard as no repairs are to be done in dockyard to avoid delay to submarine construction.
Saw men from OSTFRIESLAND and MOLTKE June 20 on leave in Berlin.
Only one man saved from WIESBADEN.
Many men from WESTFALEN, MOLTKE and GROSSER KURFURST in Hamburg, so they are probably there.
According to Bremen sailor two submarines lost.
Very large number of torpedo boat lost seems everywhere conceded.[23]

Two days later a report was received from Agent D.2 in Copenhagen about the cruiser *Stettin*:

Cruiser STETTIN arrived Flensburg damaged from North Sea Battle which sailors say will take 2 months to repair.[24]

The Effect of Gunfire From British Super-Dreadnoughts

Another source of information for the Admiralty was the letters sent by relatives to German prisoners-of-war being held in the United Kingdom.

One from a Dr Greveler of Cassel, which was sent to his son Max on 7 July, must have been particularly sweet music to the ears of those who had argued successfully for the introduction of 13.5-inch and 15-inch guns. After telling his son that the German losses at Jutland totalled one battlecruiser (*Lützow*), one old battleship (*Pommern*), four light cruisers and five torpedo-boats he then wrote:

> An engineer from the 'Lützow' told me that in the evening their ship was battered to pieces by the fire of the enemy's Super–Dreadnoughts.[25]

Clearly, no amount of armour would protect a ship against well-directed 13.5-inch and 15-inch gunfire and this point will not have been lost of the sailors manning the High Seas Fleet's capital ships.

The Germans may have lost fewer ships at Jutland but some of those which survived had taken a fearful battering without being able to reply. In November 1918 after the surrender of German warships, Captain Persius, an informed and regular contributor to the *Berliner Tageblatt* wrote that 'On 1st June, it was clear to any thinking person that this battle must, and would be the last one. Authoritative quarters' he declared 'said so openly.'[26]

Making the Grand Fleet More Combat Capable

On 4 June Jellicoe appointed committees of Grand Fleet officers to examine the gunnery lessons to be learnt while at the same soliciting suggestions for increasing protection against plunging fire.

Additional committees were also set up to report on torpedoes, wireless telegraphy in action, construction of new ships, preparation for battle and the protection of officers and men in action, anti-flame, anti-gas and fire extinguishing apparatus required in H.M. ships for use in action.

There were also committees reporting on fire control, the experiences of light cruisers at Jutland and the perennial problem of weight reduction in H.M. ships. During Jutland the Germans had demonstrated that they were far in advance of the Royal Navy in the use of searchlights and star shell and consequently a committee was established to examine searchlights and searchlight control.

The outcome of their deliberations would have a dramatic effect on the operational capability of the Royal Navy's warships.[27]

Lessons From Grand Fleet Committees

Jellicoe summarised the five major aspects of materiel needing improvement identified by the Grand Fleet Committees as follows:

> The urgent need for arrangements to prevent the flash of cordite charges, ignited by the explosion of a shell in a turret or in the

positions between the turret and the magazine, being communicated to the magazine itself. It was probable that the loss of one, if not two, of our battlecruisers was due to this cause, after the [turret] armour had been pierced.[28]

Better measures were required to prevent the charges of smaller guns from being ignited by bursting shells, and to localise any fires due to this cause, in the case of guns of the secondary battery in large ships, and in the main armament of small ships.

Increased deck armour protection in large ships had been shown to be desirable in order that shell or fragments of shell might not reach the magazines. This need was particularly felt in all our earlier ships of the Dreadnought type, since their side armour was not carried to the upper deck level. The long range at which most modern sea actions are fought, and the consequent large angle of descent of the projectiles made our ships very vulnerable in this respect.[29]

The pressing need for a better armour piecing shell with an improved fuse was also revealed.

Improved arrangements for flooding magazines and drenching exposed cartridges had to be made.[30]

The Gunnery Committees of both the Grand Fleet and the Battle Cruiser Fleet addressed the issue of how to improve fire control so as to improve methods of correction of fire thereby enabling enemy ships to be straddled with greater rapidity. Hitherto, there seems to have been a widespread and simplistic belief that the number of hits was a function of the rate of fire whereas in practice this is only true once the target has been acquired by the guns.

On 7 June Rear Admiral W.C. Packenham aboard the battlecruiser *New Zealand* wrote:

I have the honour to bring to your notice the advisability of considering without delay the relative values of the British system of obtaining hits as compared with that apparently used by the Germans.

2. The part to which I particularly refer is to the 'straddle' as opposed to the concentrated salvo. Observation of the almost irresistible effect of two or three shots striking together has impressed me with the view that without adequate reason we may now be denying ourselves the benefit of a very powerful weapon.

3. I also think the principle of the straddle has been abused. Of late gunnery practice had not expected hits. Gunnery officers have been pressed only to straddle, and this has acted as a premium on increase

of longitudinal spread. Hence spreads of over 300 yards have been accepted as satisfactory. Great longitudinal spread has obtained so much sanction, indeed, that it has been stated 'Barham' was actually ordered to increase a spread which she had reduced to 70 yards because so moderate a spread reduced the prospects of straddling.

4. It appears to me that when we have done everything possible to obtain concentrated fall and to eliminate every error, we shall still have a spread sufficient for all gunnery purposes. Concentrated fall would facilitate spotting. The principle on which ranging is done would have to be changed; but Lieutenant Commander Smith of 'New Zealand' has a proposal which promises well, and no doubt discussion would elicit many other instructive suggestions.[31]

The same day Captain Green of *New Zealand* wrote a more detailed account noting that:

The Germans appeared to fire about three salvoes in rapid succession without waiting for the fall of shot. These salvoes appeared to fall about 400 yards apart, each successive salvo falling beyond the one before. The result is a ladder of salvoes about 1000 yards in length with three stops, and by watching the fall of each step in turn a very close estimate of the true range can be obtained and far more rapidly than our bracket system.

If the ladder straddles, the enemy has a very approximate range within a minute and a half of opening fire. If the ladder fails to straddle another ladder is probably fired with a mean range of 500 to 600 [yards] more or less than the original ladder.

This method would appear to be very much quicker than our bracket system and the following modification [of the bracket system as outlined above] of it is suggested.[32]

Subsequently, on 22 June, in his report to the Battle Cruiser Fleet Committee *Lion*'s Commanding Officer, Captain Chatfield, recommended the adoption of the ladder system to promote early hitting.[33]

The Gunnery Committees also recommended the installation of improved rangefinders throughout the Fleet which happened during 1917-1918. However, merely upgrading the equipment available was only one aspect of solving the problem of hitting moving targets at long range. As Jellicoe observed, 'the developments introduced in the fire control arrangements of the Grand Fleet after the Battle of Jutland did not affect the *instruments* already in use, which fully met our requirements, but the *methods* of using these instruments and particularly the system of correction of fire'.[34]

Fire Concentration by Multiple Ships

One consequence of Jutland was that the British realised that firing opportunities in the North Sea would be brief and hitting rates low. Consequently, efforts were made to standardise spotting rules using a ladder ranging system, and for this Director control proved to be essential, especially at long range against a target taking avoiding action.

However, Jutland also demonstrated the need for ships to be able to continue engaging a target even if the latter had become obscured. This was achieved by the adoption of the Henderson gyro firing gear which utilised a gyro-stabilised prism in the trainer's telescope linked to the Director control-system. The most external features of the 'concentration system', in which one ship of a group may see a target not visible to the others, were range clocks at the mastheads and bearing markings on 'B' and 'X' turrets for ships with superimposed guns or 'A' and 'Y' turrets for earlier Dreadnoughts. The Grand Fleet tried out a four-ship concentration, with the battleship *Colossus* acting as the master ship on 27 February 1917 with each dreadnought firing in sequence at fifteen-second intervals using ranges provided by *Colossus*.[35]

Anti-Flash Procedures – the Vengeance Trials

As a result of experience gained in the Battle of Jutland action was taken to fit all H.M. Ships with improved anti-flash arrangements with a view to preventing successive ignition of cordite charges and to ensure that flash could not reach the magazines, except as a result of structural damage. The principal measures taken were:

> Doors of magazines were kept closed and only opened when necessary to pass out charges. As a temporary measure, deadlights with fearnought sleeves were fitted in the access doors to do duty as handing[36] scuttles and so prevent the necessity for opening the doors when supplying ammunition.
>
> Steel boxes were supplied for the protection for the protection of ready use rectangular cordite cases at gun positions to protect the contents of these cases from ignition by flash or penetration by shell fragments.
>
> Clarkson's cases for transport of charges between the interior of the magazine and the gun were reintroduced into the Service in order to provide complete protection for each individual charge against flash.

In open battery ships 'fearnought' screens were used to isolate guns as much as possible.

Special procedures were put in hand to avoid a continuous train of charges to the magazine as far as possible.

The tops of hoists in the working chambers of the older turret mountings were enclosed.

Leather aprons were fitted between the fixed and revolving trunks in the walking pipe space and at the top of the magazine to prevent flash finding its way to the magazine by this route.

Orders were issued that bare charges were not to be sent up in dredger hoists, and in some cases dredger hoists were removed and replaced by whip and tackle in order to enable this order to be complied with, the dredger hoists not being suitable to allow of any sort of case being used for the charges.

Handing rooms were built for all B.L. magazines and a flap type of handing scuttle was fitted. In certain classes of ships handing rooms were fitted at the top of the supply trunks as well as at the lower ends.

Anti-flash clothing was supplied to H.M. Ships.

The above precautionary measures were proceeded with at once without ship trial, and it was therefore decided in 1917 to carry out trials to ascertain whether the arrangements that had been fitted were entirely satisfactory and what further action, if any, was required. The pre-dreadnought *Vengeance* was selected for the purpose of these trials as she was available and her turrets were similar in many respects to those in the more modern ships, and included a revolving trunk extending down to the shell room.

As expected, trials in *Vengeance* were carried out under the supervision of the gunnery school H.M.S. *Excellent* between 8 August 1917 and 3 January 1918 in Cawsand Bay. Six separate series of trials were carried out during which thirty-seven different conditions were tested. The trial showed that the whole of the measures already taken were completely successful. It was also found that:

Magazine doors are not necessarily flashtight even when tightly closed.

Ventilating trunks are liable to conduct flash to a magazine.

Ignition of the contents of a cordite case in a magazine need not necessarily cause the magazine to blow up.[37]

New Armour Piercing Shells

In the days following the Battle of Jutland, Beatty and his subordinates must have found it hard to believe that they had achieved so little during their engagement with Hipper's battlecruisers. Thus, the battlecruisers had expended a huge amount of ammunition and claimed many more hits than they had actually achieved without any apparent result. It must have been difficult to admit that the Battle Cruiser Fleet's failure was down to the shortcomings of the personnel manning ships and the procedures by which the latter were operated. Fortunately, a possible cause of their failure to inflict more damage to the German battlecruisers was revealed by a Swedish naval officer. Captain Chatfield recalled:

> In August 1916, David Beatty had a luncheon party on board the *Lion* for several important visitors. Among the party was a Swedish naval officer, who had been attached to the Swedish Legation in Berlin. I arranged to sit next to him to see if I could extract anything out of him. I told him a good deal about the damage to our ships, when he volunteered the information that the German naval officers had told him, that our shell were 'laughable'. When asked if our heavy shell had penetrated their armour he replied 'The German officers told me they had broken to pieces on it.'[38]

Chatfield wasted no time in compiling a report for the Admiralty.

> It is customary for all authors to decry the performance of the British shells used at Jutland and it is often said that they broke up without penetrating, or if they did penetrate the explosion was ineffective.
>
> However, a great deal of damage was done to German ships by British shells which pierced thick German armour. Furthermore, the kinetic force of the impact of the large calibre 13.5-inch and 15-inch shells was such that even if the shell did not penetrate it still caused damage. In effect, armour plate was no longer fully effective against the damaging effect such heavy shells.

These facts can be reconciled using Grand Fleet gunnery orders which recommended the use of common (CPC) rather than armour piercing (AP) shell for the opening salvoes because the splash was more easily seen and the range could be corrected more quickly. At Jutland, where only fleeting glimpses of the enemy were seen, some ships fired little if any armour piercing shell and it is not to be wondered at that common shell broke up on contact with thick armour.

The Jutland Despatches only detail the ammunition fired for a few ships:[39]

Iron Duke	Capped Common shell only
Hercules	94 Common and 4 AP
Agincourt	144 Common only
New Zealand	Lyddite and Common only
Indomitable	98 AP, 66 Lyddite Common, 10 Powder Common
Inflexible	Common at *Seydlitz* and some Lyddite AP
Vanguard	15 Common 42 HE
Orion	51 AP
Thunderer	3 salvoes of Common then AP
Marlborough	24 CPC and 138 Common Lyddite
St Vincent	88 AP Lyddite and 8 Common Lyddite

The 2nd Battle Squadron remarked that it was usual to open with common shells before switching to armour piercing. In view of the above it is unsurprising that Scheer, in his autobiography, remarked on seeing broken British shells with 'black powder' running out:

> A number of bits of shell picked up clearly showed that powder only had been used in the charge. Many shells of 34- and 38-cm calibre had burst into such large pieces that, when picked up, they were easily fitted together. On the other hand, the colour on the ships' sides, where they had been hit, showed that picric acid[40] had been used in some of the explosive charges.[41]

The above figures are a small but representative sample from the Grand Fleet and it is therefore highly likely that many shells fired were not armour piercing. Thus, when any of these hit armour they would break up and it is certain that most of the shells which were seen to fail were of this type. To open fire with common shell was quite a sensible procedure and even in the poor visibility of Jutland it was reasonable to balance the increased chance of a hit inflicting minor but visible damage with common shell against the probability of inflicting any damage with armour piercing.

The question remains as to whether the armour piercing shells which were fired and penetrated German armour were in a fit state to explode once inside. During the attack of the 1st Scouting Group at 19.15 onwards, both 'C' and 'D' turrets of *Derfflinger* were penetrated at about 12,000 yards by 15-inch shells which exploded within, causing cordite fires which killed 152 men.[42]

A total of nine turrets were hit on German battlecruisers and in only in the case of *Von der Tann's* 'A' turret did the shell fail to explode after penetrating. A 13.5-inch shell hit on *Lützow* at 19.15 at 19,800 yards from *Orion* which penetrated the former's 'B' turret wall destroying the right gun and causing a cordite fire. Another shell penetrated the armour deck and exploded below – no German shell exploded below a British armour deck.

British shells therefore did indeed explode inside German armour but it is not easy to determine the percentage of the 3,160 armour piercing shells fired that day which behaved as expected. The defects in British APC were caused by the use of unstable lyddite as the burster, a role for which it was totally unsuitable, as well as brittle shell casings and fuzes which had no delayed action.[43]

On 25 July Jellicoe requested that experiments should be undertaken as soon as possible using armour piercing shells filled with trinitrotoluene (trotyl) and an exact copy of the German delayed-action fuse. However, the shell problem wasn't solved until Jellicoe became First Sea Lord. New armour piercing shells were designed in May 1917 and began to equip the fleet from April 1918. The new shells, which were painted green and given the soubriquet 'Greenboys', were not used in action during the war but, in Jellicoe's opinion, they certainly doubled the offensive power of the fleet's heavy guns.[44]

Although not used in the First World War , the 15-inch successors to the 'Greenboys' worked exactly as designed at Mers-el-Kebir on 3 July 1940 when two shells pierced *Dunkerque*'s thick, inclined 225mm armour belt at an oblique angle and penetrated deep into her hull before exploding. The French battlecruiser was completely disabled and, had she been at sea rather than in harbour, there can be no doubt that she would have been sunk.[45]

Clearly, one unexpected outcome of the Battle of Jutland had been to improve the materiel quality and fighting capability of the Grand Fleet which already had a considerable numerical superiority over its German opponent. However, none of this would have been anticipated by anyone reading the world's newspapers in early June 1916.

After the Battle:
British Press Reports

*We do not know nearly as much as we want to know about the
battle in the North and until we do anxiety will be intense.*[1]

For many in this digital age of more-or-less instantaneous world-wide
communication it must appear strange that a mere 100 years ago the
British public had to wait for several days for news of a major naval
battle that took place in the North Sea just 400 miles from London.

The Germans were fortunate because their bases were little more than
100 miles from the position of the High Seas Fleet at 03.00 on 1 June. At
15.00 that day the High Seas Fleet flagship *Friedrich der Grosse* anchored
in Wilhelmshaven Roads and within hours the German Naval Staff
were able to piece together the main events of the battle and issue a
statement claiming victory over the hitherto unbeaten Royal Navy. The
German legend of victory was carefully crafted and nurtured with the
British tactical mistakes that had allowed the High Seas Fleet to escape
being represented as a refusal to renew the action after the first clash of
the battleships. There was no mention of the shocked surprise with
which the German battle squadrons had recoiled from the concentrated
fire of the Grand Fleet – that would only become apparent once the
action was analysed and detailed charts prepared.

The Germans were also fortunate that their enemy's heavy losses had
been seen by ships of the High Seas Fleet as well as being confirmed by
British prisoners of war and consequently could not be denied. Most
German losses, which were considerably less than those of the British,
had occurred unseen or at night and therefore could be concealed in the
interests of security. Furthermore, the return of a weaker fleet, which
had survived contact, albeit brief, with the mighty Grand Fleet and
returned to harbour with relatively few losses, could also be regarded

as a success. Unsurprisingly, on the evening of 1 June the German newspapers proclaimed 'Great Victory at Sea'.

The British Public Relations Disaster

In comparison, the ships of the Grand Fleet had to travel about 450 miles from the site of the battle to reach their home bases and it was only after the Grand Fleet had arrived at Scapa Flow during the morning of 2 June that the Admiralty could get hard information about the battle. In the meantime, in London, strict censorship prevailed with only a few officials even aware that the Grand Fleet had been in action. Until a report was received from Jellicoe at 10.35 on 2 June, the Admiralty could not give out any communiqué but unfortunately, Jellicoe was at sea still collecting details of the action that for the most part out of sight of his flagship.

Unfortunately, by the evening of 1 June sensational rumours, which originated in Rosyth dockyard of a British defeat, were spreading all over the country. Clearly it had become dangerous to conceal news of the battle. As the sensational German communiqué began to appear in the neutral press in Europe on 2 June, British authorities soon realised that they would be unable to prevent these reports from 'leaking' into the United Kingdom and consequently decided to release the German statement without comment. The nation was stunned and the British Press clamoured for more information. Unable to resist Press pressure, the Admiralty released Arthur Balfour's tersely-worded and brutally-honest communiqué later that evening. This unfortunately-worded document gave the impression to those prepared to read between the lines that the Germans claims were essentially true and that the Grand Fleet had therefore been defeated.

Jellicoe had no liking for the Press believing that they were little more than source of information for the Germans, and therefore, had little appreciation of the consequences to be drawn from the failure to respond in full to the initial German communiqué. Thus, Jellicoe and his staff must take some of the blame for this public relations disaster not least because they failed to report that the Grand Fleet had twice caused its opponent to turn away rather than face the sustained gunfire of Jellicoe's battleships. Furthermore, there was no reference to Scheer's single-minded determination to escape to harbour once the main fleets had made contact.

Six hours later, after receiving more information from Admiral Jellicoe, the Admiralty issued a revised communiqué in an attempt to calm an agitated Press and a worried populace. Jellicoe's much amplified second report corrected these deficiencies showing that after the initial defeat of Beatty's battle cruisers, the High Seas Fleet had been overpowered and forced to flee by the intervention of the Grand Fleet's battleships. Despite the availability of more information, the Admiralty's second communiqué was limited to details of losses on each side without attempting to discuss the implications of the German refusal to accept battle. HM King George V succinctly put the matter into its correct perspective when he signalled Jellicoe on 3 June:

> I regret that the German High Seas Fleet, in spite of its heavy losses, was enabled by the misty weather to evade the full consequences of an encounter they have always professed to desire but for which, when the opportunity arrived, they showed no inclination.

The Admiralty refusal to claim Jutland as a victory coupled to their lacklustre statements left an innately suspicious Press dissatisfied and looking for someone to blame for what must have been a British defeat.

Jellicoe's antipathy to journalists made him the perfect scapegoat and allowed the Press to promulgate the legend that Beatty had gallantly fought against overwhelming odds to deliver the High Seas Fleet into Jellicoe's hands only to see the splendid opportunity wasted by excessive caution. The reality was quite different because if anyone had been defeated at Jutland it was Beatty who with six battle cruisers and four fast battleships against five battlecruisers had lost two and suffered heavy damage to others without commensurate reply.

Furthermore, Beatty was the national hero of the battles of Heligoland Bight and Dogger Bank and it was inconceivable to the Press and public that he could have been defeated. In fact, Beatty's battle cruisers were almost unable to obtain hits during the early stages of the battle, a fact that the Germans stressed continually while at the same time admitting that the shooting of the 5th Battle Squadron was outstanding. In comparison, Hipper's battle cruisers shot superbly throughout the action.

Newspaper Reports 2-8 June 1916

On 2 June the *Dundee Evening Telegraph* carried the official statement released earlier that day by the Admiralty under the headline:

GREAT NAVAL BATTLE In the North Sea. RIVAL FLEETS
ENGAGED.
HEAVY LOSSES.
Famous British Ships Sunk.
The following official statement was issued by the Press Bureau to-night:— the afternoon of Wednesday, May, a naval engagement took

place off the coast of Jutland. The British ships on which the brunt of the fighting fell were the Battle Cruiser Fleet and some cruisers and light cruisers, supported by four fast battleships. Among those the losses were heavy. The German battle fleet, aided by low visibility, avoided prolonged action with our main forces, and soon after these appeared on the scene the enemy returned port, though not before receiving severe damage from our battleships. The battle cruisers *Queen Mary, Indefatigable, Invincible,* and the cruisers *Defence* and *Black Prince* were sunk. The *Warrior* was disabled, and after being towed for some time had to be abandoned by her crew. It is also known that the destroyers *Tipperary, Turbulent, Fortune, Sparrowhawk,* and *Ardent* were lost, and six others are not yet accounted for. No British battleship or light cruisers were sunk.

The enemy's losses were serious. At least one battle cruiser was destroyed and one severely damaged. One battleship reported sunk by destroyers during night attack. Two light cruisers were disabled and probably sunk. The exact, number of enemy destroyers disposed of during the action cannot ascertained with any certainty, but it must have been large.

THE LOST VESSELS.

The *Queen Mary* was a battleship [battlecruiser] of 27,000 tons. She was commissioned at Portsmouth 4th September, 1913. The *Indefatigable* was battle cruiser of 18,750 tons. She was re-commissioned at Devonport on 17th June, 1913. The *Invincible* was a battle cruiser of 17,250 tons. She was commissioned at Portsmouth on August, 1914. The *Black Prince* was cruiser of 13,550 tons. She was recommissioned at Portsmouth in April, 1914. The *Defence* was cruiser of 14,600 tons. She was recommissioned at Devonport 2nd September, 1913. The *Warrior* was a cruiser of 13,550 tons. She was recommissioned at Devonport on 1st July 1913.

On 3 June, British newspapers were full of articles about the battle with most expressing concern that the Royal Navy may have been defeated and speculating about the causes and consequences of such an outcome. For example, the *Manchester Evening News* contained an article which voiced these fears and speculated on how the High Seas Fleet may have been able to achieve success:

THE NORTH SEA BATTLE. EVENING NEWS.

We do not know nearly as much as we want to know about the battle in the North and until we do anxiety will be intense. On duty on board the British ships which have been sacrificed were about 5,000 men; fine experienced sailors, the pick the earth. How many of them are drowned? How many saved? All other questions are subsidiary to these.

The Admiralty may be trusted to tell the terrible tale soon as they are fully acquainted with the facts. What happened, as far as we can gather from the necessarily scanty dispatches, was that our battle cruiser fleet, while off the coast of Jutland, was attacked by the German battle fleet. Air scouting probably told the German admirals of the presence of the British and determined them to leave their harbours and risk fight, in the hope that they would be able to dispose of the British cruisers before the British Grand Fleet could come from the north. The Germans never had any idea of risking a battle with the British Grand Fleet. Partially, at any rate, German strategy succeeded. The British cruisers found themselves opposed by superior force as Admiral Cradock was opposed at Coronel, and as, in turn, Admiral von Spee was opposed by Admiral Sturdee off the Falklands. But in one important respect the position differed from that at these past naval engagements. Both Admiral von Spee at Coronel and Admiral Sturdee the Falklands were anxious to get the battle over as quickly as possible.

The commander of the British cruisers off Jutland had a different purpose, and was prepared take great risks in order prolong the battle. The longer he kept it going the better was the chance of Admiral Jellicoe rushing up with an overwhelming force and totally destroying the German fleet. No doubt most of the heavy losses were sustained in the endeavour to carry out this purpose. The tactics were only partially successful. Jellicoe and his men did come on the scene in time to deliver smashing blows at the German ships, but not soon enough to prevent the escape of most of them.

The *Daily Mirror* of 3 June carried a series of articles about the battle including:

2 GERMAN DREADNOUGHTS SUNK. Foe Battle Cruiser Blown Up, Another Disabled and Stopping, and Third Seriously Damaged.

ENEMY CRUISER AND 6 DESTROYERS SUNK. Our Losses Include *Queen Mary, Indefatigable. Invincible, Defence, Black Prince; Warrior* Abandoned.

FOE FLEET AVOID LONG ACTION WITH OUR MAIN FORCE Three German Battleships Hit Repeatedly. Two Cruisers Disabled. U Boat Rammed and Sunk. (BRITISH OFFICIAL.) Press Bureau, Friday, 7 p.m. —The Secretary of the Admiralty makes the following announcement:— On the afternoon of Wednesday, May 31, a naval engagement took place off the coast of Jutland. The British ships on which the brunt of the fighting fell were the battle-cruiser fleet and some cruisers and light cruisers, supported by four fast battleships. Among these the losses were heavy.

The German battle fleet, aided by low visibility, avoided prolonged action with our main forces, and soon after these appeared on the scene the enemy returned to port, though not before receiving severe damage from our battleships. The battle cruisers *Queen Mary*, *Indefatigable*, *Invincible* and the cruisers *Defence* and *Black Prince* were sunk. The *Warrior* was disabled, and, after being towed for some time, had to be abandoned by her crew. It is also known that the destroyers *Tipperary*, *Turbulent*, *Fortune*, *Sparrowhawk* and *Ardent* were lost, and six others are not yet accounted for. No British battleships or light cruisers were sunk.

The enemy's losses were serious. At least one battlecruiser destroyed and one severely damaged; one battleship reported sunk by our destroyers during night attack; two light cruisers were disabled and probably sunk. The exact number of enemy destroyers disposed of during the action-cannot be ascertained with any certainty, but it must have been.

ADMIRAL SIR JOHN JELLICOE'S ESTIMATE OF GERMAN LOSSES IN JUTLAND FIGHT.

Admiralty, 1.5 a.m. —Since the foregoing communique was issued a further report has been received from the Commander-in Chief of the Grand Fleet stating that it is now possible to form a closer estimate of the losses and damage sustained by the enemy fleet. One Dreadnought battleship of the Kaiser class was blown up in an attack by British destroyers, and another Dreadnought battleship of the Kaiser class believed to have been sunk by gunfire.

Of three German battle cruisers, two of which is believed were the *Derfflinger* and the *Lützow*, one was blown up and another heavily engaged by our battle fleet, and was seen to be disabled and stopping, and the third was observed to be seriously damaged. One German light cruiser and six German destroyers were sunk, and at least two more German light cruisers were seen disabled. Further, repeated hits were observed on three other German battleships that were engaged. Finally, a German submarine was rammed and sunk.

Like all British newspapers that day, the *Daily Mirror* reported Jellicoe's inflated claims of the sinking of two German dreadnoughts as well as reporting the sinking of one or more U-boats even though none of the latter actually participated in the action.

This newspaper also reported the official German account of the battle which had been 'picked up' from Central News in Amsterdam. In this communiqué the Germans erroneously claimed to have sunk the battleship *Warspite*, a light cruiser and a destroyer leader named *Alcaster*, while at the same time hiding some of their own losses. In just a few days, this deception would completely undermine their initially successful propaganda campaign:

(GERMAN OFFICIAL.) Amsterdam, Friday. —The following official account of the North Sea battle was issued in Berlin to-day:— During an enterprise, directed towards the north, our High Sea Fleet on Wednesday last met a considerably superior main portion of the British Battle Fleet. In the course of the afternoon, between the Skagerack and the Horn Reef, a number of severe, and for us successful, engagements developed and continued all night. In these engagements, as far as is at present ascertained, we destroyed the great battleship *Warspite*, the battle cruisers *Queen Mary* and *Indefatigable*, two armoured cruisers of the Achilles class one small cruiser, and the new destroyer leaders *Turbulent*, *Nestor* and *Alcaster*.

According to trustworthy evidence a great number of British battleships suffered heavy damage from the artillery of our vessels, and the attacks of our torpedo-boat flotillas during the day battle and during the night. Among others, the great battleship *Marlborough* was hit by a torpedo, as is confirmed by the statements of prisoners. A large portion of the crews of the British vessels that were sunk were picked up our vessels. Among them are two sole survivors of the *Indefatigable*. On our side the small cruiser *Wiesbaden* sunk by the enemy's artillery. During the night the *Pommern* was sunk by a torpedo. Regarding the fate of the *Frauenlob*, which is missing, and some torpedo-boats which have not returned to the present, nothing is known.

The High Sea Fleet returned to our harbours in the course of to-day.—(Signed) Chief of the Naval General Staff. —Reuter. [Note. — It should not be forgotten that the British official statement points out that NO British Battleships or light cruisers were sunk].

FOE ADMIRAL'S VERSION OF THE BATTLE. Amsterdam, Friday.— The Director of the Naval Department declared in the Reichstag that, according the latest information, the whole of the German battle fleet, under command of Vice Admiral Scheer, found itself, the afternoon of

May 31, faced by the British Battle Fleet, including thirty four modern units. The battle lasted until nine o'clock in the evening, being followed by a series of reciprocal attacks during the night between cruisers and torpedo boats. 'The result of the fighting is a significant success for our forces against much stronger adversary,' said the Rear Admiral, amid cheers. He went to report the British losses already known, and added that nine or ten destroyers were destroyed, six of them being accounted for by the battleship *Westfalen*.

It was evident that some of the German ships had been considerably damaged, but the major portion of the fleet had returned to harbour.— Central News.

Amsterdam, Friday.—At a meeting of the Reichstag the President said 'In the North Sea a big naval battle has taken place- the first collision between our naval forces and pick of the English Fleet. Detailed messages are still lacking, but it may already said that our young navy has gained a great and splendid success. Several of our fine ships, indeed, have been lost, and many of our brave sailors have perished, but the enemy losses are several times greater. Above all, proof has been given that our fleet [is] able face a superior British naval force and gain a victory.[2]

In another article entitled 'The Naval Battle', the newspaper commented on such hard information as it had received while at the same time reminding its concerned readers that the Royal Navy had been the nation's sure shield for more than 300 years and would continue to perform this role regardless of the sacrifices involved:

The British Empire will receive the news of the important naval action in the North Sea off the coast of Jutland with traditional calmness and a steadfast resolution that are in themselves as inherent qualities of sea power as are battleships and guns. In the statement issued by the Secretary of the Admiralty we learn that on the afternoon of May 31 a naval battle took place in which that portion of the British Fleet winch was engaged sustained serious losses. The brunt of the fighting fell upon our battle cruiser fleet, supported some cruisers and light cruisers. Of these the battle cruisers Queen Mary, Indefatigable, Invincible and the cruisers Defence and Black Prince were sunk with a number of destroyers.

The appearance of our battleships upon the scene the enemy returned port, having suffered severe losses, of which at the present moment the evidence must of necessity be of a fragmentary nature. This is the sum total of the news in regard to the naval battle as revealed in the British official communication. It would be idle to deny that the news of these heavy naval losses will be read with very grave feelings throughout the country.

The Navy is the Briton's favourite branch of the Service. We love the sea and those heroic souls who rule the seas for Great Britain. We cherish their valour deeply, and we shall feel the losses which they have incurred with a peculiar keenness. A generation bred up in naval peace has become so inured to the tradition of British supremacy on the seas that some few souls may well be pardoned to-day if they realise this tradition can only be bought and secured by great sacrifices with something of the shock of surprise. From the days the great Armada to the days of Nelson the British race was establishing the tradition of British sea supremacy by an endless vigil and by incessant sacrifice. Some of us who live in these later days may have been prone to accept the heritage of sea power as something bequeathed to us by right without a just realisation of the fact that it is a heritage which can only be maintained the price of sacrifice such as our forefathers so gladly made endow us with an inheritance of freedom. Such losses as were incurred by our battle-cruiser squadron off the coast of Jutland on the 31st of last month must serve to remind us all that victory on the sea in this greatest of all wars will only be purchased, as victory on the land, by a grievously heavy toll.

The Empire will unite as one man in mourning the loss of those valiant sons of Britain who have given up their lives for England in battle on the high seas. But in our grief for those who are gone—and whom we may assured exacted the heaviest possible penalty from the German foe—the British people will show no sign of weakness. If possible this news will harden the national resolution and give steadfastness to the national purpose. We will spare nothing in ships and men, will hesitate before no hardships, we will shrink from no sacrifices that may be called upon to endure, now and in the future for the maintenance a supremacy on the seas, which is not only in the fine words of the King, Britain's 'sure shield,' but living guarantee to all humanity of freedom and justice between free peoples.

In its last article on the subject that day, the *Daily Mirror* used material obtained from Amsterdam to give British readers a sense of the German response to the Battle of Jutland:

JOY AND JUBILATION IN GERMANY.
Battle Regarded a Great and Brilliant Victory.
Amsterdam, Friday.—The naval battle off the Jutland coast is

regarded in Germany a brilliant victory for the German Fleet and great joy prevails. Captain Persius, writing in the Berliner Tageblatt, says: 'The English losses were very heavy, but ours were very small, extraordinarily small indeed compared with the success achieved. In an open battle, without any support from the coast batteries, our fleet has victoriously fought the most powerful fleet in the world. The whole [of] Germany thanks its admiral, commanders and crews.'—Central News. Amsterdam, Friday.—The Tagezeitung describes the fight as the greatest naval battle of modern times, and adds:— 'Against the loss of three of the most powerful British Dreadnoughts we have no similar loss to set. The success, moreover, was achieved against forces which were considered superior. Our young navy has shown great superiority against the greatest fleet in the world.' The papers assert that the British losses represent more than 100,000 tons of big units, whereas the German losses amount to only 13,200 tons.

That day, the *Aberdeen Journal* opted for a similar tone by carrying an article, which after criticizing both the British and German communiqués, laments the British losses and then goes on to remind its readers of the vital, if largely unseen work being carried out by the Royal Navy. It concluded with the stirring statement that should the High Seas Fleet encounter the Grand Fleet at some time in the future it would meet the same fate as the Spanish and French fleets in times past:

The naval battle which took place off Jutland in the North Sea on Wednesday, resulting in the definite sinking of fourteen British warships—six cruisers and eight destroyers —is the greatest sea fight which has occurred between the British and German forces during the present war. Indeed, it is not only the greatest naval engagement, but it is the most costly that has yet befallen the British Fleet. By comparison with it, the Coronel coast disaster was a small affair, and the Dardanelles losses of insignificant importance. The British account is scrappy, and the German report is even less satisfactory, but it is evident that the German losses, although not greater in number of ships, were more serious in regard to the type of vessel that was sunk.

The enemy admits the loss of eleven vessels, including two Dreadnoughts and a battle cruiser. Roughly, our loss in tonnage is 115,000 tons, and the German tonnage loss is by no means light. The disparity against us in tonnage is unfortunate, and unhappily it carries with it the more melancholy loss of life entailed. How serious that loss evidently is may be gauged by the German report that there are only two survivors from the battle cruiser Indefatigable. During the past three days the country has been seething with rumours regarding a great engagement in the North Sea.

It was known that the Battle-cruiser Squadron had left its base, but as to the circumstances leading up to the fighting the Admiralty leaves the country in doubt in the meantime. It may be that our cruiser fleet was caught by the sudden emergence of the enemy battleships from the Heligoland area, or it may be that the enemy ships were enticed out, and that 'something happened' which led to the outgunning of the cruiser squadron before our Dreadnought Fleet were able give assistance. While the losses to our Fleet are distressing, it is unnecessary to be unduly disappointed.

As the Coronel coast disaster was speedily wiped out by the Falkland Islands victory, and the Scarborough baby-killing bombardment was followed by the sinking of the Blucher in an open fight, we may be sure the Jutland misadventure will in due season be retrieved in a battle, it may be hoped, in which the possibility of German retreat within its mined area will be impossible. The German naval strategy, so far, has been able, and not without skill, and the Jutland engagement warns us that neither on sea nor on land can the enemy be regarded lightly. When the full story of the fight comes out, the probability is that it may reveal even heavier losses on the German side than we have yet been allowed to know, but in any case our Navy is still strong enough to bear much heavier losses and hold the supremacy of the sea.

At the commencement of the war the aggregate naval superiority of the Allies was not less than four to one, and our superiority is proof against much heavier losses than we have yet sustained in battle, and by submarine, mine, and mishap. Our building programme, too, on Mr Churchill's assurance, has been going on at the rate of six tons to one ton by the enemy. Even taking into consideration the ex-First Lord of the Admiralty's tendency to extravagance, we know on official authority that at the outbreak of hostilities the Allies were building forty-one Dreadnoughts against six by Germany and Austria. Since the commencement of the war, however, Germany is understood to have greatly accelerated her shipping speed, and one naval authority has even contended that Germany could build twenty-five Dreadnoughts simultaneously. Germany, however, in the Jutland battle, however strong her Dreadnought squadron may now be, did not choose to give battle [against] our biggest ships. While admitting that our Battle cruiser Squadron had an uncomfortable experience on

Wednesday, we have every confidence that when the veil is lifted and the full story is told, it will show that British seamen have lost none of their ingenuity, skill, or bravery.

The luck of battle was against our cruiser fleet, which did not imitate the German plan of running away when discretion appears to be the better part of valour. Our Navy has not yet been challenged to definite stand-up fight by the German Fleet, although a large portion of the enemy ships were evidently engaged in Wednesday's battle. Nor must the stupendous work which the British Navy has done and is still doing in other spheres than that of fighting [be] forgotten in the disappointment at our loss of this week. From the English Channel to the Dardanelles, and from the Levant the Tigris, they have given our army generals supplies of men and, therefore, freedom of operation which otherwise they would not have possessed. It was the Fleet that secured the safe evacuation of Gallipoli, and that provided the new base at Salonika. It is the British Fleet that has ensured the Allies their munitions and other necessaries, and it is our Navy on which we depend for our existence in our Island home. Our seamen, in short, control the food supply of our civilian population at home, and, the fortunes of all our land forces. Napoleon a century ago remarked, 'Your marine is the real force your country, and one which, while you preserve it, will always render you powerful.' Our Navy may have its losses, but nothing has or is likely to happen to affect our confident belief that Germany's Fleet, if the opportunity arises, will yet meet the fate of the Spanish Armada and Napoleon's naval efforts.

The *Western Daily Press* of 3 June opted to tell the story of the Jutland battle using reports received from Danish merchant ships including *N.J. Fjord*, whose interception by two German torpedo-boats signalled the start of the action:

News has been received here of the naval action the North Sea. Early on Wednesday morning, fishermen from Thyboron, when about 45 miles out at sea, saw two Zeppelins and about ten warships. At four o'clock in the afternoon the steamer N. J. Fjord, which arrived from Leith at Fredrickshaven, yesterday, reported that 125 miles west of Hanstholm she was stopped and searched by a German destroyer. Four British destroyers appeared, and pursued the Germans. The steamer afterwards met four large and 30 small German warships going at full speed towards the British destroyers, at which they fired. Off the Skaw the steamer met two Zeppelins hurrying westwards.

Another report from Friedrikshaven states that the steamer N.J. Fjord was stopped by British torpedo boats, and as the mate was taking the papers for inspection five German Dreadnoughts and some cruisers and destroyers were sighted. The mate was ordered to return to his ship. About midnight a Zeppelin passed over the west coast of Jutland, going from north to south, and at six Thursday morning a Zeppelin and an aeroplane were sighted at Fano. Towards mid-day the Z 24 passed Sonderho towards Hielding, flying low, and apparently damaged. Off Naerre Lyngvig Ringkobing, a German destroyer sighted. She was damaged aft, and unable to move. In the afternoon she was towed south by another destroyer. Ten German destroyers passed through the Little Belt, proceeding slowly from north to south, on Thursday evening. A violent cannonade was heard along the west coast Jutland at Bovbjerg and Ringkobing from six o'clock Wednesday afternoon, and Fano from four to eight on Thursday morning. Fishermen of Esbverg who were off the Horn Rocks saw what they took to be British and German warships moving south. The atmosphere was misty.

Reports of the action were not published until to-day, as yesterday, being a holiday here, there were no evening papers. The steamer Naesburg has arrived from Sunderland. According to the captain's report, the action began between three and four on Wednesday afternoon. The Naesburg was 95 miles west-north-west Hanstholm, and saw a squadron of 45 warships, some of them very large, steering north-east. Suddenly fire was opened, and squadron turned south. Eleven warships approached from the north, and later eight more intervened in the action. The cannonade continued violently. Various sailing ships were sighted nearer the scene, one apparently in the middle of the fray. At seven o'clock [a] Zeppelin passed the Naesburg going north-westwards. The steamer Moskow has arrived from Newcastle. It passed through the same region Wednesday night, and saw 20 or 30 warships, and heard a violent cannonade, which decreased to the south. On Thursday morning the captain sighted ten warships off Jutland Bank steering east-north-east towards the Skagerrak. He thought the warships were German.

The same issue of the paper also contained a short piece noting that the German claim of victory initially had an adverse effect on the New York Stock Exchange:

On the stock market here a break of one to four points followed the announcement from Berlin of the naval battle in the North Sea, but later the statement from London of the facts started a rapid recovery. A good part of the losses were made up before the close.

In its leading article, entitled 'The Naval Fight', that day the *Western Daily Press* reminded its readers that:

> Month after month since the commencement of the war the British North Sea Fleet has maintained its vigil, and, although there have been occasional excitements and serious fighting on more than one occasion, the great work of the Navy has been done silently by the economic pressure it has been able to maintain. From time to time stories have been sent out from German sources that their Fleet has cruised in the North Sea, but been unable to find the enemy. Everyone has known what value to attach to such reports, for the absence of fighting has been due to the exercise by the foe of that discretion which is said to be the better part of valour. But at last, unexpectedly, an encounter on a large scale and of a desperate character has taken place, and while only the bare outlines of the story have been supplied by the British Admiralty, it is clear that a section of the British Fleet has suffered very severely, and that a deplorable loss has occurred in men and ships. A familiar phrase reminds us that it is impossible to make omelettes without cracking eggs.

After speculating about the relative strengths of the squadrons involved and the desperate nature of the fighting the editorial observes that:

> The British story, while lacking in details, indicates that the punishment inflicted on the enemy was far more severe. This probably the case, and in a telegram received late last night Rear-Admiral Stebbinghaus is said to have admitted that some of the German Fleet were considerably damaged. Our adversary is not accustomed to make the worst of matters of this kind, and the bald British announcement consequently appears worse by comparison. It is therefore all the more necessary to reserve judgment until the facts are more fully known. The inconsistency of the German statement appears on its face, and it will be only as the true story comes through by indirect channels that the nature of their loss will be ascertainable. Wednesday's naval battle the greatest that the war has produced, and, while the loss of life is a matter for the gravest regret, happily the British naval superiority is so pronounced that the sinking of the ships—serious although the number is—will not appreciably affect the situation.

Above: *Lion* leading the battlecruisers during the Battle of Jutland. By the end of the battle, *Lion* had been hit a total of fourteen times and suffered ninety-nine dead and fifty-one wounded. (Historic Military Press)

Below: The funeral pyre of *Queen Mary* during the Battle of Jutland. All but nine of her 1,266 crew were lost – two of the survivors were picked up by German ships. (Historic Military Press)

Above: Taken from the deck of *Inflexible*, the next ship astern, this picture shows the massive plume of smoke caused when *Invincible* exploded after she was hit five times by shells from the German battlecruisers *Derfflinger* and *Lützow* during the Battle of Jutland. (Historic Military Press)

Below: A salvo of heavy shells falling near the light cruiser *Birmingham*. (Author's Collection)

Above: *Invincible* photographed underway on 31 May 1916. (Author's Collection)

Below: *Invincible* blowing up after being hit amidships. This picture and a very similar one held by the Imperial War Museum may actually be fakes derived from the previous picture of *Invincible*. Faking was an easy, if time consuming task with the photographer 're-touching' on a print using inks ranging from black to white with the shades of grey in between. Once re-touched, the new picture was simply photographed to make a new negative. (Author's Collection)

Below: The bow and stern of *Invincible* sticking out of the water as the battlecruiser sinks. The destroyer *Badger* is desperately searching for survivors. (Author's Collection)

Above: A view of the starboard (engaged) side of the light cruiser *Southampton* after her return from the Battle of Jutland. Note the splinter damage to her hull and funnels. During the point-blank range encounter with Commodore Reuter's 4th Scouting Group at about 22.35 on 31 May 1916, *Southampton* was hit by twenty 4.1-inch and 5.9-inch shells which knocked out three of her guns and two searchlights as well as destroying her radio. The action lasted for about 3½ minutes during which time thirty-five of her crew were killed and forty-one wounded. A torpedo fired from one of *Southampton*'s submerged torpedo tubes sank the old German cruiser *Frauenlob*. (Author's Collection)

Below: *Royal Oak, Acasta, Benbow, Superb* and *Canada* in action during the battle. *Canada* fired forty-two shells from her 14-inch guns and 109 6-inch shells during the battle. She suffered no hits or casualties. Amongst the targets engaged was the cruiser *Wiesbaden*. (Historic Military Press)

Above: A pre-war view of the forward 13.5-inch guns of the battlecruiser *Queen Mary*. The Royal Navy's adoption of 13.5-inch and 15-inch guns gave it a huge advantage over its German opponents which was squandered by faulty shells. However, despite their shortcomings these heavy shells caused massive damage to German battlecruisers and battleships during the Battle of Jutland. (Author's Collection)

Below: 'Birthday presents for Kaiser Bill' – new 15-inch shells aboard the battlecruiser *Renown* in 1918. These 'Greenboy' shells, issued to the Grand Fleet in 1918, would have inflicted lethal damage to the battlecruisers and battleships of the High Seas Fleet as was shown at Mers el Kebir on 3 July 1940. (Author's Collection)

Above: The four Super-Dreadnoughts of the Orion-class comprised the Royal Navy's 2nd Division of the 2nd Battle Squadron at the Battle of Jutland, 31 May 1916 to 1 June 1916. (Historic Military Press)

Below: Beatty's flagship *Lion* pictured at Rosyth in 1917 along with two 15-inch gun armed Queen Elizabeth-class battleships of the 5th Battle Squadron. The latter's excellent shooting inflicted heavy damage on the German battlecruisers and the modern battleships of the 3rd Battle Squadron. (Author's Collection)

Above: *Indefatigable* sinking on 31 May 1916. (Author's Collection)

Above: An aerial view of the battlecruiser *Inflexible* in the Firth of Forth in 1918. Note the awkward arrangement of 'P' and 'Q' turrets amidships and the aircraft on the turret tops. (Author's Collection)

Below: An amidships view of *Lion* in June 1916. Note that the 'Q' Turret has been landed for repair. (Author's Collection)

Above: The newly completed destroyer *Narborough* and other destroyers awaiting orders to attack. (Author's Collection)

Below: The crippled destroyer *Spitfire* after her return from the battle. Note the damage to her bows which was caused by collision with the German battleship *Nassau*. The damage to *Spitfire*'s bridge and fore-funnel was caused by *Nassau*'s 11-inch guns. (Author's Collection)

Below: Rear Admiral Arbuthnot's flagship *Defence*, which was armed with four 9.2-inch guns in two twin turrets and ten single 7.5-inch guns, got too close to the High Seas Fleet's battleships and was heavily hit. She blew up and there were no survivors. (World Ship Society; Abrahams Collection)

Above: The Arethusa-class light cruiser *Phaeton* (seen here) and her sister *Galatea* investigated a cloud of smoke and steam rising from the Danish steamer *N.J. Fjord*, which had been stopped by two German torpedo boats, and in so doing sighted cruisers and destroyers belonging to Hipper's 1st Scouting Group. (Author's Collection)

Below: *Black Prince*. At about 00.10 on 1 June the armoured cruiser *Black Prince* strayed too close to the German battleships. The latter raked the cruiser from stem to stern causing a massive explosion and loss of all 857 of *Black Prince's* complement. (World Ship Society; Abrahams Collection)

Above: The newly commissioned light cruiser *Chester*, which was armed with ten 5.5-inch guns, survived an ambush by Bödicker's light cruiser squadron. Chester's young and inexperienced crew displayed great courage and determination under fire with Boy First Class Jack Cornwell being awarded a posthumous Victoria Cross. (Author's Collection)

Below: The 25-knot light cruiser *Southampton*, which was Commodore Goodenough's flagship at Jutland, was armed with eight 6-inch guns. Goodenough's 2nd Light Cruiser Squadron was the only one of the British cruiser squadrons which fulfilled its expected scouting duties. (Author's Collection)

Below: The armoured cruiser *Warrior* was a half-sister to *Black Prince*, being armed with six single 9.2-inch and four single 7.5-inch guns. She was badly damaged by gunfire from German battleships and sank the following morning. (World Ship Society; Abrahams Collection)

Above: *Iron Duke* serving as a gunnery training ship in 1937. Note the prototype 5.25-inch Dual-Purpose gun mounting on 'Y' Barbette. (Author's Collection)

Below: The newly completed *Iron Duke* in dock in 1913. (World Ship Society)

Above: The destroyer HMS *Fortune* in 1914. British destroyers were painted black which made them particularly visible during night actions, especially if combined with substandard black-out procedures. (World Ship Society)

Below: The battlecruiser *Tiger*, pictured here in 1915, was the most heavily hit British battlecruiser and demonstrated that these ships were every bit as tough as their German counterparts once safe magazine practices were adopted. Despite being hit by fifteen 11-inch shells, *Tiger* was ready for action, if required, two days after the battle. (World Ship Society)

Above: The DFDS steamer *N.J. Fjord* whose interception by two German torpedo boats triggered the Battle of Jutland. (DFDS)

Below: The newly completed battlecruiser *Renown* in 1916. The double row of scuttles betrays the absence of side armour above the main deck and led Jellicoe to insist that these ships be given additional protection over their magazines thereby delaying their entry into service. In reality the magazines of *Renown* and her sister *Repulse* were not vulnerable to plunging fire from German shells of the period. The Director of Naval Construction was confident that both ships were entirely battle-worthy as completed once safe cordite handling procedures had been adopted. (World Ship Society; Abrahams Collection)

Above: The destroyer *Ardent* at sea in 1914. (World Ship Society)

Below: The flotilla leader *Turbulent* was savaged by the German battleship *Westfalen*'s port 5.9-inch gun battery during the night action. (World Ship Society)

Above: The 'M' class destroyer *Nestor* on trials. (World Ship Society)

Above: The battleship *Erin* in 1918. Note the bearing markings on 'B' and 'X' turrets and the regrouped searchlights around the after funnel. (World Ship Society; Abrahams Collection)

Below: The Queen Elizabeth-class fast battleship *Valiant* in 1915-16. (World Ship Society)

Above: A pre-war view of the destroyer *Shark*. (World Ship Society)

Above: The battleship *Marlborough* in 1918 showing bearing markings on 'B' and 'X' turrets, flying-off platforms on 'B' and 'Q' turrets and regrouped searchlights on the after funnel. (Author's Collection)

Below: A mid-war view of the battlecruiser *New Zealand*. (Author's Collection)

On 4 June the tone of British Press reporting about the Battle of Jutland changed when the *Weekly Despatch* ran a highly critical leading article entitled 'The Lesson of it all' in which it expressed the disillusionment of a nation brought up to believe in the invincibility of British naval power and the expectation of a second Trafalgar:

> We have learned to trust the Fleet. We have bestowed our increasing millions ungrudgingly upon it, built for it the ships it wanted and as many as it wanted, provided it with every artifice of modern science that could increase its efficiency, and trained for its service a personnel unequalled in the world for its courage and competence.
>
> Then what went wrong last week? It is no use to try and deceive ourselves that there was nothing wrong.
>
> The Germans succeeded in giving battle to a part of the Fleet with their full strength … And then returned to their ports before our main fleet could force a decisive action …
>
> The sorrow that we feel at the loss of so many brave men and such fine ships is not relieved by the thought that we had the opportunity, had our dispositions been correct, to bring about a decisive naval battle in which the advantage, because of our superior strength, would have been on our side.
>
> Why did we fail? Why were the Germans able so to dispose their forces as to be able to attack when our battle-cruisers were unsupported, and to retire comparatively unscathed when the 15-inch guns came up?
>
> The answer in one word – Zeppelins.
>
> The fight itself was mismanaged … The battle-cruiser is venturesome ship, and our battle-cruisers are under a venturesome commander – more power to him. But those responsible seem to forget that that the Germans can see when we are blind, otherwise they could never have so disposed their forces as to leave the cruisers to withstand the attack of the entire German fleet alone …
>
> It is not what we expect. Nor after the disaster of Coronel, do we expect our ships to be caught between the enemy and the sunset, leaving themselves silhouetted and their foes enshrouded. Nor when we have armed ships with better, heavier and longer-reaching guns than the enemy possess do we expect these costly and valuable advantages to be thrown away by engaging in close action.
>
> We want practical seamen at the head of affairs … Put Fisher in his right place at the head of the Admiralty. Bring Jellicoe down to Whitehall with the wisdom of twenty-two months' war and let him advise his old chief out of his hard-earned knowledge.

> Give the Fleet over to younger men. Beatty would need no instruction in its handling, nor would Madden, Jellicoe's Chief of Staff.

The content of this leader suggests that the writer may have been privy to information from a participant in the battle not least because Jellicoe's despatches had not then been released. Jellicoe was most displeased with the article observing that it was 'most hurtful to discipline and morale and discouraging to the officers and men of the fleet' and consequently wrote to the Admiralty on 6 June requesting that 'immediate steps be taken to prevent publication of such statements'.[3]

By 5 June more information had been made available from British sources and consequently, *The Times* was able to report that:

> The fuller accounts of the great naval battle which reach us to-day confirm, the conclusions we drew from the communiques of Saturday. We have suffered heavy losses in men and in ships, but after this, the most terrible action ever fought, our command of the seas is unimpaired. That is the one all-important fact which is past dispute. The German newspapers loudly vaunt the 'victory' which they claim to have won but where are the fruits of their victory? They are limited to our losses on the field of battle – from which the High Sea Fleet precipitately retired so soon as Sir John JELLICOE'S ships came up.
>
> We know now that the British Admiral swept the scene of action backwards and forwards all Thursday morning and found no foe to encounter him. He then steamed leisurely homeward. Our main Fleet is again ready for action; our blockade is intact; our transports and our merchant vessels pass and repass as before. Broad facts like these speak for themselves, and from all Allied and neutral countries comes proof that they are understood. The public abroad are already asking the obvious questions why the Germans hurried back to their base, and why they have not broken through the blockade of which they complain with so much bitterness, if their encounter with Sir David Beatty and Sir John JELLICOE has really filled them with the confidence they profess.
>
> The Dutch and the Danes, nations with a long experience of seamanship hundreds of years before Prussia was heard of in European politics, have seen through the German claims at once. So has prosaic Wall Street. So, too, have our French and Russian Allies. To many Frenchmen, our Paris Correspondent tells us, this battle has brought home for the first time how great is the price that England pays to insure the mastery of the seas for the common cause, and it

has led them, he adds, to appreciate the significance of that mastery. Questions of the same kind must presently suggest themselves to the reflective German intellect.

Obviously much more must be learned before anything even approaching a final judgment in this immense conflict can be formed. We have nothing like full and authentic reports of the fighting itself or of the circumstances which led up to it, and we cannot congratulate the Admiralty on the way in which they have given us such reports as we have. The first *communiqué*, issued on Friday evening, had an effect which was unduly depressing – not at all because it was untrue, but because it gave only one side of the picture, the side of the heavy British losses. We do not complain of this, because we attribute it to a frankness and honesty which have not always been shown by the Government in dealing with the public. The second *communiqué*, issued in the early hours of Saturday morning, was admittedly but an estimate of the German losses, and an estimate from the nature of things cannot be so trustworthy as a report. Certain obvious attempts were then made to set them against each other, and these culminated in many quarters during Saturday in a ridiculous 'balance sheet' which included all the German ships believed to have been hit or disabled, while it excluded all British ships except those actually sunk.

Next, well had MR. CHURCHILL [been] allowed to issue an appreciation of the action through the official Press Bureau, after seeing the reports of the Admirals and having access to other Admiralty information, while we had no appreciation at all from the Admiralty themselves. We do not challenge his conclusions; but surely this use of MR. CHURCHILL – who has no association whatever with the Government, who apparently aspires at this moment to lead an Opposition, and whose strategical utterances during the war have hardly been models of accuracy – was the most amazing confession of weakness on the part of the Admiralty?

Finally, at a late hour last night, came a third official *communiqué* which gave a still higher estimate of German losses. The present position is that the Admiralty have 'the strongest ground for supposing' that the German losses are not merely relatively, but absolutely, heavier than our own. We trust it may be so, but there are signs of a certain official anxiety to counteract the supposed effects of their first blunt announcement.

We look forward anxiously to the evidence in SIR JOHN JELLICOE'S 'full dispatch'. Meanwhile, first-hand accounts from individual ships are beginning to reach the public direct, and there is one feature in this action, on which all witnesses agree, that will be read with boundless pride and gratitude by the nation. Our sailors fought with a coolness, a daring, and a dauntless endurance unsurpassed in all the glorious annals of our naval wars.

Astonishing stories, in particular, are told of the audacity displayed by the destroyers. They were intended to sacrifice themselves in order to protect the larger vessels, and they made the sacrifice with a magnificent alacrity. Whether an excess of this fine spirit has not been shown in the higher command, where it may become a fault, is a matter which remains to be judged. Impetuous valour in the first attack, at sea as on land, is bound to be robbed of its fruits if the supports and reserves are not in place. With our present information there is an inevitable impression that the course of the action reveals a certain want of cohesion and of cleverness, coupled with over-confidence in protracting the fight against the battleships of the German High Sea Fleet before SIR JOHN JELLICOE could come up. We may pay tribute to the heroism of our men, and fairly claim our continued mastery of the seas, without going to the new extreme of being satisfied that all went as it should have gone. There are clearly many lessons on technical points – on gunfire, for instance, on armament, and on torpedoes – to be learned from this unprecedented conflict between fleets of the most modern ships of war. It is as yet too soon even to suggest what these lessons may be, but there seems no question about the teaching of the battle of Jutland in regard to combined action by sea and air. The Germans, with their Zeppelins, had 'eyes', and we had none.

What we have to do now is to take to heart, not only these technical lessons, but also the larger lessons of this tremendous battle. It has cost us dear, but the net outcome is plain. The Germans, in the words of the gracious message which our SAILOR-KING has addressed to ADMIRAL JELLICOE and the Grand Fleet. 'have robbed us of the opportunity of gaining a decisive victory' by retiring as soon as the general engagement began. But our hold of the sea is unshaken, the discipline and spirit of our sailors have never stood higher, and SIR JOHN JELLICOE was again ready to put to sea on the evening of June 2. When will the Germans be ready to meet him?

In contrast, however, the *Daily Mirror* of 5 June picked up the critical and questioning tone developed the previous day by the *Weekly Despatch* and in an article under the headline 'Questions':

THE mood of the country, during this last week-end, was, we think, one of complete mystification in regard to the action off the Jutland coast. Needless to say, the usual experts [were] swiftly mobilised into explanations. But who, at this stage in the war, pays the slightest heed to the always refuted expert? Meanwhile, the first Admiralty message was a bald statement of our great losses. That being so, people asked themselves and one another the following inevitable questions:—

1. Is it possible that the action and its result represent a false strategical move, symptomatic of a new policy, inspired by the silly superstition that the Fleet has till now not been doing enough to win the war? Mr. Balfour's regrettable Lowestoft letter led us to suppose that such new policy might be instituted. We can only say that, if it is so, it is lamentable. The country trusts Sir John Jellicoe. The country knows that he has hitherto done all and more than all that could have been expected of him. No new policy is needed in the Navy. The Navy all through, in regard to the blockade, has been hampered by Whitehall. There is where new policy is needed. The Declaration of London and other imbecilities required reform—not the strategy of the British Fleet. In the midst of our ignorance, that is the first question.

2. The second is; Why are we hampered by the low visibility of the German Fleet? Mist storm or sunshine are conditions that affect them as they affect us. Why then do they suffer less from them? The answer presumably is: We lack Zeppelins. Before the war, in our incurable aversion from new ideas, we sneered at Zeppelins. As sea scouts they are invaluable. Where are our Zeppelins? Here again—too late. The seaplane, so unwieldy in getting at sea, is no substitute. The wide radius of action, and the greater control of the Zeppelin make it far and away superior for observation purposes. For aided low by visibility in the Admiralty report, then, may we substitute aided by expert stupidity extending over a term of years in England?

3. The third question that many bereaved but brave people asked was in the nature of a supplication, a hope, that the Admiralty will refrain from excuses, and official people from the absurdity of trying to pretend that have won big victory disguise. Nothing can so blind a long deluded public this humbug. To say that the German Fleet would have been utterly defeated had ours come up in time is to say that we should have won had they not won; [to] say that the German Fleet turned tail and ran after achieving its object —the Object of all naval battles—in sinking many of the finest of our ships is to say with truly fatuous complacency that they did what they should have done, in Escaping safely instead of staying to get Sunk. Lastly it remains to be said—on the good doubtful side—that the German enterprise, whatever it may have been, was obviously countered, at great cost, by our Intervention. What was that enterprise? Was the countering worth

the cost? Those final questions can only be answered when know more.

Meanwhile German versions of the battle continued to appear in the Dutch and Danish Press and these stories made their way into the columns of papers such as the *Daily Mirror* which on 6 June carried two such accounts. The first, from a Dutch source via Reuter's, ended with a grossly exaggerated claim of success during the night fighting:

NAVAL BATTLE THROUGH GERMAN GLASSES.
Embroidered Story a Fight Against Odds.
Amsterdam, Monday [5 June].
The following semi-official description of the naval battle, in addition to what has already been published in the official telegrams, has been issued in Berlin: 'At 4.30 Wednesday afternoon some seventy miles off the Skagerrak four small cruisers of the Calliope class were sighted by our cruisers. The latter at once pursued the enemy, who ran away with all speed. At 5.20 our cruisers sighted in the west two enemy columns, consisting of six battle cruisers and a large number of small cruisers. The enemy turned towards the south.

During the battle two British battle cruisers and one destroyer were destroyed. After half an hour's fighting more powerful enemy forces were sighted north of the enemy columns. Soon afterwards the German main force entered the fight. The enemy at once turned to the north, and the five [only four present] vessels of the Queen Elizabeth class followed the English battlecruisers. The enemy attempted to evade our extremely effective fire by assuming echelon formation, trying thereby an eastern course to overtake our advanced end. Our fleet followed at top speed the movements of the enemy. In the course of this phase of the fighting one cruiser of the Achilles or Shannon class and two destroyers were destroyed.

The battle against superior British forces lasted until darkness fell. Besides numerous light forces, at least twenty-five British battleships, six battle cruisers and at least four armoured cruisers were engaged against sixteen German battleships, five battle cruisers, six older ships of the line and no armoured cruisers. After dark our flotilla opened a night attack. During the night cruiser engagements and numerous torpedo boat attacks took place, resulting in the destruction of one battle cruiser, one cruiser of the Achilles or Shannon class, one and probably two small cruisers, and at least ten destroyers.'

The second article from a Danish newspaper describes the loss of the

German torpedo-boat *V 84* from the viewpoint of some of her survivors:

GRAPHIC STORY BY GERMAN SURVIVORS.
Battle Was a Confusion of Ships. Bursting Shells and Smoke.
Copenhagen, Monday [5 June]
The Stiftstidends of Aarhus, Jutland, publishes an interview with the three German sailors brought into that port by the Swedish steamer Para. The men, who belonged to the destroyer V 84, state that a German fleet consisting of about fifty ships, large and small, left the ports of Cuxhaven and Wilhelmshaven as early as Monday last. In the evening of Wednesday last six British destroyers were observed. Shortly afterwards British cruiser squadron made its appearance, and, one of the men said : 'very short time there seemed to be nothing but a hell like confusion of ships, bursting shells, thundering guns and smoke.' This opening part of the battle took place in the north eastern area of the North Sea. The V 84 took part in it for only half an hour, at the end of which time she was split in two a shell from a cruiser. An explosion followed, which hurled the destroyer's commander 60ft. into the air, and within a couple minutes the ship went down with 102 men. By this time about sixty or seventy ships on either side were engaged, the Germans also having received reinforcements. Of the crew of the V 84 twenty-eight men succeeded in reaching some rafts, but during the night all of them disappeared except the three rescued by the Para. These said that they passed a terrible night. The sea was continually sweeping the rafts. There was a cannonade around them all the time, and from the water came the screams of wounded and drowning men. They saw one after another go down, unable to hold out any longer.

By now, accounts from British participants at Jutland were beginning to emerge and these, together with a natural scepticism bred from a long-experience of official communiqués, meant that the world's Press were beginning to challenge the initial German statements.

In particular, there was a growing belief that the Germans had not revealed all their losses or the extent of the damage sustained by the High Seas Fleet. For example, on 6 June the *Daily Mirror* also carried two articles which challenged the German communiqué of 2 June:

GERMANY HIDING HER NAVAL LOSSES
Berlin Keeps Secret Second Report of Battle
More Lies About our Ships

SEYDLITZ SEEN IN A SINKING STATE.
German Survivors' Vivid Stories of the Great Fight British Sailors Believe Foe Lost 22 Ships. Berlin, according to a message from Rome, has received second report of Germany's losses in the great naval battle, which is being kept secret. It is significant, too, that no visitors to Wilhelmshaven will be allowed for some months.

Messages from the East Coast say that returned sailors are confident that the Germans lost not less than 22 vessels. The Admiralty have already announced 18 against 14 lost by us. Reports that came to hand yesterday from merchant ships tell of the sinking of the huge German super-Dreadnought Hindenburg[4] and of the pursuit by British ships of the badly mauled German battle-cruiser Seydlitz.

The Germans have now stated that May 31 they submarined a British destroyer off the Humber, and that in the great battle the Euryalus was sunk. Both these statements are lies.

The first story of the battle from German survivors has been received from men who were on the V 28. They make an interesting statement to the effect that the German Fleet was out two days before the battle occurred. Germany's great naval victory was short lived. In spite of all the efforts of her great statesmen and publicists, the world remains profoundly unimpressed.

The command of the North Sea continues in the hands of the British, and this is the fact which tells with all other countries. According to a statement issued by Reuter's Agency, the German Fleet came out in a real attempt to break the blockade, being forced thereto by growing discontent caused by the pressure of British sea supremacy.

The second report derived from Danish sources further developed the theme that the some of the High Seas Fleet had received a severe mauling:

SECOND GERMAN REPORT KEPT A SECRET.
Wilhelmshaven Governor's Drastic Step to Hide Losses and Damage. Rome, Monday.—According to reliable information which has come to hand, Germany has received a second report regarding the losses she sustained during the night of the North Sea battle. This report is being kept secret.—Wireless Press. Copenhagen, Monday.—The Wilhelmshavener Zeitung contains a significant and prominent announcement in big type signed by the governor of the fortress of Wilhelmshaven. It informs the public that permission for temporary

visits to the town will only be granted in cases of the utmost urgency during the next few months, and that written applications must be sent to the police beforehand.—Reuter. Copenhagen, Monday.— Scandinavian steamers have saved number of Germans from the warship Wiesbaden German mariners report that their losses were colossal. The German sailors say that several of their torpedo-boats and submarines were completely capsized-by British shells. — Exchange.

An article in the *Aberdeen Journal* of Tuesday, 6 June discussed the Germans as naval opponents, castigated the author of the first British report before reminding its readers that the criticism expressed in the British Press would be good for German morale:

JUTLAND SIDE-THOUGHTS.

The Germans have issued a semi-official version of the Battle of Jutland, which, however, they seem to regard as the Battle of Skagerrack, and the public is anxiously awaiting Admiral Jellicoe's account of the fighting. There are many points still to be cleared up before the public can arrive at a definite understanding of the significance of the fight.

The idea that the result of the combat was a British reverse is undoubtedly difficult to eradicate from the public mind, although they know that the command of the sea belongs to Great Britain not one whit less than it did on the 30th of May. If singeing his Britannic Majesty's beard meant victory the Germans might claim victory, but as the British Fleet remained on the scene of the battle at the close, after forcing the enemy to flee, Jellicoe thus won the day. The naval engagements the war in which the Fleets or portions of the Fleets have met are the Battle of the Bight and the Battle of Jutland, and in each case the Germans have admittedly proved worthy of their masters. The German Navy is modelled on that of Britain. The British have taught the Germans how to fight at sea, and the British seamen concede the skill and the courage of the Teutons. The Hun seaman, in spite of the submarine campaign, with its dastardly attacks on unoffending fishermen, is not an unclean fighter, like his land brother, but while he may dispute, the sovereignty of the sea with Britannia, he will require to try a fight to the finish, and be in at the end, before drawing conclusions for the consolation his own and the consumption of neutral peoples.

Nelson himself admitted that anything may happen in a sea fight, and the unexpected happened on the 31st of May, but, the Press

Bureau hints in a communication which we publish to-day, that does not warrant certain London Liberal newspapers from calling for complete re-arrangement of the Admiralty and the Naval headquarters staff.

Whoever drew up the first British report has certainly good deal to answer for, but, after all, we have not come to the stage when we call for the head of a Department because he told the truth too bluntly to the people, and failed to make out the enemy's losses worse than knew them to be at the time. Yet, notwithstanding the fact that the position at sea is unaffected by the Battle of Jutland, there are critics who are now calling for the retirement of Mr Balfour from the Admiralty, and Sir John Jackson from the position First Sea Lord.

In their place they would put Lord Fisher, whose ability and genius very few question, and Sir John Jellicoe, and while re-arranging the Naval heads in Whitehall, they are equally prepared to rearrange the high commands at sea. Every word of criticism will no doubt be gulped up as greedily as a good meal in Germany, and is greatly to be deplored. If bricks are to be hurtled about this particular moment, it might be better to concentrate on a certain War Minister who some half-a-dozen years ago 'forgot the air,' and declined to think of Zeppelins.

By 7 June, with no new information available, newspapers such as the *Nottingham Evening Post* felt able to discuss issues Zeppelins and the use of gas shells:

There is nothing that is fresh concerning the North Sea battle, and it now seems that ten days may elapse before Admiral Jellicoe's report comes to hand. With regard to the rumoured participation of enemy aircraft [in] the battle, it is now known that Zeppelins took no important part in the action, and that probably not more than one, or perhaps two, were present. Further, it is pointed out that even the German communique makes no claim in this particular. There is stated to be not a word of truth in the report that a Zeppelin dropped on the Queen Mary and was wrecked with her. As to the reported use of gas, there were poisonings, but these were probably due to the ordinary effects of explosive shells. It is not regarded likely that asphyxiating shells were employed.

On 8 June the *Daily Mirror* reported a major speech given by the First Lord of the Admiralty to the British Imperial Council of Commerce at the Cannon Street Hotel under the headline 'The "Whole Truth" of the Naval Fight – Mr Balfour's Striking Defence of Admiralty Bulletin':

> 'There is no doubt whatever that we have told the truth and the whole truth. No attempt has been made to conceal any facts with regard to the losses of our ships.' Thus spoke Mr Balfour, the First Lord of the Admiralty, yesterday in an important speech on the recent naval battle.

After outlining the difficulties faced by Admiral Jellicoe in the compilation of his eagerly-awaited despatches, Mr Balfour addressed the criticism directed against the Admiralty communiqués saying that 'he was entirely responsible for all that was done and he did not know what other course could have been pursued.' Turning to the German claims of victory he observed:

> If it is true that the German Fleet had met the British Fleet and really inflicted defeat upon it according to the German account, and had inflicted this great loss, how was it that the next thing they did not do was to improve the occasion, and complete the discomfiture of a beaten foe – how comes it that their next procedure was to rush off when the main battle fleet under Admiral Jellicoe appears on the scene?

Balfour completed his address by discussing the possibility of a German invasion of the United Kingdom pointing out that one outcome of the Battle of Jutland was the elimination of this prospect:

> 'The German Headquarters Staff knew they could not meet our fleet on even terms, and the Germans were not to be blamed for withdrawing when Admiral Jellicoe's fleet came up. As all inferior foes must withdraw, the Germans were relatively far inferior now to what they were before the battle. Neither in the North Sea nor the Baltic could they for many months attempt any kind of organised fleet effort which might have been within their power before the battle. We had not merely carried off the honours of the day, but had carried off the substantial fruits.'
>
> In conclusion Mr Balfour said if any 'man seriously entertained the view that invasion was possible, did he not now regard it one of the many unfulfilled dreams which the war has dissipated for ever?'

Immediately beneath the account of Balfour's address there appeared a report showing one of the consequences of the British blockade imposed by the power of the Grand Fleet on German maritime trade:

LESS GERMAN MEAT.
Drastic Regulations for Controlling the Huns' Diet.
Berne, Wednesday.—
Drastic new regulations regarding the consumption of meat for the whole country came into force in Germany today. Henceforth the proprietors of hotels, restaurants, and all public eating houses are forbidden to offer to their clients the choice of more than two meat dishes in any one meal. The amount of meat permissible in a portion will be fixed from week to week. The huge dinners eaten at all restaurants all over, many often comprising four or five meat courses, must now disappear.

The reality was, that irrespective of having suffered greater losses in both men and materiel during the Battle of Jutland, British control of the sea communications remained unimpaired and consequently, the German war machine and its people were being starved of the resources to wage a successful war against the Allies.

The situation was summed up succinctly by one newspaper just four days after the battle:

Will the flag-waving German people get any more of the copper, rubber and cotton their government so sorely needs? Not by a pound. Will meat and butter be cheaper in Berlin? Not by a pfennig. There is one test, and only one, of victory. Who held the field of battle at the end of the fight?[5]

German Lies Exposed

The revised bulletin was issued on 8 June and circulated rapidly round Europe and North America where the belated admission of these losses had an adverse effect on German credibility and their propaganda effort.

The German claim to victory was based on a simple calculation, namely that fourteen British ships of 111,000 tons had been lost as against eleven German totalling 62,000 tons.

From a British perspective the loss of three obsolete, slow, vulnerable armoured cruisers was irrelevant because by 1916 they were little more than a relict species which could neither fight nor run away. The loss of three battlecruisers was potentially more serious although, it was appreciated that both *Invincible* and *Indefatigable* were first generation ships which had become outclassed by more modern construction and would be replaced by the 15-inch gun-armed *Renown* and *Repulse* within a matter of months.

In comparison, *Queen Mary* was a relatively new and much more powerful ship than either *Invincible* or *Indefatigable* and there was no replacement under construction. Despite these losses, by the end of 1916, the British Battle Cruiser Fleet would still outnumber their German counterparts by 9:5 having started the 1916 with ten ships to the German five.

The Germans Issue a Revised Communiqué

For about a week after the battle, the Germans had not admitted losing the brand new battlecruiser *Lützow* which was, by far, the most powerful ship lost by either side. They had also lost three modern light cruisers which they could ill-afford including *Rostock* whose loss was not admitted.

However, information filtering out of Germany through neutral nations meant that their initial communiqué had to be amended to include these losses. The revised bulletin was issued on 8 June and circulated rapidly round Europe and North America where the belated admission of these losses had an adverse effect on German credibility and their propaganda effort.

The British Press Response

The relieved British Press took full advantage of the German public relations blunder with the *Daily Mirror* of Friday, 9 June reporting the under banner headlines:

> GERMANS ADMIT TO 28,000-ton Cruiser Founders on Her Way to Harbour. ROSTOCK ALSO LOST.
> Berlin Says News Was 'Withheld for Military Reasons.'
> WARSPITE LIE REPEATED.
> Germany has issued a new official account the battle, in which it breaks the news gently to its cheering millions that their new 28,000 ton Dreadnought cruiser *Lützow* and the light cruiser *Rostock* were sunk on their way to harbour after the battle. 'For military reasons we refrained till now,' says this latest made-in-Germany story 'from making public the loss of the vessels *Lützow* and *Rostock*.' In announcing their loss Berlin once again claims that the Warspite and other ships were sunk, and once again the Admiralty have issued emphatic denial. President Poincare has sent message congratulation to the King on 'the happy results of the success achieved' in the Jutland battle, and the Japanese Minister of Marine has sent a congratulatory telegram to the Secretary of the Admiralty.
> SHIPS LOST ON THEIR WAY TO HARBOUR.
> Germans' First Admission Loss of *Lützow* and *Rostock*. For military reasons we refrained till now from making public the loss of the vessels Lützow and Rostock is the amusing manner in which Berlin announces the loss of those ships for the first time. The official German communique goes to say that, in view the wrong interpretation of this measure, and, moreover, in order to frustrate English legends about gigantic losses on our side, these reasons must now be dropped. Both vessels were lost on their way to the harbour after attempts had failed to keep the heavily damaged vessels afloat. The crews of both ships, including all severely wounded, are in safety. While the German list of losses is hereby closed, positive indications are to hand that the actual British losses are materially higher than established and made public.

In the same edition the *Daily Mirror* was able to give its British readers a feel for the changed reaction in neutral Europe following the release of the revised German bulletin:

> The whole of Holland is laughing at the German communique which stated that for military reasons the biggest losses of the German Fleet in last week's naval battle had been concealed.
>
> By keeping the loss of the *Lützow* secret Germany, instead of influencing neutrals in her favour, has furnished neutrals with the best proof of the scope of the British victory. It goes without saying that no credence will now be attached by them to any further German statement.

On 9 June *The Times* published a letter to the Editor from retired Rear Admiral S. Eardley-Wilmot RN[1] who, on 24 April 1891, had been appointed to revise the Gunnery Manual and other handbooks under the Director of Naval Ordnance and Torpedoes:

> Sir, - Until the publication of the official dispatches dealing with the recent action in the North Sea it is not possible to arrive at any accurate conclusion as to the result of this tremendous conflict. It is not only a question of respective losses – however great and grievous – but the bearing this meeting of the two opposing Fleets has upon the general issue of the war. So far we can only say that the German Fleet put to sea in great strength with some definite object, which could hardly be merely exercise, and returned to port with a heavy list of casualties and defects.
>
> Whether the intention was to endeavour to break through the blockade and reach the Atlantic, or to bid for naval supremacy in the North Sea, failure resulted on either assumption. A victorious fleet is not usually the first to quit the scene of action. The German admiral will probably strenuously deny that he ran away when our main Fleet appeared. Let us concede, then, that he only went as fast as possible in the opposite direction and this took him to his own ports!
>
> To me the incident is significant of the condition on land. I expressed an opinion 18 months ago that when affairs began to look hopeless for Germany on land – where she looked for a successful issue – only then would her main fleet be sent out – the reason being obvious. Whether this so-called victory will encourage her to try again after refitting remains to be seen, but it is very satisfactory to hear from the Gunnery Officer you quote that our guns and their handling leave little to be desired. Also, that the big calibre justified its existence.

In an article entitled 'The Jutland Battle' the *Aberdeen Weekly Journal* of 9 June observed that 'Our sea victory is no longer doubted' and then went on to discuss the German motives behind taking the High Seas Fleet to sea speculating that they may have wanted to break through the blockade, bombard the British coast or even launch an invasion.

The paper then turned to consideration of the Admiralty's original communiqué observing:

> With noteworthy unanimity, the Admiralty is being scolded for the tenor its original announcement. Everybody knows this time what an erroneous impression it gave. It has been characterised as 'ambiguous', 'unfortunate', 'baselessly depressing', and 'an apology for defeat'. Truth, partial though it was, is admitted, and by many people admired. It was the phraseology that was at fault. 'Written without focus,' says one critic. The whole question is one of the form in which the facts were related is suggested that in the absence fuller news it would have sufficed announce the battle and say that the Germans had been driven back into harbour.
> BATTLE NAME WANTED.
> What should we call the Battle? The query is one which is solving itself for the moment. Common usage it is becoming known Battle of Jutland. I fancy that is because Jutland was the place mentioned in the Admiralty communique. But will official history know it such that is a moot point. In all their reports the Germans allude to the Battle the Skager Rack. It may be that long after peace returns the histories the two nations may continue to differ their nomenclature.

The *Daily Mirror* of 10 June wondered why the Germans had both lied and made such extravagant boasts of naval victory using material supplied to a Dutch newspaper by its Cologne correspondent:

> German Boasts of Naval Victory Made to Impress the World. German papers reproduce the latest official admission by the German Admiralty the loss of the *Lutzow* and the *Rostock* without any comments. Amsterdam, Friday.—*The Tyd* has received from its Cologne correspondent an account of the battle of Jutland, showing how the battle is really regarded in German naval circles. One of the correspondent's friends, who participated in the battle and who was later in position to learn more about it, gave it as his opinion that the engagement's great significance lay in the fact that the German Fleet had not been beaten by the British. The boasting in some papers of a

brilliant victory off Jutland and the extravagant jubilation over the event and the unmeasured language of even high-placed Government officials were the result of a desire to maintain at abroad and home the belief in German strength rather than of love of truth.

By 12 June enough information from participants in the battle had become available for British newspapers to undertake a detailed refutation of some of the German claims.

The *Western Times* was one such publication and was able to publish evidence that the battleship *Warspite* was still very much afloat despite claims to the contrary:

THE JUTLAND BATTLE.
'Unsuccessful Submarine Attack on the Falmouth'.
GERMAN LIES NAILED.
An officer of one of the light cruisers in the recent battle, writing home, says the Germans have the trick of spreading clouds of whitish-yellow smoke, behind which they can manoeuvre without being seen. The Falmouth was the object an unsuccessful submarine attack, and a Zeppelin was driven off gunfire. One of the Warspite's crew, on leave in Birmingham, ridiculed the German claim to have sunk that vessel. She is safe and sound in harbour, ready for the next dust up. She was hit by many German shells when she was interposed between the Germans and the Warrior, and had her wireless apparatus shot away and some shot holes in the funnels. Shells mostly smashed against her armoured sides. She received serious injury, and steamed home herself after bearing a full share in the great fight.

Speculation that Other German Dreadnoughts May Have Been Sunk
Meanwhile, the belated German admission of the loss of the battlecruiser *Lützow* made various newspapers seek out evidence that other German capital ships may also have been sunk as had been suggested by the Admiralty's second communiqué.

Thus, on 14 June the *Birmingham Gazette* speculated that *Thuringen* may have been sunk:

THE JUTLAND BATTLE. SUGGESTED LOSS OF ANOTHER GERMAN DREADNOUGHT.
The Rotterdam correspondent of the 'Daily News' telegraphed last night:— trawler arriving at to-day reports having fished up in the neighbourhood of the Jutland battle two caps of German sailor bearing the name S.M.S. Thuringen, sister ship to the Ostfriesland,

the flagship of one of the German squadrons. The Thuringen is a Dreadnought 21,000 tons, with twelve 12-inch guns; built Bremen, and completed in 1911.

The *Manchester Evening News* also picked up this story and even went on to explain the political significance of the Helgoland-class of dreadnoughts:

BATTLE OF JUTLAND.
Mystery of Two German Dreadnoughts. Dutch Sailor's Find.
Ymuiden, June 13.—
A sailor of steam trawler just arrived reports having picked up near the scene the battle Jutland two caps bearing the name of the German Dreadnought (a sister ship to the Helgoland) ... Thuringen is—or was, for they may disappear or change their names—a Dreadnought of the 1908 class, eldest sister of group of four vessels, each of 21,000 tons, with a complement over 1,000 men. They carry 12-inch guns. It was the building these four ships which went furthest to the raising-the political cry in London 'We Want Eight' Dreadnoughts, at the time when Britain, unknown to Germany and to most Britons, was building Super-Dreadnoughts. Over and over again it has been asserted by neutrals that a vessel 'of the Ostfriesland class' was lost in the Jutland battle. Some reports said, definitely, the Ostfriesland— which was supposed to be flagship. Since the battle great display has been made in Germany of the fact that the Ostfriesland is still to be seen, safe and sound. 'She did not receive single hit,' they say. We have not heard so much about the Thuringen, one Ostfriesland's three sisters.[2]

The *Sheffield Evening Telegraph* of 15 June used reports of debris recovered from the west coast of Jutland to speculate on the veracity of German admissions about their losses:

A Copenhagen correspondent on the west coast of Jutland reports that every returning fishing boat brings flotsam from the battle off Horn Reef. Many caps have been recovered. On them are the following names:—Tipperary, Sparrowhawk, Ardent, Westfalen, Seydlitz, Lutzow, and Frauenlob ... It is worth noting that all British wreckage hitherto washed up belongs to warships actually lost. If the same be the case in regard to the German wreckage an interesting light is thrown on the trustworthiness the statements of the losses issued officially from Berlin.

Thirteen days the later the same paper reported that 'Among great quantities of wreckage washed ashore yesterday at Frederikstad were number of articles marked 'Seydlitz'.

The Birmingham Mail published a more detailed account of the same story, finishing with the discovery of a 'German wreck':

RELICS OF JUTLAND BATTLE. WERE THE SEYDLITZ AND KOENIG WILHELM SUNK?
Copenhagen. Tuesday.
Among great quantities of wreckage washed ashore yesterday at Fredrikstad were number of articles marked Seydlitz. Fishermen report having seen body in uniform of an admiral, according the description, some miles off ashore. Torpedo boats have gone out to recover it if possible.—Press Association. Copenhagen, June 27 The special correspondent of the 'National Tidende' at Rotterdam telegraphs that Dutch steam trawler arriving reports that in the North in latitude 35deg. longitude 6deg. E., during trawling the wreck of the sunken German warship Koenig Wilhelm[3] was discovered. The Koenig Wilhelm was a cruiser 9.800 tons, with a crew 1,150 men.[4]

Hampshire and *Marlborough* at Jutland

Letters from serving officers and men to their families were another source of news for an information-starved Press which was trying to get to the bottom of the Jutland mystery. One such letter from a subsequently drowned seaman was published in the *Newcastle Journal* of 17 June:

The ill-fated *Hampshire*'s part the recent naval battle is told in a delayed letter from Seaman J. Johnstone, who watched the fight from advantageous position in the foretop. Johnstone, who later was drowned with Lord Kitchener, says:—'The *Hampshire* first encountered a German three-funnelled cruiser, which caught the second salvo from the *Hampshire* right in her inner regions, bursting into clouds smoke and steam. After receiving a few other rounds the German turned tail and fled.'

Whilst the battleships were fighting, the *Hampshire* was the look-out for submarines, and from the foretop Johnstone saw five. The *Hampshire* settled two—one firing and another ramming. Johnstone adds that the next morning a Zeppelin passed over the scene.

The old armoured cruiser *Hampshire* had been very much on the fringes of the fighting and although she may have fired at the German cruiser

Wiesbaden it is doubtful that she obtained a hit with so many other vessels shooting at the same time. Furthermore, as no U-boats were present at Jutland it is unclear as to exactly what *Hampshire* shot at or rammed – if anything. However, the whole Grand Fleet was infected with 'submarinitis' and there was a tendency to see periscope wakes and torpedoes in every wave.

Unlike the obsolete *Hampshire*, the modern 13.5-inch gun armed battleship *Marlborough* had been at the centre of both of the brief contacts between the battlefleets, and her gunnery had been excellent. Reports of her performance at Jutland began to appear in the Press towards the end of June and that in the *Western Gazette* of 30 June is typical:

> Judging by communications received at Southampton, H.M.S. Marlborough acquitted herself magnificently the North Sea She first engaged a German ship of the Kaiser class, and registered distinct hits with her salvoes, a flame springing from the victim. Later her heavy guns were trained on an enemy light cruiser, which was blown clean out of water. Shortly afterwards the Marlborough was struck by a torpedo but without affecting her firing efficiency for she subsequently engaged [a] cruiser of the Roon class,[5] whose side was ripped open, and was seen burning from end to end. As matter of fact, the Marlborough s fire was more deadly than ever after she was struck. Within the space of six minutes four distinct hits were registered another German battleship. During the night-fighting took place all round the Marlborough, but she was never once hit [by shellfire].

British Admirals enter the Debate

Two weeks after the battle the hysteria generated by the stunning German claim of victory and the Admiralty's lamentable response had begun to die down as wiser counsels prevailed. In particular, the newspapers began to carry pieces from former and active senior naval officers who were able to put the battle in its true perspective both in terms of its outcome and the expectations of the British public.

One such article appeared in the *Liverpool Daily Post* of 17 June:

> Still harping on the stupid and misleading Admiralty announcement of the Jutland battle, Lord Beresford[6] remarks that we are an extraordinary race, in that if we never know when we are defeated, neither do we ever know when have won a victory. Admiral Henderson[7] said the other day that one difficulty with the British

public is their demand that every naval battle should be a Trafalgar. In Lord Beresford's opinion our last battle was a Trafalgar, and if Admiral Beatty had not acted as did there would have been an end of our blockade. Admiral Beatty acted on the fine old British tradition of risking all for the possible achievement of definite aim of military importance.

What did follow is succinctly conveyed in Admiral Henderson's suggestion for such an announcement as would have been made if there had been anyone at Whitehall with a spark of imagination or knowledge of human nature. 'A modest, firm, and expressive announcement,' he says, might have concluded with the plain statement that 'the German Fleet, as soon our main body got into action, retreated with precipitation, and returned to its home ports, pursued by our whole Fleet and flotillas, reports from whom have not yet been received. The command of the sea is not only unshaken, but more firmly established.'

About five weeks later, on 24 July, *The Times* printed an authoritative article derived from an un-named British Admiral who had been interviewed by a Reuter's correspondent:

THE JUTLAND BATTLE.
A BRITISH ADMIRAL'S VIEWS.
The German claim to have sunk the Warspite receives a further contradiction by a British admiral, who has been interviewed by a representative of Reuter's Agency. The Warspite was to be seen in the middle of a certain waterway not a whit the worse for the damage that she suffered in the Jutland battle and 'ready for sea at' any moment. She re-turned from the battle at a speed of 21 knots and a few days later she was once more ready for action. When he was shown the latest German account of the fight the admiral said:- 'The whole version is nonsense.

Whether the British report has been coloured, as the Germans say, to suit British tastes you can, judge for yourself. You have seen, ships which have either been sunk or hopelessly damaged according to the enemy, and have seen that one, and all are now, and have been for some time, repaired to the smallest particular and ready for sea. But, apart from this, many of the vessels received damage of such a non-vital character that there was nothing to prevent them from going to sea weeks ago.

Now it seems that the Germans declare that their fleet was the aggressor from the beginning to the end. Why, if they were the aggressors, did they turn away, and why did they throughout use smoke screens to conceal their retreat? That does not somehow look like an aggressor. Then they declare that they never avoided battle after Sir John Jellicoe's Battle Fleet had appeared on the scene. This is too ridiculous. They steamed away as soon as we appeared. One ship I fired on turned tail and skedaddled for all she was worth. The others did the same.

As to our losses, the Germans have ceased to talk about the loss of the Warspite, which is, perhaps as well in view of the fact that you have seen the Warspite yourself. They still assert that the British lost one Dreadnought of the Queen Elizabeth class. It is wholly untrue, as is also their assertion that we have lost a vessel of, the Cressy class, two small cruisers, and 13 destroyers. We have lost no ship of the Cressy class, no small cruisers, and it has already been stated that we lost nine[8] destroyers. The evidences of the disorganization that had set in among the Germans were clear.

Unpalatable Truths

Meanwhile, the Germans continued to restate their claims of success using evidence in the form of the greater number of ships sunk and the British failure to pursue the High Seas Fleet to support their assertion. On 4 July the *Western Times* reported:

> Through the Berlin correspondent of the Associated Press of America, the German Admiralty publishes a detailed report of the battle of Jutland. The results of the engagement seem indeed to become more favourable to Germany each time the tale is retold.

After discussing the German claims for ships sunk on either side, the *Western Times* notes that the present German official report is as follows:

> The High Sea Fleet, consisting three battleship squadrons, five battle cruisers, a large number of small cruisers, and several destroyer flotillas, were cruising in the Skagerrack on May 31 for the purpose, as on earlier occasions, of offering battle to the British Fleet. The vanguard of small cruisers at 4.30 in the afternoon suddenly encountered 90 miles west of the Hanstholm a group of eight of the newest cruisers of the Calliope class and fifteen to twenty of the most modern destroyers. While the German light forces, and the first cruiser squadron under Admiral von Hipper were following the British retiring to the north-west, the German battle cruisers sighted to westward Admiral Beatty's battle cruiser squadron of six ships,

including four of the Lion type and two of the Indefatigable class, which formed into battle line on a southeasterly course. Admiral Hipper formed line ahead on the same general course, and approached for [a] running fight, and opened fire at 5.49 p.m. with his heavy guns at a range of 13.000 metres against a superior enemy.

About 620 p.m. five[9] ships of the Queen Elizabeth class, coming from the west, joined the British battle cruiser line, powerfully reinforcing it with 15in. guns. While this engagement was in progress mighty explosion caused by a big shell destroyed the Queen Mary, and a third ship in the line at 6.30. Soon afterwards the German main battleship fleet was sighted southwards, steering north. The hostile fast squadrons thereupon turned northward, closing the first phase of the fight lasting about an hour.

Although this account does not mention the loss of *Indefatigable*, it is clear that the Germans were well aware that the 1st Scouting Group, consisting of five battlecruisers, had inflicted a significant defeat on Beatty's numerically superior force before the arrival of the High Seas Fleet's battleships. Understandably, this unpalatable truth was either glossed over or ignored by the Press and public at the time. The German account continued:

The British retired at high speed before the German fleet, which was following hotly. With the advent of the British main fleet, whose centre consisted of three squadrons of eight battleships, with fast divisions of three Invincibles on the northern wing and three of the newest Royal Sovereigns armed with 15in. guns, at the southern end, began, about, eight in the evening, the third phase of the engagement, embracing the combat of the main fleets.

Vice-Admiral von Scheer determined to attack the British main fleet, which, as is now recognised, was completely assembled, and about doubly superior. After the first violent onslaught against the mass of superior enemy force the opponents lost sight of one another in the smoke and powder cloud. After a short cessation of the artillery combat Admiral von Scheer ordered a new attack of all available forces of German battle-cruisers. A bitter artillery fight was again interrupted by smoke from guns and funnels, and several torpedo flotillas, which we ordered to attack somewhat later found after penetrating into the smoke-cloud that the enemy fleet was no longer before them, nor when the fleet commander again brought the German squadrons upon a southerly and south-westerly course could the enemy be found.

165

Only once more, shortly before 10.30 p.m. did the battle flare up for a short while in the twilight when the German battle-cruisers sighted to the northward four enemy capital ships and opened fire immediately. As the two German battleship squadrons attacked the enemy turned and vanished in the darkness. This ended the day of battle.[10]

Just as the British failed to admit that Beatty's battlecruisers had been defeated by a numerically weaker force, so the Germans did not admit that the High Seas Fleet had been stunned by brief cannonades from some but not all of Jellicoe's battleships. The unpalatable truth for the Germans was that their battlefleet had twice turned away in confusion and disorder rather than face the might of the Grand Fleet, but this was not mentioned in any of their communiqués, for obvious reasons.

Although newspaper reports were continually reminding the public of the battle and in particular of the British ships and their crews lost, there were occasional 'good news' stories that emanated from the continual reports of carnage. One such appeared on 5 July in several newspapers including the *Taunton Courier and Western Advertiser*:

THE JUTLAND BATTLE.
SEAMAN'S MARVELLOUS ESCAPE.
The parents of Alfred Thomas Sherwood, A.B., only son of Mr. and Mrs. Sherwood, Highstreet, Twyford, Berks, who was reported lost on the Queen Mary on the occasion of the recent naval battle, now learn that is alive and well, a prisoner of war in Germany. Sherwood had a miraculous escape from death. When the magazine of his ship exploded he was blown considerable distance into the sea without injury.

Publication of Jellicoe's Despatch and the German Riposte
Admiral Jellicoe's long-expected despatch about the Battle of Jutland was published on the evening of 6 July and the *Daily Mirror* reported that it showed that:

Twenty-one ships were lost by the Germans. The Kaiser's navy was brought to action, severely trounced, crippled, and chased off the seas in twelve hours. The enemy fought with the gallantry that was expected of him.

But for Sir David Beatty's gallant leadership, determination, and strategic insight our success would not have been possible. Admiral Beatty proceeded on a course towards the rapidly approaching ships of Admiral Jellicoe.

Of the Bulldog Breed. —Admiral Beatty mentions incidentally two glorious feats of daring. One, of the Onslow, a torpedo-boat destroyer, which sighted an enemy light cruiser about to attack the Lion with torpedoes.

Onslow at once closed and engaged her, firing fifty-eight rounds at range of from 4,000 to 2,000 yards, scoring a number of hits. Onslow then chased the enemy battle cruisers, and orders were then given for all torpedoes to be fired. At this moment she was struck amidships by a heavy shell, with the result that only one torpedo was fired. Thinking that all his torpedoes had gone, the commanding officer proceeded retire at slow speed. Being informed that he still had three torpedoes, closed with the light cruiser previously engaged and torpedoed her. The enemy's battle fleet was then sighted, and the remaining torpedoes were fired at them ... Damage then caused Onslow to stop.

The same day the *Western Daily Press* ran a long and very patriotic article intended to reassure its war-weary readers that despite Jutland being an indecisive action its strategical consequences were immensely favourable to the Allied cause:

WHAT THE BATTLE OF JUTLAND MEANS. A FAMOUS NAVAL VICTORY.

It is well known that nearly all our great Naval battles—not even excepting Trafalgar itself—have been the subject of controversy after the event. In many cases every aspect of the action became a matter of debate—the strategy, the tactics, the conduct of subordinate commanders, the actual way in which was fought, and the true estimate of its results. The, debate was not confined to the public or the Press. As often as not opinion was divided both as to the facts and the conclusions amongst officers who were present and had the best means of knowing. Many of the discussions were premature, but many continued long after all the available facts were known, and are even still alive. It would be idle, therefore, so soon after the late battle in the North Sea, and a time when so little of its detail can disclosed, without giving undesirable light to the enemy, to attempt anything like a final [account]. All that can be. done is to point out certain aspects of the battle which seem to detach themselves from the mass of half-disclosed detail, and which, so far as can be judged at present, are likely to remain its salient features.

Seen in its broadest aspect, it stands out as a case of tactical division of the Fleet, which had the effect of bringing an unwilling enemy to battle. Such method of forcing an action is drastic, and necessarily attended with risk, but for great ends great risks must be taken, and in this case the risk was far less great than that which St. Vincent accepted off Cadiz, and that division gave us the battle of the Nile, the most complete and least debated of British victories. Then the two portions of St. Vincent's Fleet were divided strategically with no prospect of tactical concentration for the battle. In the present case there was only an appearance of division. The Battle Fleet was to the north, and the Battle Cruiser Fleet to the south, but they formed in fact one Fleet under a single command acting in combination. They were actually carrying-out, as they had been in the habit of doing periodically, a combined sweep of the North Sea, and Admiral Beatty's Fleet was in effect the observation or advanced squadron.

The measure of the risk, should he have the fortune to find the enemy at sea, was the length of the period which must necessarily elapse before the Commander-in-Chief would be able to join the battle. It was a risk that would be measured mainly the skill with which Admiral Beatty could entice the enemy northward, without being overwhelmed by superior force.

In the light of this outstanding feature the action will be judged, and the handling of the Battle Cruiser Fleet, and the splendid group of four battleships that was attached it, appraised. When Admiral Beatty got contact with the German battle cruisers they were proceeding northward, and being inferior to his force, they turned to the southward. The inference was they were either trying to escape [or] bent on leading him into danger. When such doubt occurs there is in the British tradition, a golden rule, and that is to 'attack the enemy in sight'. It was the rule that Nelson consecrated, and it was good enough for Admiral Beatty. He engaged, and continued to engage, as closely he could, till he found the enemy's battle fleet coming north. Then he turned, but he did not break off the action. The enemy was in overwhelming force, but by the golden rule, it was his duty to cling to them as long as his teeth would hold. They had spread a net for him, and it was for him to see that they fell into the midst of it themselves. It was a task that demanded some courage. Yet he did not flinch, but continued the fight to the northward, and signalled the four Queen Elizabeths to turn 16 points [i.e. reverse course].

Now was the hour of greatest risk, but he was well disposed for concentrating on the van of the enemy's line, and the Commander-in-Chief was hurrying down at full speed. For an hour and a half the unequal battle raged as Admiral Beatty and Admiral Evan Thomas led the enemy on, before Admiral Hood could appear with his Battle

Cruiser Squadron. The action was then at its hottest, but Admiral Hood, without a moment's hesitation, and a manner that excited the high admiration of all who were privileged to witness it, placed his ships in line ahead of Admiral Beatty's squadron. No Admiral ever crowned an all too short career more devotedly or in a manner more worthy of the name he bore. With his fine manoeuvre the risk was in a measure reduced, but there still remained the more delicate work of the Grand Fleet effecting its junction and entering the ill-defined action.

With the exact position of the enemy's fleet shrouded in smoke in the gathering mist, the danger of interference was very great, and before the Commander-in-Chief lay a task as difficult any Admiral could be called upon to perform. To the last moment he kept his Fleet in steaming order so as to preserve up till the end the utmost freedom of deployment, but by what precise manoeuvres the deployment was carried out must for obvious reasons be left in a mist as deep as that which was hiding all that was most important for him to know. Suffice it to say that the junction was effected with consummate judgment and dexterity so nicely timed that the deployment was barely completed when at 6.15 p.m. the First Battle Squadron came into action with the enemy, who had that time turned to the eastward, and was already attempting to avoid action. Thus the fine combination had succeeded, and the unwilling enemy had been brought to action against the concentrated British Fleet. They had fallen into the midst of the net which had been drawn about them, but in the plan of the sweep there was inherent the inevitable limitation that the time left for completing the business could but barely suffice. There, were hardly three hours of daylight left, and as darkness approached the action must be broken off unless a needless chance were to be given to the enemy for redressing his battle inferiority. Still our Battle Fleet was between the enemy and his base, and there would have been little hope of his escaping a decisive defeat but for the mist that robbed those who had prepared for the chance, and those who had seized it with so much skill and boldness, of the harvest they deserved.

It was a beaten and broken fleet that escaped the trap. It had lost many units, its gunnery had gone to pieces, and no one can blame its discretion if it fairly ran for home and left the British Fleet once more in undisputed command of the North Sea. For that, in a word, was the result of the battle. What it was the enemy hoped to achieve we cannot tell. Whatever their effort meant, it failed to shake our hold upon the sea, and that is what really matters. We have fought many indecisive actions, but few in which the strategical result was so indisputable, few which more fully freed us of all fear of what the enemy's fleet could do. It is by such standards that history judges victories, and such standards the country cherishes the memory of the men that prepared and won them.

Current opinion will always prefer the test of comparative losses. Let this be applied, and it will be found that the battle off Jutland will well hold its own against all but few of our most famous victories—none of which obtained on a first attempt. From another aspect it is clear the battle can rank beside any in our history. In the fringes of the fight, in the work that is of cruisers, light cruisers, and destroyers, officers and men had chances such as their ancestors never knew, and they seized them with all the daring, skill, and the devotion that the greatest of their predecessors could have hoped. From the vigorous offensive against the enemy's cruisers, which cost Admiral Arbuthnot his life, to the least conspicuous the destroyer exploits, all was the same pattern. It is impossible to read of what they did and what they failed to do without feeling there is one thing least which the battle has given us, and that is the assurance that the old spirit is still alive and vigorous. It is able and willing to do all the old Navy could do, and in the battle of Jutland, as we now know, it has done it.

The eventual publication of Jellicoe's despatches also triggered a robust series of denials in Germany. This included reports and statements from Berlin which had been received from the wireless stations of the German Government and subsequently circulated by the Reuter's News Agency on 7 July 1916:

The English Admiralty Staff has at last published the report of Admiral Jellicoe, of which the long delay occasioned astonishment throughout the entire world. The report circulated by Reuter is specially remarkable inasmuch as it differs very much from earlier English reports, and is proved by a comparison of the estimated German losses in the present report with statements published immediately after the battle.

It was stated in the 1st English report that the British losses were heavy whilst those of the Germans were merely serious. On June 4, Jellicoe estimated the German losses at one battle-cruiser sunk, one battleship sunk, one battle-cruiser seriously damaged, two small cruisers put out of action, probably sunk, a large number of destroyers put out of action. Now, on the contrary, the estimate is, five weeks later, three battleships of the Dreadnought type sunk, one vessel of the line of the Deutschland class sunk, five small cruisers sunk, one 'U' boat sunk. Heavily damaged: Two ships of the line, one Dreadnought type battleship, three torpedo-boats, six ships so badly damaged as to make arrival back in port doubtful.

As a matter of fact the German losses amount to one battle-cruiser, one old ship of the line, four small cruisers, and five torpedo-boats.

Like the rest of the British Press, the *Daily Mirror* received information about the response of the German Press via its sources in Amsterdam and duly published the material on 8 July:

> One learns so much from the report – namely, that the British naval authorities at last admit the intervention of their biggest naval forces in the battle. To sum up the report can only strengthen our knowledge that we can record the naval battle of the Skager Rak a glorious achievement of our young Navy.
>
> The evening edition of the *Kölnische Volkszeilunq*, which has just arrived here, publishes Admiral Jellicoe's report on the Battle of Jutland as it appeared in the Dutch Press. It says:
>
> Too systematic endeavour to remove the scene of the battle as far south as possible to the neighbour-hood of the German coast in order to create the impression that the German fleet had the advantage of the British fleet does not trouble us. We maintain that the conditions of the battle in this respect were virtually the same for both sides. In spite of the unmistakable window-dressing of Admiral Jellicoe's report to suit the British public, we cannot say that it bears the stamp of the proud conviction of victory. We are entitled to translate this report, which is adapted to the necessities of war, into everyday language, and what it says once again is, 'The battle of the Skager Rak was a British defeat.'

On 9 July the *Frankfurter Zeitung* reported that:

> It is difficult to dispute with Admiral Jellicoe the main question of the battle of the Skager Rak, namely the total respective losses of the two sides. Assertion is opposed by assertion. We can state both, and say to which of the two we attach the greater credence, but we have no possible means of proving our case. Any further discussion of the question whether the relation of the total losses is more favourable to us than the ratio of one-to-two would be entirely useless.

The following day *The Times* waded into the debate, using material obtained from an interview with a Japanese Admiral to add weight to their arguments:

> Rear-Admiral Saneyuki Akiyama, of the Japanese Naval General Staff, who is on a special mission to this country, whither he has come from Russia, is going on to France and Italy. Discussing the Jutland fight Admiral Akiyama said:-
>
> Even when I saw the first announcement of the battle I was convinced that it only meant one thing – a British victory, but on studying Admiral Jellicoe's dispatch I find that the battle of Jutland was the most brilliant victory and the greatest success ever achieved by the British Fleet, though it must be said that the Germans fought very well, and put forward their utmost effort. The reasons for my view are:-
>
> (1) The superior force of the British Fleet was very well concentrated on the battlefield from its distant bases. This is a most difficult operation in naval warfare, and constituted Admiral Jellicoe's first strategic gain in the battle.
>
> (2) Neither on the battlefield as a whole nor in any part of it was there any strategical or tactical mistake committed by the British Commander-in-Chief or any of his subordinate commanders.
>
> (3) The British Fleet remained master of the battlefield and has maintained the effective control of the sea.
>
> (4) The German losses are much heavier than the British. It is a common thing in discussing a battle to see which side had the heavier loss, but this loss is not the principal element of the result of war, and the victor may often lose more than the vanquished. Anyhow, I am sure that the German losses are much greater than those reported by Admiral Jellicoe. Although I was responsible for the preparations of the plans for the Tshushimni battle, the conditions as to both distance and weapons have so entirely changed that I found it difficult to make a comparison of the two actions. I firmly believe that the German fleet cannot again take the sea, for their loss in battle-cruisers and light cruisers is so great that it is impossible for them to employ their Dreadnoughts and other capital ships that need the support of smaller vessels of great speed.
>
> Admiral Akiyarna added that the strength of the Russian Fleet in ships, men, and efficiency had doubled within a year.

The debate about ships sunk and losses in general became rather more subtle as a consequence of information about damage to German ships that survived the battle began to filter across the Channel. For example, on 14 July the *Western Daily Press* published the following account:

> The 'Daily News' correspondent at Rotterdam has learned from a reliable source some of the losses received the battle of Jutland. Here, he says, is a list of important ships now in hospital, with many having been riddled far as the superstructure is concerned, and one having had the whole of her superstructure swept clear. DREADNOUGHT BATTLESHIPS (5). Konig, Grosser Kurfurst, and Markgraf (25,000 tons each); Kaiser and Kaiserin (24,700 tons each). BATTLE CRUISERS (4). Derfflinger (28,000 tons), Seydlitz (24,640), Moltke (22,640) and Von der Tann (19,400)—all but the last named are Dreadnoughts. OLDER BATTLESHIPS (2). Hessen (13,200) and Rheinland (18,600), SMALL CRUISERS (4) Regensburg (5,000 tons). Stettin (3,450), Frankfurt (unknown), Koln, (4,280).
>
> The Seydlitz is little better than a wreck. She suffered the most withering fire possible for ship to receive, and yet kept afloat. All her superstructure was swept away in the hurricane of shells, and a great portion the crew went with it. She was taken in tow, and every effort was made to reach port during the night; but the tow parted, and she sank in shallow water when very near home. She has since been salved and placed in dock. The story goes (says the correspondent) that the 30.5 centimetre (12in)[11] guns proved unsatisfactory during the battle and that as far as possible measures are being taken re-arm the vessels.

With the passage of time the Press furore over Jutland gradually died down. That said, newspapers continued to carry occasional items relating to the battle, usually news about those who had been present and their comings and goings.

Every so often, an item about the battle and its consequences would appear, such as that in the *Hull Daily Mail* of 28 July which reported the remarks of a captured German soldier who brother was serving in the German Navy:

> THE BATTLE OF JUTLAND. AN INTERESTING ADMISSION.
> Writing from the British Headquarters in France Wednesday Reuter's special correspondent says:-'heard interesting admission from very intelligent German prisoner today. His brother is a lieutenant in the German navy, and the one subject which interested him more than all others was the Battle of Jutland – he would have it that our losses were bigger than those his own fleet, upon which he would naturally

know only a much as his countrymen have been told. But when I said that the Pommern, the sinking of which Germany admits, was not the old pre-Dreadnought, as Wilhelmstrasse had officially stated, but new battleship, he answered coolly that he knew that well enough; that, in fact, everybody in Germany knew it. I asked him when his brother thought the German fleet would be ready to come out again, and merely laughed ironically, shaking his head.'

From time to time the newspapers took the opportunity to state that, thanks to the work of the Royal Navy at the Battle of Jutland, the German war effort would continue to be hamstrung by the British blockade. Once such item appeared in the *Daily Mirror* on 4 August under the title 'Our Tighter Sea Grip':

An error, however, is to suppose that the naval victory changed the situation: what it did was to confirm it. Before Jutland, as after it, the German fleet was imprisoned and the battle was an attempt to break the bars: it failed and with its failure the High Seas Fleet sank again into impotence. It may perhaps be objected that this is but a British view of British triumphs. But this is not so. Study Mr. A. J. Balfour, and the German utterances with care, and you will find that they give precisely the same general impression [of] British sea power and the naval position that which I have just expressed.

The object of naval battle is to obtain the command the sea, or keep it; it is certain that Germany has not obtained it, and that we have not lost it. Is it, or is it not, becoming more difficult for the Germans to import raw material and food stuffs; and to pay for them by the export their manufactures? The Germans themselves will admit that it is becoming more difficult.

Four days later the same newspaper carried a report of the award of a medal for bravery to Lieutenant Frederick Joseph Rutland during the evacuation of the sinking armoured cruiser *Warrior* on 1 June:

DRAMA OF OFFICER'S DIVE.
The King's Reward for Thrilling Act After Jutland Naval Battle.
After the naval battle of Jutland a wounded sailor was accidentally dropped overboard while being transhipped from one vessel another.[12] Two officers wanted to jump overboard to save the poor fellow, but the two ships were working most dangerously, and the commanding officer had forbid their doing so. He considered it would mean certain death. Unobserved, however, Lieutenant Joseph Rutland, R.N. jumped overboard from the fore part of the ship with

a bowline, which he put around the wounded man. When drawn on board, however, the man was dead. Lieutenant Rutland had a miraculous escape from death. In last night's London Gazette it stated that the King has conferred upon him the Albert Medal of the First Class. 'His bravery,' it is explained, 'is reported to have been magnificent.'[13]

During September various newspapers printed articles showing the hitherto unadvertised beneficial effects of the Battle of Jutland. That written by Alfred Noyes[14] and published in the *Daily Mirror* of 4 September was clearly intended to show a nervous British readership that regardless of the state of the war on other fronts, the nation's maritime capability was going from strength-to-strength:

BUSINESS—AS BEFORE.
On my return journey down the Clyde I saw one very significant thing—a quite unadvertised result of the Jutland battle. For two years previously work upon merchant ships had almost been abandoned. All the energies of the shipwrights were concentrated upon the Navy. Since the Jutland battle, however, work had been resumed on merchant ships. The hammers were rattling on the sides of a dozen great liners. Cargo-boats of all kinds were keeping hundreds of men busy; and, unless my eyes grievously deceived me, the transatlantic service would soon considerably improved.

England lost eight destroyers in the Jutland battle. I saw a shipyard whence, in that same week, they had launched fifteen new destroyers. And, what is more, I saw brood after brood of ships, in yard after yard, ready to follow. No sooner was one ship launched than another was laid down. I saw, nearing completion in this one cradle of ships, a fleet of destroyers, a fleet of submarines, a fleet of battle-cruisers, that in themselves would have constituted a formidable navy for any country. Here, too, were certain 'mystery ships'; ships of a new type, round which special screens had been built to guard them from too inquisitive eyes. And if mere size be quality, I saw several submarines larger than any hitherto built; and battle-cruisers that would outstrip any ship in the world, and were considerably larger than any battleships in existence.

In mid-September Sir John Jellicoe's recommendations regarding honours and promotions for officers and men for their services in connection with the Battle of Jutland, and the consequent nominations by the King, appeared in a Supplement to *The London Gazette*.

The *Nottingham Evening Post* of 16 September carried the following report of the honours awarded:

JUTLAND HONOURS.
VICTORIA CROSS FOR JACK CORNWELL.
ORDER OF MERIT FOR ADMIRAL JELLICOE.
How splendidly officers and men behaved on that memorable occasion is sufficiently shown by the fact that Admiral Jellicoe confesses that he finds it invidious to mention any, in view of the fact that 'all did well'. The chief awards are: V.C. Boy, First Class, John Travers Cornwell, O.N. J. 42563 (died June 2nd, 1916). Mortally wounded early in the action, Boy, First Class, John Travers Cornwell, remained standing alone at a most exposed post, quietly awaiting orders, until the end of the action, the gun crew dead and wounded all round him.

Comr. the Hon. Edward S. B. Bingham (Prisoner of War in Germany). For extremely gallant way in which he led his division in their attack, first on enemy destroyers and then on their battle-cruisers, finally sighted the enemy battle-fleet, and, followed by the one remaining destroyer of his division (Nicator), with dauntless courage he closed to within 3,000 yards of the enemy in order to attain a favourable position for firing the torpedoes. While making this attack Nestor and Nicator were under concentrated fire of the secondary batteries of the High Sea Fleet. Nestor was subsequently sunk.

Major Francis J. W. Harvey, R.M.L.I. Whilst mortally wounded and almost the only survivor after the explosion of an enemy shell in 'Q' gunhouse, with great presence of mind and devotion to duty, ordered the magazine be flooded, thereby saving his ship. He died shortly afterwards.

O.M. Admiral Sir John Jellicoe awarded the Order of Merit. Vice-Admiral Sir David Beatty becomes G.C.B. The C.M.G. is given to Rear-Admiral O. de B. Brock and Captain A. S. M. Chatfield.

The D.S.O. goes to 16 commanders, nine lieutenant-commanders, one lieutenant, four engineer-commanders, two engineer-lieutenant-commanders, three fleet-surgeons, two staff-surgeons, one staff paymaster, one paymaster, one assistant-paymaster and one captain of the R.M.L.I.

CHAPLAIN'S HEROISM.
The Distinguished Service Cross awarded to the Rev. Anthony Pollen (Roman Catholic Chaplain), who 56, and who, although severely burned, carried men injured by severe burns from the battery deck to

176

the distributing station), four lieutenants, R.N., one flight-lieutenant. R N., one Lieutenant , R.N.R., one lieutenant, R.N.V.R., one carpenter-lieutenant, one sub-lieutenant, R.N., one surgeon-probationer, R.N.V.R., one chief artificer engineer and one artificer engineer. A large number officers are commended for their service, among them Sub-Lieutenant Prince Albert. Many others have received promotion, and yet more are noted for early promotion.

LOWER DECK DISTINCTIONS.

Twelve men are awarded the Conspicuous Gallantry Medal Among them Petty-Officer W. John Adlam Willie, who brought his gun into action after himself and the whole of his gun's crew had been wounded. The Distinguished Service Medal has been given to 177 persons, including First-Class Boy J. E. W. Worn and S.J. Keen and Signal Boy John Postles. Chief Writer Samuel George White has won a bar to his Distinguished Service Medal gazetted in March last year. There is also very long list of petty officers and men who have been commended for their service.

V.C.'s WIFE'S EXPERIENCES.

The Hon. Mrs. Barry Bingham, the wife of one the new V.C.s, has had two curious experiences. She was able to discard her widow's weeds when she was officially notified that Commander Bingham had been saved by the Germans and was prisoner after had been reported Last Tuesday she gave away her mother when she was married, at St. Martin's-in-the-Fields to Lieut.-Colonel Allanson.

Establishment of a Naval Department of Publicity

Captain (later Rear Admiral Sir) Douglas Brownrigg, who was the Chief Naval Censor throughout the First World War, was able to exercise a more consistent and efficient censorship compared to that of the Foreign Office and the War Office.

Brownrigg considered that the attempted concealment of the loss of the Super-Dreadnought *Audacious* in 1914 was the one foolish mistake made by the Admiralty in its dealings with the Press, not least because the event was witnessed by many American citizens. He also believed that the blunt statement of losses released on 2 June, a mere two days after the Battle of Jutland when the Admiralty had no real knowledge of the details of the action, was the result of intense discussion between the First Lord, Mr Arthur Balfour, the First Sea Lord, Admiral Sir Henry Jackson and the Chief of the Naval war Staff, Rear Admiral Sir Henry Oliver. The unfavourable response to the Admiralty's communiqués led Brownrigg to invite Winston Churchill, who was then out of office, to write a statement about the battle.[15]

The unfavourable criticism of the Admiralty's bungled post-Jutland communiqués led to the Foreign Office and the War Office suggesting that, in future, the Admiralty would be wise to adopt a less terse style of writing. On 2 July Rear-Admiral Brownrigg replied to these suggestions:

> From the wording of Sir E. Grey's Minute (Proposal for writing up communiqués by Mr John Buchan – with War Office Minute by Sir William Robertson), I take it that the Foreign Office considers it necessary to depart from the blunt style of Communique, or preferably to supplement it by a 'semi-official' of more pretentious style to be written up in all cases by Mr Buchan.
>
> Before suggesting anything at all it would be well to be clear that it is the wish of the Government or War Committee, and not only the Foreign Office. If it is accepted that the Government wish an alteration in our methods, in order to influence American opinion, then I submit that:
>
> This view should be made known to all members of the Board and Heads of Departments, in order that they may give decisions consistently when I approach them for permission to arrange interviews and/or visits, it being always clearly understood that whatever is written is submitted to this Office for censorship. I share to the full the dislike of publicity which all Naval Officers feel, but if it is accepted that a change of policy is necessary, then it should be clearly impressed on all concerned.
>
> While admitting that Mr Buchan is a fine writer on military subjects, he has not so far as I know specialised in naval matters, and so far as the Admiralty concerned, I submit it would be better to ask C.I.D to allow Mr Julian Corbett to 'dress' our 'semi-officials' for us, he being certainly the greatest authority on Naval History, Lecturer at War College, etc., etc. and we can give every facility in the way of reading despatches, etc, etc., and also keep him under our roof while he is temporarily employed;
>
> For the lighter (if I may use such a word) treatment of subjects for the Press, I propose that Mr Rudyard Kipling be invited to help us, as he has already done in the matter of submarines, I may add that I am in the process of approaching Sir John Jellicoe to try and obtain permission for him to go up to the Fleet to interview Commanding Officers and 'write up' the stories of the Torpedo Boat Destroyer actions in the Jutland Battle.[16]

On 13 July 1916, the First Lord, Arthur Balfour, wrote to Sir Edward Grey, observing that while the consensus of opinion at the Admiralty agreed with a need for more positive communiqué, this might not always have the desired result:

> It is considered that however good Mr Buchan or other writers utilised by the Foreign Office may be, they have not the knowledge of naval conditions which is essential to the production of articles of real value on naval subjects and a great deal of the advantage of fine writing would be lost if the writer exposed himself to criticism on account of his evident ignorance of the ways of the sea.[17]

Brownrigg's suggestion that Rudyard Kipling be invited to 'write up' the stories of the destroyers at Jutland bore fruit in October 1916 when several newspapers, including the *Daily Mirror*, published his semi-official account:

> DESTROYER WORK IN THE JUTLAND BATTLE.
> By RUDYARD KIPLING.
> HOW is a layman to give any coherent account an affair like the battle Jutland, where a whole country's coast-line was background to battle covering geographical degrees? There were many torpedo attacks in all parts of the battle, including [a] quaint episode [of an] enemy light cruiser who looked as if she were trying to torpedo one of our battlecruisers while the latter was particularly engaged. A destroyer of ours, returning from a special job which required delicacy, was picking her way back at thirty knots through batches of enemy battle-cruisers and light cruisers ...[18]

Thereafter, in 1917, the Admiralty Board established a Department of Public Information to liaise with the Chief Censor in the Department of Information as well as assisting the Department of Information in the presentation of the Royal Navy and Mercantile Marine in a suitable way to the Allied, and Neutral Press and the Public. Captain Sir Guy R.A. Grant K.C.M.G., C.B., R.N. was appointed as the first Director of Naval Publicity (D.P.N.).[19]

The 'Typewriter War' in The United States' Press

The German Navy is still a navy in jail which assaults its keeper now and then with great fury, but which remains in jail nevertheless.

On 16 June 1916, Count Johann Heinrich von Bernstorff[1], who had been the German Ambassador to the United States of America since 1908, sent a letter[2] to the Imperial Chancellor Theobald von Bethmann-Hollweg[3] in Berlin in which he discussed the response of the America Press to the German naval victory off the Skagerrak.

Since the outbreak of the First World War, Count von Bernstorff's position in Washington had been strained by the espionage and sabotage activities of Fritz von Papen[4], Military attaché and Captain Karl Boy-Ed[5], the Naval Attaché both of whom were expelled in December 1915.

Count von Bernstorff reported that a deep impression had been made on American public opinion by the receipt, on the afternoon of 2 June, of the first news of the German naval victory off the Skagerrak. He reported that the news found extraordinarily free expression in the American Press:

> The evening papers [of 2 June] published the transatlantic report of the wireless news of the result of the naval battle, in thick type in a conspicuous position, and added the rather subdued report of the battle from London. The familiar headlines in letters two or three inches high, right across the page, announced the German naval victory. Only the *Evening Telegram*, the most anti-German of the New York yellow journals, unblushingly described the battle as a British victory. Its headline read: 'British Win Sea Battle at Big Cost'.[6]

The papers of 3 June devoted their two first pages almost exclusively to the more detailed reports of the battle which had in the meantime come in from Europe – a fact that is worthy of note, as during the last fortnight the news from the European theatre has been relegated in most of the papers to the third or fourth page, by the reports of the National Conventions in Chicago and St. Louis.

The news columns of the New York and Washington papers, in addition to the reports from London, Paris, Amsterdam, Copenhagen and Berlin on the progress of the battle and the losses on both sides, published innumerable interviews with American naval critics on their impressions and opinions regarding the battle. Especially noteworthy among these are the anonymous statements of various officers of the American Navy, who paid the highest tributes to the achievements of their German confreres, such as that in the *World*, by an American admiral whose name is not given, who in the course of a lengthy discussion of the reports which had come to hand, said: 'The Germans are better tacticians and more scientific fighters'.[7]

The Ambassador noted that nearly all the other papers of good standing also discussed the naval battle in their leading articles, and their almost unanimous verdict was a great German success adding that:

> It goes without saying that this German success called forth no enthusiasm whatsoever from these papers are avowedly pro-British, but on the contrary, was only reluctantly admitted. In some of the neutral papers here, and in the majority published outside New York and Boston, however, a certain satisfaction over the British defeat was apparent. Too often has America already felt the iron grip of the British Fleet, and too often has Britain, when reproached with leaving the conduct of the war to her Allies, called attention to the 'great silent might' of this fleet, for the American Press to be able to refrain from sarcastic comments on the breakdown of this fleet in its first great battle with the German Navy. Winston Churchill's famous boast: 'If the German, fleet does come out to fight, we will dig it out like a rat out of a hole', provided a favourite theme for many of the papers, with ironical remarks about the success of the rat-hunt.[8]

Turning to the outcome of the result of the naval battle and regardless of whether the individual papers exalted or minimised the achievement of the German Navy, von Bernstorff observed that there was but one opinion, namely that Britain's command of the sea was in no way weakened.

Furthermore, many of the papers emphasised the fact that the battle could not be regarded as decisive, commenting that in spite of the German victory, the British blockade remained unimpaired and is still strangling the economic life of Germany. He noted that:

> For example, the *Springfield Republican* remarked in this connection 'The British Empire could not survive many naval battles like that of the Danish coast' and the *Albany Journal* wrote: 'That the British Navy is not crippled is due to its magnitude; but a series of engagements having similar results would soon cripple it!'

Having surveyed the extraordinary wealth of press comments on this subject, von Bernstorff went on to quote a few extracts from articles in the leading papers, so as to provide the German Chancellor with an overview of Press opinion in the USA:

> *New York Times*: 'However unfavourable to the British the conditions were, the results cannot fail to be humiliating to English naval pride and in a corresponding degree heartening to the Germans ...This is the first big, open naval battle of the war. The British had put themselves in position to invite it, and they have come off badly.'

> *New York World*: 'Germany has won the greatest sea fight in modern history ... Although the victory is in no sense decisive, its moral effect on the German people will be immeasurable ... It is plain that the British fleet was out-manoeuvred, outshot and outfought by its adversary ... Incidentally, the victory may help teach the German people a much-needed lesson as to the true functions of a navy. How mean and paltry and contemptible now seem in comparison with the undying glory that had their men and ships have won this North Sea fight!'

> *New York Sun*: 'The German Fleet has come out and scored a brilliant victory in the North Sea. Compared with it the engagement in which Vice-Admiral Sturdee destroyed Admiral von Spee's squadron off the Falkland Islands and the running fight in the North Sea in which *Blücher* was sunk now appear like insignificant tests of sea power and are of minor importance.'

> *New York Evening Sun*: 'The British cruiser fleet has been caught and soundly beaten by superior admiral-ship, in waters where the British flag has been supreme for centuries. To find a greater naval triumph

of an inferior enemy at England's expense, it would be necessary to go back to Suffren's victory over Byng.'

New York Tribune: 'With all due allowances for the discrepancies in the two accounts of the battle off the coast of Jutland, it is clear that the Germans are justified in claiming the most important naval victory of the war ... This event will probably cause more dismay in England than any of the disasters that have befallen British arms since the war began ... The result was a clean victory, and a victory of no insignificant magnitude.'

New York Herald: 'Measured by reported losses, the Germans inflicted the greater damage; gauged by strategic results, the fortunes or misfortunes of the day and night can have no effect on the conduct of the war ... Whether honours are easy is for each individual to determine: both fleets put up a sturdy, sound fight; the Germans inflicted the greater damage, possibly against a superior force, but the British held and are still holding the field of battle.'

Brooklyn Daily Eagle: 'The German sea victory in the North Sea is distinctly one of the Pyrrhic sort ... Half a dozen such triumphs would leave German no navy at all and England would still have a good fighting force. We are offering no congratulations to Kaiserdom.'

Springfield Republican: 'There is more shock for the British and their allies in the naval action of May 31 than in any previous reverse on land and sea ... The Germans inflicted a stunning blow and ship for ship and man for man they can no longer be considered any less than the equal of the British in Britain's own element. At sea as on land, they [i.e. the Germans] are masters of their machines.'

Boston Evening Transcript: 'The Germans may not have won a great victory but the British have suffered a severe defeat.'

Philadelphia North American: 'Germany's exultation over her first great naval adventure is abundantly justified ... There was a decisive demonstration that in courage, seamanship and gunnery the Kaiser's fighters – men and ships – are the equals of the traditional rulers of the waves ... After full credit has been given to the Germans for their achievements the fact remains, of course, that the ultimate victory remained with the British ... the battle of Jutland, despite its dramatic accomplishments, was not more decisive in its ultimate results than the capture by the Germans of a few hundred yards of trenches in France.'

Philadelphia Public Ledger: 'The damaging character of the blow administered to the pride of the "Mistress of the Seas". The victory is not decisive, but its moral effect will be far-reaching.'

Baltimore Sun: 'The naval battle off the coast of Jutland on May 31st constituted a great victory for the German sea forces ...The great lesson of this battle – and it is a reassuring one – is that superior force does not necessarily spell victory ... The moral effect of the German victory will be enormous.'

Detroit News: 'The Germans made their utmost best of their opportunity, whether that opportunity came through accident or by their own design. The effect of the battle is largely moral. Whatever the reason, British ships have not proved themselves invincible. And the blow dealt to British belief in the fleet's invincibility is a more violent one than the loss of ships and men.'

Louisville Times: 'If it was the German fleet's purpose to break through and reach the coast of England, and was stopped and driven back, then Great Britain can rightly claim a victory. If not, the laurels are all with Germany.'

St Louis Globe-Democrat: 'The Germans have every reason for satisfaction over the battle. It demonstrated that the Germans are as efficient sea fighters as they are land fighters, a fact that is not surprising, in view of the previous achievements of German raiders and submarines.'

San Francisco Chronicle: 'If the German attack resulted disastrously to the British fleet, the Allies may be inclined to listen to peace proposals. They have leaned almost as much upon that fleet as upon the line of defence through Belgium through Frances to Vosges. Even though Britain's sea losses leave her with superior numbers of Warcraft, the moral effect of her defeat will be as inspiring to Germany as depressing not only to England, but to France, Russia and Italy.'[9]

In view of the meagre initial reports of the battle which had been received, many papers speculated as to how such a British defeat was possible. Unsurprisingly, these speculations were mostly based on the assumption that the German battle fleet had lured the British Battlecruiser Fleet into a trap, and defeated it, but on being warned by Zeppelins of the approach of the far superior British Dreadnought fleet, had retired to its home waters. The Ambassador wrote that:

> A number of avowedly pro-British papers, as was to be expected, had nothing but disparaging comments to make on the strategy of the German Commander-in-Chief. Impartial journals, however, held the view that Admiral Scheer's retirement before the full force of the numerically superior British battle ship squadron, was an overwhelming proof of the superiority of German naval strategy. Thus the *New Orleans Daily* states: 'Of course, the British will say that if the Germans had stayed until the full force of the former had been brought into action, instead of heading home after the first brush, there would have been a different tale to tell. But German strategy required that the German ships should escape to port after inflicting more damage than they suffered, and there can be no doubt that they succeeded.'
>
> The *North American*, already quoted, in this connection, after a tribute to the courage, magnificent seamanship and splendid shooting of the German fleet says, 'But far more significant and tactical efficiency. The Germans won their advantage by skilful disposition of their forces – by striking one part of the enemy's fleet with preponderant strength and evading a counter-blow by withdrawing after having inflicted a maximum amount of damage.'

Count von Bernstorff reported that King George V's telegram to the Grand Fleet, which was freely reproduced in the USA, and in which he expressed his regret that the rapid retirement of the German forces robbed Britain of a decisive victory, triggered the following comment from *The North American*:

> Such regrets are natural, but they really constitute a tribute to German strategy … The victory of the Germans lay in outmanoeuvring the foe, partially crippling one of his divisions, and extricating themselves before he could bring full pressure to bear.

Prior to Jutland many American newspapers had discussed the probable effects of a victory for German arms on the United States and the German claim of victory over the Royal Navy, which had been perceived as more or less invincible for 100 years, also made some newspapers address these concerns once again. On this occasion von Bernstorff noted that, anxiety is expressed as to the future of America in case of a by no means improbable, decisive, victory of German arms at sea. The Denver *Rocky Mountain News* is very frank on this subject: The day of miracles has not passed; we cannot tell what a day or night may bring forth. The British fleet is not invincible ... Change the command of the sea, endanger it even and the allies would not be the only sufferers. This country has staked an immense sum on this one card. For eighteen months we have been gambling with destiny and in twenty-four hours there has been a marked shortening of the odds which were placed at the beginning on an open thorofare on the Atlantic Ocean.

The foregoing press opinions, which did not do much towards raising British prestige – already long since on the down-grade – in the United States, form a representative collection of journalistic utterances on one day alone. The Ambassador must then have been disappointed, but not surprised, to report that on the following day, Sunday, 4 June, the largely pro-Allied American Press seemed to have begun a campaign, 'the like of which has surely never been seen':

After short reports in the Saturday evening papers, that the German Navy had lost more large battleships than had been announced from Berlin, that 8 German battleships were 'stuck' in Danish waters, that several Zeppelins had been destroyed, and that 'the feeling in England' was excellent, the New York Sunday papers published 12 to 20 columns of news and matter of every kind, the object of which was simply and solely to represent the outcome of the battle in more unfavourable light for Germany. Long cabled reports from the London correspondents of the Associated Press and International News Service, and from the Special Correspondents of the *New York Times*, *World*, *Sun*, and the *New York Herald*, gave the official statements of the British Admiralty and other London sources, to the effect that as a matter of fact, only a small portion of the British fleet had attacked the entire German fleet and forced it to retire to its own waters. Semi-official statements from the same sources, said to be based on the evidence of eyewitnesses, reported the losses of several German Dreadnoughts, in particular the *Hindenburg*, *Derfflinger*, *Lützow* and *Westfalen*. Further, it was suggested that the *Pommern* mentioned in the Berlin report as having been lost was not the old battleship of this name – which was known to have been sunk by a British submarine in the Baltic last summer! – but a quite new ship of the same name, of the most modern construction and armament.

In an article extending over two columns, the British naval critic Archibald Hurd implied that the German losses were heavier in proportion than those of the British. In an interview with the correspondent of the *New York Times*, Admiral Cyprian Bridge represented the naval battle as a 'virtual British victory'.

Winston Churchill in an interview with the Associated Press, pointed out that Britain's command of the sea was not in the slightest degree endangered, but that Germany's power of offensive at sea had been absolutely broken for some time to come. The quintessence of this and other opinions and conclusions was certainly that both London and America had been entirely mistaken as regard the result.'

The *New York Times*, in a leading article on this date, wrote: 'When the German High Seas Fleet did really meet the British Grand Fleet, the naval supremacy of the English was immediately incontestable.'

At the same time the *World* 'corrected' its opinion on the results of the battle, as follows: 'The Germans have won a smashing victory, but it is a victory that puts them nowhere so far as sea power is concerned … The German Navy is still a navy in jail which assaults its keeper now and then with great fury, but which remains in jail nevertheless.'

On the same date the *New York Times* set forth in a tabular statement on its front page, that Britain had lost 14 ships aggregating 114,110 tons, Germany on the other hand, 13 ships aggregating 79,015 tons. On the following day this paper and several others here deliberately and purposely went a step further: they announced to an astonished world that Germany's losses were not merely relatively, but absolutely, heavier than British losses. The whole German victory was nothing but a myth!

At this point in his letter to the German Chancellor, Count von Bernstorff alludes to the power of the American Press writing that:

The *New York American*, with priceless irony, in an article headed: 'The Deadliest Weapon of Naval Warfare', stigmatises the frantic efforts of the British publicity organs to give the British defeat another complexion. The article, which does not admit of abbreviation, reads as follows:

'As fuller details of the great sea battle come to hand, we are more and more convinced of the superiority of the typewriter as a naval weapon over dreadnoughts and battle cruisers.

'The first phase of the battle off the Danish coast began on Wednesday, and was a fleet action between battle cruisers, destroyers and submarines. The second phase was an all-night battle, consisting of individual fighting between dreadnoughts, cruisers, destroyers and submarines. At the conclusion of this second phase on Thursday morning the British Admiralty announced the defeat of the British fleet.

At this stage the third phase of the battle began with a mobilization of the whole available London correspondents' auxiliary naval reserve, and after seventy-two hours of heroic action the defeat of Thursday was converted into a glorious victory of Sunday. The empire [British] certainly owes an immense debt of gratitude to the dauntless heroes of the press, both in London and New York, who have again restored the prestige of the British navy by thus winning the most unique victory which history has yet recorded.

We can recall nothing in the annals of naval warfare to equal the superb gallantry and skill with which the journalistic auxiliary naval reserve has demolished ship after ship of the Teutonic enemy during the past four days and the astonishing success with which it has converted a depressing defeat into a glorious triumph without the loss of even so much as an ink pad. The only thing which invites criticism is the undue moderation of the conquering heroes of the typewrite squadron in not demolishing the whole enemy fleet while they were about it and so ending the war in one magnificent buzz of glory'.

The *New York Evening Post*, which is by no means pro-German, took a much more serious tone towards the British attempts to claim a victory for the British fleet in the battle off the Skagerrak. This paper said: 'Until London's counter-claims are based on something more concrete than "the strongest reasons for supposing", we must refrain from changing a German success into a British victory ... The British boast that the German fleet was forced to seek refuge in harbour is justified against the extravagant claims from Berlin concerning the loss of British control in the North Sea, and the Kaiser as Admiral of the Atlantic. But is must be recalled that up to May 31 the British would not have been content with a mere encounter between two grand fleets that ended in the Germans being driven back into port. England has been hoping since the beginning of the war that the German fleet would "come out". The assumption was that if it did fairly come out, it would never get back again. The German fleet did come out, and it did get back again'.[10]

At this point the belated admission of additional losses at Jutland had a dramatic effect on the attitude of the American Press. The Ambassador described its adverse effects thus:

Into the midst of this newspaper controversy, which was by no means unfavourable to Germany, the cable report here on 8 June via London, of a long official statement, admitting the loss of the battlecruiser *Lützow* and the light cruiser *Rostock*, fell like a bomb. From the Communiqué of the Chief of Admiralty Staff, a lucid and detailed exposition of the magnitude of the German success, the press over here selected merely the belated admission of the loss of the last two ships, adding comments thereon which not only effaced to a considerable extent the great impression of the German victory, but must have seriously shattered the hitherto unquestioned reputation for reliability of the German official war bulletins. The following extracts from a leading article in the *Evening Post* indicate the impression which the above-mentioned announcement made on public opinion here:

'By Berlin's own admission of the loss of the battle cruiser *Lützow* and the light cruiser *Rostock* in the battle of May 31, the legend of a German 'victory' has been totally destroyed ... The prime significance of the latest statement from Berlin is, of course, in the doubt it throws on all German claims, with the indirect confirmation of further British assertions regarding the loss of German first-class battleships.

There will be much less scepticism now with regard to the British claim that the *Hindenburg* was among the ships that went down. The first official announcement from Berlin, on June 1, conceded the loss only of the *Pommern*, the *Wiesbaden* and the *Frauenlob*. Two days later the loss of *Elbing* was announced. On June 4 the [German] Admiralty issued a curt statement that no 'German naval units were lost except those mentioned in the official despatches'. Today comes news of the *Lützow* and *Rostock*.

'Extraordinary, indeed, is the German Admiralty's explanation that for military reasons we refrained from making public the loss of the *Lützow* and the *Rostock*. It is a confession of suppression of truth such as no War Office hitherto has pleaded guilty to. But more than that, it is an explanation that incurs odium without even explaining. What were the military reasons, the necessity of letting loose an outburst of

German patriotism which subsequent confessions would not altogether destroy?'

The *World*, *Globe*, *New York Tribune*, *Brooklyn Eagle*, and a number of other papers, some of them in a very malicious or at least sarcastic tone, point out that Germany's 'lies for military reasons' cast doubts on the whole report. Even the respected and always dignified *Springfield Republican* wrote:

'The German Admiralty weakens one's confidence in the truthfulness of any of its official reports by stating that the facts had been hitherto suppressed for military reasons. The same kind of reasons may be causing the denial of the loss of still more warships; indeed, one cannot ever be sure that the whole truth concerning German losses has been told. A presumption is at least created that British estimates of the German losses are nearer to the facts than any official statement coming from Berlin.'

The *New York Times* wrote in a spirit of hatred which is absolutely typical of all this influential paper's editorial utterances regarding Germany:

'The utmost doubt and suspicion rest, and must rest, upon the veracity of the German Admiralty. The exaggeration, still persisted in, of the British losses, the minimising of the German losses, the breaking gently to the German people of news prudently held back in order not to chill their transports and prevent the passage of credit: the convenience of the cloak of "military reasons" – all this looks like a deliberate plan to feed the popular imagination, to assure honest Hans and Michel that the German Navy, if a bit costly, is more than a match for "the gigantic British fleet", to keep the truth from the people and fire them with new energy for a struggle which the master caste may have begun to regard as hopeless. The great German victory is petering out ... And what is the plight of a Government afraid to tell its people the truth? But how can the truth be kept from leaking out? A Government suspected that buy the rest of the world of unveracity [*sic*] cannot permanently dupe its own people. At any moment Max Harden[11] may blab the inconvenient truth.'[12]

This devastatingly perceptive critique of the failed German propaganda effort must have distressed Count von Bernstorff who was an opponent of unrestricted submarine warfare while at the same time working very hard to keep the United States of America from entering the conflict on the Allied side. He pointed out in his letter to von Bethmann-Hollweg that the belated admission of the loss of *Lützow* and *Rostock* more than overcame adverse publicity generated by the British failure to admit the sinking of the battleship *Audacious* which had been witnessed by many Americans traveling aboard the White Star liner *Olympic*.[13]

> The American public in general for some time past has not swallowed everything as credible which the 'pro-Ally' papers dish up for it; especially since the experience of *Audacious*, it has by no means convinced of the reliability of the British Admiralty's statements. With regard to the naval battle off the Skagerrak, it must regretfully be admitted that the British Press Bureau and its American myrmidons have to a very large degree succeeded in effacing the first impression, so unfavourable to our enemy's prestige here, of a severe British defeat, and that the tardy German admission of previously concealed losses was of considerable service to them is this respect.[14]

The marked shift in American public opinion following the Germans' belated admission on 8 June of the loss a modern battlecruiser and a fourth light cruiser was detected by correspondents for British newspapers and reported back to their readers even before Count von Bernstorff had finished compiling his letter to the German Chancellor. For example, the *Newcastle Journal* of 14 June contained the following piece:

> New York correspondent the *Daily Telegraph* says: 'Strange as it may seem Europeans, it is only during the last day or two that Americans have been able to realise the true significance of the battle off the Skagerrak. The Germans had a big start in announcing the world their 'unexampled naval victory', and it was a long time before the British version, tardily issued, succeeded in removing the erroneous impression first credited. To-day, however, Americans realise, completely that the Germans deliberately falsified their returns with the object of influencing neutral opinion, and also of 'bull-dozing' the Germans at home into passing the extra credits. These, of course, were the 'military reasons' of the German Government for holding back the publication of big losses of their own, and of exaggerating the losses of the enemy. Nobody here, except the German-Americans, believes that Berlin even now has issued the final list, and whether it is officially supplemented or not, the utmost doubt and suspicion rest, and must rest, upon the veracity of the German Admiralty.'[15]

191

Just over a month later, the former German Naval Attaché to the United States, Captain Karl Boy-Ed, wrote to Colonel Willard Church of the *Army and Navy Journal* at New York commenting on the hypocrisy of the English Press while at the same time admitting that the attempt to hide some German losses at Jutland was a mistake:

> As for the belated announcement of the sinking of *Lützow* and *Rostock*, I may confidentially tell you that I was very much against the procedure chosen by those competent in this case and that I voted strongly against such procedure. However, there were strong reasons for those who dissented from my opinion for acting as they did and it is ridiculous, that particularly the English press belittles the German Admiralty so much for its attitude in this case. Apparently the English have quite forgotten that the *Audacious* sank on 27th October 1914 and the sinking until this very day has been always denied even officially by the English.[16]

German Perspectives

The spell of Trafalgar has been broken.[1]

By 1914 the German High Seas Fleet had become the world's second most powerful navy, but its ability to express that power was severely hampered by geography which greatly favoured the British. Thus, the Royal Navy could remain in its own waters and shut off all German sea communication except for that in the Baltic, while, unless the Germans could almost annihilate the Grand Fleet, the British would be able to protect their maritime communications.

From a German perspective, even the destruction of a detached British battle squadron or the winning of an indecisive battle in the North Sea would be merely the first of many such actions before they could break the British blockade. The cumulative effect of the latter on the German economy and population was becoming more decisive. Clearly, time was on the side of the British in so far as the naval campaign in the North Sea was concerned.

The configuration of the North Sea also favoured the Royal Navy because the Germans could only launch their offensive operations in the North Sea from a single point which was largely blocked by minefields and could be monitored easily by British submarines. Of necessity, any retreat would have to be through these same very restricted channels and consequently, the High Seas Fleet ran the risk of being cut off and hemmed in against a neutral coast. Furthermore, because many of the German sites of egress were adjacent to neutral Danish and Dutch territory British agents would have been able to gain news of German operations very quickly.

In comparison, because the British southern naval bases were too small to accommodate the entire Grand Fleet, the latter had to make use of more distant bases at Scapa Flow and Cromarty and this meant that it was difficult to intercept the High Seas Fleet in the southern North Sea.

The Need for a German Naval Victory

The Battle of Jutland took place at a very difficult period for Germany with the Verdun campaign, which cost them at least 340,000 casualties, drifting into a bloody stalemate, a looming Russian offensive in Galicia, and Romania about to enter the war on the Entente side.

Clearly, the time had come for the High Seas Fleet to justify the enormous amount of money and materiel invested in it by demonstrating that it could at very least take the war to the British. Furthermore, even if it had no effect on the battle for command of the sea, the defeat of an isolated British battle squadron or even an indecisive victory could be exploited at home and abroad. Finally, it had become necessary to demonstrate once and for all whether the High Seas Fleet had any chance of breaking the British command of the sea before the Kaiser would be convinced of the need to resume unrestricted U-boat warfare and the attendant risk that the United States would be dragged into the conflict on the side of the Allies.

After the Battle

On the afternoon of 1 June, soon after the High Seas Fleet had returned Wilhelmshaven, Scheer assembled his admirals to receive their reports. Their evidence was impressive, not least because in addition to standing up the full might of Jellicoe's battleships, they had also witnessed British battlecruiser and armoured cruisers blow up in front of them. Scheer passed the information to the Naval Staff in Berlin who compiled the official communiqué, released early that evening, announcing a famous German victory at the *Skagerrakschlacht* (Battle of the Skagerrak) and Admiral Scheer became the 'Victor of the Skagerrak'.

Neutral Reaction

The German communiqué was distributed worldwide and caused a sensation while in Germany many newspapers produced special editions with stunning headlines announcing 'Great Victory at Sea', 'Many English Battleships Destroyed'. A huge placard was hung above the entrance to *Tageszeitung* proclaimed that 'Trafalgar is Wiped Out'.[2]

The Germans must have been delighted by the impression that was produced on neutral minds by the first official communiqué from London which appeared to confirm the German account of the fight published twenty-four hours earlier. The newspapers thereupon published articles under such headings as: 'Great Britain admits defeat at Sea'.

However, as more information was released by the British Admiralty, the same newspapers began to speculate as to the actual outcome. For example, on 4 June the Oslo-based paper *Verdens Gang* published an article under the headline *The Sea Battle*:

> A start of astonishment went through people when the first telegram from Berlin came with the result of the great fight in the North Sea.
>
> The German High Seas Fleet, or a greater portion of it, had inflicted upon a considerably superior English squadron, a very heavy defeat. And as the hours went by throughout the Friday and no telegram came from London about the battle and its result, people were forced to believe that England, the mistress of the seas for centuries, had suffered defeat in the first sea fight of the war in which many ships of every type in a modern fleet took part. And when, on Friday night, the first English telegram about the battle came, belief was changed to certainty.
>
> The telegram gave this account of the losses which England had suffered: 5 of the best ships in the English fleet were sunk; more rendered incapable of fighting, and a large number of smaller vessels destroyed. The Admiralty announcement contained very little about German losses, and their statements were indefinite. The impossible appeared to have happened: England's prestige at sea had after all, so far as one could judge, received its deathblow.
>
> But yesterday there came a telegram which made it clear that the German announcements of victory were considerably exaggerated. The English Admiralty gave detailed information about the German losses: 3 of the German High Seas Fleet's largest and newest had been destroyed by torpedoes or by cannon fire, and many of the larger vessels as well as the smaller fighting vessels had been severely damaged. It is true that the English losses are large, larger than the German, but looked at relatively it is the German Navy which has suffered most.
>
> There is also another sign that the Germans have not indicated their losses correctly: after the first express-telegram of Thursday night from Berlin, in which Germans characterized their losses as inconsiderable, there was not, from German source a single world about the German losses apart from the announcement of the sinking of the small cruiser *Frauenlob*; this had already been foreshadowed in the first telegram from Berlin.
>
> This silence can only be read as pointing to the fact that the German losses have been far greater than was first announced by the German Admiralty Staff.

According to the information which is now in our possession, Germany's announcements of victory have been premature.

The losses of the English Fleet have been heavy, but, as is pointed out in another article today's issue, the English remained master of the field, and when the principal forces of the English battle fleet made their attack, the tables were turned.

The Germans have fought gloriously; the new German fleet has shown itself to be a battle fleet in the word's best and modern sense, but England's position as the world's strongest sea-power does not seem, as was originally supposed, to have been shaken.[3]

The German communiqué of 7 June admitting the loss of *Lützow* and *Rostock* made an unfavourable impression in all shades of opinion in the Swedish Press. Thus, on 9 June the *Stockholm Tidning*, which, although a Liberal paper, had often been unfriendly to the Allies, made some very caustic comments about the German communiqué writing that the

tardy recognition by the German Admiralty of their losses must have afforded a painful surprise to those, both within and without the boundaries of Germany, who have uncritically accepted the dogma of the defeat of the British Battle Fleet. They can hardly avoid thinking that the losses of the German Fleet in the battle perhaps do not even stop with those now admitted.

The article concludes by saying that the value of the German statements as to British losses and of their asseveration that the battle was a German victory, might thus be discounted before adding,

that a certain passage in the German communiqué looks like an attempt to throw dust in the eyes of their readers. It moreover points out that the German quotation of the British communiqué that Admiral Jellicoe with the Grand Fleet had already on June 1st returned to their base at Scapa Flow, over 300 miles away from the scene of the Battle [i.e. the British fled the field on 31st May], was actually false.[4]

Kaiser Wilhelm II visits the High Seas Fleet
In his history of the High Seas Fleet during the First World War, Admiral Scheer wrote that:

The first honour paid to the fleet was a visit from His Majesty the Emperor on June 5, who, on board the flagship, *Friedrich der Grosse,* made a hearty speech of welcome to divisions drawn from the crews of all the ships, thanking them in the name of the Fatherland for their gallant deeds. In the afternoon the Emperor visited all the hospitals where the wounded lay, as well as the hospital ship *Sierra Ventana*, where lay Rear-Admiral Behncke, Leader of Squadron III, who was wounded in the battle, and who was able to give the Emperor a detailed account of his impressions while at the head of the battleships. Several of the German princes also visited the Fleet, bringing greetings from their homes to the crews and expressing pride in the Fleet and the conduct of the men.

Apart from the inspection of the ships, these visits also offered an opportunity of gaining information respecting the general duties of the Fleet and plans for the impending battle that was expected, for, as those visits proved, the battle had greatly enhanced the interest in the Fleet throughout the whole country.[5]

In view of the scale of the British losses, the euphoric Kaiser, who had an excellent knowledge of English naval history, declared that 'The spell of Trafalgar is broken'. He went on to add that 'the British were beaten. You have started a new chapter in world history.'[6]

The Kaiser wanted the battle to be known as the *North Sea Battle of June First* in an imitation of the *Glorious First of June* named after Admiral Howe's victory over the French in 1794. Apparently the German Navy had great difficulty in getting the Kaiser to accept the far less historical name *Battle of Skaggerak* by which the indecisive encounter became known and celebrated as a great victory.[7]

Reports in German Newspapers

On 6 June the *Danziger Neueste Nachrichten* carried a report out the experiences aboard the battleship *Ostfriesland* – an account written by an 'eye-witness aboard the ship'.

The article established a format that was to be repeated many times as it contained a detailed description of the action as well as refutations of points made in British official communiqués:

> Our squadron was proceeding in line of battle, and everyone on board was awaiting the coming events. At 6.20 we proceeded at utmost speed, and, about 10 minutes later, I was able to distinguish four enemy cruisers and four super-dreadnoughts of the Indomitable and Marlborough classes respectively. Our range finders gave the distance as 26 kilometres [28,434 yards]. Nevertheless, I was able to observe the ships very clearly, because the visibility was extraordinarily good.

The British reports are wrong in attributing their defeat to the misty weather.

The first rounds were exchanged at about 6.40 pm. We had approached to within 19 kilometres [20,779 yards] of the enemy. The dreadnoughts were proceeding in line ahead and could be easily observed by us. We soon saw that the salvoes from our port side were all hitting the enemy. We also noticed that some ships were on fire, but they were quickly extinguished. After about an hour, we could see the second ship of the enemy's line was dropping astern. We also saw clearly that after about another hour the enemy turned away. We supposed that he was going home. But he soon returned with reinforcements.

Observation now became more difficult, as it had now become dusk and the visibility became considerably worse. But from the violence of the cannonade which now commenced and from the flashes of the guns it was soon apparent that there were now many more ships than before firing on the side of the enemy. The British has alleged that Zeppelins played a great part in our reconnaissance work. That is an error. They did not arrive till 1 June, when it was all over.

The shortest distance from the enemy attained by our squadrons was slightly less than 10 kilometres [10,936 yards]. The battle reached its height at about 10.30 pm. The entire fleets were then assembled and it may be assumed that the battle was fought over a space of about 15 nautical miles. Salvo after salvo was fired until nearly 11.30. As the visibility was now very low, we could with difficulty observe the effect of our salvoes. On the other hand, we could easily see that the British fire mostly fell short, and we had a strong sense of our own superiority of gunnery.

At about 11.30, our torpedo boats were ordered to attack en masse. They drove the main body of the British fleet eastwards. The firing gradually died away. We turned back, long after the British had already done so. The British assertion that the German fleet took flight is untrue. The contrary is the truth. Our ships remained on the spot for a time, but of course there was no use in us staying on the scene of the battle without the enemy. There was no further fighting the next morning. Our impression was that the British fleet was so seriously damaged that it was unable to follow us. During the night a number of isolated actions took place. A portion of the British cruisers tried to harry us, to cover the retreat of their ships. But, more especially, we were pursued by several flotillas of torpedo-boats destroyers. Many of these were destroyed by our fire. I heard on good authority that the WESTFALEN alone sank six destroyers.[8]

On 10 June the *Hamburger Fremdenblatt* published a message from Berlin purporting to be a full description of 'The German Naval Victory at the Skagerrak'. It claimed the strategic importance of the German victory for their war position in the North Sea.

After describing the clash between the battlecruisers and mistakenly claiming that all five Queen Elizabeth-class ships were present, the article states:

> Meanwhile, there approaches from the North, presumably coming from Norwegian waters, the English main force consisting of more than 20 battleships. The climax of the battle is reached while the English Cruiser Fleet continues its attempts to catch up the head of our line, Admiral Jellicoe is striving to put himself with his large battleships like the cross of a T in front of the head of our line. As the head of our line thus comes for a time under fire from both sides, Admiral Scheer throws the German line round on to a westerly course, and at the same time our torpedo boat flotillas are ordered to attack the enemy, and they do so three times in succession with splendid vigour and visible success. A number of large English battleships suffer severe damage and one sinks before our eyes.
>
> By these attacks the English Main Fleet is driven away to the east, whence it will afterwards have taken a north-westerly course homewards. The German Fleet ceases its violent cannonade at 11.30 as the English had already stopped firing, and after nightfall there was nothing but the flash of their salvoes to give us a target. As the enemy cannot be found again the main battle is broken off.
>
> During the night numerous cruiser fights and torpedo-boat attacks develop against individual enemy ships, which either had gone astray or had been ordered to worry us and to cover the retreat of the English. In these actions an enemy battlecruiser, a cruiser of the Achilles or Shannon class, several small cruisers and at least 10 destroyers are sunk – six of them by *Westfalen* alone.
>
> A squadron of English battleships came up from the south, but not until June 1, after the battle was over and it turned away without coming into action or even coming in sight of the main German force. It was observed by one of our Zeppelins, which, as is well known, owing to the weather on the previous day, could not undertake reconnaissances until June 1.[9]

Many papers always carried discursive articles which not only described the battle but also wrote glowingly about the results achieved by the High Seas Fleet. One such, entitled *The Naval Victory off The*

Skaggerak and written by a Captain Hollweg and published initially in the Berlin paper *Die Woche*, was also reproduced in the *Wilhelmshaven Tageblatt* of 18 June started by reminding readers about *The Glorious First of June.*

Thereafter, the author lambasts the British Press, British pride and British brutality before asking some very pertinent questions of the Royal Navy's scouting and signalling performance:

> 122 years ago, on 1 June 1794, 400 miles from Ushant, after several days of preliminary skirmishes, the British Admiral Lord Howe, with 25 ships of the line, decisively defeated a French republican fleet of about the same strength commanded by Villaret.
>
> The memory of this victory is preserved in British naval history under the sonorous name of 'the glorious first of June'. The victory is almost as well known in England as Aboukir and Trafalgar, not so much by reason of its strategic and tactical importance as on account of its name, which remains in one's memory.
>
> The first of June 1916 will cause the splendour of this day to fade somewhat in England. The memory of the glorious day in 1794 will in future be accompanied by the unpleasant after-taste of 1 June 1916. Germany too now has its 'glorious first of June', though the Germany victory will be known to history by another name.
>
> In spite of what appears to be official support and of the efforts of a Churchill and a Reuter, the British press will not succeed by its lies in turning the honourably won victory of the German fleet into a defeat and into the 'greatest British naval victory since Trafalgar'. Happily neutrals have better means of learning the truth, for the purposes of impartial historical inquiry, than Reuter's reports and Churchill's boasts. Let it be said the honour of the British press that a considerable part of it is beginning to abandon the distortion of the facts, and speaks in all earnest of the battle off the Skagerrak as a 'most costly disaster for British sea-power'.
>
> It is not out of the question that someday, when even French people again can look at things objectively, they may feel a certain malicious pleasure over this failure of the arrogant sea-power of their very brutal Ally.
>
> A portion of the British press has been attempting to portray the course of the battle off the Skagerrak as follows. The German fleet had some secret strategic objective. The British fleet, unfortunately being unprovided with air-scouts, was not sufficiently well informed of the German's departure from harbour to be able to attack them in full strength. The 'impetuous' cruisers of the British fleet this met the

entire German fleet in superior strength. They thus suffered considerable loss in their action with the latter, who had the assistance of submarines, minefields, gas bombs, aircraft and other 'unfair' means. When the British main fleet was brought on the scene by the masterly leadership of the British, the German fleet unfortunately fled to the protection of its harbours from the punishment and annihilation prepared for it. Result: strategic object unattained, complete tactical defeat of the Germans by superior British gunnery, no loss of British prestige. The victorious British fleet commands the North Sea as it did before the action.

The day will come when England itself will be ashamed of much perversions of the truth. Impartial historical research will make short work of such self-deceptions.

The German official report, which states precisely the place, time and course of the action, clearly shows what was intended and what was achieved. The German fleet had no secret object. It wanted to fight, and it went to seek the enemy at the place where he had been frequently reported. The German fleet had often been at sea with the same object. It was not its fault of the British fleet was not there.

The result of the battle shows that, thanks to skilful dispositions on the part of the Commander-in-Chief, the German objective of fighting under tactically advantageous conditions was attained. Wind, weather, the position of the sun and the geography of the scene of action are important factors in such tactical calculations. The attacker, and that was the German fleet, has, as always, the option of being able to decide the time and place of the battle, and thus to turn many of the above mentioned factors to his own advantage. That is invariably the advantage which the offensive possesses over the defensive.

British pride seems unable to conceive why the German fleet, barely half the strength of the British, did not station itself somewhere or other and wait patiently for the entire British fleet to assemble undisturbed around it, so as to be able to complete without risk the task of utter annihilation, which has been so frequently threatened. That was not the intention. The German Commander-in-Chief had no wish to make a present of cheap glory to his British opponent.

The British assert that the essential part of the battle consisted merely of a partial engagement between the cruiser forces on both sides. The German official report completely refutes this contention. The entire British battlefleet was engaged with the Germans. In consequence of repeated attacks by our torpedo-boat flotillas on the head of the line of battleships led by Admiral Jellicoe in person, the

British admiral broke off the engagement. The only possible explanation of this is that the British battle squadrons also suffered such severe losses by gunfire and torpedoes that the British admiral thought it dangerous to complete the movement of his line which he had begun. The German Commander-in-Chief from that moment was able to carry out undisturbed the movements of his squadrons, which he had already commenced, the same precision as at manoeuvres, and he set his course for the night.

The feebleness of the contention that submarines, Zeppelins, mine-fields and poisonous gases were the source of the victory won by the Germans in honourable fighting has already been adequately exposed from German official quarters. The object of these British assertions is quite obvious: although they are obliged to admit to neutrals that the immensely superior British fleet, which commands the sea, has suffered such extraordinary and unexpected losses, it must never be admitted that this German success was won in the natural way by 'sheer hard fighting' with men-of-war armed with the gun, the queen of all weapons, and the torpedo; some German devilry or other must be found to account for the want of success. British pride cannot and will not admit that any other fleet is equal to its own and in effect of its weapons.

Finally as regards the 'flight' of the German fleet to its harbours. Which fleet, the British or German, was superior in the number of warships, especially cruisers and torpedo-boats, and in the average speed of its squadrons? Both fleets were closely engaged almost until dusk, as already mentioned. The German fleet was in the open sea more than 150 miles from its nearest base. There is no choice of route from there to the corner of the 'wet triangle'. It is practically a straight line from the scene of the battle to Heligoland. There could scarcely be any doubt about the course chosen by the German fleet. A short June night fell, with barely five hours of darkness. Does any British professional seaman seriously expect to persuade the world, that an energetic British admiral, anxious to fight and with his hands free, could not during the night have kept touch, by means of his light vessels, with the German fleet, if he still cherished the desire to annihilate it and if he still had the power to do so?

Has not the British fleet learnt, in the long years of hard training in peace, to keep in touch with an enemy main fleet of about 30 vessels during a short night with the aid of its numerous fast cruisers?

Admiral Jellicoe undoubtedly knew the course taken by the main German fleet from the reports of his forces, either from those which were sunk by the German anti-torpedo gun, or from those which successfully attacked the 'Pommern' and 'Frauenlob'. Like blazing torches, the British cruisers and destroyers beaten off in the night attack, marked the course of the German fleet.

Since it was his duty and his ardent desire to annihilate the German fleet, why did he not throw the completely intact fresh squadron of 12 ships approaching from the south, across the enemies' path: this compelling them to fight, until he himself should be able to reach the scene of the new battle? The fact is that he did not do so, and did not feel strong enough to renew the battle. The victorious German fleet and the British admiral both headed for their home ports. And, on the way, the German ships still found time to pick up and bring back as prisoners many brave British seamen from sunken vessels.

The German Commander-in-Chief and the entire German fleet had fully expected to meet the British fleet, strengthened by fresh squadrons ready for action, on the morning of the 1 June when they were on their way to inner German Bight. But, when the sun rose on the 1 June, there was nothing in sight; the sea was clear of the enemy and remained so. There was no reason why the German Commander-in-Chief should again seek out the enemy and remain at sea for that purpose. He had attained his object and performed his task. His action is fully explained by the desire to complete his supplies of stores and coal, to give his gallant crews a well-earned rest, to land the wounded and at once be ready for fresh-fighting.

The German fleet also claims that it did not owe the victory of 31 May and 1 June 1916 to chance, but to the courage and efficiency of all who were engaged. Until the battlefleet gained the long-awaited opportunity of proving in this war its powers and the need for its existence, there were many in the German nation who felt a measure of doubt, whether it was right to build up the Empire's sea-power on powerful squadrons of battleships.

Many people in our country have wondered, in quiet moments, whether the millions spent under the Fleet Law would bear fruit and interest in this war. There were even naval experts who thought it their duty to publish their notions regarding the 'cheap' submarine. But now all doubts have been swept aside by the thunder of the battleships' guns on the last day of the spring month of 1916. The winter of our discontent vanished before the sun of the 'glorious first of June'.

Germany's fleet will now live, Germany's sea-power will now endure for all the time![10]

Demands For The Resumption of Unrestricted Submarine Warfare
During a meeting of the German Navy League, which was reported by
the *Berliner Tageblatt* on 19 June, Grand Admiral von Koester was
strikingly modest in his reference to the battle of 31 May-1 June:[11]

> Thanks to the determination of our officers, the bravery of our seamen
> and the excellence of the materiel, the first sea-power of the world
> suffered such great losses in the first great naval battle of the world
> war, the battle of the Skagerrak, that it has been considerably
> weakened in spite of a numerical superiority. This battle proved how
> much can be accomplished, even against a first class enemy, by
> thorough tactical training, united action on the part of the leaders,
> harmonious co-operation of the separate units and faultless handling
> of guns and torpedoes.

Thereafter, the true scale of the German victory at Jutland can be seen
in his arguments about the need to resume unrestricted submarine
warfare which he believed was the only way by which Germany could
win the war. In effect, he admitted that German surface fleet was quite
incapable of either breaking the crippling British blockade or disrupting
Britain's vital maritime trade.

> Unfortunately, the enemy have completely succeeded in cutting off
> our overseas trade, owing to the unfavourable geographical position
> which restricts us in the North Sea to a small triangle. The disturbance
> of Foreign [i.e. British, French & Italian] trade has been chiefly the
> work of submarines. At first, when our submarines became active,
> the English took a sporting interest in the result. But, when the
> shortage of tonnage increased and freight prices rose, they began to
> realise the strategical and political object of the weapon.
>   When the Allies declined the United States proposal to disarm all
> merchant vessels, they actually deprived our chivalrous submarine
> officers of all possibility of showing the consideration they would
> have wished to show to the crews of ships which they intended to
> torpedo, because the time necessary to ascertain if a ship were armed
> or no would be the most dangerous moment for the submarine.
> Therefore England and her Allies must be held guilty for what must
> now occur, namely the endangering of human lives. We must make
> full use of the weapons at our command. When the enemy employs
> mines and aircraft against us by sea and land, when the greatest
> possible cruelties have been perpetrated in the East, and when Mr
> Wilson, the champion of humanity and justice, has made the

204

prolongation of the war possible simply and solely by supplying our enemies with munitions, why should not we employ this new and, for us, most successful weapon, which is certainly no more open to the charge in inhumanity that the methods just mentioned.

As far as it is possible we must go forward energetically in full consciousness of our aim, however, greatly the United States consider that the holy and unimpeachable laws of humanity are jeopardised. We must use our whole weight as a lever in this direction, especially as the weapon is wielded in so wise, well-considered and determined a manner by our incomparable submarine seamen, whom God protects (Loud cheers). If it is considered necessary to restrict the employment of our submarines, there must undoubtedly be important political and economic reasons which are beyond our judgement. We submit to them, but we do so with a heavy heart, knowing that the Navy is thus making a great sacrifice. We know that we are in a position to wound the enemy to the heart in a comparatively short time by using our submarine weapon without scruple or mercy (Loud cheers). We can best judge the weight that has lately been taken off the minds of our enemies by the abatement of our submarine warfare when we note the consequent decrease of marine insurance rates.[12]

On 20 June the *Tägliche Rundschau* published a long article under the headline 'What Can We Learn From the German Naval Victory off the Skagerrak?':

The naval victory achieved by the German High Seas Fleet over its numerically far superior British enemy on 31 May 1916, and the following night, has been hailed with hearty rejoicing throughout Germany. And yet it would not be too much to say that the German nation has not yet sufficiently grasped the full extent of this veritably historic event. Since the beginning of the war, i.e. for nearly two years, people had waited in vain for an encounter between the two main fighting forces, the actual battle fleets, and gradually they became tacitly convinced that such an encounter would never take place. And now the long-expected has happened at last, and not merely happened, but – what we scarcely dared to hope – resulted in a glorious victory for the German fleet.. The belief in the invincibility of the British Navy, which remained unshaken in England, amongst her Allies and throughout all the neutral countries, notwithstanding Coronel, the Dogger Bank, the Dardanelles, and the successes of our submarines, has been proved to be a superstition. What the battle of

Trafalgar (21 October 1805) achieved, has been seriously impaired 111 years later by the Battle of the Skagerrak.

Thereafter the writer recites the bare facts of the battle and its results noting that 'Admiral Beatty's famous battlecruiser squadron, the pride of Britain, was in a bad way' soon after the commencement of the battle. The article continues the fiction that the British lost the new battleship *Warspite* and a light cruiser of about 5,000 tons before undertaking some crude analyses of the relative losses suffered by each fleet:

> In view of these facts, it is truly pitiable that the British should attempt to minimise the defeat, either by stories of suppressed German losses, or by casting the blame on to the thick weather, which prevented full use being made of their heavy guns. The weather in the North Sea is hardly ever clear enough to suit the convenience of the English, and if this circumstances enabled the Germans to come up closer, so as to make full use of their medium calibre guns, this merely shows that the construction of their ships was better suited to the normal weather conditions of the North Sea.
>
> What are the lessons to be learnt from the results of the naval battle? The victory over a superior British force shows us that our side was the more efficient. The spirit and the material of the German fleet proved superior. In the first place, our shooting was better and more effectual, for the enemy's heaviest losses were caused in the earlier part of the battle by the guns of our battlecruisers. With all due respect to the valour of the British, the greater dash, the more daring offensive, was displayed on our side. This was shown by the successful torpedo-boats in broad daylight, three of which were carried out in succession by the same squadron. Further we had better leaders, and the tactical discipline and solidarity of our squadrons was gloriously demonstrated.
>
> In short, our Emperor's conception of the Fleet and the life-work of Admiral von Tirpitz have been gloriously vindicated. The apparent inactivity to which our High Seas Fleet seemed to be doomed, its inability to attack the British foe, who never showed himself outside his home waters and protected stations, led many people to suppose that the capital expended on the construction of a battle fleet had been thrown away, and that in view of the submarine successes, large battleships were altogether obsolete weapons.[13]

The Sinking of the Old Cruiser *Frauenlob*
The obsolete cruiser *Frauenlob* had been sunk during the night action

by a torpedo fired from one of the cruiser *Southampton*'s submerged tubes. *Frauenlob*'s eight survivors were rescued by a Dutch steamer after drifting for about ten hours.

A correspondent from the *Norddeutsche Allgemeine Zeitung* was despatched to Holland and interviewed the two senior survivors namely Midshipman Stolzmann and Engine Room Warrant Officer Max Müller, about the last hours of the ship. Their story was published on 25 June. Midshipman Stolzmann described the sinking of his ship:

> After darkness had fallen about 1.30, the searchlight of a ship at the end of our line suddenly illuminated a cruiser which looked like a destroyer, and the ship opened fire. It was soon clear that there were five cruisers of the Aurora type, only about 800 metres distant. A few minutes later we altered course to starboard. I at once switched on both available searchlights on to the cruiser opposite us. The guns immediately opened fire. This was followed by such a furious rain of shell, which nearly all hit the after part of the ship, that it looked as several enemy ships were concentrating their fire on us.
>
> A very few seconds later, a terrific crash there, with the characteristic tremor of a ship which has been hit by a torpedo. We had been torpedoed. The light went out. The searchlights, which till then had fulfilled their mission well, went out also, and the gunlayers continued firing independently. As all my functions of range-finding, searchlight and signal officer had now come to an end, I left the upper bridge. The ship had already a heavy list to port. I hurried to the after bridge, to give any help I could. As I passed the conning tower, I heard orders given to the engine-room and quartermaster with a view to turning the ship to starboard. It was all in vain ... only the rudder seemed still under control.
>
> From now on the searchlights did not play on us and the bombardment ceased. Owing to the machinery having been put out of action by the explosion, we were soon left behind. For the first minute the ship merely seemed to sink slowly, but after that it went down rapidly. On reaching the after bridge, I barely had time to fasten on a lifebelt, and glance hastily at the havoc in the after part of the ship a shapeless mass of wreckage, cowls and corpses ... before the water reached the deck of the after bridge, and I threw myself onto a raft which was floating in the angle between the fore-and-aft bridge. I found two men who with great difficulty helped me to clear the raft from the fore-and-aft bridge and the after bridge, so as not to be caught in the latter. A few seconds later we saw the ship sink without any internal explosion.

Some of our guns continued firing when the gunlayers were already standing in the water and the ship was sinking. As the last tremor ran through the vessel, three cheers for H.M. the Kaiser ran out.

The Engine Room Chief Warrant Officer described what happened after the torpedo exploded:

At about 12.40 [a.m.] there was a tremendous explosion in the after part of the ship, which could only have been caused by a torpedo. At the same time, both engines stopped, probably owing to damage to the propeller-shafts, the light went out and there was a roar of water pouring in.

As I followed the sound, to find out where the hole was, the water was already rushing over the floor-plates, so that it was no longer possible to locate the hole. I went on deck and enquired through the speaking tubes to the starboard engine-room, whether the engine-room was still intact. The chief engineer replied: 'We will try and get rid of the water from the port engine-room'. This took some time, and meanwhile the action was proceeding on the port side with unabated fury. The ship had a heavy list to port.

At the same time, the water was rushing over the deck and flooding the port side. Just then I saw the chief engineer coming up from the starboard engine room – probably he was the last to leave. I just had time to put on a lifebelt, and was then carried away by the sea and washed overboard, after becoming entangled several times in the open hammock lockers. After swimming about for some time, I reached a raft, and just as I climbed on to it, with some difficulty, I saw the funnels of the *Frauenlob* disappear. For some time an acetylene buoy marked the place where she sank.[14]

On 28 June the *Tägliche Rundschau* published an account of the battleship *Thüringen* in the Battle of the Skagerrak by an officer who was on board at the time. The article contains a dramatic account of the sinking of the British armoured cruiser *Black Prince*:

We had just passed a blood-red flaming British armoured cruiser with which SMS *Nassau* had been engaged, when a vessel approached the *Thüringen* on the opposite course, like a great white spectre. Friend or foe? What an immense responsibility there is at such a trying moment! We made some absolutely secret recognition signals, known only to German ships. The enemy, for such she must have been, returned no answer. Searchlights and guns were laid on her. 'Switch on the searchlights!' The beams of light fell at once on their objective. Almost at the same instant came the word: 'British! Salvo – fire!' Our broadsides roared out, and fell with a mighty crash into the stern of the enemy, who was seen to be an old, four funnelled cruiser. An immense column of fire blazed up, and a devastating fire was now opened on the whole of the enemy ship, raking her from stem to stern, before the enemy could come to her senses. We were only 700 or 800 metres away from her. He failed to put up any effective defence, so quickly was she overwhelmed. As we had fired a few salvoes from our broadside, SMS *Ostfriesland* and *Friedrich der Grosse* also joined in, and helped valiantly to give the enemy the finishing stroke. Another lofty flame blazed up, and then the vessel sank in silence.

About an hour later, another ship was seen burning a long way to port. The light of a rocket showed her to be an enemy cruiser of medium size, which was on fire in the stern, but she seemed otherwise unharmed. She was going against the wind, in order to restrict the fire as far as possible to the stern. Our very first salvo straddled her, i.e. the range was so exact that no further alteration was needed. The fire presented a good [aiming] mark, and when, after firing a few more salvoes, we sent up another light rocket, we saw the ship listing with a heavy list to starboard, so that the upper deck was almost touching the water. We then left the enemy to her fate.[15]

Perhaps the most comprehensive article about Jutland to appear in the German Press was that in the *Frankfurter Zeitung* under the headline 'The Naval Action off the Skagerrak 31 May–1 June' and which was serialised in four parts on 30 June, 1 July, 3 July and 4 July. One of the issues was that of possession of the battlefield as a measure of victory:

On the British side, in first embarrassment, with obvious desire of offering a by no means pampered public a morsel of comfort, the curt announcement was repeated that the British battlefleet 'was left in possession of the battlefield'. Attention has been called elsewhere to the absurdity of this amateurish phrase. There is no such thing as holding the sea or conquering it, in the sense of land warfare. 50 square kilometres [31 square miles] of the North Sea cannot be conquered. A naval battle is decided by result. However, in order to do full justice to the British point of view, let us follow up the idea. The criterion which British officialdom offered to the world for 'possession of the battlefield' on 24 January 1915, after the Battle of Dogger Bank, was the fact that the prisoners were left in the hands of the British, On 31 May the survivors of nearly all the British ships sunk were picked up by us. It will therefore be necessary on this occasion to find some other evidence of 'victorious possession of the battlefield'.

The article concluded with the following:

It is clear to every German that the battle of the Skagerrak did not have a decisive result. It is not our fault that the battle was not fought to a finish, but that of our enemy, who, although in far superior force, in every way, did not attempt to fight it out. On the other hand, it is established for all time that the battle resulted in a very considerable success for us against overwhelming odds.

Those who had the good fortune to take part in this battle, will acknowledge with a grateful heart that God's protection was granted us in abundant measure. It is an old historical truism however, that luck is usually on the side of the most efficient.[16]

Reality Returns

Despite all the euphoric claims of victory that appeared in the German Press it didn't take long for a more sober assessment of the outcome and the prospects for success in any future surface confrontation with the Grand Fleet. The unpalatable truth which, could not be concealed, was that although three British battlecruisers had been sunk, it had not changed the balance of naval power in any way. Thus, 'the Royal Navy continued its centuries-old tradition of mastery of the sea, against which the German fleet had been as powerless to act as if it had lain on the seabed'.[17]

Admiral Scheer recognised the truth of Germany's predicament in his final impressions of the battle in a written report dated 4 July 1916 to Kaiser Wilhelm II. He wrote:

The success achieved is due to the eagerness in attack, the efficient leadership through subordinates, and the admirable deeds of crews full of an eminently warlike spirit. It was only possible to the excellence of our ships and arms, the systematic peace-time training of the units, and the conscientious development on each individual ship. The rich experience gained will be carefully applied. The battle proved that in the enlargement of our Fleet and the development of the different types of ships we have been guided by the right strategical and tactical ideas, and that we must continue to follow the same system. All arms can claim a fair share in the success. But, directly or indirectly, the far-reaching heavy artillery of the great battleships was the deciding factor and caused the greater part of the enemy's losses that are so far know, as also it brought the torpedo-boat flotillas to their successful attack on the ships of the Main Fleet. This does not detract from the merits of the flotillas in enabling the battleships to slip away from the enemy by their attack. The big ship – battleship and battlecruiser – is therefore, and will be, the main strength of naval power. It must be further developed by increasing the gun calibre, by raising the speed and by perfecting the armour and protection below the waterline.

Finally, I beg respectfully to report to Your Majesty that by the middle of August the High Seas Fleet, with the exception of the *Derfflinger* and *Seydlitz*, will be ready for fresh action. With a favourable succession of operations the enemy may be made to suffer severely, although there can be no doubt that even the most successful result from a high sea battle will not compel England to make peace. The disadvantages of our geographical situation as compared with that of the Island Empire and the enemy's vast material superiority cannot be coped with to such a degree as to make us masters of the blockade inflicted on us, or even of the Island Empire itself, not even were all the U-boats to be available for military purposes.

A victorious end to the war at not too distant a date can only be looked for by the crushing of English economic life through U-boat action against English commerce. Prompted by convictions of duty, I earnestly advise Your Majesty to abstain from deciding on too lenient a form of procedure on the ground that it is opposed to military views, and that the risk of the boats would be out of all proportion to the expected gain, for, in spite of the greatest conscientiousness on the part of the Chiefs, it would not be possible in English waters, where American interests are so prevalent, to avoid consequences which might force us to make humiliating concessions if we do not act with the greatest severity.[18]

Scheer's experience at Jutland had shown him that the Grand Fleet was unconquerable and therefore control of the sea would remain in British hands.

Consequently, the increasingly damaging starvation blockade of Germany's maritime trade would continue unchecked. Germany's hopes of knocking the United Kingdom out of the war and thereby being able to impose a 'German Peace' on the Entente powers therefore rested on 'unrestricted' submarine warfare as the decisive weapon with the High Seas Fleet reduced to a fleet in being. The fleet, which was isolated by the distant British blockade, lay more-or-less useless at anchor in Wilhlemshaven and Kiel and its few operational sorties in the North Sea achieved nothing.

In November 1918 Korvettenkapitän Ernst von Weizsäker summed up the contribution of the High Seas Fleet thus:

> The Navy! It sprung forth from the hubris of world power, and for 20 years it has been ruining our foreign relations. It never kept its promises in wartime. Now it sparks the revolution.[19]

.

13

Scapegoating The Battlecruiser

Something wrong with our system.[1]

The genesis of the battlecruiser can be traced back to Admiral Fisher and his naval revolution which led to first the all-big gun battleship *Dreadnought* in 1905. In the early years of the twentieth century British battleships had a mixed armament of 12-inch and 9.2-inch guns and while their faster armoured cruiser contemporaries were equipped with a mix of 9.2-inch, 7.5-inch and 6-inch guns.

Typically, these large armoured cruisers were protected by 6-inch belt armour which would deflect all 6-inch shells, most 9.2-inch shells and even larger HE shells thereby allowing them to form a fast squadron capable of supporting battleships fighting the van or rear of the enemy line. Once the decision had been made to adopt an all 12-inch gun armament for *Dreadnought* and her successors, it was logical to eliminate the mixture of gun calibres in future armoured cruisers. Thus was born the *Invincible* design which featured eight 12-inch guns in four clumsily arranged turrets and a speed of twenty-five knots but only 6-inch belt armour. Despite their 12-inch guns, these ships were not expected to engage in single-ship combat with battleships and until November 1911 they were referred to armoured cruisers rather than battlecruisers.

Subsequently, the Germans also adopted the large armoured cruiser armed with battleship-calibre guns but their designs featured significantly more armour than their British contemporaries. Following the outbreak of war in August 1914, both navies used their battlecruisers as fast scouting groups operating ahead of the main battlefleet.

The Development of Lax Magazine Practices
In the Royal Navy it was axiomatic that victory would inevitably go the

ship which hit the target first and then kept on hitting. This led to the idea that a faster rate of fire would increase the number of hits but far too many forgot that this was only true once the guns had acquired the target. It was also appreciated that as battle ranges increased it would become necessary to expend a considerable amount of ammunition before any decisive results would be achieved. As this was likely to require more ammunition than the official allowance of eighty rounds per gun (rpg), in early 1914, this was increased to 100 rpg in battleships and 110 rpg in battlecruisers. By the outbreak of war, each battlecruiser was actually carrying 120 rpg in addition to the fifty per cent increase in the number of cordite charges necessary to propel these shells towards their targets. These additional charges were stowed on the magazine gangways in flash-proof boxes known as 'Clarkson cases' which caused congestion in the magazines.[2]

Rapid firing exercises conducted in 1914 showed that the rate of supply to the guns depended on the rate of removal of cordite charges from their Clarkson cases and that this was a tedious and time-consuming process. These exercises also suggested that the most effective way of preventing delay in the delivery of propellant to the guns was to remove a proportion of cordite from its flash-proof container well before the action started and the place it close to the magazine door. By the outbreak of war, the practice of stockpiling unprotected cordite charges ready for use in the magazine passages, handing room, cordite cage and turret had become widespread and was tolerated by senior naval officers in the pursuit of enhancing the rate of fire.[3] Predictably, the empty Clarkson cases caused congestion at the bottom of hoists with a concomitant decrease in the rate of fire and gunnery officers partly solved this problem by removing the anti-flash doors between the magazines and the spaces so that cartridges could be passed out more quickly.

British capital ships had been designed such that explosion and fire in the turrets should not lead to explosion of the magazines and therefore detonation of the latter would require a shell to penetrate and explode within. However, removal of anti-flash doors and the stockpiling of unprotected cordite effectively converted the turrets, their associated working chambers, cages, handing room and magazines into giant ready use lockers vulnerable to a single shell that penetrated the turret armour.

Early War Experience 1: The Battle of the Falklands, 8 December 1914
During the Battle of the Falklands the armoured cruiser *Kent* was struck

by a shell in A3 casemate which ignited one or more charges. This caused a flash of flame that went down the ammunition hoist into the ammunition passage at the bottom of which was a charge in the hoist. Fortunately, Sergeant Charles Mayes, RMLI had the presence of mind to throw away the charge and flood the magazine thereby saving his ship, an act of heroism for which he was awarded the Conspicuous Gallantry medal.[4]

In February 1915 the Admiralty issued a memorandum to the fleet pointing out 'the great danger of allowing cordite to accumulate in gun positions and causing severe fires.'[5] By then, the fleet had received further warnings that it would chose to ignore.

Early War Experience 2: The Battle of Dogger Bank, 24 January 1915
The Battle of Dogger Bank is famous for the lesson that should have been learnt from the damage inflicted on the German battlecruiser *Seydlitz* which was hit by a 13.5-inch armour piercing shell from Beatty's flagship *Lion*. The shell struck *Seydlitz*'s 'Y' turret barbette and penetrated the reloading chamber causing a huge propellant fire which spread to 'X' turret. The magazines were flooded and the ship remained in action without suffering any loss of speed, although 'X' and 'Y' turrets were put out of action. The fire aboard *Seydlitz* was seen by Beatty and his staff aboard *Lion* but no thought seems to have been given as to implications for British ships.

During this action *Lion* was hit by sixteen 11-inch or 12-inch shells plus one 8.2-inch projectile. Four shells struck below her waterline and one of these on the 9-inch belt drove a piece of armour plate inboard thereby flooding a feed water tank and so immobilizing the battlecruiser. Much less well known is that an 11-inch shell, from either *Seydlitz* or *Moltke*, burst against the armour of 'A' barbette causing a small fire in 'A' turret lobby. Although the fire was extinguished with little difficulty, in the confusion a message was sent to the bridge that there was a grave danger of a magazine explosion. The order was passed to flood the magazine, and there were two feet of water in the compartment before the alarm was realized to be false and flooding stopped. The most critical effect of it was to flood the main switchboard and short-circuit two of *Lion*'s three dynamos. In 1921, Filson Young, who was a journalist aboard *Lion* at Dogger Bank wrote:

> The faultiness of our turret and magazine design was revealed by the fact that the charges in 'A' turret magazine had become ignited; and that if that could happen it was a mere chance that the whole ship be

215

blown up at any moment. This was pointed out; but nothing was done towards remedying the defect until after Jutland, when three battle cruisers actually were blown up from the same cause.[6]

Filson Young recorded that after Dogger Bank the Battlecruiser Fleet set up committees of their experts to consider every aspect of the action and produced a mass of very valuable material which would have occupied the attention of a proper Naval Staff, such as that operating in the Second World War, for many months and which, in due course, would have promulgated instructions throughout the fleet. Instead, in Filson Young's words:

> The Admiralty, having acknowledged its receipt of the masses of material presented to it, made no further sign. Doubtless throughout the Fleet there were hundreds of officers who were keen to get all the information and technical data that they could, but there was no means of furnishing them even with the results arrived at in our own [i.e. the Battle Cruiser Fleet] force.[7]

However, *Lion* did do something to remedy this defect because her Commissioned Gunner, Alexander Grant (later Captain A. Grant, CBE, DSC, RN), who joined the ship shortly after Dogger Bank, was, with the support of Captain Chatfield, able to put strict limits on the quantities of shells and propellant allowed outside the magazines:

> I brought all this to the notice of the Gunnery Officer and suggested drastic alterations in the supply of cordite. These were (1) One magazine only to be in use during action. (2) Not more than one full charge to be in the handing room. (3) Charges to be taken out of their cases only as required. (4) Crews not to wear boots or shoes. (5) During any lull in the demand for charges the magazine door to be closed and watertight clips put on. (6) On no account should the magazines be flooded except on receipt of an order from a responsible officer.[8]

Despite reservations from *Lion*'s turret officers, Grant trained the magazine crews and was able to demonstrate that his new arrangements proved that the supply of cordite was faster than the guns could take it.

Thanks to Grant, on 31 May 1916, there were only eight charges exposed to ignition in *Lion*'s 'Q' turret trunking and when they deflagrated they were not powerful enough to sink the ship.

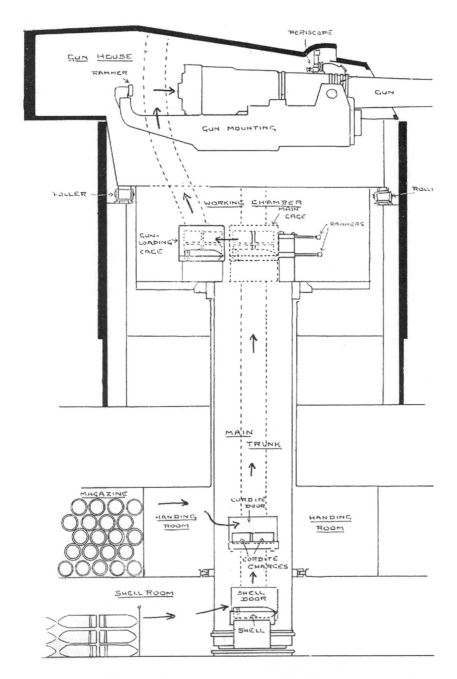

Above: Figure showing the typical layout and relative positions of a British heavy gun turret and its associated magazine and shellrooms.

It is odd that none of *Lion's* squadron mates took such precautions or, more importantly, was instructed by Vice-Admiral Beatty to implement them.

Dogger Bank and the Need for a Properly Functioning Naval Staff

Twenty-five years later, a fully formed Admiralty Staff system would have received information from all relevant sources, sent it to the appropriate Departments for evaluation, comment and recommendation prior to promulgating the action to be taken in a Confidential Admiralty Fleet Order. To quote James Goldrick:

> The change to a staff organization came too late for the Royal Navy in the First World War. Moving from a situation in which the war plans were literally locked within the brain of the First Sea Lord, the British did not have the time to develop a fully functioning staff by the beginning of the war. Misunderstanding of staff concepts led to tactical and material problems and deprived the Royal Navy of many considerable technological advantages. Since there was no system before the war to collate and analyse information, or even to devise the questions that would elicit such data, the Admiralty, collectively, had little appreciation of the capabilities of submarines, aircraft and other technology.[9]

Thus, the lack of a proper Naval Staff meant that the Admiralty made no attempt to develop tactical doctrine based on operational experience or seek remedies in response to material deficiencies which soon became apparent.

Similarly, small lessons, including those of *Lion* which took measures to improve the flash-tight conditions of magazines and turrets, were not passed on to other units – including those under the same operational commander, in this case, Vice Admiral Beatty. Because of the lack of a Naval Staff, the Admiralty failed to realize that the command could not function effectively in the absence of information while, tactical and material superiority could only be ensured by the continual evaluation of experience.

As a consequence, the Royal Navy was unable to wage war as effectively as it should have because nobody was monitoring its overall performance let alone defining the basic problems to be overcome. This failure to develop and promulgate best practice to the fleet would become apparent at Jutland.

Unfortunately, the main lessons that Beatty drew from the Battle of Dogger Bank was that German 11-inch shells were not very effective and that a faster rate of fire would have enabled him to annihilate the German battlecruisers. He was wrong on both counts as Jutland would show.

Disaster at Jutland

During the afternoon and early evening of 31 May the battlecruisers *Indefatigable, Invincible* and *Queen Mary* suffered magazine explosions and sank having suffered very little damage prior to their loss. In each case, the ship was hit on, or near to, a turret resulting in a colossal explosion after which what was left of the battlecruiser quickly disappeared beneath the waves.

As already recounted above, Beatty's flagship *Lion* had nearly been lost after a shell penetrated 'Q' turret and exploded and with this in mind he sent a revealing signal to Jellicoe:

> Vice-Admiral Battle Cruiser Fleet to C-in-C 3rd June 2.58 pm Urgent. Experience of *Lion* indicates that open magazine doors in turrets are very dangerous. Present safety arrangements of flash doors are ineffective when turret armour is penetrated. Flash from shell may reach cordite in main cages and thence to handing rooms. This occurred in *Lion* when turret roof was penetrated, but magazine doors being at once closed saved magazine from catching fire. Almost certain that magazines of three lost battlecruisers exploded from such cause. Consider matter of urgent necessity to alter existing communications between magazine and handing rooms by reverting to original system of handing room supply scuttles, which should be fitted immediately. Meanwhile considered imperative to maintain small stock in handing room for magazine, doors being kept closed with one clip and only opened for replenishment of handing room. Proposed handing room supply scuttles should be capable of being made watertight at will. Commander Dannreuther of *Invincible* will report personally on this matter at Admiralty to-morrow Sunday.[10]

On 3 June Beatty also contacted the Admiralty on the subject of magazine doors in turrets which he considered to be both most urgent and of vital importance. He wrote:

> Commander Dannreuther confirms the conclusions of Captain of *Lion*. Undoubtedly loss of *Invincible* was due to magazine doors being left open. All evidence of witnesses in other ships points to the destruction of *Queen Mary* and *Indefatigable* being due to exploding magazines, following shell striking of turrets or beneath turrets.[11]
> 2. Witnesses from *Queen Mary*, a Midshipman and Gunlayer of 'Q'

turret, report that 'Q' turret was hit, an explosion following which wrecked the turret. Turret was evacuated, upper deck being below water. Another explosion occurred, sinking the ship.

3. Pending Admiralty action as to fitting supply scuttles to all magazine doors, with watertight provision, I have given orders to battle-cruisers that magazine doors are to be kept closed on one clip and only opened to replenish handing room from time to time. This will necessitate four or five full charges being kept in handing room, but will minimise danger of magazine explosions.[12]

Master Gunner Alexander Grant, whose re-organisation of *Lion's* cordite handling procedures probably saved the battlecruiser, proposed two theories the second of which posited:

> A fire may have been caused by the first shell that put the turret out of action. If so, then the strong draught of air being forced down ignited the cordite in the gun-loading cages and supply trunk. It is this second theory that has always made me regret not going up into the turret to see that no fire was about. It was by the providence of God that the hatchway leading from the flat to the magazine handing room was open. This opening formed a vent through which the gases set up by the ignition of the cordite could escape. As it was the bulkheads were found to be saucer-shaped on examination from the force of the explosion. It is difficult to say what might have happened had the hatchway been closed, or charges of cordite been left in the handing room at the time of flooding. As it was, the grim fact remained that over sixty of my shipmates lost their lives in tragic circumstances without an opportunity to escape.[13]

The Legend of the Battlecruisers' Indifferent Protection

However, despite evidence to the contrary, on 5 June Jellicoe signalled the First Sea Lord Sir Henry Jackson suggesting an alternative explanation:

> The heavy casualties among the battlecruisers are I fear largely due to inadequate protection. Of course the German battlecruisers are battle*ships* in protection. That is the whole story and the public ought to know it for the sake of the reputations of our officers and me, and also for the information of *neutrals*.[14]

The consequences of this signal were summed up succinctly by Marder who wrote, 'Thus was the legend of the battlecruisers indifferent protection born and it originated with Jellicoe, Beatty and most other commanding officers of the Grand Fleet in the post-Jutland investigations.'[15]

The development and dissemination of this legend was in part due to the results of the deliberations undertaken by the committees of experts set up after Jutland by the Grand Fleet and the Battle Cruiser Fleet. Thus the reports of the Gunnery Committees set up by both fleets discuss how to increase the rate of hitting, enhanced armour protection and the design of future battlecruisers, made no mention of lax magazine procedures. However, amongst the recommendations made on 1 August by the Battle Cruiser Fleet Gunnery Committee led by Captain Walter Cowan of *Princess Royal* is the intriguing phrase: 'Turret magazines – hoped that by limiting the number of charges in the handing room high [cordite deflagration] pressures will be avoided [in the event of a fire].'[16]

The Battle Cruiser Fleet's Battlecruiser Committee report of 18 June further developed the idea that British battlecruisers lacked adequate armour protection stating that they 'consider that British Battle Cruisers whether in service or about to be commissioned, are unequal to the duties assigned to them, as deficiency of protection renders them unable to encounter the capital ships of the enemy without incurring grave risk of destruction.' The Committee went on to describe the role of battlecruisers as indispensable, recommending the adoption of the fast battleship type although the armoured decks of the Queen Elizabeth-class were not considered to be strong enough to resist plunging fire. However, the Committee observed that the 'Queen Elizabeth-class would be a good starting point and that in reality HOOD was a fast QE'.[17]

Clearly, both Jellicoe and Beatty had strong incentives to find alternative explanations to that of lax magazine procedures so as to avoid personal censure of themselves and other senior officers which would be bad for morale. Obviously, these dangerous practices were eliminated as soon as possible but thereafter they searched assiduously for alternative explanations. Beatty in particular opted for an altogether more simple explanation, namely that the British battlecruisers lacked armour and, in this scenario, he envisaged that long range German shells plunged through deck armour to explode in or near magazines thereby causing a catastrophic explosion.

Thus, on 14 July Beatty wrote to the Admiralty from *Tiger* discussing the loss of the battlecruisers observing that because German ships never blew up even when heavily hit and went on to conclude that either our methods of ship construction were faulty or our ammunition was far too unstable. Beatty believed that German ships had 'adequate protection which ensures the burst of an A.P. shell before it reaches the immediate vicinity of a magazine.' Beatty elaborated further in a distinctly self-serving manner:

> I therefore most strongly urge that it should be accepted that a radical fault does exist, and that the best brains in the country are necessary to assist in its speedy removal in existing ships and its prevention in new construction. To this end I suggest that Committees of the greatest experts should be formed, and no expense or trouble be spared to thoroughly investigate the following amongst other points. I assume that the measures taken by the Admiralty since the action are not in any way final or other than temporary expedients; to my mind the cure is farther to seek.

Several of the thirteen points listed by Beatty related to improving flash tight measures and the provision of 'a separate explosion trunk from all handing rooms to the upper deck to provide some egress for gas pressures other than through the turret and trunk'.

The Vice Admiral observed the 'need of additional protection to the roof plates, glacis, trunk of all turrets and particularly 'Q' turret since most hits occur on this central part of ships'. Beatty also stressed the need to investigate the protection of magazines from shell fire and torpedoes noting 'that the penetration of one hot splinter to a magazine may be sufficient to cause explosion of the contents'.[18] Clearly, Beatty had changed his mind about consequences of lax cordite handling opting instead to place the blame elsewhere.

As it happened both Jellicoe and Beatty were right to be concerned about turret armour as a contemporary German report made clear:

> The large number of hits in the turrets is remarkable, and it is generally considered that turret armour should be appreciably stronger, especially in the lower part of the barbettes; for it is not only the disablement of the guns that comes into question, serious though this might be, but also the blowing up of magazines and the total destruction of the ship, as the wide shaft down to the magazines cannot possibly be made completely flash-proof. This is the most vital part of the ship. It is only owing to the small explosive charges in British shells that there were no explosions of magazines in the German ships.[19]

The Admiralty's Response

Beatty's missive reached the Admiralty a few days later and was rejected soon after by Departmental experts including the Director of Naval Ordnance and Torpedoes (DNO) and the Director of Naval Construction (DNC), not least because of evidence of lax procedures given by *Invincible's* gunnery officer Commander Dannreuther eight days after Jutland. Furthermore, in a letter Jellicoe admitted that the drill in force at the time of the battle 'was to keep all cages and waiting positions loaded and magazine doors open and all the evidence seems to show that if a turret was pierced by a shell which exploded inside it, the magazine was almost certain to blow up'. Despite making this statement, Jellicoe and Beatty agreed that 'there was no evidence that in the ships lost, the precautions essential to the safety of cordite charges, as then we knew them, were neglected'.[20]

In the light of the above, it was hardly surprising that in a minute written on 3 August, the DNO, Rear Admiral Morgan Singer, commented on Beatty's observations about ammunition handling:

> While not wishing to minimise in any way the seriousness of the events of 31st May, I am convinced that the blowing up of our ships in that action was caused not so much by the greater inflammability of our propellant as by the system of supply which we unfortunately practised i.e. magazine doors open, lids off powder cases, all cages and waiting positions loaded; thus should a shell burst in a working chamber or trunk, as I have no doubt occurred at least in one case, 'Invincible', there was every possibility of the flash being carried direct to the magazine.
>
> The Vice Admiral appears to think that cordite if ignited in the open or only lightly confined will explode, this is not so, it burns rapidly giving off a large quantity of gas; in the 'Lion' the charges did not explode but the evolution of gas was sufficient to carry flash down the trunk, as the nearest vent, into the shell room igniting some charges in the handing room en route, had the magazine been open and the lids off the powder undoubtedly the magazine would have blown up.[21]

The DNC, Sir Eustace Tennyson D'Eyncourt, was equally dismissive in a minute dated 7 October. In this he pointed out that:

> The methods of ship construction adopted for warships are very little different in any navy, and for a new navy like that of the German it is doubtful if they have done any other than follow our practice as nearly as they can; and this has been practically admitted in debates in the Reichstag.

It is considered that our losses must be put down to the cause stated in par. 1 of the DNO's remarks. As the outcome of years of battle practice firing, it was the general and accepted opinion that a good supply of ammunition near the guns, also in ammunition passages etc., was most essential, and that the risk of cordite fires must be accepted – and although after the engagement on the Coronel Coast and at the Falklands, this opinion was corrected by Gunnery Order G.043-15 dated February 1st 1915 there is little doubt that accumulations did exist in turrets and gun batteries during the battle.

That the charges in 'Lion's' turret, hoists and working space were not sent back into the magazine before the doors were closed is an indication of the manner in which loose cordite was regarded on our ships.[22]

The DNC then went onto to discuss British design practices and British magazine positions before comparing British and German practices showing them to be very similar. In doing so he refuted allegations that Jutland had demonstrated that horizontal armour over magazines was too thin by pointing out the much larger machinery spaces were protected by similar thicknesses as that over magazines.

Was it plausible, he argued, that plunging German shells only struck British battlecruisers over their magazines whilst at the same time always missing the much larger boiler and engines rooms? Thus, because there was no evidence that any surviving British battlecruiser had suffered damage, caused by plunging shells, to machinery spaces it was unlikely that magazines had been penetrated by such projectiles.[23]

In fact deck protection in both British and German ships was very similar and there was no evidence that any shell at Jutland penetrated a British armoured deck. The battle did however demonstrate that turrets and barbettes needed heavier armour because turrets could not accommodate internal splinter protection. The DNC also observed that thick belt armour could not keep out large-calibre shells – and if they did resist the shell, there was a considerable battering effect on the receiving ship.

On 26 October the Third Sea Lord, Rear Admiral Tudor, wrote that:

There is little doubt in my mind that in the great anxiety to attain a rapid rate of fire, the ordinary precautions for safety of cordite cartridges have been gradually relaxed, until at last the test of the enemy's shells has proved the danger of what was being done.

Stringent orders and precautionary and protective measures have now been taken to safeguard charges; and I feel confident that they will have the desired effect.

It seems desirable that a reply should be carefully drafted embodying the gist of DNO's and DNC's remarks, and laying great stress on the undoubted improper exposure of cordite during this [Jutland] action.[24]

Admiral Sir Henry Jackson, the First Sea Lord, was convinced, and instructed the Secretary of the Admiralty to inform Beatty that:

I have laid before the Lords Commissioners of the Admiralty your letter of 14th July last No.240/B.C.F.05, in which you offered observations on the causes of explosion in British Warships and suggested matter for investigation.

Their Lordships took immediate and far-reaching steps after the action of the 31st May to introduce improvements in the construction of armoured ships with the object of securing a greater measure of immunity from explosion and, they have caused much attention to be devoted to the majority of the points which you placed before them.

Having given careful consideration to the reports and opinions available to Them, My Lords are forced to the conclusion that in some of the ships engaged in the action of 31st May the precautions essential to the safety of cordite cartridges were to a certain extent subordinated to the great desire necessarily felt to achieve a rapid rate of fire. My Lords consider the stringent instructions and measures, precautionary and protective, which have now been instituted will have the effect of safe guarding charges and sensibly diminishing the risk of explosions.

Your proposal for the establishment of a Committee of experts does not commend itself to Their Lordships. They have the greatest confidence in the opinions of Naval Officers whose experience is able from time to time to suggest expedients as a result of their practical knowledge of the issues at stake.[25]

The Admiralty assertion that three battlecruisers had been lost because of magazine regulations had been contravened on 31 May infuriated Beatty who took this to be a personal affront to him and his beloved Battle Cruiser Fleet.

On 17 November the Vice-Admiral re-entered the fray denying that cordite handling was the cause:

With reference to Admiralty Letter S.01146/16, dated 4th November 1916, I would like to submit that as regards their Lordships' conclusion, stated in Paragraph 3, there is no evidence that, in the ships lost, the 'precautions essential to the safety of cordite charges' (so far as the Admiralty at that time had defined them) were neglected, neither is there any proof of irregularities in the then prescribed drill for cordite supply.[26]

He then went on to restate his belief that there is a case to consult the greatest experts on high explosives so as to provide a causal explanation to the disasters that befell his battle cruisers. On 17 November, Jellicoe, aboard *Iron Duke*, wrote to the Admiralty supporting Beatty:

I entirely concur with the Vice-Admiral Commanding the Battle Cruiser Fleet, that there is no evidence that, in the ships lost, the precautions essential to the safety of the cordite charges, as we knew them, were neglected.

2. The drill and custom then in force was to keep all cages and waiting positions loaded and the magazine doors open, and all the evidence seems to show that if a turret was pierced by a shell which exploded inside it, the magazine was almost certain to blow up. I therefore submit that their Lordships may reconsider the conclusion stated in paragraph 3 of their letter S.01146/16 of 4 November, 1916.

3. It is quite realised that absolute immunity from explosion cannot perhaps be expected in action in a ship carrying hundreds of tons of explosives in a confined space, but it is considered that every possible means should be taken to investigate the causes that may lead to these explosions so that they may be overcome, if possible, and the method suggested by the Vice-Admiral Commanding, Battle Cruiser Fleet, appears to be the one most likely to meet with success.

4. Fourteen German ships – battleships to light cruisers have been sunk by gunfire alone and none of them have blown up. Nine British ships – battleships to light cruisers, have been sunk by gunfire, of which six blew up. From a study of these figures it is difficult not to conclude that the Germans have the advantage over us in either fuzes, explosives or ship construction.[27]

Jellicoe becomes First Sea Lord

On 28 November Jellicoe left Scapa Flow for London to take up the post of First Sea Lord and was succeeded as C-in-C Grand Fleet by Beatty. Once in office, he ordered Rear Admiral Tudor to set about quashing the criticism implied in the Admiralty's letter of 4 November. Tudor replied to Jellicoe on 16 December stating that:

> The wording of the Admiralty reply to that of the Vice-Admiral [Beatty] appears to have conveyed the impression that some censure was implied.
>
> This if course was never intended; my remarks (pencilled in red) on which the letter was largely based are on the attached paper, S. 01146/16. They were founded on the conviction that of late years there had been a general tendency towards relaxation of safety precautions with cordite charges in order to get increased rapidity of fire; also on the verbal evidence given in my Room by the Gunnery Commander of INVINCIBLE 3 days after the Battle, upon which the first precautionary instructions to the Fleet were issued; and further because it is hardly possible to provide adequate Officer supervision of all sources of cordite and shell supply in view of the large personnel required for control of fire.[28]

Three days later Rear Admiral Tudor then wrote to the Secretary of the Admiralty telling him that the first action should be to draft a letter to C-in-C to remove the impression that any censure of the officers of the Fleet was implied. The letter read:

> With reference to your predecessor's submission of 24th November, No. 2791/H.F. 1187, relative to the causes of Explosion in British Warships, I am etc. to acquaint you that They have learned with regret that the wording of Admiralty Letter S.01146/16 of 4th November, was construed as implying that the precautions essential to the safety of cordite charges as laid down in Admiralty Regulations and the authorised drill had been neglected, and I am to state that this was not the intention of the remarks in paragraph 3 of the letter.
>
> Their Lordships were of the opinion that the regulations then in force were insufficient to ensure that a desire to achieve rapid rate of fire might not, in some cases, tend to reduce the precautions to ensure the safety of cordite cartridges, which later experience has shown to be required.[29]

Although the Senior Officers in the Battle Cruiser Fleet had managed to escape what would have been fully justified censure, there is evidence that some, if not all of Jellicoe's battleships had an equally careless attitude to cordite.

For example, Constructor Lieutenant Victor Shepheard, who was DNC from 1951-1958, served as a supernumerary aboard the battleship *Agincourt* at Jutland and is reported to have been alarmed at the number of unprotected cordite charges strewn around the turret working spaces. He also observed that the turret manned by Royal Marines was the worst offender.[30]

The Need for More Armour
The Grand Fleet Committees had concluded that long-range fire was decisive and therefore more attention to need to be given to defence against plunging shells. The fiction that German shells had penetrated British battlecruiser magazines gained further traction when Jellicoe became First Sea Lord and he insisted on additional side and deck armour plate being added to all British capital ships.

Worse still Jellicoe was adamant that *Renown* and *Repulse* were no better armoured than the Invincibles and therefore not battle worthy and consequently their entry into service was delayed by several months while additional armour was incorporated over magazines. The DNC disagreed pointing out that given proper magazine practices, these ships would prove to be successful in action.

The battlecruisers were the first priority for up-armouring with *Tiger*, *Repulse* and *Renown* being the first to be taken in hand. Jellicoe also demanded that these changes be incorporated into the incomplete *Hood* thereby delaying her completion until after the war.

Battlecruisers from Japan?
Another consequence of the Grand Fleet's unnecessary obsession with increasing armour protection was a paper entitled *Battle Cruiser Strength* which was compiled in July-August 1917 for presentation to War Cabinet. The paper, which has all the hallmarks of Jellicoe's innate pessimism, explored the relative strength of the British and German battlecruiser fleets assuming that the latter was composed of almost invincible 'superships':

> The Board of the Admiralty desire to draw to the attention of the War Cabinet to the serious situation which will arise by the end of this year in regard to the comparative strength of the British and German Battle Cruiser Forces.
>
> Owing to their superiority in armour protection and speed, raids can be carried out with comparative impunity by German Battle Cruisers on our coasts and East Coast shipping and successful scouting work for the Battle Fleet by the Battle Cruiser Force becomes

a matter of considerable difficulty and places the Battlefleet at a disadvantage on joining action with the High Seas Fleet. The Board suggest that the only way of meeting this danger is by using Japanese Battle Cruisers. The Japanese are unlikely to consent to such craft joining the Grand Fleet, and in any case, it is doubtful whether, manned by Japanese, they would be a match for the German Battle Cruisers. The Board suggests for the consideration of the War Cabinet that the Foreign Office should be asked to instruct the Ambassador at Tokio to sound the Japanese Government as to whether they would sell two Battle Cruisers.

The First Sea Lord has prepared a comparative statement of the fighting strength of British and German Battle Cruisers of approximately the same date, which shows that the German craft are much superior in protection and that their heavy guns have considerably greater range than the British. In speed the slowest German Battle Cruiser exceeds our fast ships ahead of the slower ones.

The First Sea Lord groups the Battle Cruisers thus:

MANTEUFFEL	PRINCESS ROYAL
HINDENBURG	LION
DERFFLINGER	TIGER
	NEW ZEALAND

And

SEYDLITZ	AUSTRALIA
MOLTKE	REPULSE
VON DER TANN	RENOWN
	INFLEXIBLE

And has little doubt that in either group the advantage would lie with the enemy.

(As one of our Force would certainly be refitting at the German selected moment, our weakest Battle Cruiser – INDOMITABLE – is omitted).

(MANTEUFFEL is expected to commission in a few months; MACKENSEN, the next Battle Cruiser about November 1918[31]; our next HOOD, December 1920. ANSON, HOWE and RODNEY are stand-by jobs.)

On a detailed comparison, taking vessels of approximately the same age, the First Sea Lord remarks that RENOWN and REPULSE are absolutely outclassed by and not fit to engage the MANTEUFFEL and

HINDENBURG: that TIGER and DERFFLINGER, PRINCESS ROYAL, LION and SEYDLITZ are fairly matched except for very inadequate torpedo protection in our ships: that NEW ZEALAND and AUSTRALIA are badly outclassed by MOLTKE: and that INFLEXIBLE and INDOMITABLE are considerably inferior to VON DER TANN in protection and speed, though somewhat superior in armament. The all-round superiority of the VON DER TANN is shown by her 2,000 tons greater displacement.[32]

On 5 October 1917, Sir William Graham Greene, Secretary of the Admiralty, reported that:

Minister for Foreign Affairs has delivered to me written reply regretting inability of Ministry of Marine to meet our wishes. Handing me this paper Minister for Foreign Affairs said that Japan had only four battle cruisers; that public took greatest pride and interest in those and that the Government would be unable to defend themselves in Parliament or before public if they consented to any part with any of them.

In a later paragraph the Japanese Minister observed that 'In any case the relative superiority of Great Britain to Germany in this branch was already assured and addition of two Japanese vessels could not materially affect it'.[33]

Ten days later the Ambassador in Tokyo confirmed the initial response and an alternative Japanese proposal,

to say that the reasons which caused the Japanese Government to be loth to dispose of two of their Battle-Cruisers are fully appreciated; and to suggest that instead of this course being adopted they should attach two of their Battle-Cruisers to our Battle-Cruiser Force for the period of this war.[34]

The proposal to acquire two Japanese battlecruisers was discussed at War cabinet on 16 October where Jellicoe's arguments were restated and the suggestion made that 'our Ambassador at Tokio may be requested to sound the Japanese Government as to their willingness to sell to us two of their Battle Cruisers. If our Ambassador finds that it would be unwise to actually make the proposition, he might stop short after sounding the Japanese Government.'[35] Nothing came of the proposal.

Just How Fragile Were the British Battlecruisers at Jutland?

The battlecruiser *Tiger* was one of the most heavily hit ships at Jutland being struck by fifteen 11-inch shells – all but one of which was from *Moltke*. A former Royal Navy Constructor considered that of these hits:

> Three hit the main belt and failed to penetrate, one hit the 6-inch side armour and penetrated. One hit 'Q' turret roof, failed to pierce it but did considerable damage. The rest hit unarmoured structure. *Tiger* remained in action with one turret out of use but unimpaired speed. *Lion* with about 12 hits was still very much a fighting ship despite the loss of one turret.
>
> It is worth considering the allegation that German battlecruisers were 'tougher' than their British contemporaries. The most heavily hit were *Lützow* (24 hits), *Derfflinger* (17 hits) and *Seydlitz* (21 hits) of which the first sank and the last 'was supported by the sea bottom'. *Moltke* and *Von der Tann* had 4 hits each apiece and the *Von der Tann* rendered incapable of effective fighting.
>
> Neither British not German turret armour was adequate to keep out shells and prevent them exploding inside. British deck armour was adequate to keep out the German shells of 1916.
>
> The cordite explosions obscured the fact that the British battlecruisers could take a great deal of punishment and remain in action.[36]

Shortly after Jutland the Germans had just one battlecruiser, *Moltke*, which could be made ready for action at short notice. Of the remainder *Derfflinger* and *Seydlitz* would be under repair for many months while, *Von der Tann*, which had been disabled as a fighting unit by just four hits, was under repair for eight weeks.

In comparison, on 2 June Beatty was able to report that the damaged *Lion*, *Princess Royal* and *Tiger* were available for action if required. In other words, providing safe magazine procedures were followed, British battlecruisers were every bit as tough as their German counterparts.

Post-War Echoes

Soon after the war various newspapers addressed the issue of Jutland and the controversies arising from this indecisive and highly unsatisfactory battle. In particular, the issue arose of how and why three battlecruisers exploded during this action. For example, little more than a month after the Armistice, on 20 December 1918 the *Ballymena*

Observer contained an article with the dramatic headline 'Losses in the Jutland Battle – How Were the Battle Cruisers Sunk?':

> One of greatest naval mysteries of the war is the loss of Admiral Beatty's three great battle cruisers, the Queen Mary, Indefatigable and Invincible, in the Battle of Jutland. Two of these magnificent fighting ships were lost in the engagement within few minutes of each other, the third being sunk later in the day. All three sank with great rapidity after being hit, suggestions being that their magazines were exploded by a lucky enemy shot.
>
> Conflicting theories have been advanced as to what occurred. A well-informed correspondent, writing in the Pall Mall Gazette, observes that what actually occurred will never be known with absolute certainty, but the charge of the critics of the Admiralty has always been that flash tight doors of the ammunition hoists were faulty, and that explosions in the turrets caused by enemy shells communicated with the magazines and resulted in the destruction of the ships. Explosions preceded the sinking of each cruiser—that is known but there is very high authority for the belief that explosions did not take place in the magazines. No unchallengeable evidence exists, but the theory of the cause of these grave disasters is that the defiance of all rules and regulations, but animated by intense zeal and anxiety, the officers responsible, in preparing for immediate action, had assembled in turrets the cordite which should have come up the hoists as required for serving the guns but as the enemy was engaged the turrets were struck and the cordite fired. Among the experts who accept the theory that the magazines exploded there are those who are convinced that the magazines were reached owing the inadequacy of the protective desk.
>
> This is another charge but in common fairness it must be recalled that the Queen Mary, Indefatigable, and Invincible, which were designed under Lord Fisher, were the first battle cruisers in the world, just as the Dreadnought was the first dreadnought. Speed was the main essential, and they were not designed fight in the [battle]line all.[37]

This wide-ranging article, which must have had input from naval officers, explored all the various possibilities including that of inadequate armour and lax magazine procedures without coming to any definite conclusion. Sadly, there appear to be no surviving documents in official archives that provide positive evidence of how cordite was routinely mishandled in British turrets and associated working chambers, cages, handing room and magazines. However, from time-to-time strong hints emerged that this was indeed the case.

One such concerns Captain (later Vice-Admiral) C.V. Usborne who is reported to have mentioned casually at Greenwich in 1923 that, due to better magazine arrangements ships were no longer tinderboxes, as they had been at Jutland. Interestingly, he made no distinction between the battleships and battlecruisers thereby fuelling speculation that dangerous magazine practices were widespread in the Grand Fleet at the time of Jutland.[38]

More evidence can be found in the diaries of Sir Stanley Goodall who wrote on 1 January 1934 that,

> DNC (Arthur Johns) lent me Pastfield on Jutland. He rightly concludes that cordite fire were our sole trouble.[39]

Goodall was heavily involved in the design of the *King George* V-class of battleships which involved meetings with the Controller, Sir Reginald Henderson, and the First Sea Lord, Sir Ernle Chatfield. The latter, who had been the Captain of *Lion* at Jutland, had witnessed the destruction of *Queen Mary* and was determined that no ship for which he had responsibility would be sunk by detonation of a magazine.

Goodall's diary entry for 13 March 1936, provides an interesting insight into both Chatfield's views and what really happened at Jutland:

> Controller I gather is thinking he won't get Chatfield to walk back and agree the 14O study. He put Chatfield case very politely and said it was the psychological shock of what he saw at Jutland. I pointed out that *Queen Mary* and co went up through cordite fires and Controller said 'Yes; Chatfield knows and I know. Nevertheless the effect on Chatfield is such that he feels under no circumstances will he be responsible for a ship that has the faintest chance of blowing up.' This is the constructors' tragedy.[40]

Thus was Henderson's case for heavy armament at the expense of armour over-ridden by the First Sea Lord and the King George V-class were completed with ten 14-inch guns instead of the twelve recommended by the Controller.

14

Echoes of Jutland

I was not alone in a feeling of disappointed when we sighted the German ships coming to meet us, not to fight, but to be escorted as prisoners into the Firth of Forth.

Whatever the misgivings of Jellicoe, Beatty and other Senior Naval Officers as to the battle worthiness of British battlecruisers at Jutland, the United States Navy was impressed, believing that, but for their presence, Jellicoe's battleships would never have entered the fray.

At about the time of Jutland, the United States Senate was considering whether or not to embark on the construction of a large fleet of modern dreadnought battleships and battlecruisers. The lobbying for the construction of American battlecruisers even reached the British Press as can be seen in a report in the *Aberdeen Journal* of 18 July 1916:

> The battle cruiser more than justified itself in the battle of Jutland, according to the opinion which Admiral Knight has just given officially in response to a request made to him by Mr Daniels, the Secretary of the Navy. 'Had the success, which Admiral Sir John Jellicoe claims was almost within his grasp, been actually attained,' says Admiral Knight, 'it would have been entirely due to the battle cruisers, and the loss of three of them was small price to pay. In my view the value the battle cruiser has been somewhat enhanced by the results of the Jutland fight. If the United States builds four capital ships this year, 1 recommend that they be all battle cruisers.[1]

Three days later the US Senate passed the Naval Act of 1916, the so-called 'Big Navy Act', which agreed to the construction of ten dreadnoughts including five battlecruisers of the Lexington-class.

Honouring the Danish S.S. *Vidar*

At 22.00 on 31 May the Danish S.S. *Vidar* picked up six survivors from the sunken destroyer *Shark* about seventy miles from the Danish coast. The water had been very cold and the survivors gradually succumbed until about 22.00 when only seven were alive, one of whom, Chief Stoker (Pensioner) Francis Newcombe, died soon after getting aboard *Vidar*. His body and the six survivors were taken to Hull. While aboard the survivors were treated very well by the Captain and crew of *Vidar*.[2]

The Captain of *Vidar* (O.H. Christensen) was awarded a gift of an inscribed gold watch as a measure of thanks by a grateful Admiralty. In a reply to the letter notifying him of the award Captain Christensen pointed out that his Chief Officer and four of his sailors played a major role in rescuing the survivors of *Shark* because the personnel concerned had to go in a boat and steer clear of mines.[3]

The Germans regularly intercepted neutral Danish ships which traded with Britain and searched them for contraband. Consequently, it was no great surprise on 16 August 1916 when Rear Admiral Stuart Nicholson at Hull received a report that:

> Danish S.S. VIDAR was reported at Copenhagen as having been seized by a German Torpedo Boat on a voyage from Copenhagen to Hull and taken to Cuxhaven about 26th July last. By the latest report from Copenhagen, dated 4th August, she is still at Cuxhaven.[4]

Subsequently, S.S. *Vidar* was released by the Germans on 29 August, arriving at Copenhagen on the following day.[5] With *Vidar* now back in service it was possible to arrange a date for the presentation to be made during one of the ship's visits to Hull. In due course, the presentation was made by Rear Admiral Stuart Nicholson to her officers and men at Hull during a ceremony held on 6 November but unfortunately Captain Christensen was unable to attend – proceedings being reported in the *Hull Daily Mail* of 6 November. On 8 November Captain Christensen sent a letter acknowledging receipt of his watch.[6]

The inscription on the back of the gold watch read:

> Presented by the Lords Commissioners of the Admiralty to Ole Hansen Christensen, Master of the Danish S.S. 'Vidar' for his services in rescuing survivors of the crew of His Majesty's Ship 'Shark' after the Battle of Jutland Bank 31st May 1916.

The *Hull Daily Mail* of 6 November 1916 recorded that:

Rear Admiral Stuart Nicholson, CB, MVO, at Hull today made several presentations on behalf of the Lords Commissioners of the Admiralty. The ceremony took place in the Council Chamber at the Guildhall, the chamber being filled with a representative gathering of the public and the two services.

The gifts were a gold watch for Capt. O.H. Christensen, a handsome silver cup for Chief Officer A.P. Anderson, and gifts of money to four sailors, Ola Nelson, Otto Nelson, R. Jensen and A. Hamalalden. All belong to the Danish steamer *Vidar* and the awards were in recognition of their praiseworthy act in rescuing seven survivors of the destroyer *Shark*, sunk in the Jutland Battle. It was also recalled by the Rear-Admiral in the course of his interesting speech that the *Vidar* was the vessel which brought home the bodies of the British submarine *E.13*, which grounded at Saltholm Island and was fired on.

Captain Christensen unfortunately was prevented from attending owing to ill-health, and telegraphed from Copenhagen: 'Please present Admiralty my best wishes. Should have appreciated attending presentation, but regret my health does not permit my presence.'

A Survivor of Jutland?

Every so often reports that appeared in the Press highlighted the activities of men who claimed to have been at the Battle of Jutland. For example, on 2 December 1916 *The Times* reported that:

At Westminster Police Court yesterday, before Mr Horace Smith, George Winterbourne, who wore the uniform of stoker in the Navy, was charged on remand as an absentee. He appeared to be dazed, and there was a medical certificate from Dr Dyer, of Brixton Prison, to the effect that he was suffering from shock. Inspector Emptago said that the defendant had declared he was a survivor from H.M.S. *Defence*, which was sunk at the Battle of Jutland Bank. The official report was that there were no survivors, but the defendant asserted that after the ship was blown up he was in the water for hours, supported by an air-belt, and was picked up unconscious by a collier, which subsequently landed him near Newcastle. Since then he had wandered about the country living on money – some £20 –which he had on him in his belt.

Mr. Horace Smith directed Inspector Emptago to take the defendant to the Admiralty for his story to be investigated. The inspector returned with the sailor and gave the Court further particulars. He said that the man's memory seemed to be defective, but he had given some corroborative details. He stated that he had only just been transferred to the *Defence* before the naval action, and that when in the sea after the explosion a midshipman with an arm blown off gave his name and his last message. 'If you get through, Jack, tell father we are winning.' The authorities ascertained that there was a midshipman on board of the name given by the defendant. They were so far satisfied that they desired the defendant to be detained and sent to Portsmouth. Mr. Horace Smith made an order to that effect.

Unrest in the German Fleet

On 6 June 1917 sailors aboard the battleship *Prinzregent Luitpold* went on hunger strike in protest at their extraordinarily bad rations. The strike was quickly resolved when the officer in command ordered a more substantial meal for the men.

Emboldened by their success, the men proceeded to form a sailors' council to press for more reforms. Events escalated, until in August of 1917, another strike on the *Prinzregent Luitpold* was labeled a mutiny and was met with harsh punishment by Admiral Scheer. Dozens of men were court-martialled and nine were slated for execution although all but two of these sentences were later commuted. The combination of lax regulation by officers of the sailors during their free time and a desire to gain small concessions resulted in actions by the sailors that were inherently chaotic and spontaneous in nature. The unrest among sailors continued for several months following the August 1917 mutiny.

In the latter part of the war British Newspapers frequently carried reports, derived from continental sources, of unrest in the German military. Two such articles about the German Navy appeared in the *Liverpool Daily Post* of 12 October 1917 and must have been a welcome relief for British readers who had been subjected to the seemingly endless casualty lists associated with the long-running Battle of Passchendaele. More perceptive readers will have realised that these German difficulties were a consequence of the unceasing work of the Royal Navy:

> A traveller from a German port recently informed me that his talk with German sailors convinced him that the battle of Jutland had considerable adverse effect on them. Sailors of the Grand Fleet show they know that in the British Fleet they have such superior foe that going out fight means something like going into trap. Again, long enforced idleness has tended to sap the men's activity and spirit, seeing that it is accompanied by unnecessarily hard conditions. The

Dusseldorf *General Anzeiger* yesterday referred to what is called the 'Wilhelmshaven insubordination case,' and says that rumours have been going round about it for some time. They were exaggerated, of course, declares, but, it 'the seriousness of the matter is sufficiently clear.' Prominent naval men have made efforts in interviews to dispel those rumours. One of the most significant was a statement Admiral von Scheer, which telegraphed August 31, One curious statement made was; 'It is true things have sometimes gone somewhat badly with us and that they are going altogether well with us now.'

The second article in the *Liverpool Daily Post*, under the heading 'Acts of Sabotage – Trouble Also in the Army', stated:

The *Excelsior* gives further details of mutiny in the German fleet, which was due to continued inactivity, bad and insufficient food, severity punishment, the influence of Russian Revolution (news of which had been brought by mutinous sailors), and action of certain civil elements on shore. The mutiny showed itself, first, aboard a battle cruiser. Officers were threatened and sailors refused to obey orders. Court martial sentences of death for mutineers were passed. Subsequently revolt broke out in battleship, and commanding officers were thrown into the sea. Another body of sailors complained at their treatment, went the officers' quarters and took possession of them. The sailors then left their ships without permission, and committed several acts of sabotage.

Conman Caught-Out Lying About Jutland

From time-to-time the papers would also report on the activities of criminals who claimed to have performed heroic deeds in battle so as to obtain money by deception. In one such case, described in the *Daily Record* on 28 December 1917, the conman claimed, amongst other things, to have been present at Jutland:

Only three cases were down for settlement at the High Court in Glasgow yesterday. An unusual career of deception was unfolded in the evidence relating to Francis Kelly, a middle-aged man, against whom were preferred two charges of obtaining by fraud. According to George Moncur riveter, the accused, in October last, alleged that he was a naval lieutenant, that he was about to get married, and that he had inherited a farm in Ireland, with £600. To purchase part of the bride's trousseau he borrowed £8 explaining that the loan would be repaid as soon as handled the money from the inheritance. By way of proving that he had been in the Battle Jutland, Kelly bared his arms and showed scars.

The man's landlady averred that he told her he was a naval lieutenant, that he had knocked out a couple of U-boats, and that he had been awarded the Victoria Cross. He proposed marriage. She discovered a paper, however, which showed that Kelly had been discharged from Peterhead Prison, and she at once put him out of the house. John Campbell, 218 Cambridge Street, Glasgow, stated that Kelly visited his shop, stated that a sister was about be married, and that wished two pairs boots, one for himself and the other for the lady who was to act as best maid. Calling several days later, while the witness was absent for dinner, Kelly approached the shop woman, and told her that he needed £5 for the purpose settling a lawyer's bill. The money was given him. Repayment was promised for that evening, the accused explaining that he had £1800. The sum was never repaid. No evidence was led for the defence.

The jury returned a verdict guilty on both charges. Kelly was afterwards charged with being a habitual criminal. The sentence was seven years' penal servitude, with seven years' preventive detention. Lord Guthrie remarked that the case was a bad one. The crimes which the accused had committed since 1910 involved deliberation and variety of arts, including that of good personal appearance, good address, and plausible stories which made men like the prisoner real danger to society.

Captain Persius Pays Tribute to British Naval Strength

By June 1918 it must have been clear to everyone that German attempts to win the war in a series of offensives starting in March of that year had failed and, that sooner or later, the Central Powers were going to be defeated.

That the real consequences of Jutland had been understood in Germany was apparent in a report that appeared in the *Daily Mirror* on 3 June:

'BRITAIN HAS NEVER YET LOST A WAR'
Remarkable German Tribute to Our Naval Strength Amsterdam, Sunday.—Captain Persius, the well-known naval critic, writing in the *Berliner Tageblatt* on the anniversary of the battle of Jutland, points out that the writers of boastful Press utterances about British naval domination having been completely shaken, have realised now that it was wrong put such thoughts to paper. 'The battle proved that British naval power is not invincible, that if the necessary material

strength is produced by the other party, the domination of one State will no longer exist. Today, on the anniversary of the battle of Jutland, it is opportune again to realise how seriously Britain is to be taken as an enemy. She has never yet lost a war. She has triumphed at the end of every campaign. She is now sacrificing blood in streams. Words like "The British realise that if they experience second Skaggerak it will be all up with their naval domination" are worthless in these bitterly hard times.'

A little over five months later the war was ended on 11 November by an Armistice. Under its terms the German Fleet had to be interned in Allied and neutral ports.

Unsurprisingly, Scapa Flow was chosen eventually as the most suitable place in which the bulk of the German Fleet was to be interned, and on 19 November, five battlecruisers, nine battleships, seven light cruisers and fifty torpedo boats left Wilhelmshaven for the last time.

Early on 21 November they were met by the light cruiser *Cardiff* which led the German ships past all 370 ships and 90,000 men of the Grand Fleet prior to anchoring off Rosyth where they were inspected to confirm that no weapons nor ammunition was on board. The event, which was staged by Admiral Beatty as a grand pageant, was widely reported in the British Press. The *Dundee Evening Telegraph* recorded the event in a series of articles:

SURRENDER OF GERMAN HIGH SEA FLEET. BEATTY'S MESSAGE TO THE ADMIRALTY
22 Vessels Taken Over Thirty Miles Off May Island.
The following communique was issued by the Admiralty this afternoon:— The Commander-in-Chief of the Grand Fleet has reported that at 9.30 this morning he met the first and main instalment of the German High Seas Fleet, which is surrendering for internment.
GREATEST DAY IN NAVAL HISTORY. DREADNOUGHTS AND CRUISERS HANDED OVER FOR INTERNMENT
This is one of the greatest days in the history of the British Navy. Admiral Beatty at sunrise this morning accepted the surrender of the German warships and battle cruisers in the North Sea, some miles east of May Isle, which lies in the broad estuary of the Firth of Forth. The German High Seas Fleet consisted of eight[7] super-Dreadnought battleships, six[8] battle cruisers, and eight light cruisers. It was eight o'clock that the ceremony opened. The enemy ships were manned by navigating crews only, and also, under, the terms of surrender, no ammunition of any kind was on board. After our naval authorities

had satisfied themselves that the conditions of the armistice had been complied with to the letter the German vessels were convoyed by the Grand Fleet for internment. Thus ended the greatest and most humiliating naval surrender in history. Official pictures were taken of the pageant, the film to be shown on the screen.

ALLIED FLEET CAST ANCHOR FROM THE FORTH

At 4 o'clock This morning. (By a Naval Correspondent.) H.M. Battle Cruiser *Ajax*[9], Thursday.

The Grand Fleet, the American battle squadron, a French light cruiser and her attendant destroyers pushed off from the anchorage above and below the Forth Bridge [at] four o'clock this morning for the rendezvous named by Admiral Beatty where the Imperial German High Seas Fleet is to make its surrender. The named place is about thirty miles east of the May Isle.

To those who may have wondered how we could allow the vast number of German ships to approach our shores so closely while our fighting ships remained anchorage and the ceremonial of the King's visit take place, I may say that we have never, relaxed for a moment our network of patrols, and that if any nonsense was attempted, the fleet, which for four years has kept steam up, has still the steam full up and ready for action should the signal be given at any moment.

Last night the fog cleared away before a westerly breeze, and we had fine moonlight evening. This morning the weather is dull, with a slight haze hanging over the Firth.

HUN FLEET PASSES ELIE FLYING THE WHITE ENSIGN

Great Crowds Watch Spectacle from Seashore. (By Our Special Representative.) Elie, Thursday Afternoon. 'They didn't intend to come in like this,' observed a breezy son of the sea as he viewed from Elie Point this afternoon the greatest and most momentous pageant ever witnessed in the Firth of Forth.

SURRENDERED FLOWER OF THE GERMAN NAVY

There was expectancy in every eye on the south-east shore of Fife this morning, and from daylight on the sea was eagerly scanned for the first signs of the return of the Grand Fleet that went out in the early hours of this morning to pick up the surrendered flower of the German navy.

GLORIOUS PANORAMA OF SEA POWER

Shortly after noon the first of the vessels was sighted, one of the great battleships of the British Navy, and immediately, with destroyers on either side, followed one of the newest of the German battleships. There followed in rapid procession the most glorious panorama of sea power that has ever been witnessed from the shores of the kingdom … A good view of the vessels was obtained on the shore as they were sailing fairly close to the north side. All the vessels flew a white ensign at the masthead, with their own flag underneath. The German ships that passed up under escort of British and French ships consisted of battleships cruisers and torpedo [boat] destroyers and U-boats. There were three divisions, the last one passing Elie shortly after two o'clock. All along the Fife shore great crowds witnessed the pageant.

The surrender of the German ships, intact and afloat, showed that the Grand Fleet had failed to achieve the 'Second Trafalgar' expected by the British public and consequently, for many serving officers and men viewing the event, it felt like a hollow triumph. Captain William 'Ginger' Boyle, the commanding the battlecruiser *Repulse*, described his feelings on witnessing the surrender of the High Seas Fleet:

> It was a great event to take part in, but I am sure that I was not alone in a feeling of disappointed when we sighted the German ships coming to meet us, not to fight, but to be escorted as prisoners into the Firth of Forth. It was difficult to analyse one's feelings. It was the first tangible sign of the nation's victory, and so to be rejoiced at, but it was also the blighting of our hopes to substitute a veritable triumph that no one could question, for the unsatisfactory result of the Battle of Jutland.[10]

Admiral Sir David Beatty's disappointment at the tame surrender of the German High Seas Fleet was apparent in an address given on board his old flagship *Lion* on 24 November to the officers and men of the ship and the 1st Battle Cruiser Squadron. Beatty's pride in 'his battlecruisers' and the desire to have had one more chance to decisively defeat his German opponents' shines through:

> I have always said in the past that the High Sea Fleet would have to come out and meet the Grand Fleet. I was not a false prophet; they are out, and they are now in. They are in our pockets, and the 1st Battle-Cruiser Squadron is going to look after them. The 1st Battle-Cruiser Squadron, in fact the Battle-Cruiser Force, has more intimate acquaintance with the enemy than any other force of the Grand Fleet.
>
> It has been their great fortune, to cast their eye upon them on several occasions, and generally with very good effect. But we never expected that the last we should see them as a great force would be when they were being shepherded, like a flock of sheep, by the Grand

Fleet. It was a pitiable sight, in fact I should say it was a horrible sight, to see these great ships that we have been looking forward so long to seeing, expecting them to have the same courage that we expect from men whose work lies upon great waters – we did expect them to do something for the honour of their country – and I think it was a pitiable sight to see them come in, led by a British light cruiser, with their old antagonists, the battle-cruiser, gazing at them.

I am sure the sides of this gallant old ship, which have been well hammered in the past, must have ached – as I ached, as all ached – to give them another dose of what we had intended for them.[11]

The Grand Scuttle

Thereafter, the German fleet was transferred to Scapa Flow during 23– 25 November where it was joined by several more ships including two battleships.

There it remained, swinging uselessly at anchor in the challenging Orkney weather, while crew morale and discipline was eroded steadily by poor food and lack of employment. The misery was ended on 21 June 1919 when Rear Admiral Reuter gave the order to scuttle, and all the capital ships sank except for *Baden* which was beached. The *Taunton Courier & Adver*tiser of 25 June 1919, carried a series of reports describing the dramatic event and its consequences:

The German Fleet, which surrendered ingloriously to Admiral Sir David Beatty in November, and was interned at Flow, in the Orkneys, now lies the bottom of the sea. In accordance with the terms the armistice, skeleton German crews were left on the ships as caretakers, and guards, British or otherwise, were on board. There were altogether 70 vessels at Scapa Flow, 47 have been sunk, including nine battleships, five battle cruisers, five light cruisers, and 28 torpedo-boats. The whole Fleet, valued at nearly £50,000,000, and consisting some seventy vessels, only one battleship, the Baden, a light cruiser, the famous Emden [not the famous raider of 1914 but a new ship of the same name] and a few destroyers remain.

After scuttling the ships the Germans took to their boats. According to an official statement issued by the Admiralty, some boats from the ships refused to stop when ordered, and were fired on, and a small number of Germans were killed and wounded. It is officially stated that the German Admiral, von Reuter, at Scapa Flow, was alone responsible for the sinking of the interned ships, and that there was no collusion with the Berlin Government. Von Reuter is to be tried by court martial for a breach the armistice terms. Joy, mingled with fear of possible unpleasant consequences, marked the reception of the news in Germany. The scuttling is 'an example of the German sense of duty and honour.' Feeling in France, mirrored in the Paris Press, is very bitter over the scuttling, and there is a tendency in some quarters to blame England for not having taken the precautions necessary prevent such action.'

ADMIRAL AND CREWS CUSTODY

BOATS WHICH REFUSED TO STOP FIRED ON

The Secretary of the Admiralty announced on Saturday:— This afternoon certain of the interned German ships Scapa were sunk and abandoned by their crews. The crews will be detained in safe custody. 21 VESSELS BEACHED. The Admiralty issued the following on Saturday night: According to the latest reports received from Scapa Flow, all interned German battleships and battle cruisers have sunk, except the battleship *Baden*, which was still afloat. Five light cruisers have sunk, but the other three have been beached. Eighteen destroyers have also been beached by the local tugs, and four destroyers were still afloat. The rest of the destroyers have sunk. The German rear-admiral and most of the Germans from the ships are in custody on board H.M. ships.

EYE-WITNESS'S DESCRIPTION OF SCUTTLING

The 'Glasgow Herald' states that an eye-witness gave a graphic description of the scuttling of the German vessels. He stated that while a party of children were being taken on a sail round the interned vessels they suddenly saw that something was wrong. They were warned by a drifter to keep away from the German ships, which began to fly the German Eagle. The vessels gradually began to settle in the water, some sinking slowly and others turning turtle and going down rapidly. The German sailors took to boats and rafts, many of which were, flying white flags.

OPINION IN AMERICA 'A GOOD RIDDANCE'

New York, Sunday. 'A good riddance and a God-send to the Allies,' 'The best thing that could have happened,' 'A Naval incubus removed,' 'All parties now satisfied.' such are headlines taken at random from America's leading papers, indicating that the United States are not profoundly moved by the sinking of the German vessels, and that the uppermost feeling is one of relief rather than consternation. Admiral Benson. Chief of Naval Operations, who has just returned to Washington, said the spirit of the work in Paris was in favour of ultimate disarmament. There were some reasons for distributing the vessels as prizes of war, but overwhelming reasons were they should be sunk or destroyed.

Kaiser's Famous Victory Speech Deceived No One

With the ending of the war various reports began to emanate from Germany as to how the populace felt about particular facets of the conflict which had just ended.

One such report, written by Cecil Roberts on 9 December 1918 about his experiences with British troops entering Germany post Armistice, concerned the response to the Kaiser's claim of victory at Jutland soon after battle:

> The Jutland Defeat. There is no doubt whatever that the Germans have finished with the war. They are aware of their complete defeat, and their one anxiety is to control the immense revolutionary feeling now, stimulated by the stories of returned soldiers, and the official revelations that are being made. The landlord's son at the hotel Duren, where I lunched, was in the German Navy, and fought in the Jutland battle. He was present when the Kaiser made his famous victory speech, and told me that it deceived no one. The whole fleet knew they had suffered an overwhelming defeat, and the speech was received with sullen silence, although the papers in their reports said that the Emperor was repeatedly cheered. The collapse in the morale in the fleet began from that day, and the Government was forced to send large drafts of men into the dockyard to maintain discipline through severe labour penalties.

Returning PoW Speaks of Hardships in Germany

The end of the war meant that prisoners of war were released and sent home. One such was Seaman G.W. Watson who had been captured at Jutland and then endured more than two-and-a-half years' captivity.

His story was told on 3 January 1919 by the *Yorkshire Post & Leeds Intelligencer*:

> CAPTURED AT JUTLAND. YORKSHIRE SEAMAN'S HARDSHIPS GERMANY. HEAVY WORK UNDER. BAD CONDITIONS.
> Seaman G.W. Watson has returned to home in Cross Street, The Falls, East Ardsley, near Leeds. Watson was taken prisoner during the Battle Jutland, and during, his enforcement in Germany underwent many interesting experiences some of which he described to a representative of 'The Yorkshire Post' yesterday. Prior to the war Watson was an employee of the Great Northern Railway at East Ardsley, is well known in the district and his home-coming on Wednesday evening being the occasion for much jubilation in the village. One of his treasured relics of his captivity is a hunk of evil

smelling black bread, which represents one-tenth of a loaf, this amount being his daily bread ration while in Germany. Aged 23, and single, he enlisted August, 1915, and went into action May 31, 1916, onboard a destroyer.

After describing how his destroyer was lost he then explained how survivors were rescued by German torpedo boats:

We were swimming about in the water when our own motor boat picked us up. There we remained until a German T.B.D. picked us up. The destroyer came alongside as if she was going ram us, but the fine seamanship of those board brought us safely alongside of her. We were pulled aboard, and the captain and other officers went aft the officers' quarters, and the men forward. The German captain told his men look after us and give clothes and food to eat and drink. The man who took me in hand opened his locker, and motioned me to get what I liked. Cigarettes, and English at that, were supplied to every man. They treated us with every kindness. We switched on the gramophone and set out to enjoy ourselves during the rest of the fight, telling one another the experiences we had gone through. We were heavily shelled by our own Fleet, but now the Germans were making with all possible speed to harbour and got safely into Wilhelmshaven on June 1st, about three o'clock in the afternoon.

We moored alongside a hospital ship, and there we saw plenty of evidence how the Germans had been knocked about. The sights board the hospital ship were terrible. In the harbour we saw only four big ships and a few destroyers: the rest had not returned the base, and there were all sorts of rumours as to their fate. We were taken board the hospital ship and given food of curry and rice.

Defeated at Jutland – A German Admission

By 1920, German versions of the then recent war were beginning to be disseminated in the British media. One such was published in the *Dundee Evening Telegraph* of 9 December, having first been printed in the *Vossiche Zeitung* the previous day.

It contained an admission that the Germans did not win the Battle of Jutland despite their strident claims made just three and a half years earlier:

Admiral Sheer's secret report to the Kaiser has been published in most papers here, but few venture on any comment. The *Vossische Zeitung*, however, is quite frank about the matter. 'What was the result?' it asks. 'The German Fleet was put out of condition to fight for ten weeks at least. Certainly the British losses were greater, but a little blood-letting is nothing to the giant, though fatal to the weaker adversary.' The German Fleet fought out the fight honourably against superior forces. That it did not achieve victory is not a reproach which should be levelled against it, any more than that the unfortunate result of the whole war should regarded the fault of the German people.

H.M.S. *Chester* to be Preserved as a Memorial to the Battle of Jutland? With the return to peace and peacetime budgets, it was inevitable that the enormous and bloated Royal Navy would be reduced by the wholesale scrapping of surplus ships including all those built prior to the construction of HMS *Dreadnought* as well as a large number built thereafter.

Amongst those slated for disposal in 1921 were the modern light cruisers *Birkenhead* and her sister *Chester*, which despite their relative youth were armed with 5.5-inch guns instead of the 6-inch guns which were then standard for such cruisers. *Chester*'s claim to fame was that during Jutland she had suffered heavy casualties whilst engaging three German light cruisers and that one of her crew, Boy Jack Cornwell, had been awarded a posthumous Victoria Cross. By 1921, *Chester*, was laid up on the Medway awaiting disposal and this stimulated the Mayor of Chatham to propose that she should become a memorial of the battle of Jutland. The story was told in the *Dundee Evening Telegraph* on 27 December 1921:

> The Mayor of Chatham (Alderman H.F. Whyman) is making an effort to induce the Admiralty to preserve, as a naval war relic, H.M.S. *Chester*, the light cruiser on which Jack Cornwell won his V.C. at the Battle of Jutland. Alderman Whyman has written to their Lordships pointing out that as the *Chester* is now lying in the Medway on the disposal list, the opportunity might be seized of preserving her at Chatham as a national memorial to the glorious heroism shown the men of the fleet at the Battle of Jutland. 'I believe the whole nation would be gratified,' says the Mayor, who states that the *Chester* could be made available for public inspection, just as is the case with the *Victory*. 'Chatham would consider it a great privilege,' he adds, 'to obtain possession of the ship for such a purpose, and to know that the gallant little, vessel, instead of being ignobly broken up, were to remain in the Medway to bear silent, if strangely eloquent, tribute to the Cornwell spirit.' The Mayor has also written to Commander-in-

Chief of the Nore, Admiral Sir Hugh Evan Thomas, asking for his support in matter.

Sadly, nothing came of the proposal and *Chester* became just another ship that made that melancholy final journey to the breaker's yard.

Will on Identity Disc

On 8 July 1922, the *Cheltenham Chronicle* reported on a curious will, described as a relic of the Jutland battle, which had just been admitted as probate and filed at Somerset House:

> It is in the form a Royal Navy identification disc, about the size of a half-crown and bearing on one side in the usual deeply punched letters, the name, number, rating, and religion of the man to whom was issued. On the other side appears first be just a piece polished brass, but at a certain angle of light there can be clearly seen some neatly engraved words which become quite clear under a microscope. This document 'is the will of William Henry Thorn Skinner, H.M.S. Indefatigable, plumber, R.N', who was lost with that ship in the Battle Jutland May 31, 1916. The disc was recovered from the sea and on being cleaned the words of the will were revealed. In the words of the grant, the testator (being a sailor on active service) is officially stated have 'made and duly executed his last will and testament.' This will reads follows: Feb. 1, 1916. Everything I possess and all the moneys, property due to me by Wills, Wages, Banks or any other sources, I bequeath my Darling Wife, Alice Maud Skinner, signed. This Ist Feby. 1916 H.M.S. Indefatigable, Wm. H. Skinner. Witnessed W. H. Taylor, H. J. Way.

The Lord Alfred Douglas Libel Trials

During 1923, Lord Alfred Douglas[12] was involved in libel trials against Winston Churchill and the Morning Post Ltd. These cases arose from articles published in the fiercely anti-Semitic magazine *Plain English* that Douglas had founded in 1920.

The articles alleged, amongst other things, that Churchill, who was then out of Government, had falsified the Jutland report so that Jewish financiers could make a 'killing' on the stock exchange and in return Churchill was given £40,000. In addition to suggesting that Jews were responsible for the death of Lord Kitchener and were attempting to destroy the 'Christian Race', Douglas went to allege that he had 'the statement of an intelligence officer, who said that during the battle of Jutland he detected wireless messages passing between the German Navy and our Admiralty, in which arrangements were made prevent the Harwich destroyers going on to give the German Fleet its *coup de grace*'.[13]

This latter charge, that the Germans had escaped at Jutland because a spy in the Admiralty had sent a radio message to the High Seas Fleet telling the Germans of British plans to entrap them, triggered considerable correspondence between the Secretary to the Admiralty and the lawyers appointed by the Crown to defend Winston Churchill. For example,

> From: Reginald Ward Poole (of Lewis & Lewis Solicitors of Holborn, London) to Sir Oswyn Murray 16.5.1923
>
> Dear Sir Oswyn Murray,
>
> I shall doubtful hear from you in due course as to what Captain Pound can say but I am rather assuming that he could give evidence that he had examined and could produce all the original telegrams in connection with the Battle of Jutland and that he could speak also as to the messages which were translated from the German code. This is important because you will remember one of the allegations Lord Alfred Douglas makes is that the German code was decoded by someone in the Admiralty who made use of his knowledge of its terms to communicate with the Germans and so enable the German Fleet to escape from our Battle Fleet.

In a later exchange of letters, it emerged that Commander J.A. Slee CBE RN (Retired) was able state that:

> He was in charge of the Admiralty Wireless Telegraphy Station at the date of the Battle of Jutland. That the crew consisted of a Divisional Chief Officer of Coast Guard and a number of Coast Guard and Royal Naval Reserve ratings, a list of whose names and rates he produces. That no one of them ever came under suspicion of treachery or corresponds in any way to the description contained in the extracts from 'Plain English'. That the Admiralty Wireless Station was only used on a very rare occasions for communicating with the Fleet at sea, or for outgoing messages of any kind, its ordinary duty being that a receiving station. That it was his duty to visit the Wireless Station constantly and to examine the log containing the messages dealt with and on no occasions was there any indication of any message other than a properly authorised Service message having passed through the Station either inwards or outwards.[14]

On 7 November 1923, the *Exeter and Plymouth Gazette* reported the start of the libel case under the headline 'Jutland Echo Criminal Libel Charge'. It stated the following:

> The Hon Alfred Bruce commonly called Lord Alfred Douglas, was charged at Bow-street yesterday with criminally libelling Mr. Winston Churchill in a pamphlet entitled 'The murder of Lord Kitchener and the truth about the Battle of Jutland and the Jews'. The prosecution was at the instance of the Public Prosecutor, and pamphlet been on sale for three months. Mr. Churchill was in Court during the opening of the case by Sir Richard Muir for the prosecution. Counsel said the pamphlet alleged that Mr. Churchill was given a large sum by the late Sir Ernest Cassel after Mr Churchill had issued a false report of Jutland.

Douglas lost his case and was sentenced to six months' imprisonment.

Maimed Man's Story of Ten Years in a German Asylum

Probably the most unusual Jutland 'echo' to appear in the British Press was that recorded in the *Dundee Evening Telegraph* of 12 September 1927, under the banner 'Jutland Survivor – Maimed Man's Story of Ten Years in German Asylum':

> A hopelessly-maimed man wandered into Brighton Police Station and related a remarkable story. He described himself as Patrick Terence O'Malley (52), of Curraghmore, County Wexford. His left leg was off to the thigh, his right leg was off to the knee, both his arms were paralysed, and a silver plate had been fitted in place of his jaw. He stated that he was first-class petty officer on the Queen Mary at the Battle of Jutland. His family were informed that he had been killed in action, but two days after the battle O'Malley, who had lashed himself to a mess table, was picked up by the Germans, was raving mad.
>
> For ten years, he says, has been in Wilhelmshaven Asylum, where, he asserts, he had only one meal a day, no amusements, and was not allowed to write to Britain. Gradually his mind became normal, and he was repatriated few weeks ago, being sent to Tilbury. The Germans, who gave him the equivalent of £2 in British money, with some of which he paid his fare to this country. He has in his possession a pair of crutches and a cork leg, both made in Germany. The Brighton police are sending O'Malley back to London so that, he may be interviewed by the Admiralty.

The Passing of the Leviathans

From a British perspective of the period, the two most famous survivors of the Battle of Jutland were Beatty's flagship, the battlecruiser *Lion*, and Jellicoe's flagship, the battleship *Iron Duke*.

The fates of *Lion* and *Iron Duke* were determined by the provisions of the Washington Treaty and consequently, both ships were withdrawn from service some years earlier than might have otherwise been expected. In the case of *Lion*, the *Hartlepool Northern Daily Mail* of 21 October 1922 reported that:

> The battle cruiser *Lion*, which is among the ships earmarked for scrapping under the terms the treaty, has, been temporarily removed from the disposal list. This has given rise to reports that given the Admiralty intend to retain the vessel a national relic of the War. Inquiry at the Admiralty, however, has elicited the information that the original decision to scrap the ship is unchanged; her temporary removal from the disposal list being for the sole purpose of removing some articles which will be preserved as relics. The Admiralty made it quite clear in their message to the Press a short while ago that the Washington treaty specifically named the *Lion* among the capital ships which must, without fail be completely scrapped within 18 months of the ratification of the Treaty.

Ten months later the Dunfermline correspondent of the *Western Morning News* speculated, in the edition of 30 August 1923, that *Lion* might be preserved as training ship:

> The Admiralty has called for estimates for the conversion of the battle cruiser Lion into a training ship for stokers. The famous battle-cruiser, our correspondent adds-, was in the shipbreakers' hands, although dismantling has not started.
>
> The news was a welcome surprise to Rosyth. Owing to her distinguished services in the Great War, the announcement that the *Lion* is be saved from the shipbreakers will give the greatest satisfaction, and nowhere will the gratification be keener than at Devonport, where the vessel was built. The *Lion* was one of the 24 ships specified for destruction by the Washington Treaty, and was the only one on the list not disposed of.
>
> From time-to-time there have been petitions for utilizing her while with the terms of the treaty, but was that the cost of maintaining her as a 'show ship' would absolutely prohibitive, and there was the further important consideration that many other ships had splendid

war records. It probable that the process of scrapping her would have been in advanced stage but for the fact that it was desired to retain her long possible in order that certain mementoes the war might be removed for preservation.

Alas, it was not to be as the *Dundee Courier* of 28 December 1925 reported that '*Lion* was sold for £77,000 in [January] 1924. Anyone can buy a battleship or light cruiser provided he gives a guarantee that it will be broken up and not used for war purposes.'

Jellicoe's flagship was demilitarised as a training ship in 1931-32 with 'B' and 'Y' turrets and her belt armour removed and sufficient boilers made inoperable so as to reduce her speed to eighteen knots. In 1939, a prototype twin 5.25-inch dual purpose gun mounting was installed aft and to starboard of 'Y' barbette for trials.

During the Second World War, she was used as a base ship at Scapa Flow and on 17 October, four Junkers Ju 88 bombers attacked Scapa Flow, damaging *Iron Duke* with several near misses. To prevent her from sinking, the ship was run the ship aground. *Iron Duke* was later repaired and returned to service as a base for the rest of the war, although she remained beached.

She remained on the Navy list until March 1946 when she was sold for scrapping to Metal Industries, while still beached in Scapa Flow. The ship was re-floated on 19 April 1946 and transferred to Faslane on 19 August. The *Dundee Evening Telegraph* of 19 August 1946 reported that:

> *Iron Duke* Reaches New 'Graveyard' A new 'graveyard' for ships was inaugurated on the Clyde today when the battleship *Iron Duke* (21,250 tons) arrived from Scapa Flow to be broken up. Jellicoe's flagship is to be reduced to scrap at Metal Industries' new shipbreaking establishment at Faslane, the £5,000,000 war emergency port on the Clyde. Built 34 years ago, the *Iron Duke* took part in the Battle of Jutland in 1916.

In September 1948, *Iron Duke* was re-sold and the ship moved to Glasgow, arriving on 30 November 1948 where she was demolished. At the time of writing, the last survivor of the Battle of Jutland, the light cruiser *Caroline* is in Belfast undergoing preservation to become a museum ship.

Jutland: The Most Unsatisfactory Battle that Assured Victory
There can be no doubt that to some, from a nation brought up to believe

in the invincibility of British naval power, the First World War was, from the perspective of the war at sea, a massive disappointment. Not only had the Royal Navy failed to deliver a 'Second Trafalgar', but the flower of the nation's young manhood had been sacrificed on the battlefields of Belgium and Northern France.

Unsurprisingly, in the face of such horrendous casualty lists, the Navy's vital and understated role in securing the essential sea communications while at the same time preventing invasion, was undervalued not only by the general populace but also by professional naval officers as well.

Writing in 1942, 'Ginger' Boyle's thoughts about the perceived role of the Royal Navy in the First World War were summed up in a single, telling sentence:

> We of the past generation of naval officers whose active life has finished are grateful to our successors for having taken the opportunity in this war [i.e. Second World War] of reinstating the reputation of our service at an even higher level than it occupied in 1918.[15]

Fortunately, a former Prime Minister Herbert Henry Asquith put Jutland into it proper context during a speech delivered at Lincoln on 9 October 1918 when he said that:

> The Battle Jutland was one of the turning points of the war. The Germans received such a lesson that their great fleet—the Armada on which many millions had been spent —had remained skulking in its harbours ever since. With all deference to our soldiers, this war had been won by sea power.[16]

Appendix I

Letter from Sir John Jellicoe to the Admiralty,
30 October 1914[1]

'Iron Duke',
30th October 1914.

The experience gained of German methods since the commencement of the war make it possible and very desirable to consider the manner in which these methods are likely to be made use of tactically in a fleet action.

2. The Germans have shown that they rely to a very great extent on submarines, mines and torpedoes, and there can be no doubt whatever that they will endeavour to make the fullest use of these weapons in a fleet action, especially since they possess an actual superiority over us in these particular directions.

3. It therefore becomes necessary to consider our own tactical methods in relation to these forms of attack.

4. In the first place, it is evident that the Germans cannot rely with certainty upon having their full complement of submarines and minelayers present in a fleet action, unless the battle is fought in waters selected by them, and in the Southern area of the North Sea. Aircraft, also, could only be brought into action in this locality.

5. My object will therefore be to fight the fleet action in the Northern portion of the North Sea, which position is incidentally nearer our own bases, giving our wounded ships a chance of reaching them, whilst it ensures the final destruction or capture of enemy wounded vessels, and greatly handicaps a night destroyer attack before or after a fleet action. The Northern area is also favourable to a concentration of our cruisers and torpedo craft with the battlefleet; such concentration on the part of

the enemy being always possible, since he will choose a time for coming out when all his ships are coaled and ready in all respects to fight.

6. Owing to the necessity that exists for keeping our cruisers at sea, it is probable that many will be short of coal when the opportunity for a fleet action arises, and they might be unable to move far to the Southward for this reason.

7. The presence of a large force of cruisers is most necessary, for observation and for screening the battlefleet, so that the latter may be manoeuvred into any desired position behind the cruiser screen. This is a strong additional reason for fighting in the Northern area.

8. Secondly, it is necessary to consider what may be termed the tactics of the actual battlefield. The German submarines, if worked as is expected with the battlefleet, can be used in one of two ways:—

(a) With the cruisers, or possibly with destroyers.

(b) With the battlefleet.

In the first case the submarines would probably be led by the cruisers to a position favourable for attacking our battlefleet as it advanced to deploy, and in the second case they might be kept in a position in rear, or to the flank, of the enemy's battlefleet, which would move in the direction required to draw our own Fleet into contact with the submarines.

9. The first move at (a) should be defeated by our own cruisers, provided we have a sufficient number present, as they should be able to force the enemy's cruisers to action at a speed which would interfere with submarine tactics.

The cruisers must, however, have destroyers in company to assist in dealing with the submarines, and should be well in advance of the battlefleet; hence the necessity for numbers.

10. The second move at (b) can be countered by judicious handling of our battlefleet, but may, and probably will, involve a refusal to comply with the enemy's tactics by moving in the invited direction. If, for instance, the enemy battlefleet were to turn away from an advancing Fleet, I should assume that the intention was to lead us over mines and submarines, and should decline to be so drawn.

11. I desire particularly to draw the attention of their Lordships to this point, since it may be deemed a refusal of battle, and, indeed, might possibly result in failure to bring the enemy to action as soon as is expected and hoped.

12. Such a result would be absolutely repugnant to the feelings of all British Naval Officers and men, but with new and untried methods of warfare new tactics mast be devised to meet them. I feel that such tactics, if not understood, may bring odium upon me, but so long as I

have the confidence of their Lordships I intend to pursue what is, in my considered opinion, the proper course to defeat and annihilate the enemy's battlefleet, without regard to uninstructed opinion or criticism.

13. The situation is a difficult one. It is quite within the bounds of possibility that half of our battlefleet might be disabled by under-water attack before the guns opened fire at all, if a false move is made, and I feel that I must constantly bear in mind the great probability of such attack and be prepared tactically to prevent its success.

14. The safeguard against submarines will consist in moving the battlefleet at very high speed to a flank before deployment takes place or the gun action commences. This will take us off the ground on which the enemy desires to fight, but it may, of course, result in his refusal to follow me. If the battlefleets remain within sight of one another, though not near the original area, the limited submerged radius of action and speed of the submarines will prevent the submarines from following without coming to the surface, and I should feel that after an interval of high speed manoeuvring, I could safely close.

15. The object of this letter is to place my views before their Lordships, and to direct their attention to the alterations in pre-conceived ideas of battle tactics which are forced upon us by the anticipated appearance in a fleet action of submarines and minelayers.

16. There can be no doubt that the fullest use will also be made by the enemy of surface torpedo craft. This point has been referred to in previous letters to their Lordships, and, so long as the whole of the First Fleet Flotillas are with the Fleet, the hostile destroyers will be successfully countered and engaged. The necessity for attaching some destroyers to Cruiser Squadrons, alluded to in paragraph 9, emphasizes the necessity for the junction of the 1st and 3rd Flotillas with the Fleet before a fleet action takes place.

17. It will, however, be very desirable that all available ships and torpedo craft should be ordered to the position of the fleet action as soon as it is known to be imminent, as the presence of even Third Fleet Vessels after the action or towards its conclusion may prove of great assistance in rendering the victory shattering and complete. The Channel Fleet should be accompanied by as many destroyers, drawn from the Dover or Coast patrols, as can be spared. I trust that their Lordships will give the necessary orders on the receipt of information from me of an impending fleet action.

18. In the event of a fleet action being imminent, or, indeed, as soon as the High Sea Fleet is known to be moving Northward, it is most desirable that a considerable number of our oversea submarines should proceed towards the Fleet, getting first on to the line between the

Germans and Heligoland in order to intercept them when returning. The German Fleet would probably arrange its movements so as to pass Heligoland at dusk when coming out and at dawn when returning, in order to minimise submarine risk. The opportunity for submarine attack in the Heligoland Bight would not therefore be very great, and from four to six submarines would be the greatest number that could be usefully employed there. The remainder, accompanied by one or two light cruisers, taken, if necessary, from the Dover patrol, should work up towards the position of the fleet, the light cruisers keeping in wireless touch with me.

I have the honour to be. Sir,
Your obedient servant,
J. R. JELLICOE

Appendix II

Letter from the Admiralty to Sir John Jellicoe, 7 November 1914[2]

Admiralty,
7th November 1914.

I HAVE laid before My Lords Commissioners of the Admiralty your letter of the 30th ultimo. No. 339/H.F. 0034, and I am commanded by them to inform you that they approve your views, as stated therein, and desire to assure you of their full confidence in your contemplated conduct of the Fleet in action.

2. My Lords will, as desired, give orders for all available Ships and Torpedo Craft to proceed to the position of the Fleet Action on learning from you that it is imminent.

I am, Sir,
Your obedient Servant,
W. GRAHAM GREENE.

Appendix III

Data on the Short Type 184 Seaplane Serial Number N8359

TECHNICAL DATA[3]

Description:	Two-seat reconnaissance, bombing and torpedo-carrying seaplane. Wooden structure, fabric covered.
Manufactured by:	Westland Aircraft Works, Yeovil.
Power Plant:	One 225-h.p. Sunbeam later changed for one 240-h.p. Sunbeam engine.
Dimensions:	Span, 63 feet 6¼ inches; Length, 40 feet 7½ inches; Height, 13 feet 6 inches; Wing area, 688 square feet.
Weights:	Empty, 3,703lb.; Loaded, 5,630lb (both figures for machines with a 260h.p. Sunbeam engine).
Performance:	88½ m.p.h. at 2,000 feet; 84 m.p.h. at 6,500 feet; Climb, 8 minutes 35 seconds to 2,000 feet; 33 minutes 50 seconds to 6,500 feet; Endurance, 2¾ hours; Service ceiling, 9,000 feet (all figures for machines with a 260h.p. Sunbeam engine).
Armament:	One free-mounted Lewis machine-gun aft and provision for one 14-inch torpedo or various loads of bombs up to a maximum of 520lb.

SERVICE HISTORY OF N8359[4]

22.6.1916	Delivered to the Seaplane School Calshott Grain
4.3.1916	Accepted
30.3.1916	Naval Air Station (NAS) *Killingholme* then HMS *Engadine*.

10.5.1916	NAS *Killingholme* (storage)
13.5.1916	HMS *Engadine*
16.5.1916	Dundee
26.5.1916	HMS *Engadine*
31.5.1916	Reconnoitred before Battle of Jutland whilst crewed by Flight Lieutenant F.J. Rutland RN and Assistant Paymaster E.S. Trewin RNR
3.8.1916	Dundee
7.9.1916	HMS *Engadine*
1.3.1917	Dundee (fitted with 240-h.p. engine)
26.3.1917	HMS *Engadine*
7.5.1917	Dundee
28.6.1917	HMS *Engadine*
30.7.1917	Rosyth
16.9.1917	HMS *Furious*
23.9.1917	HMS *Engadine* (ship at Buncrana 27.9 – 18.11.1917, at Liverpool 19.11.1917)
	Packed at Buncrana by 2.12.1917 and despatched to Imperial War Museum store week ending 29.12.1917
	Exhibited pre-Second World War
	2.2016 undergoing restoration in Fleet Air Arm museum in Yoevilton

Appendix IV

The British Grand Fleet at Jutland, 31 May 1916

Battleships (in order from the van to rear when deployed)

Second Battle Squadron

King George V	Captain F.L. Field (Flagship of Vice-Admiral Sir Martyn Jerram)
Ajax	Captain G.H. Baird
Centurion	Captain M. Culme-Seymour
Erin	Captain The Hon. V.A. Stanley
Orion	Captain O. Backhouse (Flagship of Rear-Admiral A.C. Leveson)
Monarch	Captain G.H. Borrett
Conqueror	Captain H.H.D. Tothill
Thunderer	Captain J.A. Fergusson

Fourth Battle Squadron

Iron Duke	Captain F.C. Dreyer (Fleet flagship of Admiral Sir John Jellicoe)
Royal Oak	Captain C. Maclachan
Superb	Captain E. Hyde-Parker (Flagship of Rear-Admiral A.L. Duff)
Canada	Captain W.C.M. Nicholson
Benbow	Captain W.H. Parker (Flagship of Vice-Admiral Sir Doveton Sturdee)
Bellerophon	Captain E.F. Bruen
Temeraire	Captain E.V. Underhill
Vanguard	Captain J.D. Dick

First Battle Squadron

Marlborough	Captain G.P. Ross (Flagship of Vice-Admiral Sir Cecil Burney)
Revenge	Captain E.B. Kiddle
Hercules	Captain L. Clinton-Baker
Agincourt	Captain H.M. Doughty
Colossus	Captain A.D.P.R. Pound (Flagship of Rear-Admiral E.F.A. Gaunt)
Collingwood	Captain J.C. Ley
Neptune	Captain V.H.G. Bernard
St Vincent	Captain W.W. Fisher

Battlecruisers (Temporarily attached to the Grand Fleet)

Third Battlecruiser Squadron

Invincible	Captain A.L. Clay (Flagship of Rear Admiral The Hon. H.L.A. Hood)
Inflexible	Captain E.H.F. Heaton-Ellis
Indomitable	Captain F.W. Kennedy

Armoured Cruisers

First Cruiser Squadron

Defence	Captain S.V. Ellis (Flagship of Rear-Admiral Sir Robert Arbuthnot)
Warrior	Captain V.B. Molteno
Duke of Edinburgh	Captain H. Blackett
Black Prince	Captain T.P. Bonham

Second Cruiser Squadron

Minotaur	Captain A.C.S.H. D'Aeth (Flagship of Rear Admiral H.L. Heath)
Hampshire	Captain H.J. Savill
Cochrane	Captain E. La T. Leatham
Shannon	Captain J.S. Dumaresq

Light Cruisers

Fourth Light Cruiser Squadron

Calliope	Commodore C.E. Le Mesurier
Constance	Captain C.S. Townsend
Caroline	Captain H.R. Crooke

Royalist	Captain The Hon. H. Meade
Comus	Captain A.G. Hotham

Attached Cruisers (Mainly for repeating visual signals between units of the Battle Fleet)

Active	Captain P. Withers
Bellona	Captain A.B.S. Dutton
Blanche	Captain J.M. Casement
Boadicea	Captain L.C.S. Woollcombe
Canterbury	Captain P.M.R. Royds
Chester	Captain R.N. Lawson

Destroyers

Fourth Flotilla

Tipperary (Captain C.J. Wintour), *Acasta, Achates, Ambuscade, Ardent, Broke, Christopher, Contest, Fortune, Garland, Hardy, Midge, Ophelia, Owl, Porpoise, Shark, Sparrowhawk, Spitfire* and *Unity*

Eleventh Flotilla

Castor (light cruiser, Commodore J.R.P. Hawksley), *Kempenfelt, Magic, Mandate, Manners, Marne, Martial, Michael, Milbrook, Minion, Mons, Moon, Morning Star, Mounsey, Mystic* and *Ossory*

Twelfth Flotilla

Faulknor (Captain A.J.B. Stirling), *Maenard, Marksman, Marvel, Mary Rose, Menace, Mindful, Mischief, Munster, Narwhal, Nessus, Noble, Nonsuch, Obedient, Onslaught* and *Opal*

Miscellaneous destroyers

Abdiel (minelayer) and *Oak* (destroyer tender to fleet flagship *Iron Duke*)

The Battlecruiser Fleet

Battlecruisers (in order from van to rear)

Lion	Captain A.E.M. Chatfield (Flagship of Vice-Admiral Sir David Beatty)

First Battlecruiser Squadron

Princess Royal	Captain W.H. Cowan (Flagship of Rear-Admiral O. de B. Brock)

Queen Mary	Captain C.I. Prowse
Tiger	Captain H.B. Pelly

Second Battlecruiser Squadron
New Zealand	Captain J.F.E. Green (Flagship of Rear-Admiral W.C. Pakenham)
Indefatigable	Captain C.F. Sowerby

Fast Battleships (temporarily attached to Battlecruiser Fleet)

Fifth Battle Squadron
Barham	Captain A.W. Craig (Flagship Rear-Admiral H. Evan-Thomas)
Valiant	Captain M. Woollcombe
Warspite	Captain E.M. Phillpotts
Malaya	Captain The Hon A.D.E.H. Boyle

Light Cruisers

First Light Cruiser Squadron
Galatea	Commodore E.S. Alexander-Sinclair
Phaeton	Captain J.E. Cameron
Inconstant	Captain B.S. Thesiger
Cordelia	Captain T.P.H. Beamish

Second Light Cruiser Squadron
Southampton	Commodore W.E. Goodenough
Birmingham	Captain A.A.M. Duff
Nottingham	Captain C.B. Miller
Dublin	Captain A.C. Scott

Third Light Cruiser Squadron
Falmouth	Captain J.D. Edwards (Flagship of Rear Admiral T.D.W. Napier)
Yarmouth	Captain T.D. Pratt
Birkenhead	Captain E. Reeves
Gloucester	Captain W.F. Blunt

Destroyers

First Flotilla
Fearless (light cruiser, Captain C.D. Roper), *Acheron, Ariel, Attack, Badger,*

Defender, *Goshawk*, *Hydra*, *Lapwing* and *Lizard*

Ninth & Tenth Flotillas (combined)
Lydiard (Commander M.L. Goldsmith), *Landrail*, *Laurel*, *Liberty*, *Moorsom*, *Morris*, *Termagent* and *Turbulent*

Thirteenth Flotilla
Champion (light cruiser, Captain J.U. Farie), *Moresby*, *Narborough*, *Nerissa*, *Nestor*, *Nicator*, *Nomad*, *Obdurate*, *Onslow*, *Pelican* and *Petard*

Seaplane Carrier

Engadine   Lieutenant Commander C.G. Robinson

Appendix V

The German High Seas Fleet at The Skagerrak, 31 May 1916

The Battle Fleet

Battleships (in order from van to rear when deployed)

Third Battle Squadron

König	Captain Brüninghaus (Flagship of Rear-Admiral Paul Behncke)
Grosser Kurfürst	Captain E. Goette
Kronprinz	Captain C. Feldt
Markgraf	Captain Seiferling
Kaiser	Captain F. von Kayserling (Flagship of Rear-Admiral Nordmann)
Kaiserin	Captain Sievers
Prinzregent Luitpold	Captain K. Heuser

First Battle Squadron

Friedrich der Grosse	Captain T. Fuchs (Fleet flagship of Vice-Admiral Reinhard Scheer)
Ostfriesland	Captain von Natzmer (Flagship of Vice-Admiral E. Schmidt)
Thüringen	Captain H. Küsel
Helgoland	Captain von Kameke
Oldenburg	Captain Captain Höpfner
Posen	Captain Lange (Flagship of Rear-Admiral Engelhardt)
Rheinland	Captain Rohardt
Nassau	Captain H. Klappenbach
Westfalen	Captain Redlich

Second Battle Squadron

Deutschland	Captain H. Meurer (Flagship Rear-Admiral Mauve)
Hessen	Captain R. Bartels
Pommern	Captain Bölken
Hannover	Captain W. Heine (Flagship of Rear-Admiral F. von Dalwigk zu Lichtenfels)
Schlesien	Captain F. Behncke
Schleswig-Holstein	Captain Barrentrapp

Light Cruisers

Fourth Scouting Group

Stettin	Captain F. Regensburg (Broad Pennant of Commodore von Reuter)
München	Commander O. Böcher
Hamburg	Commander von Gaudecker
Frauenlob	Captain G. Hoffman
Stuttgart	Captain Hagedorn

Torpedo boats

Rostock	Captain O. Feldman (Broad Pennant of Commodore Michelson)

First Flotilla (half)
Four boats under Commander C. Albrecht in *G39*

Third Flotilla
Seven boats under Captain Hollmann in *S53*

Fifth Flotilla
Eleven boats under Captain Heinecke in *G11*

Seventh Flotilla
Nine boats under Captain von Koch in *S24*

The Battlecruiser Force

Battlecruisers

First Scouting Group

Lützow	Captain Harder (Flagship of Vice-Admiral Franz Hipper)
Derfflinger	Captain Hartog
Seydlitz	Captain M. von Egidy
Moltke	Captain von Karpf
Von der Tann	Captain Hans Zenker

Light Cruisers

Second Scouting Group

Frankfurt	Captain T. von Trotha (Flagship of Rear-Admiral Bödicker)
Wiesbaden	Captain Reiss
Pillau	Captain Mommsen
Elbing	Captain Madlung

Torpedo boats

Regensburg (light cruiser) Captain Herberer (Broad Pennant of Commodore Heinrich)

Second Flotilla
Ten boats under Captain Schurr in *B98*

Sixth Flotilla
Nine boats under Captain Schultz in *G41*

Ninth Flotilla
Eleven boats under Captain Goehle in *V28*

Appendix VI

Brief Particulars of British Ships Participating in the
Battle of Jutland, 31 May 1916[5]

BATTLESHIPS

Royal Sovereign Class
Revenge and *Royal Oak*
Displacement: 28,000–31,000 tons.
Dimensions: 624ft 3in x 88ft 6in x 28ft 6in.
Machinery: 4-shaft, turbines, 40,000shp = 23 knots.
Armour: Belt 13in, turrets 13in.
Armament: 8 x 15in, 14 x 6in, and 2 x 3in AA guns; 4 x 21in torpedo
              tubes.
Complement: 997.

Queen Elizabeth Class
Barham, Malaya, Warspite and *Valiant*
Displacement: 27,500–31,500 tons.
Dimensions: 645ft 9in x 90ft 6in x 28ft 9in.
Machinery: 4-shaft, turbines, 76,000shp = 24 knots.
Armour: Belt 13in; turrets 13in.
Armament: 8 x 15in, 14 x 6in, and 2 x 3in AA guns; 4 x 21in torpedo
              tubes.
Complement: 951.

Iron Duke Class
Iron Duke, Marlborough and *Benbow*
Displacement: 25,000–29,560 tons.
Dimensions: 622ft 9in x 90ft x 29ft 6in.

Machinery: 4-shaft, turbines, 29,000shp = 21¼ knots.
Armour: Belt 12in; turrets 11in.
Armament: 10 x 13.5in, 12 x 6in, and 2 x 3in AA guns; 4 x 21in
              torpedo tubes.
Complement: 1,022.

King George V Class
King George V, Ajax and *Centurion*
Displacement: 23,000–25,700 tons.
Dimensions: 597ft 6in x 89ft x 28ft 8in.
Machinery: 4-shaft, turbines, 31,000shp = 21 knots.
Armour: Belt 12in; turrets 11in.
Armament: 10 x 13.5in, and 16 x 4in guns; 3 x 21in torpedo tubes.
Complement: 782.

Orion Class
Orion, Monarch, Conqueror and *Thunderer*
Displacement: 22,200–25,870 tons.
Dimensions: 581ft x 88ft 6in x 24ft 11in.
Machinery: 4-shaft, turbines, 27,000shp = 21 knots.
Armour: Belt 12in; turrets 11in.
Armament: 10 x 13.5in, and 16 x 4in guns; 3 x 21in torpedo tubes.
Complement: 752

Agincourt
Displacement: 27,500–30,250 tons.
Dimensions: 671ft 6in x 89 ft x 27 ft.
Machinery: 4-shaft, turbines, 34,000shp = 22 knots.
Armour: Belt 9in; turrets 12in.
Armament: 14 x 12in, 20 x 6in, 10 x 3in, and 2 x 3in AA guns; 3 x 21in
              torpedo tubes.
Complement: 1,115

Canada
Displacement: 28,600–32,120 tons.
Dimensions: 661ft x 92ft x 29ft.
Machinery: 4-shaft, turbines, 37,000shp = 22¾ knots.
Armour: Belt 9in; turrets 10in.
Armament: 10 x 14in, 16 x 6in, and 2 x 3in AA guns; 4 x 21in torpedo
              tubes.
Complement: 1,167

Erin
Displacement: 22,780 – 25,250 tons.
Dimensions: 559ft 6in x 91ft 7in x 28ft 5in.
Machinery: 4-shaft, turbines, 26,500shp = 21 knots.
Armour: Belt 12in; turrets 11in.
Armament: 10 x 13.5in, 16 x 6in, and 2 x 3in AA guns; 4 x 21in torpedo tubes.
Complement: 1,070

Neptune
Displacement: 19,680–22,720 tons.
Dimensions: 546ft x 8ft x 28ft 6in.
Machinery: 4-shaft, turbines, 25,000shp = 21 knots.
Armour: Belt 10in; turrets 11in.
Armament: 10 x 12in, and 16 x 4in guns; 3 x 18in torpedo tubes.
Complement: 759

Colossus Class
Colossus and *Hercules*
Displacement: 20,225–23,050 tons.
Dimensions: 546ft x 85ft x 28ft 9in.
Machinery: 4-shaft, turbines, 25,000shp = 21 knots.
Armour: Belt 11in; turrets 11in.
Armament: 10 x 12in, and 16 x 4in guns; 3 x 21in torpedo tubes.
Complement: 755

St Vincent Class
St Vincent, Collingwood and *Vanguard*
Displacement: 19,569–23,030 tons.
Dimensions: 536ft x 84ft x 27ft 11in.
Machinery: 4-shaft, turbines, 24,500shp = 21 knots.
Armour: Belt 10in; turrets 11in.
Armament: 10 x 12in, and 20 x 4in guns; 3 x 18in torpedo tubes.
Complement: 718

Bellerophon Class
Bellerophon, Superb and *Temeraire*
Displacement: 18,800–22,102 tons.
Dimensions: 526ft x 82ft 6in x 27ft 3in.
Machinery: 4-shaft, turbines, 23,000shp = 20¾ knots.
Armour: Belt 10in; turrets 11in.
Armament: 10 x 12in, and 16 x 4in guns; 3 x 18in torpedo tubes,
Complement: 733

BATTLECRUISERS

Tiger
Displacement: 28,430–35,710 tons.
Dimensions: 704ft x 90ft 6in x 28ft 6in.
Machinery: 4-shaft, turbines, 85,000shp = 28 knots.
Armour: Belt 9in; turrets 9in.
Armament: 8 x 13.5in, 12 x 6in, and 2 x 3in AA guns; 4 x 21in torpedo
               tubes.
Complement: 1,121.

Lion Class
Lion, Princess Royal and *Queen Mary*
Displacement: 26,270–29,680 tons.
Dimensions: 700ft x 88ft 6in x 27ft 8in.
Machinery: 4-shaft, turbines, 70,000shp = 27 knots.
Armour: Belt 9in; turrets 9in
Armament: 8 x 13.5in, and 16 x 4in guns; 2 x 21in torpedo tubes.
Complement: 997

Indefatigable Class
Indefatigable and *New Zealand*
Displacement: 18,500–22,110 tons.
Dimensions: 590ft x 80ft x 26ft 6in.
Machinery: 4-shaft turbines, 44,000shp = 25 knots.
Armour: Belt 6in; turrets 10in.
Armament: 8 x 12in, and 16 x 4in guns; 3 x 18in torpedo tubes.
Complement: 800

Invincible Class
Invincible, Indomitable and *Inflexible*
Displacement: 17,373–20,078 tons.
Dimensions: 567ft x 78ft 6in x 26ft 2in.
Machinery: 4-shaft, turbines, 41,000shp = 25 knots.
Armour: Belt 6in; turrets 10in.
Armament: 8 x 12in, and 16 x 4in guns; 5 x 18in torpedo tubes.
Complement: 784

ARMOURED CRUISERS

Minotaur Class
Defence, Minotaur and *Shannon*
Displacement: 14,600 tons.
Dimensions: 519ft x 74ft 6in x 26ft.

273

Machinery: 2-shaft, 4-cylinder Triple Expansion, 27,000ihp = 23 knots.

Armament: 4 x 9.2in, 10 x 7.5in, and 16 x 12pdr guns; 5 x 18in torpedo tubes.

Complement: 755

Warrior Class
Cochrane and *Warrior*
Displacement: 13,550 tons.
Dimensions: 505ft 4in x 73ft 6in x 25ft.
Machinery: 2-shaft, 4-cylinder Triple Expansion, 23,000ihp = 23 knots.
Armament: 6 x 9.2in, and 4 x 7.5in guns; 3 x 18in torpedo tubes.
Complement: 712

Duke of Edinburgh Class
Duke of Edinburgh and *Black Prince*
Displacement: 13,550 tons.
Dimensions: 505ft 4in x 73ft 6in x 26ft.
Machinery: 2-shaft, 4-cylinder Triple Expansion, 23,000ihp = 23 knots.
Armament: 6 x 9.2in, and 10 x 6in guns; 3 x 18in torpedo tubes.
Complement: 790

Devonshire Class
Hampshire
Displacement: 10,850 tons.
Dimensions: 473ft 6in x 68ft 6in x 24 ft.
Machinery: 2-shaft, 4-cylinder Triple Expansion, 21,000ihp = 22 knots.
Armament: 4 x 7.5in, 6 x 6in, and 2 x 12pdr guns; 2 x 18in torpedo tubes.
Complement: 655

LIGHT CRUISERS
Boadicea Class
Boadicea and *Bellona*
Displacement: 3,300 tons.
Dimensions: 405ft x 41ft x 14ft.
Machinery: 4-shaft, turbines, 18,000shp = 25 knots.
Armament: 6 x 4in guns; 2 x 18in torpedo tubes.
Complement: 317

Blonde Class
Blanche
Displacement: 3,350 tons.
Dimensions: 405ft x 41ft 6in x 15ft 6in.
Machinery: 4-shaft, turbines, 18,000shp = 24½ knots.
Armament: 10 x 4in guns; 2 x 21in torpedo tubes.
Complement: 314.

Bristol Class
Gloucester
Displacement: 4,800 tons.
Dimensions: 453ft x 47ft x 15ft 6in.
Machinery: 4-shaft, turbines, 22,000shp = 25 knots.
Armament: 2 x 6in, and 10 x 4in guns; 2 x 18in torpedo tubes.
Complement: 480.

Weymouth Class
Falmouth and *Yarmouth*
Displacement: 5,250 tons.
Dimensions: 453ft x 48ft 6in x 15ft 6in.
Machinery: 4-shaft, turbines, 22,000shp = 25 knots.
Armament: 8 x 6in guns; 2 x 21in torpedo tubes.
Complement: 475.

Fearless Class
Active and *Fearless*
Displacement: 3,440 tons.
Dimensions: 406ft x 41ft 6in x 15ft 7in.
Machinery: 4-shaft, turbines, 18,000shp = 25 knots.
Armament: 10 x 4in guns; 2 x 18in torpedo tubes.
Complement: 325.

Chatham Class
Dublin and *Southampton*
Displacement: 5,400 tons.
Dimensions: 458ft x 49ft x 16ft.
Machinery: 4-shaft, turbines, 25,000 = 25½ knots.
Armament: 8 x 6in guns; 2 x 21in torpedo tubes.
Complement: 475.

Birmingham Class
Birmingham and *Nottingham*

Displacement: 5,440 tons.
Dimensions: 457ft x 50ft x 16ft.
Machinery: 4-shaft, turbines, 25,000shp = 25½ knots.
Armament: 9 x 6in guns; 2 x 21in torpedo tubes.
Complement: 480.

Birkenhead Class

Birkenhead and *Chester*
Displacement: 5,235 tons.
Dimensions: 446ft x 50ft x 16ft.
Machinery: 4-shaft, turbines, 25,000shp = 25½ (*Chester* 31,000shp = 26½) knots.
Armament: 10 x 5.5in, and 1 x 3in AA guns; 2 x 21in torpedo tubes.
Complement: 500.

Arethusa Class

Galatea, Inconstant, Phaeton and *Royalist*
Displacement: 3,750 tons.
Dimensions: 436ft x 39ft x 13ft 5in.
Machinery: 4-shaft, turbines, 40,000shp = 28½ knots.
Armament: 2 x 6in, and 6 x 4in guns; 4 x 21in torpedo tubes.
Complement: 282.

Caroline Class

Caroline, Comus and *Cordelia*
Displacement: 4,219 tons.
Dimensions: 446ft x 41ft 6in x 16 ft.
Machinery: 4-shaft, turbines, 40,000shp = 28½ knots.
Armament: 2 x 6in, 8 x 4in, and 1 x 13pdr AA guns, 4 x 21in torpedo tubes.
Complement: 301.

Calliope Class

Calliope and *Champion*
Displacement: 4,228 tons.
Dimensions: 446ft x 41ft 6in x 14ft 9in.
Machinery: 4-shaft, turbines, 40,000shp = 29 knots.
Armament: 2 x 6in, 8 x 4in, and 1 x 13pdr AA guns; 2 x 21in torpedo tubes.
Complement: 368.

Cambrian Class

Canterbury, Castor and *Constance*

Displacement: 4,320 tons.
Dimensions: 446ft x 41ft 6in x 14ft 10in.
Machinery: 4-shaft, turbines, 40,000 = 28½ knots.
Armament: 2 x 6in, 8 x 4in, and 1 x 13pdr AA guns; 2 x 21in torpedo
              tubes.
Complement: 368.

DESTROYERS

I (Acheron) Class
Acheron, Ariel, Attack, Badger, Defender, Garland, Hydra, Lapwing and *Lizard*
Displacement: 778 tons.
Dimensions: 246ft x 25ft 8in x 9ft.
Machinery: 3-shaft, turbines, 13,500shp = 27 knots.
Armament: 2 x 4in, and 2 x 12pdr guns; 2 x 21in torpedo tubes.
Complement: 70.

I (Special) Class
Oak
Displacement: 778 tons.
Dimensions: 246ft x 25ft 8in x 9ft.
Machinery: 3-shaft, turbines, 15,500shp = 29 knots.
Armament: 2 x 4in, and 2 x 12pdr guns; 2 x 21in torpedo tubes.
Complement: 70.

K (Acasta) Class
Acasta, Achates, Ambuscade, Christopher, Contest, Midge, Owl, Shark, Sparrowhawk, Spitfire and *Unity*
Displacement: 1,072 tons.
Dimensions: 267ft 6in x 27ft x 9ft 6in.
Machinery: 2-shaft, turbines, 24,500shp = 29 knots.
Armament: 3 x 4in guns; 2 x 21in torpedo tubes.
Complement: 73.

K (Special) Class
Ardent, Fortune, Garland, Hardy and *Porpoise*
Displacement: 1,072 tons.
Dimensions: 267ft 6in x 27ft x 9ft 6in.
Machinery: 2-shaft, turbines, 24,500shp = 29 knots.
Armament: 3 x 4in guns; 2 x 21in torpedo tubes.
Complement: 73.

L Class
Landrail, Laurel, Liberty and *Lydiard*
Displacement: 950 – 1,010 tons.
Dimensions: 268ft 10in x 27ft 8in x 10ft 6in.
Machinery: 2-shaft, turbines, 24,500shp = 29 knots.
Armament: 3 x 4in guns; 4 x 21in torpedo tubes.
Complement: 73.

M Class
Maenad, Magic, Mandate, Manners, Marne, Martial, Marvel, Mary Rose, Menace, Michael, Millbrook, Mindful, Minion, Mischief, Mons, Moon, Moorsom, Moresby, Morning Star, Morris, Mounsey, Munster, Mystic, Narborough, Narwhal, Nerissa, Nessus, Nestor, Nicator, Noble, Nomad, Nonsuch, Obdurate, Obedient, Onslaught, Onslow, Opal, Ophelia, Ossory, Pelican and *Petard*
Displacement: 900 – 1,100 tons.
Dimensions: 269ft 6in – 274ft 3in x 25ft 7in – 27ft x 8ft 6in – 10ft 6in.
Machinery: 2-3-shaft, turbines, 23,000 – 27,000shp = 34 – 35 knots.
Armament: 3 x 4in, and 2 x 1pdr pom-pom; 4 x 21in torpedo tubes.
Complement: 79.

Faulknor Class Leaders
Tipperary, Broke and *Faulknor*
Displacement: 1,610 tons.
Dimensions: 330ft 10in x 32ft 6in x 11ft 7in.
Machinery: 3-shaft, turbines, 30,000shp = 31 knots.
Armament: 6 x 4in, and 1 x 1½ pdr guns; 4 x 21in torpedo tubes.
Complement: 197.

Lightfoot Class Leaders
Abdiel, Kempenfelt and *Marksman*
Displacement: 1,440 tons.
Dimensions: 324ft 10in x 31ft 9in x 12 ft.
Machinery: 3-shaft, turbines, 36,000shp = 34½ knots.
Armament: 4 x 4in, and 2 x 1pdr guns; 4 x 21in torpedo tubes.
Complement: 104.

Talisman Class Leaders
Termagent and *Turbulent*
Displacement: 1,098 tons.
Dimensions: 309ft x 28ft 7in x 9ft 6in.
Machinery: 3-shaft, turbines, 25,000shp = 32 knots.

Armament: 5 x 4in guns; 4 x 21in torpedo tubes.
Complement: 102.

SEAPLANE CARRIER

Engadine
Displacement: 1,881 tons.
Dimensions: 316ft x 41ft x 16ft.
Machinery: 3-shaft, turbines, 6,000shp = 21½ knots.
Armament: 2 x 4in, and 1 x 6pdr AA guns; 4 seaplanes.
Complement: 197.

Appendix VII

Brief Particulars of German Ships Participating at The Skagerrak, 31 May 1916[6]

PRE-DREADNOUGHT BATTLESHIPS
Braunschweig Class

Hessen

Displacement: 14,167 tons.

Dimensions: 127.7 oa x 25.6 x 8.1 metres.

Machinery: 3-shaft Triple Expansion, 17,000ihp = 18¾ knots.

Armament: 4 x 280mm, 14 x 170mm, and 18 x 88mm guns; 6 x 450mm torpedo tubes.

Complement: 743.

Deutschland Class

Deutschland, Pommern, Hannover, Schlesien and *Schleswig-Holstein*

Displacement: 13,933 tons.

Dimensions: 127.6 oa x 22.2 x 8.25 metres.

Machinery: 3-shaft Triple Expansion, 19,000ihp = 18½ knots.

Armament: 4 x 280mm, 14 x 170mm, and 20 x 88mm guns; 6 x 450mm torpedo tubes.

Complement: 743.

BATTLESHIPS
Nassau Class

Nassau, Westfalen, Rheinland and *Posen*

Displacement: 18,570–21,000 tons.

Dimensions: 146.1 x 26.9 x 8.08/8.9 metres.

Machinery: 3-shaft, 3 cylinder Vertical Triple Expansion, 22,000ihp = 19½ knots.

Armour: Belt 300mm; turrets 280mm.

Armament: 12 x 280mm, 12 x 150mm, and 16 x 88mm guns; 6 x 450mm torpedo tubes.
Complement: 1,124.

Helgoland Class
Helgoland, Ostfriesland, Thüringen and *Oldenburg*
Displacement: 22,240–25,200 tons.
Dimensions: 167.2 x 28.5 x 8.2/9.0 metres.
Machinery: 3-shaft, 4 cylinder Vertical Triple Expansion, 28,000ihp = 20 knots.
Armour: Belt 300mm; turrets 300mm.
Armament: 12 x 305mm, 14 x 150mm, and 14 x 88mm guns; 6 x 500mm torpedo tubes.
Complement: 1,284.

Kaiser Class
Kaiser, Friedrich der Grosse, Kaiserin, Prinzregent Luitpold
Displacement: 24,330–27,400 tons.
Dimensions: 172.4 x 29 x 8.3/9.1 metres.
Machinery: 3-shaft, turbines, 31,000shp = 21 knots.
Armour: Belt 350mm; turrets 300mm.
Armament: 10 x 305mm, 14 x 150mm, and 12 x 88mm guns; 5 x 500mm torpedo tubes.
Complement: 1,249.

König Class
König, Grosser Kurfürst, Markgraf and *Konprinz* (renamed *Konprinz Wilhelm* on 30 June 1918 on the 30th anniverasry of the accession of Kaiser Wilhelm II)
Displacement: 25,390–29,200 tons.
Dimensions: 175.4 x 29.5 x 8.3/9.3 metres.
Machinery: 3-shaft, turbines, 31,000shp = 21 knots (exceeded at Jutland).
Armour: Belt 350mm; turrets 300mm.
Armament: 10 x 305mm, 14 x 150mm, and 10 x 88mm guns; 5 x 500mm torpedo tubes.
Complement: 1,284.

BATTLECRUISERS
Von der Tann
Displacement: 19,064–21,700 tons.
Dimensions: 171.7 x 26.6 x 8.1/9 metres.

Machinery: 4-shaft, turbines, 43,600shp = 25 knots.
Armour: Belt 250mm; turrets 230mm.
Armament: 8 x 280mm, 10 x 150mm, and 16 x 88mm guns; 4 x
             450mm torpedo tubes.
Complement: 1,174.

Moltke Class
Moltke
Displacement: 22,616–25,300 tons.
Dimensions: 186.5 x 29.5 x 8.2/9 metres.
Machinery: 4-shaft, turbines, 52,000shp = 25½ knots.
Armour: Belt 270mm; turrets 230mm.
Armament: 10 x 280mm, 12 x 150mm, and 12 x 88mm guns; 4 x
              500mm torpedo tubes.
Complement: 1,355.

Seydlitz
Displacement: 24,594–28,100 tons.
Dimensions: 200.5 x 28.5 x 8.2/9.2 metres.
Machinery: 4-shaft, turbines, 63,000shp = 26½ knots.
Armour: Belt 300mm; turrets 250mm.
Armament: 10 x 280mm, 12 x 150mm, and 12 x 88mm guns; 4 x
              500mm torpedo tubes.
Complement: 1,425.

Derfflinger Class
Derfflinger and *Lützow*
Displacement: 26,180-30,700 tons.
Dimensions: 210.4 x 29 x 8.3/9.5 metres.
Machinery: 4-shaft, turbines, 63,000shp = 26½ knots.
Armour: Belt 300mm; turrets 270mm.
Armament: 8 x 305mm, 12 x 150mm, and 4 x 88mm guns; 4 x 500mm
              torpedo tubes.
Complement: 1,391.

LIGHT CRUISERS
Gazelle Class
Frauenlob
Displacement: 3,130 tons.
Dimensions: 105.4 oa x 12.2 x 5.53 metres.
Machinery: 2-shaft Triple Expansion, 8,500ihp = 21 knots.

Armament: 10 x 105mm guns; 3 x 450mm torpedo tubes.
Complement: 249

Bremen Class
München and *Hamburg*
Displacement: 3,756 tons.
Dimensions: 111.1 oa x 13.3 x 5.61 metres.
Machinery: 2-shaft Triple Expansion, 11,750ihp = 23 knots.
Armament: 10 x 105mm guns; 2 x 450mm torpedo tubes.
Complement: 288.

Königsberg Class
Stettin and *Stuttgart*
Displacement: 3,480 tons.
Dimensions: 116.8 x 13.3 x 5.3 metres.
Machinery: 2-shaft 3-cylinder Vertical Triple Expansion, 12,000ihp = 23 knots
                (*Stettin*: 4 shafts, turbines, 13,500shp = 24 knots).
Armament: 10 x 105mm guns; 2 x 450mm torpedo tubes.
Complement: 322.

Graudenz Class
Regensburg
Displacement: 4,912 tons.
Dimensions: 139 x 13.8 x 5.75 metres.
Machinery: 2-shaft, turbines, 29,000shp = 28 knots.
Armament: 12 x 105mm guns; 2 x 500mm torpedo tubes.
Complement: 385.

Pillau Class
Elbing and *Pillau*
Displacement: 4,390 tons.
Dimensions: 134.3 x 13.6 x 6 metres.
Machinery: 2-shaft, turbines, 30,000shp = 27½ knots.
Armament: 8 x 150mm, and 2 x 88mm guns; 2 x 500mm torpedo
                tubes.
Complement: 442.

Wiesbaden Class
Frankfurt and *Wiesbaden*
Displacement: 5,180 tons.
Dimensions: 141.7 x 13.9 x 5.8 metres.

Machinery: 2-shaft, turbines, 31,000shp = 27½ knots.
Armament: 8 x 150mm, and 2 x 88mm guns; 4 x 500mm torpedo
             tubes.
Complement: 474.

Torpedo Boats German destroyers and torpedo boats were un-named being identified by a single letter followed a number. Those present at The Skagerrak varied in size from 800 to 1,400 tons and were capable of thirty-three to thirty-six knots. Their armament consisted of up to three 88mm or 105mm guns and six 500mm torpedo tubes as well as twenty-four mines. Their complements ranged from eighty-three to 114 officers and men.

Notes and References

Foreword
1. H.W. Fawcett and G.W.W. Hooper, *The Fighting at Jutland* (Macmillan, 1921).
2. Nigel Steel and Peter Hart, *Jutland 1916: Death in Grey Waters* (Cassell, 2003).
3. *Battle of Jutland Official Despatches* (HMSO, 1920).
4. John Campbell, *Jutland, An Analysis of the Fighting* (Conway, 1986).
5. J.E.T. Harper, *The Truth About Jutland* (John Murray, 1927).
6. Innes McCartney, *Jutland 1916: The Archaeology of a Naval Battlefield* (Bloomsbury, in press, 2016).

Chapter 1: A Tale of Two Communiqués
1. The German communiqué of 1 June 1916, quoted in *Naval Operations Volume IV* by Henry Newbolt (Longmans, Green and Co., 1928), p.4.
2. ibid, pp.4-5.
3. The initial British communiqué of 3 June 1916, quoted in Newbolt, p.3.

Chapter 2: The Opening Moves
1. Peter C. Smith, *Sailors in the Dock: Naval Courts Martial Down the Centuries* (The History Press, 2011), pp.113-8.
2. Julian S. Corbett, *Maritime Operations in the Russo-Japanese War 1904–1905, Volume 1* (Naval Institute Press, 1994), pp.234-5, describes the loss of Japanese battleships *Hatsuse* and *Yashima* which were sunk by mines off Port Arthur on 15 May 1904.
3. Reinhard Scheer, *Germany's High Seas Fleet in the First World War* (Frontline Books, 2014), p.233.
4. ibid, p.239.
5. Scheer, p.134.
6. ibid.
7. Letter from Jellicoe to Admiralty 20.10.1914, *Battle of Jutland Official Despatches*, pp.601-3. See Appendix I.

8. Letter from Admiralty to Jellicoe 7.11.1914, *Battle of Jutland Official Despatches*, p.603. See Appendix II.
9. Scheer, p.133.
10. Room 40 was the Admiralty's secret intelligence department.
11. *Battle of Jutland Official Despatches*, p.5.
12. Ewart Oakeshott, *The Blindfold Game: The Day at Jutland* (Pergamon Press, 1969), p.34.
13. Stephen Roskill, *Admiral of the Fleet Earl Beatty The Last Naval Hero: An Intimate Biography* (Collins, 1980), pp.153-4.
14. *Battle of Jutland Official Despatches*, p.6.
15. ibid, p.7.
16. S. Thorsøe, P. Simonsen, S. Krogh-Andersen, F. Frederichsen and H. Vaupel, *DFDS 1866-1991 Ship Development Through 125 Years from Paddle Steamer to Ro/Ro Ship* (DFDS, 1991), p.225.
17. Langhorne Gibson and Vice Admiral J.E.T. Harper, *The Riddle of Jutland: An Authentic History* (Cassell, 1934), pp.110-1.
18. *Battle of Jutland Official Despatches*, p.172.
19. ibid.
20. 'Battle of Jutland Daring Spirit Impresses the Danes, How the Fight Began', *Western Times*, 16 June 1916.
21. Gibson and Harper, p.113.
22. *Battle of Jutland Official Despatches*, p.172.
23. Oakeshott, p.37.
24. *Battle of Jutland Official Despatches*, p.116.

Chapter 3: The Run to the South

1. *Battle of Jutland Official Despatches*, p.7.
2. ibid.
3. The Short 184 Seaplane that undertook this historic flight had the serial number N8359. The service history of N8359 can be found in Ray Sturtivant and Gordon Page, *Royal Navy Aircraft Serials and Units 1911–1919* (Air-Britain (Historians) Ltd., 1992), p.129. The aircraft is currently being restored at the Fleet Air Arm Museum, Yeovilton.
4. *The Enemy in Sight* (translated from *Skagerrak*) describing the arrival of Rutland's aircraft, ADM 137/4809, p.74.
5. *Battle of Jutland Official Despatches*, p.7.
6. Report written by Commander G.J. Mackenzie-Grieve of HMS *Birmingham*, dated 31st May-1st June and written before the cruiser returned to harbour after Jutland. In ADM 137/1644, p.18.
7. *Battle of Jutland Official Despatches*, p.7.
8. On 1 November 1914 the obsolete British armoured cruisers *Good Hope* and *Monmouth*, manned by reservists with little or no gunnery training, were sunk by the powerful armoured cruisers *Scharnhorst* and *Gneisenau* during the Battle of Coronel. The German vessels, which were crack gunnery ships, were barely

visible in the fading light while their British opponents were silhouetted against the afterglow.

9. Commander Georg von Hase, First Gunnery Officer S.M.S. *Derfflinger* at Jutland on 31 May 1916.
10. *Battle of Jutland Official Despatches*, p.7.
11. Admiral of the Fleet, Lord Chatfield, *The Navy & Defence* (Heinemann, 1942), pp.140-1.
12. John Campbell, *Jutland: An Analysis of the Fighting* (Conway Maritime Press, 1986), p.39.
13. ibid, p.40.
14. Report written by Commander G.J. Mackenzie-Grieve of HMS *Birmingham*, in ADM 137/1644, p.19.
15. Campbell, pp.40-2.
16. ibid, p.43.
17. C. Falmer, Imperial War Museum IWM), Department of Sound, AC 4096 Reel 1.
18. Report written by Commander G.J. Mackenzie-Grieve in ADM 137/1644, p.19.
19. Campbell, p.44.
20. *Battle of Jutland Official Despatches*, p.8.
21. Campbell, p.49.
22. Captain Otto Groos was the Navigator aboard *Von der Tann* at Jutland on 31 May 1916.
23. E. Francis, *Impressions of a Gunner's Mate at Jutland*, IWM Department of Documents, T.M. Field Collection.
24. J.L. Storey, typescript memoir in H.H. McWilliam Collection, Peter Liddle Collection, Leeds University.
25. E. Francis, *op. cit.*
26. ibid.
27. Lord Chatfield, p.143.
28. Campbell, pp.47-8.
29. Mackenzie-Grieve, ADM 137/1644, p.19.
30. Lord Chatfield, p.142.
31. From 'The Autobiography of Chief Gunner Alexander Grant: HMS *Lion* at the battle of Jutland, 1916', edited by Eric Grove (The Naval Miscellany, Volume VII, pp.379- 406).
32. *Battle of Jutland Official Despatches*, pp.8-9.
33. Mackenzie-Grieve report, ADM 137/1644, p.19.
34. ADM 137/1644, Jutland Later Reports, pp.12-3.
35. Campbell, p.47.
36. *Battle of Jutland Official Despatches*, p.9.
37. Campbell, pp.51-4.
38. ibid, p.54.
39. Mackenzie-Grieve report, ADM 137/1644, pp.20-1.
40. ibid.
41. ibid, pp.52-8.

42. The double florin (4/-) was one of the shortest-lived British coin denominations ever, only being produced during four mint years between 1887 and 1890. The silver coin weighed 22.6 grams (0.80 oz) and was 36 millimetres (1.4 in) in diameter. The coin was introduced as part of a short-lived attempt at decimalization of the currency, after an earlier attempt had spawned the florin. As with the sixpence, Shilling, and Florin the coin was not demonetized as part of the 1971 decimalization. Unlike those coins is has not been subsequently called in, and it remains legal tender for 20 pence. The coins are not likely spent, though, as the silver content of each coin is worth far more than 20 pence. The coin acquired the nickname of 'Barmaid's Grief' because of its similarity to the slightly larger crown coin, worth 5 shillings, 25% more than the double florin, as neither coin was marked its denomination and both used an identical portrait of Queen Victoria on the obverse (Spinks, *Coins of England and the United Kingdom*, 2007).
43. ADM 137/4808, pp.52-3.
44. ADM 137/4809, pp.16-7.

Chapter 4: The Run to the North
1. Campbell, pp.96-7 and p.102.
2. Campbell, pp.102 and 126.
3. ibid, pp.129-34.
4. ibid, pp.135-145.
5. *Battle of Jutland Official Despatches*, p.11.
6. ibid.
7. Campbell, p.59.
8. *Battle of Jutland Official Despatches*, p.14.
9. ADM 116/1484, Chester's Report on Action 31.5.1916 (written 13 June 1916).
10. *Battle of Jutland Official Despatches*, p.14.
11. ibid, pp.319-20.
12. ADM 137/1643, pp.65-7.
13. ibid.
14. *Battle of Jutland Official Despatches*, pp.317-8.
15. ibid, p.16.
16. ibid, p.11.
17. Campbell, p.117.

Chapter 5: Windy Corner
1. *Battle of Jutland Official Despatches*, p.16.
2. Campbell, p.122.
3. ibid.
4. The largest German shells fired at Jutland were 12-inch in diameter. However, many in the Grand Fleet were aware that, prior to the outbreak of war, the Germans had been constructing a 14-inch gun armed battlecruiser, to be known as *Salamis*, for the Greeks. The Royal Navy had obtained the battleships *Agincourt*, *Canada* and *Erin* by taking over ships under construction for other

navies and consequently some British officers expected to find themselves in action against the former Greek ship, hence the reference to 14-inch guns. Ironically, her 14-inch guns were ordered from Bethlehem Steel in the USA, but were sold to the British in November 1914 and were used in the Royal Navy's Abercrombie class monitors.

5. The so-called 'Russian type' cruisers reported by Captain Molteno were *Elbing* (ex-*Muraview Amurski*) and *Pillau* (*Admiral Nevlski*) which had been ordered from Schichau at Danzig in 1913 and completed in December 1914 and September 1915 respectively.
6. *Battle of Jutland Official Despatches*, pp.290-1.
7. ibid, p.65.
8. ibid. p.17.
9. ibid. pp.163-7.
10. The ship reported damaged and in sinking condition was *Lützow* and not *Derfflinger* (*Battle of Jutland Official Despatches*, pp.163-7).
11. ibid, pp.167-9.

Chapter 6: Main Fleet Action

1. *Battle of Jutland Official Despatches*, p.17.
2. Campbell, p.157.
3. *Wiesbaden*.
4. The battleship was actually *König*.
5. Gunner F.W. Potter R.N., *Battle of Jutland Official Despatches*, pp.61-2.
6. Twenty-seven ships in six and three-quarter miles including the 5th Battle Squadron.
7. Campbell, p.161.
8. Rev. J.L. Pastfield, *New Light on Jutland* (William Heineman, 1933).
9. Campbell, pp.155-6.
10. *Battle of Jutland Official Despatches*, p.18.
11. ibid.
12. Sir Julian S. Corbett, *Official History of the War, Naval Operations Vol. III* (Longmans, Green & Co. 1923), p.370.
13. Campbell, p.163.
14. ibid.
15. No German submarines participated in the Battle of Jutland.
16. ADM 137/1643, Jutland Additional Papers 1916, p.21.
17. *Battle of Jutland Official Despatches*, p.65.
18. Discussed in Roskill, p.176.
19. Campbell, p.164.
20. *Battle of Jutland Official Despatches*, p.18.
21. ibid, p.66.
22. ibid, pp.79-80.
23. The eight dreadnoughts of the Nassau and Helgoland classes were powered by steam reciprocating machinery.

24. Campbell, pp.206-7.
25. Gunner Potter, *Battle of Jutland Official Despatches*, p.62.
26. *Battle of Jutland Official Despatches*, pp.19-20.
27. Campbell, pp. 210-2.
28. Gunner Potter, *Battle of Jutland Official Despatches*, p.62.
29. Gunner Herbert D. Jehan R.N., *Battle of Jutland Official Despatches*, p.63.
30. Campbell, p.212 and pp.214-5.
31. *Battle of Jutland Official Despatches*, p.66.
32. ibid, p.20.
33. ibid.

Chapter 7: Night Action and Inaction

1. This lack of initiative is the thesis running throughout Andrew Gordon's *The Rules of the Game: Jutland and British Naval Command* (John Murray, 1986).
2. *Battle of Jutland Official Despatches*, pp.20-1.
3. ibid, pp.21-2.
4. Discussed in detail by Professor A.J. Marder in *From Dreadnought to Scapa Flow Vol. III Jutland and After: May to December 1916* (Seaforth Publishing, 2014), pp.172-5.
5. Campbell, pp.275-6.
6. Marder, p.155.
7. ibid, pp.171-2.
8. ibid, p.161
9. *Battle of Jutland Official Despatches*, pp.22-3.
10. Campbell, p.281.
11. *Battle of Jutland Official Despatches*, pp.23-4.
12. Campbell, p.286.
13. *Spitfire* assumed them to be cruisers without realising that she had been attacking the head of the German battle line.
14. Campbell, p.287.
15. ADM 137/4809, pp.136-7. In *S.M.S. Nassau off the Skagerrak* by 'One Who Was There', translated from *Norddeutsche Allgemaine Zeitung*, 26/8/1916.
16. Campbell, p.287.
17. ibid, pp.288-9.
18. Marder, p.168.
19. Campbell, p.290.
20. ibid, p.291.
21. ibid, p.292.
22. *Battle of Jutland Official Despatches*, p.26.
23. Campbell, p.293.
24. ADM 137/1644, pp.13-5.
25. Campbell, pp.294-5.
26. ibid, p.295.
27. ibid, p.317.

28. This is another example of Jellicoe using eyewitness reports to justify his claim that two battleships of the German 3rd Battle Squadron were sunk.
29. *Battle of Jutland Official Despatches*, pp.23-4.
30. Campbell, p.299.
31. ibid, p.301.
32. *Battle of Jutland Official Despatches*, pp.24-5.
33. Campbell, p.294.
34. ADM 116/1485.
35. *Battle of Jutland Official Despatches*, p.26.
36. ibid. p.25.
37. The sinking cruiser was actually *Elbing*.
38. *Battle of Jutland Official Despatches*, p.27.
39. ibid, p.22.
40. Campbell, p.315.
41. *Battle of Jutland Official Despatches*, pp.27-8.

Chapter 8: Ready For Action?

1. *Battle of Jutland Official Despatches*, pp.28-9.
2. ibid, p.29.
3. Roskill, p.204.
4. *Battle of Jutland Official Despatches*, pp.29-30.
5. ibid, pp.30-1.
6. ibid, pp.292-3.
7. ADM 137/1643, Jutland Additional Papers, p.134.
8. ibid, pp.31-2.
9. ibid. p.183.
10. ADM 137/2134, Battle Cruiser Force Records Vol. IV Miscellaneous, p.349.
11. Actually the 21,000 ton (full load) battleship *Nassau*.
12. ADM 137/4809, Letter from Captain Superintendent 5th August 1916 to Secretary of the Admiralty, p.269.
13. ibid, Letter to Captain Superintendent, Tyne 28th September 1916, p.268.
14. Newbolt, p.1.
15. Campbell, p.336.
16. ADM 137/4808, Report from R.16 sent from Rotterdam 27.6.1916 and received on 28.6.1916, pp.17-21.
17. ibid, Message from Petrograd sent on 17.6.1916 and received on 18.6.1916, p.34.
18. ibid, Report from Russian Admiralty, p.36.
19. ibid, From Naval Attaché in Copenhagen, p.41.
20. ibid, From German Agent D.15, pp.201-3.
21. ibid, Report from Agent D.3, p.206.
22. ibid, Report from Danish Secret Service 24.6.1916, p.39.
23. ibid, Report from Agent N.1 in Copenhagen, p.205.
24. ibid, Report from Agent D.2, p.206.
25. ibid, Letter from Dr Greveler of Cassel, Germany dated 7.7.1916 to his P/W son

Max Greveler, p.48.

26. *Berliner Tageblatt*, 18 November 1918, quoted by Admiral Viscount Jellicoe in *The Grand Fleet 1914-16 – Its Creation, Development and Work* (Cassell, 1919), pp.411-2.

27. ADM 137/2027, Grand Fleet Committees formed to consider experiences at Jutland.

28. The loss of all three battlecruisers was almost certainly caused by cordite fires following penetration of turret armour. The problem was caused by the lax ammunition handling procedures that had been allowed to develop throughout the fleet in the years leading up to Jutland. See Chapter 13 for a more detailed discussion.

29. Defence against plunging shell was aided was aided by the considerable depth of inessential structure above the amour deck. Almost without exception the fuses of German shell were actuated on hitting the upper deck and amongst all the hits on the decks of surviving ships only one splinter penetrated the armour deck. Consequently, it is highly unlikely that any of the ships were lost because of penetration of deck armour. The high velocity German shells did not fall very steeply (11-inch shell at 18,000 yard 10 degrees to the horizontal) and this reduced the need for British deck armour. See Chapter 13 for a more detailed discussion.

30. Jellicoe, pp.418-9.

31. ADM 137/2134, Battle Cruiser Force Records Vol. IV Miscellaneous, p.430.

32. ibid. p.368.

33. ibid. p.369.

34. Jellicoe, p.421.

35. Discussed by Norman Friedman in *Naval Firepower Battleship Guns and Gunnery in the Dreadnought Era* (Seaforth Publishing, 2008), pp.102-6.

36. 'Handing room' is the correct term although many sources have erroneously called it the 'handling room'.

37. ADM 186/229 *Vengeance Flash Trials 1917 and 1918*, pp.5-6.

38. Lord Chatfield, p.153.

39. *Battle of Jutland Official Despatches*, pp.75, 93, 100, 166, 170-1, 359, 372, 375, 69 and 94.

40. Lyddite.

41. Scheer, p.174.

42. Campbell, p.220-2.

43. ibid. p.349 and p.386.

44. Marder, p.263.

45. John Jordan and Robert Dumas, *French Battleships 1922–1956* (Seaforth Publishing, 2009), pp.81-2.

Chapter 9: After the Battle: British Press Reports

1. *Manchester Evening News*, 3 June 1916.

2. *Daily Mirror*, 3 June 1916.
3. *The Jellicoe Papers Volume I, 1893 – 1916*, Edited by A. Temple Patterson (Navy Records Society, 1966). pp.272-3.
4. *Hindenburg* was not present at Jutland and this report is referring to the sinking of her sister *Lützow*.
5. *The Globe*, 4 June 1916.

Chapter 10: German Lies Exposed

1. Quoted on www.dreadnoughtproject.org.
2. *Manchester Evening News*, 14 June 1916.
3. It is unclear as to the identity of this ship because the only ship of this name in service with the German Navy at this time was an old ironclad cruiser serving as a training hulk. She survived the war and was broken up in 1921.
4. *The Birmingham Mail*, 28 June 1916.
5. Neither of the two Roon-class ships was present at Jutland.
6. Lord Charles Beresford (1846–1919), whose later career was marked with a long-running dispute with Admiral of the Fleet Sir John Fisher, was widely known to the British public as 'Charlie B'.
7. Admiral Sir Reginald Henderson (1846–1932).
8. Eight not nine were lost.
9. *Queen Elizabeth* was in dock at the time of Jutland and therefore only four of the class were present.
10. *Western Times*, 4 July 1916.
11. *Seydlitz* was armed with 11-inch guns. There is no evidence that the German 11-inch and 12-inch guns proved in any way unsatisfactory during the Battle of Jutland.
12. The captain of the sinking *Warrior* ordered his ship abandoned after the seaplane carrier *Engadine* came alongside to take the crew off at 08.00. About 675 officers and men successfully made it to the much smaller *Engadine* including about thirty seriously wounded men who were transferred across in their stretchers. One man fell from his stretcher between the ships, but, against orders, Rutland dived overboard with a bowline to rescue him. Rutland's exploits in a Short 184 the day before earned the soubriquet 'Rutland of Jutland'.
13. *Daily Mirror*, 12 August 1916.
14. Alfred Noyes (1880–1958) was a poet and essayist who from 1916 completed his military service on attachment to the Foreign Office, where he worked alongside John Buchan on propaganda.
15. Rear Admiral Sir Douglas Brownrigg, *Indiscretions of The Naval Censor* (Cassell, 1920).
16. ADM 1/8462/170, Publicity.
17. ibid.
18. *Daily Mirror*, 19 October 1916.
19. ADM 1/8462/170.

Chapter 11: The 'Typewriter War' in the United States' Press

1. Count Johann Heinrich von Bernstorff (1862-1932) was German Ambassador to the United States from 1908-1917.
2. A copy of this letter, dated 16 June 1916, from Count von Bernstorff, Imperial German Embassy, Washington D.C. to the Imperial Chancellor in Berlin, translated into English is to be found in ADM 137/4808, pp.154-71.
3. Theobald Theodore von Bethmann-Hollweg (1856-1921) was Imperial German Chancellor from 1909-1917.
4. Fritz von Papen (1879-1969) was German Military Attaché in Washington D.C. at the outbreak of the war and was expelled on 28 December 1915. He subsequently became German Chancellor in 1932 and served as Vice-Chancellor under Adolf Hitler in 1933-1934.
5. Captain Karl Boy-Ed (1872-1930) was German Naval Attaché in Washington D.C. at the outbreak of the First War and was expelled in December 1915.
6. ADM 137/4808, p.154.
7. ibid, pp.154-5.
8. ibid, pp.155-6.
9. ibid, pp.157-61.
10. ibid, pp.151-70.
11. Max Harden (1861–1927) was a fierce critic of Kaiser Wilhelm II who by 1914 had become an ardent annexationist demanding that Germany win the war to annex most of Europe, Asia and Africa thereby making the Reich the world's greatest power. Post war he became a pacifist!
12. ADM 137/4808, pp.151-70.
13. On 27 October 1914 the British super-dreadnought *Audacious* sank after striking a mine laid by the German auxiliary *Berlin* off Tory Island. The battleship took several hours to sink and her loss was witnessed and photographed by American passengers aboard the British liner R.M.S. *Olympic*. The Admiralty imposed a news blackout to try and stop news of *Audacious'* loss getting to the Germans but American citizens on American soil were beyond British jurisdiction and consequently the Germans became aware of the sinking of *Audacious* within a few weeks.
14. ADM 137/4808, pp.170-1.
15. 'The Naval Battle – Americans and Falsified German Accounts', *Newcastle Journal*, 14 June 1916.
16. ADM 137/4809, p.161, from a communication dated 11 July 1916, by Captain Boy-Ed to Colonel Willard Church.

Chapter 12: German Perspectives

1. Kaiser Wilhelm II addressing the crew of *Friedrich der Grosse* at Wilhelmshaven 5 June 1916, quoted in *A Naval History of World War I* by Paul G. Halpern (UCL Press, 1994), p.326.
2. Robert K. Massie, *Castles of Steel, Britain, Germany and the Winning of the Great War at Sea* (Jonathan Cape, 2004), p.658.

3. ADM 137/1643, *Jutland Additional Papers*, p.145.
4. ibid, pp.167-9.
5. Scheer, pp.175-6.
6. Quoted in Gordon, p.498.
7. Quoted in Halpern, p.326.
8. ADM 137/4808, pp.210-3.
9. ibid, pp.31-2.
10. ibid, pp.75-88.
11. Grand Admiral Hans von Koester (1844-1928) was the first German to attain the rank of Grand Admiral while still serving. He retired on 31 December 1906 and was President of the German Fleet Association from 1908 to 1919. During 1916-17 he was a passionate advocate of unrestricted submarine warfare.
12. ADM 137/4808, pp.67-71.
13. ibid, pp.132-7.
14. ibid, pp.114-8.
15. ibid, pp.142-9.
16. ibid, pp.223-52.
17. Nicolas Wolz, *From Imperial Splendour to Internment, The German Navy in the First World War* (Seaforth Publishing, 2015), p.162.
18. Scheer, pp.168-9.
19. *Korvettenkapitän* Ernst von Weizsäker's diary entry for 5/6 November 1918, quoted in Seligman, M.S., Nägler, F. and Epkenhans, M. (Eds), *The Naval Route to the Abyss: The Anglo-German Naval Race, 1895-1914* (Navy Records Society, 2015), p.xxxv.

Chapter 13: Scapegoating the Battlecruiser

1. Rear-Admiral W.S. Chalmers, *The Life and Letters of David Earl Beatty* (Hodder and Stoughton, 1951), p.262.
2. Nicholas A. Lambert, '"Our Bloody Ships" or "Our Bloody System"? Jutland and the Loss of the Battlecruisers, 1916', *The Journal of Military History*, 1998, 62, p.36.
3. Lambert, p.37.
4. Quoted in Geoffrey Bennett, *Coronel and the Falklands* (Pan Books Ltd, 1967), p.165.
5. Lambert, p.39.
6. Filson Young, *With the Battlecruisers* (Birlinn, 2002), p.191.
7. ibid, pp.224-5.
8. Alexander Grant, *The Naval Miscellany Volume VII*, Edited by Eric Grove, (Navy Records Society, 2008) p.390.
9. James Goldrick, *The King's Ships Were At Sea; The War in the North Sea August 1914–February 1915* (Naval Institute Press, 1984), p.312.
10. *Jellicoe Papers Vol. I*, pp.265-6.
11. It is more likely that flash reaching magazines was the cause of the battlecruiser sinking but, this telegram is evidence that British magazine precaution were dangerously unsafe.

12. *The Beatty Papers: Selections from the Private and Official Correspondence of Admiral of the Fleet Earl Beatty Vol. I 1902-1918*, edited by B. McL. Ranft (Scholar Press for the Navy Records Society, 1989), p.318.

13. Alexander Grant, pp.400-1.

14. *The Jellicoe Papers*, p.271.

15. Marder, p.209.

16. ADM 137/2134, Recommendations of BCF Gunnery Committee, p.393.

17. ibid, BCF Records, Vol IV The BCF Battlecruiser Committee 18th June 1916, p.530-3.

18. ibid, Beatty to Admiralty, 14 July 1916, pp.502-4.

19. *The Jellicoe Papers*, p.267.

20. Quoted by N. Friedman in *The British Battleship 1906-1946* (Seaforth Publishing, 2015), p.391.

21. ADM 1/8463/176, Causes of Explosion in British Warships When Hit by Heavy Shell.

22. ibid.

23. Quoted in Lambert, pp.50-1.

24. ADM 1/8463/176.

25. ibid.

26. ADM 1/8463/176.

27. ADM 137/2134, p.514.

28. ADM 1/8463/176.

29. ibid.

30. Lambert, p.46.

31. *Mackensen* was at least a year from completion at the time of the Armistice. There was no German battlecruiser named *Manteuffel* and this name may be an Admiralty reference to one of *Mackensen*'s three sister ships (*Graf Spee, Prinz Eitel Friedrich* and *Fürst Bismarck*) which were also incomplete in November 1918.

32. ADM 137/1646, Grand Fleet Policy Special Papers 1915-1918, Proposal to Purchase Two Japanese Battlecruisers, pp.62-3.

33. ibid, p.75.

34. ibid, p.76.

35. ibid, p.77.

36. Letter from Royal Navy Constructor David K. Brown (RCNC, Ret.) to the author, 13 April 2004.

37. *Ballymena Observer*, 20 December 1918.

38. Captain, Later Vice-Admiral, C.V. Usborne (1880-1951), quoted in Norman Friedman, *The British Battleship 1906-1946* (Seaforth Publishing, 2015), p.391.

39. Reverend J.L. Pastfield, *New Light on Jutland* (1933), from ADM 52787, *The Goodall Diaries 1934* (British Museum), quoted in letter from Royal Navy Constructor David K. Brown (RCNC, Ret.) to the author, 13 April 2004.

40. ADM 52789, The Goodall Diaries 1936, (British Museum) quoted by D.K. Brown in *Nelson to Vanguard: Warship Design and Development 1923-1945* (Seaforth Publishing, 2000), p.9.

Chapter 14: Echoes of Jutland
1. *Aberdeen Journal*, 18 July 1916.
2. ADM 137/1643, p.65.
3. ibid. p.75.
4. ibid. p 78.
5. ibid. p.93.
6. ibid, p.95.
7. Actually nine battleships. *Baden* and *König* joined the interned ships some time later.
8. Only five battlecruisers.
9. *Ajax* was one of four King George V-class battleships.
10. Admiral of the Fleet, The Earl of Cork and Orrery, *My Naval Life 1886–1941* (Hutchison & Co., 1942), p.120.
11. *The Beatty Papers*, edited by B. McL Ranft (Scholar Press for the Navy Records Society, 1989), pp.570-1.
12. Lord Alfred Douglas (1870-1945), better known as the friend and lover of Oscar Wilde, was famous for his litigious nature.
13. *Hull Daily Mail*, 18 July 1923.
14. ADM 1/8637/51, Lord Alfred Douglas Trial.
15. The Earl of Cork and Orrery, p.120.
16. *Dundee Evening Telegraph*, 27 December 1921.

Appendices
1. *Battle of Jutland Official Despatches*, pp.601-3.
2. ibid, p.603.
3. Owen Thetford, *British Naval Aircraft Since 1912* (Putnam, 1961), pp.255-7.
4. Ray Sturtivant and Gordon Page, p.129.
5. *Conway's All the World's Fighting Ships 1906-1921*, pp.22-36, 50-9, 65 and 71-9.
6. ibid pp.145-62, 248-9 and 258-9.

Bibliography

DOCUMENTS HELD IN THE NATIONAL ARCHIVES (TNA), KEW, LONDON

ADM 1/8460/149   Gunnery Information drawn from the action of 31 May 1916: Report of Dreadnought Battle Fleet Committee.

ADM 1/8461/153   Complaint by Vice Admiral Sir David Beatty re: abbreviations made by the Admiralty in his despatches relating to the Battle of Heligoland Bight, Battle of Dogger Bank and Battle of Jutland.

ADM 1/8461/159   Disposal of corpses washed ashore on Norwegian Coast.

ADM 1/8462/170   Naval Publicity.

ADM 1/8463/176   Causes of explosions in British warships when hit by heavy shells.

ADM 1/8581/27   Official Record of the Battle of Jutland.

ADM 1/8582/125   Abandonment of Captain J.E.T. Harper's Official Narrative.

ADM 1/8637/51   PLAIN ENGLISH Case.

ADM 1/8722/290   Publication of the Harper Report.

ADM 116/1484   Jutland Battle Vol. 3: Losses of Battle and Armoured Cruisers, Lack of Armour Plating not borne out by evidence, Exposed Cordite etc.

ADM 116/1485   Jutland Battle Vol. IV: Reports from destroyers and destroyer leaders.

ADM 116/3188   Observations on the Narrative of the Battle of Jutland.

ADM 137/302   Jutland 31 May 1916: Reports of Flag and Commanding Officers.

ADM 137/1643   Jutland Additional Papers 1916.

ADM 137/1644   Jutland Later Reports 1916.

ADM 137/1645   Grand Fleet Post Jutland Changes.

ADM 137/1646   Grand Fleet Policy Special Papers 1915 – 1918.

ADM 137/2027   Grand Fleet Committees formed to consider experience at Jutland: Part I.

ADM 137/2028   Grand Fleet Committees formed to consider experience at Jutland: Part II.

ADM 137/2029   Grand Fleet Committees formed to consider experience at Jutland: Part III.

ADM 137/2134   Battle Cruiser Force War Records Vol. IV Miscellaneous.

ADM 137/4808   Battle of Jutland Information Vol. I.

ADM 137/4809   Battle of Jutland Information Vol. II.

ADM 186/229   VENGEANCE Flash Trials 1917 and 1918.

ADM 203/83   Article on Jutland by Admiral Dreyer.

SECONDARY SOURCES
STUDIES

Ronald Bassett, *Battlecruisers: A History 1908-1948* (Macmillan, 1981).

Geoffrey Bennett, *Coronel and the Falklands* (Pan Books Ltd, 1967).

Geoffrey Bennett, *Naval Battles of the First World War* (Pan, 1974).

Admiral of the Fleet, The Earl of Cork and Orrery (William 'Ginger' Boyle), *My Naval Life 1886–1941* (Hutchison & Co., 1942).

John Brooks, *Dreadnought Gunnery and the Battle of Jutland: The Question of Fire Control* (Routledge, 2005).

D.K. Brown, *The Grand Fleet: Warship Design and Development 1906-1922* (Conway, 1999).

Rear Admiral Sir Douglas Brownrigg, *Indiscretions of The Naval Censor* (Cassell & Co., 1920).

John Campbell, *Jutland, An Analysis of the Fighting* (Conway, 1986).

Rear-Admiral W.S. Chalmers, *The Life and Letters of David Earl Beatty* (Hodder and Stoughton, 1951).

Ernle Chatfield, *The Navy and Defence* (William Heinemann, 1942).

Julian S. Corbett, *Maritime Operations in the Russo-Japanese War 1904 -1905 Vol. 1* (Naval Institute Press, 1994).

Julian S. Corbett *History of the Great War, Naval Operations Volume I* (Longmans, Green & Co., 1920).

Julian S. Corbett *History of the Great War, Naval Operations Volume II* (Longmans, Green & Co., 1921).

Julian S. Corbett *History of the Great War, Naval Operations Volume III* (Longmans, Green & Co., 1923).

H.W. Fawcett and G.W.W. Hooper, *The Fighting at Jutland* (Macmillan, 1921).

Norman Friedman in *Naval Firepower Battleship Guns and Gunnery in the Dreadnought Era* (Seaforth, 2008).

Norman Friedman, *Naval Weapons of World War One: Guns, Torpedoes, Mines and ASW Weapons of all Nations* (Seaforth, 2011).

_____, *Fighting the Great War at Sea: Strategy, Tactics and Technology* (Seaforth, 2014).

_____, *The British Battleship 1906-1946* (Seaforth, 2015).

H.H. Frost, *The Battle of Jutland* (United States Naval Institute and B.F. Stevens &

Brown, 1936).

Langhorne Gibson and Vice Admiral J.E.T. Harper, *The Riddle of Jutland: An Authentic History* (Cassell, 1934).

James Goldrick, *The King's Ships Were at Sea: The War in the North Sea August 1914 – February 1915* (Naval Institute Press, 1984).

Andrew Gordon, *The Rules of the Game: Jutland and British Naval Command* (John Murray, 1986).

Eric Grove (Ed.), 'The Autobiography of Chief Gunner Alexander Grant: HMS LION at the Battle of Jutland, 1916', in *The Naval Miscellany Volume VII* (Susan Rose, Ed.), Ashgate for The Navy Records Society, 2008.

Paul G. Halpern, *A Naval History of World War I* (UCL Press, 1994).

J.E.T. Harper, *The Truth About Jutland* (John Murray, 1927).

Paul M. Kennedy, *The Rise and Fall of British Naval Mastery* (Macmillan, 1983).

J.R. Jellicoe, *The Grand Fleet 1914-16: Its Creation, Development and Work* (Cassell, 1919).

John Jordan and Robert Dumas, *French Battleships 1922 – 1956* (Seaforth, 2009).

Nicholas A. Lambert, *Sir John Fisher's Naval Revolution* (University of South Carolina Press, 1999).

Donald Macintyre, *Jutland* (Pan, 1966).

Arthur J. Marder, *From Dreadnought to Scapa Flow, Volume III Jutland and After: May to December 1916* (Seaforth, 2014).

Robert K. Massie, *Dreadnought: Britain, Germany, and the Coming of the Great War* (Jonathan Cape, 1992).

_____, *Castles of Steel: Britain Germany and the Winning of the Great War at Sea* (Jonathan Cape, 2004).

H. Newbolt, *History of the Great War, Naval Operations Volume IV* (Longmans, Green & Co, 1928).

_____, *History of the Great War, Naval Operations Volume V* (Longmans, Green & Co, 1931).

Ewart Oakshott, *The Blindfold Game: The Day at Jutland* (Pergamon Press, 1969).

Rev. J.L. Pastfield, *New Light on Jutland* (William Heineman, 1933).

John Roberts, *Battlecruisers* (Conway, 1997).

B. McL. Ranft (Ed.), *The Beatty Papers, Volume I, 1902-1918* (Scolar Press for The Navy Records Society, 1989).

_____, *The Beatty Papers, Volume II, 1916-1927* (Scolar Press for The Navy Records Society, 1993).

S.W. Roskill, *Hankey, Man of Secrets, Volume 1 1877-1918* (Collins, 1970).

_____, *Admiral of the Fleet Earl Beatty, The Last Naval Hero: An Intimate Biography* (Collins 1980).

Reinhard Scheer, *Germany's High Seas Fleet in the First World War* (Frontline Books, 2014).

M.S. Seligman, F. Nägler and M. Epkenhans, M., *The Naval Route to the Abyss: The Anglo-German Naval Race, 1895-1914* (Navy Records Society, 2015).

Peter C. Smith, *Sailors in the Dock: Naval Courts Martial Down the Centuries* (History

Press, 2011).

Gary Staff, *German Battlecruisers of World War One: Their Design, Construction and Operations* (Seaforth, 2014).

Nigel Steel and Peter Hart, *Jutland 1916: Death in Grey Waters* (Cassell, 2003).

Ray Sturtivant and Gordon Page, *Royal Navy Aircraft Serials and Units 1911 – 1919* (Air-Britain Ltd., 1992).

V.E. Tarrant, *Battlecruiser Invincible: The History of the First Battlecruiser, 1909-16* (Arms & Armour Press, 1986).

A. Temple Patterson (Ed.), *The Jellicoe Papers Volume I, 1893-1916* (The Navy Records Society, 1966).

_____, *The Jellicoe Papers Volume II, 1916 1935* (The Navy Records Society, 1968).

Eustace H.W. Tennyson D'Eyncourt, *A Shipbuilder's Yarn: The Record of a Naval Constructor* (Hutchison & Co., 1948).

S. Thorsøe, P. Simonsen, S. Krogh-Andersen, F. Frederichsen and H. Vaupel, *DFDS 1866-1991 Ship Development through 125 Years from Paddle Steamer to Ro/Ro Ship* (DFDS, 1991).

Nicolas Wolz, *From Imperial Splendour to Internment, The German Navy in the First World War* (Seaforth, 2015).

Filson Young, *With the Battle Cruisers* (United States Naval Institute, 1986).

HMSO PUBLICATIONS

Battle of Jutland Official Despatches (HMSO, 1920).

WEBSITES

www.Britishnewspaperarchive.co.uk
www.dreadnoughtproject,org/tfs/index.php/

Index

For ease of reference, warships are indexed under Warships, British and Warships, German.